Movies in the Age of Obama

Movies in the Age of Obama

The Era of Post Racial and Neo-Racist Cinema

Edited by
David Garrett Izzo

ROWMAN & LITTLEFIELD
Lanham • Boulder • New York • London

Published by Rowman & Littlefield
A wholly owned subsidiary of The Rowman & Littlefield Publishing Group, Inc.
4501 Forbes Boulevard, Suite 200, Lanham, Maryland 20706
www.rowman.com

16 Carlisle Street, London W1D 3BT, United Kingdom

Copyright © 2015 by Rowman & Littlefield

All rights reserved. No part of this book may be reproduced in any form or by any electronic or mechanical means, including information storage and retrieval systems, without written permission from the publisher, except by a reviewer who may quote passages in a review.

British Library Cataloguing in Publication Information Available

Library of Congress Cataloging-in-Publication Data

Movies in the age of Obama : the era of post racial and neo-racist cinema / edited by David Garrett Izzo.
  pages cm
Includes bibliographical references and index.
ISBN 978-1-4422-4129-9 (cloth : alk. paper) — ISBN 978-1-4422-4130-5 (ebook) 1. African Americans in motion pictures. 2. Race in motion pictures. 3. Racism in motion pictures. 4. Motion pictures—United States—History—21st century. I. Izzo, David Garrett, editor.
  PN1995.9.N4M68 2915
  791.43'6552—dc23
  2014019499

ISBN 978-0-8108-9534-8 (pbk : alk. paper)

∞™ The paper used in this publication meets the minimum requirements of American National Standard for Information Sciences Permanence of Paper for Printed Library Materials, ANSI/NISO Z39.48-1992.

Printed in the United States of America

Contents

Introduction   vii
    David Garrett Izzo

Part I: Resonance from the Past: Experience Is Learned Backward But Must Be Lived Forward   1

1   "I *Really* Need a Maid!" White Womanhood in *The Help*   3
    Kwakiutl L. Dreher

2   Gwendolyn Brooks's Bronzeville and Tate Taylor's Jackson: "Art hurts. Art urges voyages— and it is easier to stay at home."   15
    Blake G. Hobby

3   If Django and Lincoln Could Talk: James Baldwin Goes to the Movies   31
    Robert McParland

4   The Exceptional N*gger: Redefining African American Identity in *Django Unchained*   45
    Rodney M. D. Fierce

5   Blaxploitation in the Age of Obama: *Black Dynamite*, *Django Unchained*, Racial Reasoning, and Racial Capitalism   57
    Brian E. Butler

6   Between *The Butler* and *Black Dynamite*: Servility, Militancy, and the Meaning of Blaxploitation   67
    Andrew Grossman

7   Rednecks, Racism, and Religion: King and Darabont's Precarious Prophecy of Obama's Coming   85
    Victoria McCollum

Part II: The Present Is an Eternal Now Connecting Past and Future   103

  8 "I Am Trayvon Martin": Obama and the Black Male in Cinema   105
      Mohanalakshmi Rajakumar and Alisha Saiyed

  9 *Invictus*: South Africa as a Post-racial Fantasy in the Age of Obama   111
      Sohinee Roy

10 "Mama, I Think I Broke Something": Thinking about the Environment in Benh Zeitlin's *Beasts of the Southern Wild*   131
      Irina Negrea

11 It's Not a Wonderful Life: The Financial Crisis on Film and the Limits of Hollywood Liberalism   149
      Peter Grosvenor

12 Reimagining Barack Obama as Jay Gatsby in Baz Luhrmann's Film Adaptation of *The Great Gatsby*   171
      Cammie Sublette

Part III: The Present Imagines the Future   183

13 *The Hunger Games*, Race, and Social Class in Obama's America   185
      Sonya C. Brown

14 Rise of the Planet of the People: Contradictions and Revolution in *Rise of the Planet of the Apes*   203
      doug morris

Part IV: 2013 Academy Award for Best Picture: *12 Years a Slave*   225

15 "Under the Floorboards of This Nation": Trauma, Representation, and the Stain of History in *12 Years a Slave*   227
      Ed Cameron and Linda Belau

16 162 Years after *12 Years a Slave*: A Viewing through Double-Consciousness   241
      Salvador Murguia

17 Revoking the Privilege of Forgetting: White Supremacy Interrogated in *12 Years a Slave*   251
      David M. Jones

18 No, You Can't: Passive Protagonists in *The Blind Side*, *Django Unchained*, and *12 Years a Slave*   275
      Thomas Britt

Index   291

About the Editor and Contributors   297

Introduction

David Garrett Izzo

THE UPSIDE

More people of all colors are seeing black films in greater numbers than at any time in American history. Why? President Obama is one reason—the obvious one—but not the only one, which awaits further deliberation below.

First, it must be said that this collection was initially inspired by a *New York Times* article of the same title as this book that asserted:

> Politically and personally this president functions as a screen onto which different Americans project their fears and fantasies. From the right, the picture is often of a monster whose policies are steps on a scary road to socialism or some other exotic form of tyranny. Many liberals, by contrast, have expressed disappointment at his willingness to compromise with Republicans and his reluctance to fight. At different times and from various angles Mr. Obama is a fiery orator, an aloof intellectual, a policy nerd and a shrewd strategist. He is notoriously resistant to sketch-comedy impersonation and also, perhaps, to simple pop-cultural appropriation.[1]

He is "resistant" possibly but mirrored nonetheless, even if not so much directly, but as a zeitgeist that permeates the cultural atmosphere with a wafting aura that concludes: *things are not the same as they once were.* Some feel this tangibly; most do not intellectualize this new world order but hear/see it obliquely unless presidential news dictates a necessity that highlights the visuals and raises the volume as headlines instead of the bland buzz of elevator music that obliquely surrounds an unaligned consciousness rather than sharply impinges on it.

Movies, past and present, react to the pulse of change and respond to it: the Great Depression (*The Grapes of Wrath*), World War II (*A Walk in the*

Sun), the 1960s (*Easy Rider*). In all films there is context and there is subtext. "Race" is a dominant theme of the Obama era, either overtly contextual (*12 Years a Slave, Django Unchained*) or often as a subtext more covertly disguised (*The Hunger Games, The Great Gatsby*), that are about outsiders seeking to get inside and influence the status quo.

> This year [2013] race is firmly back on the table with movies like "Lincoln" and "Django Unchained." Yet much like Mr. Obama, who has rarely made race a topic of conversation, the current nominees for best picture speak to other issues, including war, the economy and just about everything else.[2]

Screenwriters, like the rest of the public, are affected by the new world order of a first black president; Tony Kushner explains how he adapted *Lincoln* for the age of Obama:

> Watching the Obama presidency through the lens of *Lincoln* has been a transformative thing for me. I think Barack Obama is a great president. I won't say that he's as great as Lincoln. I don't know if there'll ever be a president as great as Abraham Lincoln. But I think Obama inherited a mess as formidable as the mess that FDR inherited when he came into Washington during the Great Depression. Progressive people have not been patient enough, and thoughtful enough, in our criticisms of him. I feel it's been a blessing to be thinking about Lincoln the whole time. Lincoln reminds you that great good can come from compromise, and always from politics.[3]

Obama and movies became a theme for many more media evaluations:

"President Obama as Django"

> The film was the most liberating and empowering one that I have ever seen. Out of the hundreds of movies that I have seen in my lifetime, I do not remember one where the black man uses wit, savvy and a conspicuous bravado to outsmart and outgun whites and ride off victoriously. Sidney Poitier's wit and savvy made him a big-screen legend. But Poitier never played a character like Django.
>
> Brilliantly played by Jamie Foxx, Django is a different type of black hero. His defiance and his capacity to exact revenge by successfully fighting violence with violence is something that is uniquely foreign to the American cinematic experience.
>
> The film's statement on race is just as revolutionary as the character Django is defiant. One of the most humorous scenes in the film is when the Ku Klux Klan rides to find Django and his German bounty hunter comrade, Schultz. While looking for the two, the Klan begins to question why they are wearing white sheets over their heads, making it difficult to see. This satire of our own homegrown terrorist organization is reflective of Tarantino's fearless cinematic grit.[4]

According to a report in *Indie Wire*,[5] black-themed films are increasing in the number released, signifying that whites were/are willing to see them enter the mainstream of multiplexes. CNN, among other media sources, has taken note, as reported in October of 2013:

> This year's critically acclaimed films take audiences from places like slave plantations in the antebellum South, to packed Ebbets Field as Jackie Robinson steps up to bat, and to inner-city public housing on a scorching summer day. While set in various eras and depicting diverse stories, many of the films on the short list for the 2013 [and 2014] awards season show an emerging trend; Hollywood is making movies about the black experience in America.
> "Certainly 2013 has been a banner year with regards to the number of films that feature African-American themes," said Gil Robertson, co-founder of the African-American Film Critics Association. "Those films all really arrive at the threshold in terms of the quality that will seriously put them in the running for Oscar consideration."
> Not only do the movies portray the African-American experience, but they're also created from the ground up by today's most prominent black filmmakers and actors. Oscar-winner Forest Whitaker, who played the lead role in *The Butler*, says the trend in Hollywood allows for a more diverse storytelling. "There are so many projects where people are being able to have their voices heard," Whitaker said. "I think that's hopefully going to continue to expand in the African-American community ... and all the voices can be heard in the tapestry of who we are as people."[6]

Even the British at BBC.com are writing about the resurgence of American black cinema:

> Celebrated US movie mogul Harvey Weinstein was working the press a few nights ago at Manhattan's Museum of Modern Art where his latest film, *Fruitvale Station*, was being given its New York launch. It's a picture based on the last 24 hours in the life of a young black man fatally shot by a white police officer in California in 2009. The movie is in the vanguard of a new wave of black films arriving in American cinemas. "It should have happened a long time ago—but it's finally happening now," said Weinstein.[7]

Obama certainly is the main and culturally obvious impetus for this better-late-than-never "new wave of black films." However, it is a bit more complicated than just the impact—as large as it is—of the first black president. The psychology of *Otherness* began to change with the Great Recession of 2008—before Obama—with anti-Bush II and anti-Republicanism making Obama's election a greater probability. Yes, Obama was/is the most radically *Other* president of our generation, eclipsing JFK's Catholic *Otherness*. There was also a new "us-against-them sentiment." The Occupy Wall Street Movement helped to define a more populist form of Otherness: the 99 percent versus the 1 percent. This was a broad stroke and certainly did not include more conservative Republicans, and—as of this writing on March 3, 2014, a day after *12 Years a Slave* won the Best Picture Academy Award—it seems that there are no more "moderate" Republicans, with the Tea Party demanding and Koch money financing extreme right (and white) politics. In 2008, more progressive Democrats as a block, moderates of both parties, and many independents felt the sting of a recession that merged a unique form of Otherness engendered in a majority and not just the traditional minorities. A majority of people felt put upon by economic policies that appeared to favor Wall Street and banks that then received a massive bailout while the working class suffered. This majority of Otherness elected Obama whose own Otherness was for the moment not a detriment to his supporters but a simpatico bonding mechanism, as in: *a black guy knows what it's like to get screwed just like we've been.* This good will overlapped into a greater embrace in white appreciation of black art, including film.

This unique form of a majority collective subjectivity of Otherness—heretofore, Otherness was the appellation assigned to put-upon minorities—would find its traditional application applied by Obama's enemies to diminish the first black president. How so? By appealing to both traditional and neo-racists.

THE DOWNSIDE

"Parallels to Country's Racist Past Haunt Age of Obama"

> A recent Associated Press online poll concluded that racial prejudice in America has slightly increased since Obama's election. The survey said that a majority of Americans, 51%, express explicit racial prejudice toward blacks, compared to 48% in 2008.
>
> While the poll on its own doesn't prove the country has become more racist in the last four years, it does offer evidence that the "post-racial" world some thought Obama's inauguration would bring has yet to materialize.
>
> "We're in a racist renaissance," said Nsenga Burton, a writer for *The Root*, an online news site with an African-American perspective. "It's a rebirth of the oldest forms of racism. It's not new, not different. It's like the 1800s, the most archaic abusive terms are applied to black people every single day."[8]

"Attacks against Obama's 'Otherness' Inspired by Racism"

> Tragically, instead of unifying, justifying, and strengthening this country, the election of the first biracial president of the United States has torn us apart, exposing the nasty undercurrent of racism that runs through us. Of course, we are in denial about it. Of course, it infuriates some people to be told it exists. Of course, Americans, who pledge allegiance to "one nation, under God, indivisible with liberty and justice for all," cannot bring themselves to believe the

truth that our social fabric is terribly tattered, that all of the buzz words about President Obama's "otherness" are euphemisms for "he's black."

Continuing the refrain, Mitt Romney tries to paint President Obama as not a *real* American. We know what he *really* means. Don't be fooled!

We have come a long way as a nation in bridging our racial and ethnic divide—but far from far enough. To be sure, a potpourri of people are now on TV, in elective office, at the head of major businesses. We have changed people's minds: There are legal prohibitions against discrimination. But we have yet to change people's hearts, which is why an incident like the killing of Trayvon Martin became so explosive so quickly. We are sitting on a social powder keg. It's a miracle it hasn't erupted beyond our ability to handle it.

At times of crisis, we keep saying we need a "national dialog" about race. Remember Rodney King? But we never have it, and it wouldn't matter much if we did. Beyond words, we need to transform ourselves, one by one, into the nation "under God" we say we are. For unless you think God is a racist, we are taking her name in vain—at our peril.[9]

Black cinema in the age of Obama is a two-way mirror; those standing on one side of the mirror are looking at *12 Years a Slave* as a horrible document of American slavery eliciting tears, pity, or shame, while viewers on the other side of the mirror feel nostalgic for the "good old days."

The sting of old and neo-racism is unyielding without any amelioration or diffusion; instead, the age of Obama has seen the sharpened tips of a collective death by a thousand cuts. African Americans know it in their bones, in the marrow that harbors the old suffering now renewed as many old and new racists fear that their narrowly tenuous grasp on their isolationist de facto walls of mental segregation will enclose them within their psychological castles under siege by the new alliance of minorities near majority. They are afraid: fear of defeat becomes anger; anger is not suppressed; it is vented. Blacks receiving the anger are aware of it and not amused. How do black artists recalibrate their approaches to this old/new racism? The significance of this collection is to measure the recent past, compare it to the present, and anticipate the future: even as these films represent triumphs over suffering, they have no choice but to also recall the nature of oblivion.

Still, there is that upside of mutual commiseration that encourages hope for a future of black cinema that is no longer "black" but just "cinema."

Brad Pitt, a producer of *12 Years a Slave*, spoke about its message: "I just hope this film is a gentle reminder that we're all equal," he said, "and another's freedom is as important as our own."[10]

NOTES

1. A. O. Scott and Manhola Dargis, "Movies in the Age of Obama," *New York Times*, January 16, 2013.

2. Scott and Dargis, "Movies in the Age of Obama."

3. Jessica Koslow, "Tony Kushner Explains How He Adapted *Lincoln* for the Age of Obama," *LA Weekly*, November 12, 2013, http://www.laweekly.com-publicspectacle-2012-11-05-tony-kushner-explains-how-he-adapted-lincoln-for-the-age-of-obama (accessed February 12, 2014).

4. Renford Reese, "President Obama as Django," *Los Angeles Daily News*, February 16, 2013, http://www.dailynews.com/general-news/20130218/president-obama-as-django (accessed February 12, 2014).

5. Tombay Obenson, "Where is Black Film Today," *Indie Wire*, August 22, 2013, http://blogs.indiewire.com/shadowandact/how-far-has-black-cinema-come-this-chart-showing-annual-number-of-black-films-released-might-help (accessed February 12, 2014).

6. Jane Caffrey, "Hollywood's African-American Film Renaissance," CNN.com, October 20 2013, http://www.cnn.com/2013/10/18/showbiz/movies/african-american-film-renaissance/ (accessed February 12, 2014).

7. Tom Brook, "A Renaissance of Black Cinema," *BBC Culture*, July 18, 2013, http://www.bbc.com/culture/story/20130718-a-renaissance-of-black-cinema (accessed February 12, 2014).

8. John Blake, "Parallels to Country's Racist Past Haunt Age of Obama," CNN.com, November 1, 2012, http://inamerica.blogs.cnn.com/2012/11/01/parallels-to-countrys-racist-past-haunt-age-of-obama/ (accessed February 13, 2014).

9. Stephen Goldstein, "Attacks against Obama's 'Otherness' Inspired by Racism," *Sun-Sentinel* (South Florida), April 27, 2012, http://articles.sun-sentinel.com/2012-04-27/news/fl-sgcol-obama-critics-racism-goldstein-0427-20120427_1_president-obama-elective-office-chief-justice (accessed February 13, 2014).

10. Brad Pitt, as quoted in Melena Ryzik, "A Night That Proved to be on Message," *New York Times*, March 3, 2014, http://www.nytimes.com/projects/oscars/2014/ (accessed March 3, 2014).

Part I

Resonance from the Past: Experience Is Learned Backward But Must Be Lived Forward

Chapter One

"I *Really* Need a Maid!" White Womanhood in *The Help*

Kwakiutl L. Dreher

The premiere of Tate Taylor's film *The Help* stirred a hot debate within the community of scholars, columnists, moviegoers. Many concluded that the film was racist and that Taylor opted for a "feel good" kind of movie without a solid contextualization of the southern mentality/psychology that made for the oppressive treatment of the help in the first place. Popular culture critic Melissa Harris-Perry maintains, "The true story is that for some white people and the Black female domestics who worked for them [the reality] is much closer to a horror film than a light-hearted drama. . . . For Black maids the threat of rape was always a clear and present danger."[1] Historian Micki McElya posits:

> Primarily what this film does and what the book does is present us with a Mammy narrative for the 21st century. It refits the Mammy iconography . . . the Mammy story that a woman . . . a Black woman working in a white household loves the people she works for. She is not there for wages; she is not coerced to be there . . . she wants to be there . . . she authorizes those relationships because she loves the people there.[2]

In his review of the film, Owen Gleiberman sees the film as "a movie . . . about the low-key, day-to-day, highly ambivalent intimacy of black/white relationships in the Deep South. It's about what really goes on in middle-class households between the lines of the most seemingly ordinary encounters."[3]

Whether a dramatization of black/white intimacy, presenting the public with yet another narrative of Mammy, or the lack of the presentation of the truth of the black domestic, the film on close reading, however, reveals that

The Help really is a textbook chapter on how *white women* came of age in the South. "I *Really* Need a Maid!" examines the ways in which the presence of the black female body in the white household was necessary for white women to have social status in the community and to have access to *each other* within that community and that the *control* of the black female body made possible the vigor of white womanhood. What is more, the black maid in the white household made visible and, more importantly, legitimized white womanhood. Without the presence and a demonstration of control of the black woman's body, white womanhood was impotent.

Let me tell you a story: I visited a retired instructor on a summer visit home in South Carolina one summer. As I sat in her old worn Queen Anne Chair, and as she rolled her "medicine" (taken for her arthritis) and drank her bourbon, she commenced to give me intimate details about her life as a child in the South. "Kwakiutl, you can tell me, honestly," she begins, "you're in the witness protection program out there in Nebraska, huh?" We both laughed, and she turned her head and asked, "Have you seen *The Help*?"

"Yes, I have."

"Well, what'd ya think about it?"

"Well . . . I . . ."

"See, Kwakiutl, that was some bullshit; the film industry has to portray things of a southern nature as *all* bad . . ."

"Well, what do you . . ."

"See, Kwakiutl, I had a maid . . . hell . . . all my friends had maids; that's all who raised us. Where was the child care? Wa'n't no child care. My mother wouldn't have made it if it wasn't for Beulah; and I tell you, Kwakiutl, it was all love in the household. I knew all about her family; and you know she knew all about mine . . . we got along well . . . it was like my mother had died when Beulah passed on. You know Beulah and Daddy used to love to watch the World Series together; oh, she really enjoyed that . . . you sure you don't want some bourbon? 'Medicine'?"

"No, no . . . thank you."

"See Kwakiutl those were the times . . . when you were born into something already set up for you when you were formed in your mother's womb and that's all you see and all your friends who were born at that same time have the same thing . . . that's all you know . . ."

"Hmmmm . . ."

"And you know, Kwakiutl, we never called them 'nigger.' *Never*! My momma and daddy wouldn't allow it . . . no. You know what we called them?"

I shook my head no.

"Nigra . . . but never nigger . . ."

Through the haze of smoke, I jumped at the echo of footsteps. Arriving at the top of the stairs was a rail-thin white man who looked to be about in his late fifties, carrying a Ziploc bag of sorts.

"Me and Kwakiutl were talking about *The Help* . . . you know that movie . . ."

"*The Help?* Huh . . . I know all about the help. I wouldn'a been raised . . . humph . . . I wouldn'a even be here . . . heck if it wasn't for Pearl." He unlocked the bag and poured out the contents on a piece of newspaper. "I wouldn'a been raised . . . !"

I made a gesture that it was time for me to leave, and after the "Glad to see ya"s and the "Glad to meet ya"s, my teacher said, "Come back to see me again; I ain't goin' nowhere. I'm right here . . . always."

As I unlocked my car, I realized I was under a spell. Lush tones cloaked their words, and strong expressions of pride attended the storytelling. In the analysis of my teacher's and her partner's storytelling, historian Micki McElya adds to my inquiry that there is a "sensuality approaching the erotic" that "remains unmediated and undeterred by the authors' youth in the [textual] scenes they recollect."[4] My teacher's partner's story brought to relief that Pearl's caretaking made possible for his own parents or guardians to go about their business without any thought for him. As I listened to each anecdote, their eyes betrayed a longing for those days again, even a nostalgia for Beulah and Pearl.

That conversation reiterated, moreover, the long-held truth about the black domestic: they were the social engineers of the white familial structure. These women, specifically, instilled a legacy of child care that ensured the healthy growth of a generation of white children who "wouldn'a been raised" or "wouldn'a even be here" if it were not for the Pearls and the Beulahs. The main character of *The Help*, Aibileen Clark (Viola Davis), opens the film with: "I was born 1911, Chickasaw County, Piedmont Plantation. My momma was a maid; my grandmother was a house slave. . . . I done raised 17 kids in my life. Looking after white babies, that's what I do." As southern white writer and activist Lillian Smith writes in her autobiography, *Killers of the Dream*, "It was not a rare sight in my generation to see a black woman with a dark baby at one breast and a white one at the other, rocking them both in her wide lap."[5] My teacher's and her partner's recollections reflect a common feeling among whites for their black caretakers. They were considered members of the family but could not have ultimate freedom, nor respect for that matter. Neither the Beulahs nor the Pearls enjoyed what could be termed as the "handle of respect" of being called "Mrs. ___"; they simply were Beulah or Pearl.

The black domestic, as was her predecessor, Mammy, was bound up in surrogacy, tender loving care, and always considered loyal to her masters and mistresses, faithful to her assigned duties, and the nurturer and the embodiment of nostalgia, as McElya contends.⁶ The presence of her black body allowed for a seamless performance of white womanhood, especially in the South, since the South provided what Susan Tucker refers to as "the white housewives' utopia" wherein "the domestic . . . was often used to illustrate how the Old South worked at its best."⁷ What *The Help* reiterates—as well as its cinematic predecessors, most notably, *I'm No Angel* (1933), *Imitation of Life* (1934; 1959), and *Gone with the Wind* (1939)—is that the black domestic proved essential for the coming of age of white women (and men) and their children at different intervals in their lives, and the presence of the black domestic facilitated the stabilization of their place in their respective societies. As Ruth Frankenberg notes, female whiteness is "a mere mirroring of a mirroring, a 'not' of a 'not.' [It] comes to self-name, invents itself, by means of its declaration that it is *not* that which it projects as Other. And there is thus a level at which whiteness has its own inbuilt complacency, a self-naming that functions simply through a triumphant 'I am not that.'"⁸ The presence of the black domestic in the white household is key, then, to marking out what is *not* in the household.

A "conversation" about the black domestic deserves some knowledge of servitude across national borders that brings to relief the cultural continuities that still held sway at the time period of the film, the 1960s. During the Edwardian period (1901–1910) in the United Kingdom, Alison Maloney outlines the code of conduct for servants, which includes: "Do not smile at droll stories told in your presence or seem in any way to notice, or enter into, the family conversation, or the talk at table, or with visitors"; "keep out of sight as much as possible"; and "hand a family member or visitor a letter or parcel . . . on a silver platter to minimize the risk of physical contact."⁹ She recounts the humiliation of one servant whose mistress chided her for handing to her newspapers in her bare hands: "I thought it was terrible . . . that someone could think that you were so low that you couldn't even hand them anything out of your hands."¹⁰ Upon his visit to London in 1836, Prince Puckler-Müskau remarked that servants "appear to be considered rather as machines than as beings."¹¹ As for the arrangement of space in the household, in Victorian England (1837–1901), Scottish architect Robert Kerr notes that the separation of the servants from the quarters of the master and mistress constituted the necessary boundary for privacy. He writes,

> It becomes the foremost of all maxims, therefore, that the Servants' Department shall be separated from the main house, so that what passes on either side of the boundary shall be both invisible and inaudible to the other. . . . The idea which underlies all is simply this. The Family constitute one community; the servants another. Whatever may be to their mutual regard and confidence as dwellers under the same room, each class is entitled to shut its door upon the other, and be alone.¹²

Privacy and separation, which carries the "language of apartheid" according to Mark Girouard, were exhibited in a number of ways: "At Welbeck the Duke of Portland . . . sacked any housemaid who had the misfortune to meet him in the corridors. Housemaids in a country house in Suffolk had to flatten themselves face to the wall when they saw family or guests coming."[13] Lady Dundonald, displeased with a servant wrote, "Idleness, Dress and Insolence are their prevailing vices."[14] As for the sharing of the intimate space of the bathroom, Lucy Lethbridge notes the aristocracy of the 1930s "maintained their cheerfully ambivalent attitude towards cleanliness, and the idea of sharing a bathroom with others . . . was anathema to people whose most intimate secrets, paradoxically, had long been shared with the valet or the lady's-maid who undressed and bathed them."[15]

This domestic etiquette lodged deep into the psyche of some of the Europeans who immigrated to North America from the advent of slavery even to the present. These cultural continuities resisted change, especially in terms of interactions of servant/master/mistress, because the primary goal was to conserve and regenerate the socio-cultural core of society.

The English servants had their place. Servants knew their place, and the majority of them accepted that place, finding solace in their strong work ethic and in the name of the family for which they worked. Indeed, the upstairs/downstairs mentality of segregation ruled, and any interactions to the contrary resulted in immediate dismissal.

In North America, where property included chattel slaves, this upstairs/downstairs mentality morphed into a practice of terror on the enslaved, and its practice was passed down from generation to generation. Thomas Jefferson rightly predicted this practice when he wrote in his Query XVIII: "Manners":

> There must doubtless be an unhappy influence on the manners of our people produced by the existence of slavery among us. The whole commerce between master and slave is a perpetual exercise of the most boisterous passions, the most unremitting despotism on the one part, and degrading submissions on the other. Our children see this, and learn to imitate it. . . . This quality is the germ of all education in him. From his cradle to his grave he is learning to do what he sees others do. . . . The parent storms, the child looks on, catches the lineaments of wrath, puts on the same airs in the circle of smaller slaves, gives a loose to his worst of passions, and thus nursed, educated, and daily exercised in tyranny, cannot but be stamped by it with odious peculiarities.[16]

Katherine Van Wormer lays bare how the rules that African American domestics had to follow mirror the conventions of the English country home and rub against Jefferson's ideas on the manners of the plantation regime:

- entrance and exit by the back or kitchen door only

- given separate toilet or no toilet use
- wore a maid's uniform
- their space was in the kitchen
- addressed by first name while required to use the formal name of the employer.[17]

More specifically, Harris-Perry notes the story of eighty-seven-year-old Edith Johnson that is part of the Oral History Project from Spelman College: "I worked for a woman who would not let me sit at the table. She gave me a sandwich and I sat on the top step going to the basement." In the home in the Jim Crow South, these attitudes continued but transformed into a radical psychology all bound up in race.

In the "Bridge Club" scene of *The Help*, for example, audiences witness Jefferson's "germ of education" in the game of bridge that begins in the living room. Skeeter Phelan (Emma Stone) advises her white female cohorts that she has found a job at the *Jackson Journal*, writing for the "Miss Myrna" column. She wishes to "talk to Aibileen just to help [her] with some of the letters so [she] can get a knack for it." Elizabeth agrees "as long as it does not interfere with [Aibileen's] work." Aibileen is serving another table within earshot of conversations that center on work and gossip. When she serves at the Ms. Hilly/Skeeter/Elizabeth table, the camera focuses in on Aibileen's hand pouring tea in between Skeeter and Elizabeth. The camera only shows Aibileen from the neck to her waist, clad in the maid's uniform. Ms. Hilly moves around in her chair, uncomfortable because she has to go to the bathroom. Elizabeth encourages her to go, but she replies that it is OK. Her mother, Missus Walters (Sissy Spacek) hollers from the anteroom, "Oh, she's just upset because the nigra uses the bathroom and so do we!" Elizabeth becomes anxious: "Just go use mine and Roy's!" In the presence of Aibileen, Ms. Hilly initiates her "concern" over bathroom patronage. She replies, "If Aibileen uses the guest bath, I am sure she uses yours too!" Elizabeth retorts, "She does not!" She then tells Aibileen to go check on her child. Ms. Hilly continues,

> Wouldn't you rather them take their business outside?. . . Tell Riley every penny he spends on a colored's bathroom he'll get back in spades when y'all sell! Ugh! It's just plain dangerous; they carry different diseases than we do. That's why I have drafted *The Home Health Care Sanitation Initiative*. A disease preventative bill that requires every white home to have a separate bathroom for the colored help. It's been endorsed by the White Citizens Council. . . . I'll do whatever it takes to protect our children.

In this scene, Ms. Hilly practices her racist prowess by demonstrating a robust research agenda on home health sanitation; specifically, the possibility of the transmission of disease from the help, not to mention the economic loss that could result if a white home buyer found out the help used the family's bathroom. She continues to flex her racist muscle by informing her bridge partners of her political ambitions when it comes to the help. Such are her racist smarts, that the *White Citizens Council* has adopted them. Especial to this scene is the expression of über-distress demonstrated by Elizabeth Leefolt when Ms. Hilly suggests Aibileen uses her bathroom without her knowledge. In that moment, the streak of possibility arises that Miss Elizabeth might be gossiped about or, at worst, ostracized if, in fact, the Leefolts allow the help to use their bathroom. All the while, Aibileen has to figuratively "flatten [her] face to the wall" when listening to Ms. Hilly's perorations on domestic bathroom etiquette in the hallway after being dismissed.

The next scene illustrates how Ms. Hilly's *Home Health Care Sanitation Initiative* has come to circulate within political circles, and has caught the attention of politicians, to include Governor Ross Robert Barnett. The community of white women meets to discuss a coat drive and a raffle for baked goods (proceeds to go toward "put[ting] a dent in African children's hunger"). Ms. Hilly chairs the assembly, and there she gleefully announces, "I just found out the surgeon general has reviewed the *Home Health Care Sanitation Initiative* that I drafted, and he passed it along to Governor Barnett!" To highlight the importance of Ms. Hilly's announcement, it is necessary to give a brief introduction of Barnett.

Governor Barnett, an avowed white supremacist from Mississippi, espoused a firm stance on segregation. When Freedom Riders James Farmer and Stokely Carmichael were arrested in Mississippi and thrown into the notorious Mississippi state prison called Parchman Farm, Barnett told prison guards to "break their spirit . . . but not their bones."[18] He is best remembered for his public denial of civil rights activist and Air Force veteran James Meredith's enrollment into the University of Mississippi (Ole Miss) that sparked a riot in October 1, 1962. In his defiance of the Supreme Court's order to admit Meredith, he said, "We must either submit to the unlawful dictates of the federal government or stand up like men and tell them no." He hinged his belief upon an imagined divine design: "The Good Lord was the original segregationist. He put the black man in Africa. . . . He made the white man white and the black man black and he did not intend for them to mix."[19] He also stated, "There is no case in history where the Caucasian race has survived social integration. . . . We will not drink from the cup of genocide."[20] In February 1964, he sat in the courtroom with Byron de la Beckwith, the white supremacist accused of murdering civil rights activist Medgar Evers in 1963, and patted him on the back in support during de la Beckwith's trial.

Ms. Hilly's racist agenda and her announcement of acceptance of same are testaments to her solid place in the community of white women that now has been sanctioned by the southern patriarchy. Ms. Hilly's plan as well as her white womanhood, however, gains strength as she attempts to control the black body and where its bodily functions or its "business" can take place. More significant, her "campaign" is motivated by her vigorous desire to keep sacred the rituals of segregation. In an interview with a white woman who grew up with a domestic in the Jim Crow South, Van Wormer recounts, "[The maid] could not use the residents' bathroom because of the belief current at the time that black people had germs that whites did not have. . . . The maid would have to go across the levee and squat by the river."[21] In effect, Ms. Hilly draws a boundary between white womanhood (purity) and black womanhood (dirty and diseased). Mary Douglas would agree that Ms. Hilly deems her white body a representation of the hallowed socio-cultural convention embedded in Mississippi rule for it is "a sacred thing . . . to be kept from defilement."[22] The threat of the black female body's use of the intimate space of the bathroom, where formalities of personal hygiene are performed (i.e., cleansing via bathing and defecating), suggests the danger of pollution of the white female body and, by extension, the sacred rule of segregation. Ms. Hilly coddles her presumed purity and reinforces it by keeping it free from desecration.

The Help also brings to relief that without the black female domestic, a white woman is cast to the margins of her community because she cannot "trade the stories" necessary to demonstrate her place in that community, nor can she produce the leisure time critical to exercise the racism that she has inherited. Celia Foote (Jessica Chastain), for example, lives isolated in a house reminiscent of Tara in the movie *Gone with the Wind* (1939) away from the main community. It has five bedrooms and five bathrooms and a pool house with two beds and two baths. She "really needs a maid" to show her husband that she can perform every domestic chore all by herself. "Johnny doesn't know I'm bringing in help," she tells Minny during the interview. As Minny teaches Celia the value of *Crisco* ("the most important invention since they put mayonnaise in a jar") and its many uses ("Got bags under your eyes? Wanna soften your husband's scaly feet? . . . uh . . . hmmm: *Crisco*"), and after Minny's reminders of the boundaries between the help and the employer, Celia finds the courage to release herself from the margins and move among Ms. Hilly's circle of women. They do not accept her "because they think you white trash" Minny tells her; however, that is not the point. What matters is that the presence of the black domestic in her household emboldens Celia to such an extent that she considers herself worthy to request admission into that club of white women.

This scene also illustrates how Miss Celia, from Sugga Ditch, is willing to "pass" as the consummate housewife by pirating Minny's labor. Minny, then, is the shadow in the house but all labor produced by her body is the prop for Miss Celia's womanhood. Such is the elation over having hired her first maid, that Miss Celia figuratively has an orgasm, as the spill from the Coca-Cola illustrates.

On its other side, the presence of the black domestic in white households created a culture of the grotesque, as generally, the white female could build racist muscle in intimate settings in the company of her white female peers, children, and men. This calisthenics of racism is passed down generation to generation, as one maid named Cora (Carol Sutton) lays bare during Skeeter's interviews with the domestics:

> I worked for Miss Jolene's mother until the day she died. Then her daughter, Miss Nancy, asked me to come and work for her. Miss Nancy a real sweet lady. But Miss Jolene's Ma done put it in her will that I got to work for Miss Jolene. Miss Jolene's a mean woman—mean for sport! Lord I tried to find another job but in everybody's mind—the French family and Miss Jolene owned me . . . owned me.

When asked about Cora being willed to her, Miss Jolene (Anna Camp) laughs and replies, "Well, yes, that's not odd, is it? Happens all the time, right?"

Rather than realizing the power of gender in households economically funded by white males/husbands and using the intimacy of the home as a site of resistance against the white patriarchal order, *The Help* uncovers what Michel Foucault would term the *capillaries of power* or that power installed by, in this case, the southern white patriarchal order of the Jim Crow South to ensure products are created by that power.[23] These capillaries extend from government entities into the domestic intimate space wherein the products of power—white women—keep watch over their sacred conventions. In the scene "One More Story," Skeeter begs her mother, Charlotte (Allison Janney), for the true story of her nurse/maid Constantine (Cicely Tyson). Through flashbacks, Charlotte remembers that Constantine

> didn't give me a choice. The Daughters of America had just appointed me state regent! Gracie Higginbotham had come all the way down from Washington, D.C., to our house for the ceremony. [Constantine] had gotten so old and . . . and slow, Skeeter.

The camera relates the levity of the afternoon that is interrupted by Constantine's daughter, Rachel (LaChanze), who tries to enter through the *front* door with flowers to see her mother. Charlotte slams the screen door and tells her to "go around back and wait in the kitchen . . . go on now." Rachel waltzes through the front door anyway and, in the dining room around Charlotte's white female comrades, announces, "I'm just doing what I was told Ms. Charlotte . . . going to the kitchen . . . but I'm gonna see my mother first!" Gracie Higginbotham, mortified, rises from the dinner table and declares,

"*You* may put up with this kind of nonsense, but I do not!" Charlotte, though hesitant, tells Rachel to "get out of this house." Constantine says, "Miss Charlotte, let me take [Rachel] to the kitchen," but Gracie Higginbotham (Dana Ivey) demands Charlotte assert her white authority in the company of the Daughters. "Both of ya, leave! Now!" says Charlotte with an obvious show of regret.

The camera shifts to the dinner table and the positive nods from Charlotte's peers. Her treatment of the two black women, especially the domestic Constantine, solidifies her place in the Daughters of America, especially her new appointment as state regent of that entity. Rachel's act shovels in the "dirt" of civil rights activism into Charlotte's pure domestic space, but the white mistress of the house, to the relief of her club friends, trowels it back out through the front door to protect sacred southern customs.

Aibileen Clark (Viola Davis) and Minny Jackson (Octavia Spencer) are the help, and the casting of the dark-skinned Davis and the rotund Spencer to play against, among others, the fair-skinned, thin-bodied Howard, Camp, and Chastain, marks clearly Frankenberg's *not that* in the movie. Just as Hattie McDaniel's Mammy delineated the high contrast of Scarlett O'Hara's socioeconomic class and (Irish) ethnicity, thinness, and white womanhood, Aibileen and Minny make possible the potency of racist white womanhood. It is necessary to observe, however, Taylor's attempt to demonstrate that even though the white characters in the film rehearse their racist power, Aibileen and Minny find ways to inoculate themselves from that power. In the kitchen, the help prepare a menu of deviled eggs, ambrosia, and sweet tea for the bridge party. They share a few minutes of camaraderie that, to some degree, illustrate resistance strategies they employ to mitigate their oppressive work conditions. On Ms. Hilly's sartorial choice for the party, Minny comments, "She looks like a mini-horse at the Kentucky Derby with all of those flowers and bows. Forgive me, Lord, but I'm gonna have to kill that woman, Aibileen! Now she's gone and put pencil marks on the toilet paper!"

Aibileen hardly can control her amusement as she stirs the tea. "But I carry paper in from my own damn house! That fool don't know!" Minny continues. Aibileen lets loose her laughter, adding that, "Ms. Leefolt got so much hairspray in her hair, she going to blow us all up if she lights a cigarette!" Aibileen and Minny hardly can contain the hilarity of their own observations. This interaction is supposed to provide the audience some comfort in the fact that *at least* these two women have managed intra-relation support in spite of Ms. Hilly's very hostile attitude toward Negroes. What translates, though, is that no matter how "happy" these domestics appear to be, the *world* within which they live—segregation—demands—on a daily basis—Jefferson's "perpetual exercise of the most boisterous passions" and "unremitting despotism" from southern whites. In other words, southern rule dictates a reminder to the help—by any means necessary—that they are but props used for white womanhood to pass on the revered southern customs and traditions, for them to come of age, and for them to make hearty the ideal of white womanhood.

The Help, as a visual cultural artifact, highlights a rabid investment in racism, in particular, white womanhood, and a zealous craving for *inclusion* and social standing in this institution as shown by Celia Foote. These practices and intense desires mutate into practices of the grotesque, producing, therefore, houses of terror or houses with elements of the gothic (women in distress, women who are desperate, women terrorized by a tyrannical male; in the case of *The Help*, the tyranny is brought to bear by white women). My former teacher's parents felt that *nigra* was the lesser of the evil *nigger*, and one can only imagine the humiliation Beulah felt when her charge decided to terrorize her by calling her out of her name, a custom of whites novelist Maya Angelou described as a "hellish horror." [24] The permission granted by her parents not only made Beulah the *not that* in the family, that societal clearance facilitated her coming of age into a world of white privilege formed in her mother's womb. As Mammy was to Scarlett O'Hara; my teacher's Beulah and her partner's Pearl; and Aibileen and Minny are to Ms. Hilly and Celia Foote, "Mammy [or the help] makes possible Scarlett's [or white women's] privileged life as a Southern belle; the nurturing and labor of the black servant is indispensable for [white women] to be [their] beautiful white sel[ves]."[25] This "beautiful self," though, can only blossom in the presence of the indispensable—yet denigrated—help.

NOTES

1. Melissa Harris-Perry, "*The Help* Doesn't Help," MSNBC.com, February 25, 2012, http://www.msnbc.com/melissa-harris-perry/watch/harris-perry-the-help-doesnt-help-domestic-workers-44146755519.

2. Micki McElya, *Clinging to Mammy: The Faithful Slave in Twentieth-Century America* (Cambridge: Harvard University Press, 2007).

3. Owen Gleiberman, "Inside Movies," EW.com August 14, 2011, http://insidemovies.ew.com/2011/08/14/is-the-help-a-movie-for-white-liberals/ (accessed March 4, 2014).

4. McElya, *Clinging to Mammy*, 44.

5. Lillian Smith, *Killers of the Dream* (New York: W. W. Norton, 1994), 130.

6. McElya, *Clinging to Mammy*, 45.

7. Susan Tucker, "A Complex Bond: Southern Black Domestic Workers and Their White Employers," *Journal of Women Studies* 9, no. 3 (1987): 7.

8. Ruth Frankenberg, "When We Are Capable of Stopping, We Begin to See," in *Names We Call Home: Autobiography on Racial Identity*, ed. Becky Thompson and Sangeeta Tyagi (New York: Routledge, 1996), 7.

9. Alison Maloney, *Life Below Stairs: True Lives of Edwardian Servants* (New York: St. Martin's Press, 2011), 136–37.

10. Maloney, *Life Below Stairs*, 138.

11. Francesca M. Wilson, *Strange Island: Britain Through Foreign Eyes 1395–1940* (London: Longmans, Green and Co., 1955), 174.

12. Robert Kerr, *The Gentleman's House: Or, How to Plan English Residences, from the Parsonage to the Palace* (Teaneck: Chadwyck Healey Press, 1983), 74–75, microfiche.

13. Mark Girouard, *Life in the English Country House: A Social and Architectural History* (New Haven: Yale University Press, 1978), 285.

14. Jeremy Musson, *Up and Down Stairs: The History of the Country House Servant* (London: John Murray, 2009), 118.

15. Lucy Lethbridge, *Servants: A Downstairs History of Britain from the Nineteenth Century to Modern Times* (New York: W. W. Norton, 2013), 204.

16. Thomas Jefferson, "Query XVIII: The Particular Customs and Manners That May Happen To Be Received in That State?" in *The Works, vol. 4 (Notes on Virginia II, Correspondence 1782–1786)*, http://oll.libertyfund.org/?option=com_staticxt...%E2%80%8ELiberty%20Fund (accessed March 4, 2014).

17. Katherine Van Wormer, David W. Jackson III, and Charletta Sudduth, *The Maid Narratives: Black Domestics and White Families in the Jim Crow South* (Baton Rouge: Louisiana State University Press, 2012), 269.

18. Barnett, as quoted in David Oshinsky, *"Worse Than Slavery": Parchman Farm and the Ordeal of Jim Crow Justice* (New York: Free Press, 1996), 235.

19. Barnett, as quoted in Joseph Crespino, *In Search of Another Country: Mississippi and the Conservative Counterrevolution* (Princeton: Princeton University Press, 2007), 69.

20. Ross Barnett, "A Statewide Address on Television and Radio to the People of Mississippi," September 13, 1962.

21. Van Wormer et al., *The Maid Narratives*, 273–74.

22. Mary Douglas, *Purity and Danger: An Analysis of Concepts of Pollution and Taboo* (New York: Routledge, 2002), 9.

23. Michel Foucault, *Power/Knowledge: Selected Interviews and Writings 1972–1977* (New York: Pantheon, 1980), 39.

24. Maya Angelou, *I Know Why the Caged Bird Sings* (New York: Random House, 1993), 109.

25. Hernán Vera and Andrew M. Gordon. "Scarlett and Mammy Revisited: White Women and Black Women in Hollywood Films," in *Screen Saviors: Hollywood and Fictions of Whiteness* (Lanham, Md.: Rowman & Littlefield, 2003), 100–101.

Chapter Two

Gwendolyn Brooks's Bronzeville and Tate Taylor's Jackson: "Art hurts. Art urges voyages— and it is easier to stay at home."

Blake G. Hobby

Surrounded by made-for-Hollywood images, we create obsessional, two-dimensional self-representations. We name these images "memes," imitations of imitations for which there are no originals—often hackneyed, derivative forms paraded as *au courant* and novel. Thus, it should not surprise us that our fall from innocence might come from a similar mimetic form, such as a mass-marketed comic film like Tate Taylor's *The Help*, which acts as a meme of an utterly horrific subject matter: the exploitation of African Americans during the time of domestic terror in Mississippi before the Civil Rights Act of 1964. To restore from a flattened meme both an artistic mode and a critical stance toward American history, one can couple Tate Taylor's *The Help* in dialogue with a short 1960 poem by African American poet Gwendolyn Brooks. While Taylor's film takes place in the summer of 1962 when Medgar Evers, a civil rights activist living in Jackson seeking to integrate the University of Mississippi, was assassinated, Brooks's poem returns to 1955, focusing upon the most significant case in the history of the civil rights movement, the murder and open-casket funeral of Emmett Till, a fourteen-year-old boy whose life was cruelly taken by Mississippians seeking vengeance. By placing a 1960 poem and a 2011 film in close proximity, the intent is to arouse. As the provoker, the one who opens a dangerous conversational game: what should socially conscious and social justice–oriented artwork do?

Notably, both of the works discussed—Gwendolyn Brooks's poem "A Bronzeville Mother Loiters in Mississippi. Meanwhile, A Mississippi Mother Burns Bacon" and Tate Taylor's film *The Help*—enshrine a time when the world was focused upon civil rights abuses in Mississippi. These two representations show us how history and art transact and the way our present society self-images. Thus, while seeing a contemporary film in light of a 1960 poem, we can recognize our cultural amnesia and diagnosis it as a symptom of the age of Obama. For, as Cornel West argues, in his recent foreword to Michelle Alexander's *The New Jim Crow: Mass Incarceration in the Age of Color Blindness*, many of us falsely hold onto the myth of post-racial America:

> While the Age of Obama is a time of historic breakthroughs at the level of racial symbols and political surfaces, Michelle Alexander's magisterial work takes us beyond these breakthroughs to the systemic breakdown of black and poor communities devastated by mass unemployment, social neglect, economic abandonment, and intense police surveillance. Her subtle analysis shifts our attention from the racial symbol of America's achievement to the actual substance of America's shame: the massive use of state power to incarcerate hundreds of thousands of precious poor, black, male (and, increasingly, female) young people in the name of a bogus "War on Drugs." And her nuanced historical narrative tracing the unconscionable treatment and brutal control of black people—slavery, Jim Crow, mass incarceration—takes us beneath the political surfaces and lays bare the structures of a racial caste system alive and well in the age of colorblindness. In fact, the very discourse of colorblindness—created by neoconservatives and neoliberals in order to trivialize and disguise the depths of black suffering in the 1980s and '90s—has left America blind to the New Jim Crow. How sad it is that this blindness has persisted under both Republican and Democratic administrations and remains to this day hardly acknowledged or examined in our nation's public discourse.[1]

But how do we get from the age of civil rights to the age of Barack Obama in terms of cultural representations? Provisionally, entertainment is not the desired end. The juxtaposition of Brooks and Taylor is the opposite of spectacle and also the opposite of what Aristotle values in art: the elevation of the spirit. By neither appealing to public sentiment nor to notions of high art, we abandon the way we normally observe art forms and instead see the way art can embody radical social thought. In doing so, we encounter what I call the subjectivity of disjunction, for certainly struggle accompanies differentiation and the formation of identity. As any teenager knows, this process means confronting unknowing, facing fears, checking privilege at the door, and moving to a place of utter discomfort. In this sense, the subjectivity of disjunction leads to an ongoing conversation between us and books and films and others and art and the world. This disjunctive movement is really emblematic of the United States, a country still held in the bonds of slavery waiting to be freed, a social space that has yet to grant individual lives dignity, and a place whose ways of articulating and practicing justice are yet to be realized. In the end, such a powerful disjunction has the potential to lead to openings, what James Joyce might call "portals of discovery."

In "A Bronzeville Mother Loiters in Mississippi. Meanwhile, A Mississippi Mother Burns Bacon" (1960), Gwendolyn Brooks dwells on the highly publicized lynching of a fourteen-year-old black boy named Emmett Till. Originally born in Mississippi, Emmett Till moved to Chicago when he was two years old. In 1955, Till and his cousin traveled to Money, Mississippi, to stay with Till's great-uncle, Moses Wright. Till's mother was well aware of the racial tension in the South, especially following the United States Supreme Court's 1954 decision to end segregation in public schools: *Brown v. Board of Education*, a landmark case that overturned the 1896 Supreme Court ruling in *Plessy v. Ferguson*, which had previously allowed U.S. states and localities to mandate racial segregation. Thus, Till's mother had cautioned him about Mississippi.

On August 24, 1955, Emmett Till entered Bryant's Grocery and Meat Market in the town of Money. Till exited the store; soon afterward so did Carolyn Bryant, the storeowner's wife. Although it is not clear exactly what transpired (sources differ), the official FBI report says that Till whistled at Bryant, who told her husband of the event several days later after he returned from a trip. According to the FBI report, "On August 28, 1955, at approximately 2:30 a.m., Roy Bryant (Carolyn Bryant's husband), J.W. Milam and at least one other person appeared at the home of Moses Wright, Till's great uncle, looking for the boy who had 'done the talking' in Money and abducted Till from the home."[2] The men then drove to a plantation, where they beat him, shot him in the head, tied a cotton gin fan around his neck, and threw him into the Tallahatchie River. His body was recovered on August 31, 1955. This nationally reported event fueled the growing civil rights movement. On May 10, 2004, the Justice Department reopened the case to see if anyone else was liable. While the grand jury found no credible evidence that others were involved and decided not to press charges against Carolyn Bryant, the report provided some sense of closure to a case studied and written about for more than fifty years. In addition to Brooks's work, which memorializes the event, the case has inspired many poignant artworks, including the first play by Nobel Laureate Toni Morrison, poems by Langston Hughes and Audre Lorde, and a song by Bob Dylan called "The Death of Emmett Till."

Told primarily through the point of view of Carolyn Bryant, the white woman whose husband had just been acquitted of the murder of Emmett Till, Brooks's poem describes a mother (Bryant) as she, while performing her daily domestic routine, burns bacon, her mind wandering far from the kitchen where she cooks. The narrator describes how Bryant imagines the story in the form of a ballad. As with lyric poetry and fairy tales, she wants the story to conform to conventions, to fit her preconceived notions of the world and to absolve her of guilt. She thinks of herself as "the milk-white maid" pursued by "the Dark Villain" (Till) and ultimately rescued by "the Fine Prince," figures that might, from her dim recollection, appear in a ballad. But the poem's speaker notes, perhaps ironically, that she does not even remember what a ballad is. These thoughts, interrupted by the burning of bacon, soon leave her as she dwells on the boy's age and innocence. As she sees an image of Till's blackness, the fairy tale she has woven disintegrates, leaving her with "no thread capable of the necessary Sew-work."

Her meditation on the events turns to her husband; hatred burns within her. She fears his grotesque mouth and Emmett Till's mother's eyes: "But his mouth would not go away and neither would the / Decapitated exclamation points in the Other Woman's eyes." The image of the Other Woman, the mother of Emmett Till (Mamie Till), who insisted that her son have an open-casket funeral, saying, "I don't have a minute to hate. I'll pursue justice for the rest of my life," creates guilt that Bryant cannot dispel.[3] As the poem ends, Bryant's husband pulls her close and kisses her, but she does nothing. Her own self-loathing, her hatred for her husband, and the memory of the horribly disfigured pictures of Emmett Till burst "into a glorious flower." A jarring juxtaposition remains, with an unresolved set of observations that need to be processed, examined, and understood. For this is the way of art, not to lead us to one specific conclusion or exact location but to lead us outward, toward those things we do not understand or know, wherein we often meet our finitude and weakness. With such art and aspirations in mind, Alfred Nobel, inventor of the destructive explosive agent dynamite, specified in his will that a prize be given to "the person who shall have done the most or the best work for fraternity between nations, for the abolition or reduction of standing armies and for the holding and promotion of peace congresses."[4]

On the evening of December 10, 2009, having served ten months and twenty days as president of the United States of America, Barack Hussein Obama joined the ranks of Peace Prize Laureates Martin Luther King Jr. (1964), Mother Teresa (1979), Lech Walesa (1983), Desmond Tutu (1984), Elie Wiesel (1986), the Dalai Lama (1989), Nelson Mandela (1993), Yasser Arafat (1994), Shimon Peres (1994), Kim Dae-Jung (2000), and Kofi Annan (2001). In the October 9, 2009, formal announcement, the Nobel Foundation recognized Obama for his "extraordinary efforts to strengthen international diplomacy and cooperation between peoples."[5] On the December evening of the Nobel banquet and speech, amid all the pomp and circumstance, the Norwegian Nobel Committee introduced President Obama in grandiose hyperbole, praising him as an idealist, a civil rights champion, and a dreamer. Like so many Americans, the Norwegian prize givers believed they and the United States had transcended race, what Stanley Crouch years ago called "the All-American Skin Game." Instead of looking for the dispossessed according to characteristics or appearances, they opted instead for a veil of ignorance, a willed colorblindness wherein race was taken out of the social equation so that human beings could dwell together without the looming specter of slavery and genocide and servitude and enmity.

The committee viewed Obama as the harbinger of peace, cooperation, and compromise. Just as the United States has long venerated Lady Justice—blindly weighing support and opposition on a scale she could not see and then administering the law with objectivity through reason and justice—so also the Nobel Committee placed faith in the cool reason at work in the idea of a colorblind age that had elected a biracial president. Certainly, if anyone could enact the theory of justice John Rawls imagined and assume the "veil of ignorance" for the betterment of all, it would be Obama, and his form of justice would be egalitarian, humane, fair-minded, and objective.[6] Unfortunately, in a "post-racial" vision of the human experience, the ease of passage afforded to persons of the dominant culture and the restrictions encountered by persons of color seemed of little concern.

Meanwhile, even today, behind the walls of prisons and tenement halls, the U.S. presence in Iraq, its bold proclamations on democracy and social progress, its pride and belief in the strength of its welfare, and its obsession with Wall Street's daily gains and losses, lie people of color, the forgotten faces of America's war on drugs, wards of the juvenile detention system, students targeted as problems to be stricken from the world of possibilities at a young age by another system equally good at containment and equally good at denying self-worth and opportunity, the education system. Swept from the soil-filled carpet their mothers and grandmothers might have cleaned as domestic workers, they are housed out of sight so that "Hope" and "Change" can emerge, with roughly one out of every three black men spending time in the U.S. penal system. And, once there, not only is their humanity taken away, but also innumerable opportunities die.

Yet, the recognition of color, like the recognition of the hovering military drone ready to make its deadly assault, is vital if the age of Obama, in which films like Tate Taylor's *The Help* proliferate, is to awaken to the human atrocities done in the name of culture and sound out a loud cry for justice. The unthinkable wrongs done in the name of God and country, approved by decree upon treaty upon law upon Constitution upon Amendment upon policy, tell us it must be so, but, somehow, amid all our colorblindness and millennial optimism, we feel shame and think these are truths too unsettling to confront and that if we confront them there is nothing that can be done and that if we do confront them they will swallow us. Despite the Nobel committee's post-racial optimism and today's millennial disbelieving, apathy, and declarations that color does not matter, it really does. No matter how skeptical, stubborn, or politically incorrect it may seem, when people of color cannot exercise their "unalienable rights" as granted in the Constitution, no matter how much the mass media, the White House, and the neoliberals and neoconservatives spin it, the specter of race and the overwhelming legacy of slavery continues to affect "life, liberty, and the pursuit of happiness" for many African Americans. As Cornel West continues to argue, African Americans have little or no mobility and thus remain apart, an "undercaste" kept in check largely through the mechanisms of mass incarceration:

> What is completely missed in the rare public debates today about the plight of African Americans is that a huge percentage of them are not free to move up at all. It is not just that they lack opportunity, attend poor schools, or are plagued by poverty. They are barred by law from doing so. And the major institutions with which they come into contact are designed to prevent their mobility. To put the matter starkly: The current system of control permanently locks a huge percentage of the African American community out of the mainstream society and economy. The system operates through our criminal justice institutions, but it functions more like a caste system than a system of crime control. Viewed from this perspective, the so-called underclass is better understood as an undercaste—a lower caste of individuals who are permanently barred by law and custom from mainstream society. Although this new system of racialized social control purports to be colorblind, it creates and maintains racial hierarchy much as earlier systems of control did. Like Jim Crow (and slavery), mass incarceration operates as a tightly networked system of laws, policies, customs, and institutions that operate collectively to ensure the subordinate status of a group defined largely by race.[7]

While the prize givers might have seen Obama's potential as a leader and community builder, they may have also been blind to the racial divisions and social inequities in America today. Inspired perhaps by the *Portrait of President Barack Obama* by Shepard Fairey, which captured the "Hope" message of the 2008 Obama/Biden campaign so powerfully; by the sheer force of the campaign's simple yet effective "hope and change" rhetoric; or by the number of diverse encounters the Nobel Committee had had in a land where 94.4 percent of the people are Norwegian, 3.6 percent European, and 2 percent declared "other," the Nobel Committee helped sustain the appearance that African Americans had known concrete results, with racism a relic of the past, prejudice and judgment based upon skin color a distant nightmare, and the United States a kind of Disney World where dreams really do come true:

> Many have been awarded the Peace Prize for their courage, even when the results for a long time seemed modest: . . . When Martin Luther King Jr. received his award, he had proclaimed his dream that "my four little children will one day live in a nation where they will not be judged by the color of their skin but by the content of their character," but there was still a long way to go from dream to reality.
> Mr. President, we are happy to see that through your presence here so much of Dr. King's dream has come true.[8]

After recognizing Obama as a living embodiment of Martin Luther King Jr.'s dream, the committee went as far as to see Obama as a reflection of its own ideals: "to strengthen international institutions as much as possible; to advance democracy and human rights; to reduce the importance of arms and preferably do away with nuclear arms altogether."[9] Yet, rather than articulate these particular shared ideals as proclaimed by the Scandinavian folk or rehash a Martin Luther King Jr. sentiment, Barack Hussein Obama lined out justifications for the use of force, especially in cases of domestic terrorism.

The irony most likely was missed that evening, but the United States herself has known such horrific acts done in the name of the Militant Father, the Bigoted Son, and the Hooded Ghost for most of the twentieth century, burning fear into the hearts of African Americans who by day cleaned the houses of the dominant culture, washed their windshields, filled their gas tanks, changed their oil, fixed their tires, and took the time and care, well beyond their birthing years and their bodily capacities allowed, to raise white children and teach them to love themselves and grow and know how to master self-doubt and how to fashion a sense of authenticity that would carry them for the rest of their lives. To refer to the black women who gave their lives, their blood, sweat, and tears, for little money and for great labor, as "the help," is ludicrous, for "the help" is a kind of insider's joke of the middle to upper-middle class and the aspiring bourgeoisie. It is an expression that both trivializes what significant things are being demanded and the toll doing these things for years takes on a human psyche and body. It is a grotesque understatement that attempts to make something as puerile as bondage light and funny, something that those with capital, power, and "all the right stuff" can fling off silver-forked tongues whose not ever knowing lack or want leads them to see servitude as their right and slavery as justice. In this sense, using African Americans as domestics during the daylight hours and threatening their homes, assaulting their children and mothers and fathers during the evening, were acts of domestic terrorism. Yet no Patriot Act overriding the Constitution emerged. In fact, it took years of protest and many lives lost before the Civil Rights Act of 1964 was passed. On the night of December 10, 2009, Barack Obama chose to speak on domestic terrorism and the modern, "surgical" way it could be combated: "Terrorism has long been a tactic, but modern technology allows a few small men with outsized rage to murder innocents on a horrific scale."[10]

"Surgical," antiseptic forms of engagement distort reality, twisting things so they no longer appear as horrific as they are. For that evening and for much of his presidency, Obama has condoned the use of unmanned aerial vehicles or "drones" as ideal weapons for a "surgical" and indirect, removed, safely distant war. Although they appear to remove the remote operator from direct combat, drones create a false sense of distance and objectivity, as in Omer Fast's *5,000 Feet Is the Best*, a short film exhibited in museums and on the Internet that depicts a drone pilot as he is being interviewed in a Las Vegas hotel room, with constant interruptions from a loud "emergency-broadcasting test" tone that disturbs him so much that he reaches for some sort of pill to ease the obvious trauma induced.[11] Presumably, the pills are some form of benzodiazapam and the pilot a PTSD sufferer. But, as with the late plays of Samuel Beckett, Fast captures something quite haunting in the inhumanity we show one another. With Tate Taylor's *The Help,* the daily inhumanity of 1962 Mississippi disappears amid the almost minstrel show–like laughter the over-the-top black characters elicit. With both Obama's notion of the surgical war and Taylor's interpretation of *The Help,* reality and action are glossed over and minimized. By presenting an antiseptic view of race relations, *The Help* enables us to consume the civil rights movement easily, with the difficult aspects of its genesis, struggles, social tensions, dangers, terrors, and tragic casualties kept safely at bay. Calling Taylor's representation of the segregated South "deeply sanitized," Roxane Gay asserts, "The movie gives the impression that life was difficult in Mississippi in the 1960s for women, white and black, but still somewhat bearable because that's just how things were."[12] Further, Ida E. Jones and the Association of Black Women Historians convincingly demonstrate how *The Help* revives the stereotypical Mammy trope. In this well-known artistic representation and also societal role wherein black women sought employment in white households, black women were depicted as "asexual, loyal, and contented caretakers of whites."[13] Thus, both now and when the Mammy stereotype was so often used, the dominant culture could "ignore the systemic racism that bound black women to back-ground, low paying jobs where employers routinely exploited them."[14]

The Help (released in 2011) is the film version of the 2009 Kathryn Stockett blockbuster novel by the same name that has since been read by book clubs across the United States and with which the Obamas took great delight. Romanticizing the relationships between black domestic women and their white women employers, the film is told from the perspective of Aibileen, one of the black domestics encouraged to come forward by "Skeeter," one of the domestic employer's children who has gone to school and now seeks, by having the black women tell their own stories, to empower them. In effect, Skeeter steps out of time and space and transcends the moment, saving the day for black women through the power of the word. It is a myth of post-racial America that many millennial generation members find compelling, so much so that two researchers at UNC–Charlotte now use the film as an ideal way of teaching about diversity for the "intersectionality" the film contains.[15]

Nevertheless, although the film sure can be awfully uplifting and optimistic about the past, present, and future, it is not faithful to history, especially this well-documented period of America's civil rights age. Thus, the film may inspire, but it never challenges. It may offer facile, idealistic musing but never presents us with an art encounter to sort through, agonize over, and dwell upon, especially one so connected to historical moments. For history needs to be interrogated, especially in light of what Michel Foucault calls "subjugated knowledges": the many things left out that make history the "nightmare," as James Joyce put it, from which we are continually trying to awaken. Unfortunately, those things neglected by history are the very things glossed over and idealized by *The Help*.

Aside from the assassination of Medgar Evers, most of the civil rights movement is largely ignored. In fact, Evers's shooting by the KKK (noted incorrectly in the novel as a "bludgeoning" when in fact Evers was shot in front of his children in his driveway) occupies only a few frames of the film and never occupies enough of the story to alter its terrain of comedy. Heroes of the civil rights movement are erased or ignored; after the assassination of Medgar Evers, life goes on. After the assassination of John F. Kennedy, "a framed picture of JFK has now joined the pictures of Treelore and Jesus."[16] Where hangs the picture of Medgar Evers? Or Martin Luther King Jr.? Or any other civil rights activist whose work and words were more relevant to women like Aibileen and Minny? The danger of the 1960s is thus removed from this setting of Jackson, Mississippi, which, according to Pat Arneson,

> places the story in contradiction with the facts, ultimately crumbling the ethos of the story as historical narrative and potentially as historical fiction. When a narrative does not retain fidelity with important features of historic account, the story sacrifices believability. Stockett uses Jim Crow to contextualize her plot. She reveals segregation, but not so much that a reader/viewer might become uncomfortable. However, the very nature of societal inequalities that inhibit realizing a full democracy *should* continue to make people uncomfortable.[17]

The very premise of the film is a reimagining of history. The idea that the book Skeeter is compiling is a revolutionary undertaking negates the work of "more than thirty prominent black writers who had treated the subject in literature," as outlined in Trudier Harris's study, *From Mammies to Militants*.[18]

The film distorts history, relies upon the elements of fiction, and brings together farcical elements of fancy to create a sense of ensuing action that is not only out of sync with the time period but also at odds with the climate of fear, incertitude, and persecution that accompanied the life of a domestic worker in early 1960s Mississippi. For example, one need look no further than the sumptuous treats the film shows everyone making, devouring, and sharing. Here, one could with success compare Taylor's *The Help* with something of the sacred, one of the Dinesen *Anecdotes of Destiny*, or *Babette's Feast*, where the bread of daily life becomes something symbolic and sacramental. Thus, were one to warp 1962 Mississippi into a communal Eucharistic feast where those who do not share water fountains or restrooms now become one sacred body capable of laughing and eating shit pies together, one could get an idea of the effort needed to suspend disbelief in creating the pre–Civil Rights Act Mississippi we find in *The Help*. While from that perspective *The Help* is not credible, from another *The Help* is quite believable. Many have used domestic "others," taking their lives, their sweat, their toil, their labor without proper compensation and care. From the perspective of the exploiter, the film offers a wish fulfillment, a pat on the back and rosy-colored view of the past that assuages guilt and conscience and remorse.

After teaching Celia to cook (Miracle #1), Minny avoids the merciless hands of Mr. Johnny (Miracle #2) and is presented with an elaborate array of casseroles, fried chicken, and baked goods. This decadent spread is an expression of Celia's gratitude for Minny's efforts. As Minny is overcome with emotion at this display of kindness, we hear the voice of the writer (The Angel Aibileen beatifies her), who authenticates her, though we know all along that the voice of the writer has been mediated by another writer (The Blessed Virgin Skeeter, who saves): "That table of food gave Minny the strength she needed. She took her babies out from under Leroy and never went back."[19] This act of what will seem to us as mediation occurs because the entire story has hinged upon the help of white women to gather their strength and commit acts of courage, namely telling their stories.

But what one has to also keep in mind is the position of the twin creators, Stockett and Taylor, both of whom had African American nannies. In Stockett's case, her domestic caregiver was forced to go to the bathroom in a hot, small, enclosed outdoor facility that to this day Stockett has not entered. In the case of Taylor, his nanny nurtured him and helped him become successful. In a real sense, both had black women standing behind them as they reached their goals. They are both Skeeter figures; yet, interestingly, neither has taken the proceeds from the book or the film and returned them to those who made their artistic lives possible, those whose stories they, in essence, have co-opted. As he reveals in the August/September 2011 interview in *Garden and Gun* magazine, Tate Taylor even took the wealth acquired from his initial investment in *The Help* and purchased an old Mississippi plantation where blacks would have toiled in servitude for white masters. Thus, quite literally, the book's improbabilities and incongruities become real-life incarnations, a vision of what may be if we let *The Help* stand alone and do not challenge the world portrait it offers.

Because *The Help* has been enjoyed, discussed, received, reviewed, and debated, the ruckus it has caused and continues to generate is actually dialogue: a national conversation on the representation of race and class and the purpose and responsibility of art in an age that prides itself on being open, sensitive, and diverse. As it is most certainly bad art, unfaithful to history, and Hollywood sentimentalism marketed for a Barack Obama "post-racial" age, it is safe to say there are significant concerns many have about the film. That is not to say that the film raises these concerns. Rather, as Pat Arneson lines out so well in the *First Amendment Studies* article "Considering Social Divisiveness: Offensive Communication, Historical Fiction, and *The Help*," the film actually—through its misrepresentation of 1960s Mississippi culture, its deliberate inclusion of stereotypical behavior and language usage, its reliance upon the "great white hope" trope so often in cultural forms now seen as insensitive, distasteful, inconsiderate, and even insulting—employs offensive communication and even qualifies as a form of hate speech. For Arneson says,

> The narrative frame of white hope serves as a fundamental building block in *The Help* and the character Skeeter plays that role. Within the story, the trope gathers together several characteristics of offensive communication. The implication is that members of the out-group . . . are unwilling or unable to free themselves from the situation without the guidance of white people (who ironically were instrumental in institutionalizing Jim Crow in law and custom). Rather than working as an ally for social change, Skeeter sets out to reveal the realities of domestic work and save the black women from their situation, wrongly assuming that white people are needed to raise black people's social status. This denigrates the out-group and at the same time unreflectively conceives social change as easy to accomplish.[20]

Skeeter was raised in the same social situation as her friends, yet she does not express the hatred and racism that permeate her friends' speech and action. As a white female child supposedly born in the late 1940s and reared in the South during the 1950s, Skeeter's enculturation would typically instill some negative prejudice about race. A historically factual story would likely include a point at which Skeeter addresses her prejudices. The audience does not see or read Skeeter "confronting negative prejudicial thoughts about race because her in-group character is written as if she has none."[21]

At the film's conclusion, Aibileen and Minny encourage Skeeter, their "great white hope," to accept a job offer in New York City.[22] "I don't mean to rub salt in your wound, but . . . you ain't got a good life here in Jackson," says Aibileen, as if Skeeter's wounds and prospects in the South are as deep, dangerous, and constraining as Aibileen's own.[23]

> "You ain't got nothing left here but enemies in the Junior League. You done burned ever bridge there is. You ain't never gone get another man in this town, and everybody know it. So don't walk your white butt to New York, RUN IT!"[24]

So says Minny, echoing Aibileen's sentiments. Skeeter may have become something of a social pariah among her southern middle- and upper-middle-class social group, but her privilege still affords her more opportunities than Aibileen or Minny can ever hope to obtain. Their own potential futures are completely ignored—in fact, Minny has secured a job with Celia and Johnny for the rest of her life, as if that is the best thing a black woman can hope for in the 1960s South, and Aibileen has no job at all as the film closes with the image of her walking into the distance.

Although it may meet the formal definition of hate speech but not meet the bar of liability because of the different ways audience members have responded, the issue with the film version of Stockett's book has much to do with the way it seeks to make appeals, the actual universal appeals it makes, and the utter occlusion of historical facticity. Too often our strategy is to provide spurious contexts of Universality or of Otherness; both can be merely masks for our own values. Interestingly, when questioned about the film and about those who take issue with it, the film's director Tate Taylor defends it as a universal work of art:

> I want people to look at where they are in life, whether they are white, black, gay, straight, Asian, tall, short, they probably at one point in life felt oppressed, repressed or discriminated against. Figure out who is holding you back, and take a chance to talk to them and see what happens. Cross the line and have a discussion. That's what *The Help* is all about.[25]

But somehow, even though a nationwide conversation that includes the president and first lady is taking place, Taylor and Stockett's universalization of the Other's experience falls short of what we as artists and creators are capable of and also of what we as members of a dominant culture are responsible to care about and work together toward: the material changes and weighing of multiple perspectives that will generate genuine inclusivity and enable all members of American society to pursue justice.

The relationship between Gwendolyn Brooks's poem and Tate Taylor's film is disjunctive, not connective. Therefore, this is not an attempt to compare two radically different works dealing with prescient concerns and argue that each treats difference, inequality, racial identity, civil rights, and ignorance for the betterment of society. Rather, it is to tease out an uncomfortable relationship between two art forms, indicating how the cultural complacency and historical irresponsibility of a "post-racial" era has muffled the cry for social justice of the 1960s. As Gwendolyn Brooks urges in her powerful poem that reaches out to the pain two mothers know, we must voyage out. To do so is to embrace socially conscious art, which often objects. Here we might risk calling upon metaphor to transport us, for, as Brooks says, "Art hurts. Art urges voyages—and it is easier to stay at home."[26]

NOTES

1. Cornel West, foreword to *The New Jim Crow: Mass Incarceration in the Age of Colorblindness*, by Michelle Alexander (New York: New Press, 2010), Kindle edition.
2. "Emmett Till Part 01 of 02." FBI.gov. http://vault.fbi.gov/Emmett%20Till%20/Emmett%20Till%20Part%2001%20of%2002 (accessed April 28, 2014).
3. Mamie Till Mobley, 1955, quoted in Cornel West, *Democracy Matters: Winning the Fight Against Imperialism* (New York: Penguin Books, 2004), 21.
4. "Facts on the Nobel Peace Prize," Nobelprize.org, Nobel Media AB, 2013, http://www.nobelprize.org/nobel_prizes/facts/peace/.
5. "The Nobel Peace Prize 2009 – Presentation Speech," Nobelprize.org, Nobel Media AB, 2013, http://www.nobelprize.org/nobel_prizes/peace/laureates/2009/presentation-speech.html.
6. John Rawls, *A Theory of Justice* (Cambridge: Belknap Press of Harvard University Press), 1971.
7. Michelle Alexander, *The New Jim Crow: Mass Incarceration in the Age of Colorblindness* (New York: New Press, 2010), 13.
8. "The Nobel Peace Prize 2009 – Presentation Speech."
9. "The Nobel Peace Prize 2009 – Presentation Speech."
10. Barack H. Obama, "Nobel Lecture: A Just and Lasting Peace," Nobelprize.org, Nobel Media AB, December 10, 2009, http://www.nobelprize.org/nobel_prizes/peace/laureates/2009/obama-lecture_en.html.
11. Omer Fast, *5,000 Feet Is the Best*, co-published by Henie Onstad Art Center, Oslo and The Power Plant, Toronto, 2012, http://www.gbagency.fr/fr/32/Omer-Fast/#!/5-000-Feet-is-the-Best/site_video_listes/87.
12. Roxane Gay, "The Solace of Preparing Fried Foods and Other Quaint Remembrances from 1960s Mississippi: Thoughts on *The Help*," *Rumpus*, August 17, 2011, http://therumpus.net/2011/08/the-solace-of-preparing-fried-foods-and-other-quaint-remembrances-from-1960s-mississippi-thoughts-on-the-help/.
13. Ida E. Jones et al., "An Open Letter to the Fans of *The Help*," Association of Black Women Historians, http://www.abwh.org/images/pdf/TheHelp-Statement.pdf.
14. Jones et al., "An Open Letter to the Fans of *The Help*."
15. Eun-Kyoung Othelia Lee and Mary Ann Priester, "Who Is The Help? Use of Film to Explore Diversity," *Affilia*, November 11, 2013, 0886109913509545. doi:10.1177/0886109913509545.
16. Pat Arneson, "Considering Social Divisiveness: Offensive Communication, Historical Fiction, and *The Help*," *First Amendment Studies* 47, no. 1 (2013): 104.
17. Arneson, "Considering Social Divisiveness," 30.
18. Page R. Laws, "The Help," *Cineaste* 36, no. 4 (2011): n.p.
19. Tate Taylor and Kathryn Stockett, *The Help* (screenplay) (Universal City, Calif.), 2011, 135.
20. Arneson, "Considering Social Divisiveness," 32.
21. Arneson, "Considering Social Divisiveness," 32.
22. Arneson, "Considering Social Divisiveness," 29.
23. Taylor and Stockett, *The Help*, 137.
24. Taylor and Stockett, *The Help*, 138.
25. Tate Taylor, as quoted in "Director: People Are Too Critical of 'The Help,'" by Chris Witherspoon, *theGrio*, August 15, 2011, http://thegrio.com/2011/08/15/the-help-director-people-are-too-critical-of-this-film/.
26. Gwendolyn Brooks, *In the Mecca: Poems* (New York: Harper & Row, 1968), 40.

REFERENCES

Alexander, Michelle. *The New Jim Crow: Mass Incarceration in the Age of Colorblindness*. New York: New Press, 2010.

Arneson, Pat. "Considering Social Divisiveness: Offensive Communication, Historical Fiction, and *The Help*." *First Amendment Studies* 47, no. 1 (2013): 20–37. doi:10.1080/08997225.2012.741815.

Bolden, B. J. *Urban Rage in Bronzeville: Social Commentary in the Poetry of Gwendolyn Brooks, 1945–1960*. Chicago: Third World Press, 1999.

Brooks, Gwendolyn. *In the Mecca: Poems*. New York: Harper & Row, 1968.

———. *Selected Poems*. New York: Harper & Row, 1963.

———. *The Bean Eaters*. New York: Harper, 1960.

Crouch, Stanley. *The All-American Skin Game, or Decoy of Race: The Long and the Short of It, 1990–1994*. New York: Pantheon Books, 1995.

Fast, Omer. *5,000 Feet Is the Best*. Co-published by Henie Onstad Art Center, Oslo and The Power Plant, Toronto, 2012. http://www.gbagency.fr/fr/32/Omer-Fast/#!/5-000-Feet-is-the-Best/site_video_listes/87.

Gay, Roxane. "Bad Movie/Worse Book, Part I: Why 'The Help' Is Hopeless." *New York Daily News*. http://www.nydailynews.com/blogs/pageviews/2012/02/bad-movieworse-book-part-i-why-the-help-is-hopeless(accessed December 26, 2013).

———. "The Solace of Preparing Fried Foods and Other Quaint Remembrances from 1960s Mississippi: Thoughts on *The Help*." *Rumpus*, August 17, 2011. http://therumpus.net/2011/08/the-solace-of-preparing-fried-foods-and-other-quaint-remembrances-from-1960s-mississippi-thoughts-on-the-help/.

Gregory, Vanessa. "The Man Behind The Help." *Gun & Garden*. 2011. http://gardenandgun.com/article/man-behind-help.

Harris, Trudier. *From Mammies to Militants: Domestics in Black American Literature*. Philadelphia: Temple University Press, 1982.

hooks, bell. *Writing Beyond Race: Living Theory and Practice*. New York: Routledge, 2013.

Jones, Ida E., Daina Ramey Berry, Tiffany M. Gill, Kali N. Gross, and Janice Sumler-Edmond. "An Open Statement to the Fans of *The Help*." Association of Black Women Historians, n.d. http://www.abwh.org/images/pdf/TheHelp-Statement.pdf.

Laws, Page R. "The Help." *Cineaste* 36, no. 4 (2011): n.p.

Lee, Eun-Kyoung Othelia, and Mary Ann Priester. "Who Is The Help? Use of Film to Explore Diversity." *Affilia*, November 11, 2013, 0886109913509545. doi:10.1177/0886109913509545.

Mobley, Mamie Till, quoted in Cornel West, *Democracy Matters: Winning the Fight Against Imperialism*. New York: Penguin Books, 2004.

"The Nobel Peace Prize 2009 – Presentation Speech." Nobelprize.org, Nobel Media AB, 2013.http://www.nobelprize.org/nobel_prizes/peace/laureates/2009/presentation-speech.html.

"The Nobel Peace Prize for 2009 to President Barack Obama – Press Release." Nobelprize.org, Nobel Media AB, 2013. http://www.nobelprize.org/nobel_prizes/peace/laureates/2009/press.html.

Obama, Barack H. "Nobel Lecture: A Just and Lasting Peace." Nobelprize.org, Nobel Media, December 10, 2009.
http://www.nobelprize.org/nobel_prizes/peace/laureates/2009/obama-lecture_en.html.

Raines, Howell. "Grady's Gift." *New York Times*, December 1, 1991. http://www.nytimes.com/1991/12/01/magazine/grady-s-gift.html?pagewanted=all&src=pm.

Rawls, John. *A Theory of Justice*. Cambridge: Belknap Press of Harvard University Press, 1971.

Rosenberg, Alyssa. "'The Help': Softening Segregation for a Feel-Good Flick." *Atlantic*, August 10, 2011. http://www.theatlantic.com/entertainment/archive/2011/08/the-help-softening-segregation-for-a-feel-good-flick/243395/.

Singley, Bernestine. "Sniffing Dirty Laundry: A True Story from 'The Help's' Daughter." BeforeBarack.com, 2011. http://www.beforebarack.com/sniffing-dirty-laundry-a-true-story-from-%e2%80%9cthe-help%e2%80%99s%e2%80%9d-daughter/.

Stockett, Kathryn, quoted in "'The Help' Author Says Criticism Makes Her 'Cringe.'" *All Things Considered*, by Michele Norris. NPR.org, December 23, 2009. http://www.npr.org/templates/story/story.php?storyId=120966815.

———. *The Help.* New York: Amy Einhorn Books, 2009.
Taylor, Tate, dir. *The Help.* Burbank, Calif.: Touchstone Home Entertainment; distributed by Buena Vista Home Entertainment, 2011.
Taylor, Tate, and Kathryn Stockett. *The Help* (screenplay). Universal City, Calif., 2011.
Viola Davis's Interview for "The Help" on The Charlie Rose Show (1/4), 2012. http://www.youtube.com/watch?v=JZwxGIWP8sg&feature=youtube_gdata_player.
West, Cornel. "Cornel West on the Death of Emmett Till, 9/11, Preemptive Wars and Race in America." *Democracy Now!* http://www.democracynow.org/2004/5/28/cornel_west_on_the_death_of (accessed December 27, 2013).
Witherspoon, Chris. "Director: People Are Too Critical of 'The Help.'" *theGrio*, August 15, 2011. http://thegrio.com/2011/08/15/the-help-director-people-are-too-critical-of-this-film/.

Chapter Three

If Django and Lincoln Could Talk: James Baldwin Goes to the Movies

Robert McParland

Our myths are projected upon the screen these days. They appear in films like *Lincoln* and *Django Unchained*. We project images. Indeed, a leader like Barack Obama is a screen onto which people project their fantasies, needs, fears, and hopes. At his inauguration, Obama was sworn in with his hand on the Lincoln Bible, in a symbolic gesture, a mythic gesture. This symbolism, like that of Dr. King's "I Have a Dream" speech in 1963 before the Lincoln Memorial, deals in selective historical memory. We are not given the whole story of the quest for racial equality or popular hope for the future by the Obama inauguration or by the film *Lincoln*. We are given myth and perhaps myth gives us hope. In Steven Spielberg's film, Abraham Lincoln is presented at the center of the issue of race. Django, in Quentin Tarantino's film, likewise becomes that central figure. This mixes with our national mythology at a time when a post-racial utopian unity remains a dream rather than a reality.

The films of 2013, *Lincoln* and *Django Unchained*, interrogate, rather than merely underwrite, our myths of racial harmony. In the *New York Times*, Jonathan Rieder, writing on Dr. Martin Luther King's "Letter from the Birmingham Jail," insisted that King made "a defiant assertion of a black right to belong that rested on something more primal than, and prior to, the nation's official documents and civic heroes."[1] These films point toward that "something more primal." Beyond the violence of *Django* and the vigorous congressional debate in *Lincoln*, perhaps they help us to think further about how only the recognition of dignity, common humanity, and respectful interpersonal life will advance the American dream.

Lincoln and *Django Unchained* are films that help us to frame our American story, much as Homer once gathered stories that had passed through generations to offer the Greeks a common story. *Django Unchained*, set in the South two years before the Civil War, prompts us to look at America's past and our future. The *New Yorker* viewed this as a burlesque of violent absurdity and cruelty, parody fantasy, a mock Western followed by revenge melodrama. The reviewer claimed that, while there are arresting images, there is little actual confrontation with the issues of race or slavery in the film.[2] However, a viewer is clearly prompted by this film to reflect upon the condition of slavery. Impossible dominance and violent abuse are evident in the killing of the slave who is forced to be a boxer and can no longer fight. Equally vulgar is the abuse of Django's enslaved wife, Broomhilda (Kerry Washington). The entire role of the co-opted slave Steve (Samuel L. Jackson) is a form of commentary. He has been so completely absorbed into the structure of slavery that, as a proud house slave, he has become an enforcer of the very impositions of inhumanity that psychologically and physically imprison his race.

Steven Spielberg's *Lincoln* likewise reminds us of America's debate over slavery. The film presents a heroic Lincoln, determined to pass the Thirteenth Amendment, to extirpate slavery through constitutional means. Dealing only with Lincoln's last year in office, the film does not mention that Abraham Lincoln, as a presidential candidate, urged the maintenance of the union but, at first, did not actively promote racial political equality in Illinois or in the nation. Lincoln focused on the natural rights of African Americans. Yet, he endorsed black recolonization. He was not, upon his election to the presidency, inclined to emancipate the South's slaves. The struggle of the slaves was not his main focus. It was, of course, on his mind and the effort to achieve this came later. As the film *Lincoln* points out, some legislators were concerned that the Emancipation Proclamation could be retracted if it were not written into law in the Thirteenth Amendment. Others surmised that accomplishing this might be a way to end the war. This film, emerging during the Obama presidency, speaks to America at a time when we have been encouraged to look beyond race. Yet, to be lulled into believing that we have moved beyond race is to not face America's reality. To have Barack Obama sworn in as president with his hand on the Lincoln Bible is a noble gesture. Although this may symbolize our hopes, his presidency alone does not equal inter-racial maturity.

Lincoln comes alive for us in Daniel Day-Lewis's stirring portrayal, Steven Spielberg's sharp images and tableaux, and Tony Kushner's vital script. Their Lincoln insists upon passage of the Thirteenth Amendment to affirm "that democracy is not just a chaos." He asserts that the eyes of the world are upon them and "the fate of human dignity is in our hands now." That comment is as true today as it was in 1864–1865. The racial situation in America remains as significant as it was in the years of Lincoln. One hundred years later, novelist and essayist James Baldwin wrote, in 1963: "One is attempting to save an entire country. . . . The price for that is to understand oneself."[3] Like Abraham Lincoln looking toward reconstruction in the 1860s, Baldwin in the 1960s saw a big project ahead. He saw racial issues as poison, a problem that is structural. Ending legal segregation was the tip of the iceberg. There was a bigger problem underneath. In his essay collection *Notes of a Native Son* (1955), Baldwin wrote: "All over Harlem now there is felt the same bitter expectancy with which, in my childhood, we awaited winter; it is coming and it will be hard; there is nothing anyone can do about it."[4]

The reflections of James Baldwin from the 1960s continue to speak to the anxieties, the anger, and the suffering in our time. We might speak of both the social critique and the hope of James Baldwin. In phrases that sound current today, the author asserts being American and the importance of maintaining the nation while critiquing its flaws. Baldwin would contend that mostly we hold to myths, democratic ideals, while in practice denying minority groups rights and privileges. Baldwin addresses the need to "disrupt the comforting beat, in order to be heard."[5] Like a jazz artist, he would break rhythm. In a letter to Archbishop Desmond Tutu, he insisted that "black freedom will make white freedom possible."[6] His voice is an important one to consider, if we think of contemporary historical novels and films as a repository of myths that suggest something about our past and our present.

What both Lincoln and Baldwin clearly saw is that a great effort would be necessary to foster effective structural change. Today, years later, the United States continues to have numerous pockets of poverty in its urban areas: among them Detroit, Baltimore, Philadelphia, Newark, and many others. These are places where large sections of the urban environment are caught in a time warp, one as old as the walls around them. The days in which James Baldwin wrote still live in these walls. In some places, the brick walls of nineteenth-century industry still stand. So too do structures of inequality and matters of indignity still dwell within. Vibrant communities live and love in these places—and they endure. Walls protect and shelter and they separate and contain. Post-racialism is a veil dangled over the rough concrete face. Frequently, we will hear the question about how recession has affected the middle class. This middle class is an ever-expanding middle that appears to include most every voter in the country. We hear less about the urban or the rural poor. An abstract anti-capitalism, such as the recent Occupy Wall Street movement, does not provide school funding, desegregate urban geographies, ease the strain of police enforcement, rebuild inner cities, or put food on tables. Action is required to respond to the poverty and joblessness in our urban areas. Often enough the poor and jobless are members of racial minorities. Developing ways to provide paths to education for urban minorities may be a route to assist them in claiming and contributing their talents and skills in the wider world. Yet often in these settings, education itself may be demeaned and looked upon as "uncool." This attitude is fundamentally suicidal, as a brief poem by Gwendolyn Brooks, "We Real Cool," points out.[7] Like Django, there is a need for young African American men and women to seize opportunity and assert responsibility to reclaim justice and the love of one's life. Against all odds, one must make the effort.

James Baldwin appears to have recognized the need for a heroic journey, like that of Django. In his writing, Baldwin dealt with race and economic issues in structural terms, not merely with rhetoric. He asked what policy efforts would transform things. Baldwin grew up in Harlem and knew it well. He was the eldest of nine children, with a stepfather who was a preacher in a small church. One may substitute the name of any racially identified ghetto with Harlem in Baldwin's statement when he says: "All over Harlem, Negro boys and girls are growing into stunted maturity, trying desperately to find a place to stand, and the wonder is not that so many are ruined but that so many survive."[8]

A film like *Django Unchained* suggests this survival and endurance. Django wishes to reclaim his wife from slavery, hardship, and the sadistic treatment by Calvin Candie (Leonardo DiCaprio). Ingenuity and revenge are mixed with an effort to reclaim freedom and dignity. Jamie Foxx as Django is heroic, resourceful, and brutal when necessary. At the center is the issue of race, and like Daniel Day-Lewis's Lincoln, he is a screen onto which viewers may project their fantasies, needs, fears, and hopes.

James Baldwin approached these needs, fears, and hopes through story, as well as the discursive essay. *The Progressive* published Baldwin's essay "A Letter to My Nephew," which was written in the midst of civil rights–era issues and the centennial of the Emancipation Proclamation. In it Baldwin points out that democracy has shown limited achievements. Much like Martin Luther King in that same year, Baldwin sees evidence in the ghettos that is to the contrary. There are structural issues beyond what the political forum has moved to change. There are assertions of black ability and equality. There are white calls for "integration." But what community is there? As a social critic, Baldwin did not favor any form of violent social revolution or rebellion. Rather, his goal was "to force our brothers to see themselves as they are; to cease fleeing from reality and begin to change it."[9] The issue was to face marginalization and to make it visible. This was to confront not only southern racism and Jim Crow laws but to face the more insidious socio-economic issues that existed nationwide. For James Baldwin, this was an existential issue.

The theme of justice, in Baldwin's writing, as in that of Martin Luther King and others, is embedded in Judeo-Christian ethics. Baldwin's writing embodies the rhythms of church and the blues-jazz tradition. Voice and musicality are connected with a religion of the soul. Blues and jazz were fused with awakening to his identity as an African American man. In "The Uses of the Blues," he wrote of "the experience of life, or the state of being, out of which the blues come" and "the toughness that manages to make that experience articulate."[10] For Baldwin, blues represented liberation for the African American. The blues figure in Baldwin is symbolic of the race: the style, the soul, and the burden that is carried. This is an exile improvising in a racially troubled world. A Baldwin protagonist is often a tragic hero reflecting the cultural experience of the people. In "What It Means to be an American," Baldwin writes that the blues vocals of Bessie Smith helped him to "dig back" into his ancestral speech, his racial identity, and his feelings and experience.[11] He told Studs Terkel in 1961 that he had to clear away his feelings of being shamed by "all of the stereotypes that the country inflicts on Negroes."[12] Storytelling and digging back into that ancestral speech were his way of reclaiming dignity and integrity. Like Django, sitting tall on horseback, he made a determined journey.

To have Jamie Foxx play Django (and Ray Charles, in an earlier film) on the screen is relevant here. Baldwin often enlisted the names of Bessie Smith and Ray Charles and Billie Holiday as those who helped him to embrace his truth and sing on paper. Jazz was a voice other than the fundamentalist church in which he was raised. To prose he brought those blues notes, those inflections and calls that were part of the Negro idiom. The title of his novel *If Beale Street Could Talk* refers to the Memphis home of the blues. Beale Street recalls singers and players, suffering and rhythm and joy. It is a call for a voice in America, in the world. In *Go Tell It On the Mountain*, we read: "The Sunday morning service began when Brother Elisha sat down at the piano and raised a song. This moment and this music had been with John, so it seemed, since he had drawn his first breath."[13]

Music runs through much of Baldwin's work. Ida and Rufus in *Another Country* are musicians. In *Just Above My Head*, the situation of "Sonny's Blues" is expanded: Hall Montana reflects on the life of his brother Arthur, who is a musician. He portrays the civil rights movement in *The Fire Next Time*, *Blues for Mister Charlie*, "Going to Meet the Man," and other works. This music is communal and filled with exchange from one voice to another. Through music and story, one may look to this community and a unique individuality. The individual jazz player collaborates while bringing a unique style and improvisational voice to his or her playing. In "Sonny's Blues," for example, Sonny is a symbol of alienation; a pulsing of hurt plays in his veins, but he is also one who finds voice through his music. He suggests Bird, Charlie Parker, as the tragic hero.

A storyteller like James Baldwin is a mythmaker, just as filmmakers like Spielberg and Tarantino are. As a novelist and essayist, by summer 1961, Baldwin had become a visible, public voice for the civil rights movement in the United States. "The Negro Problem" was one that he called a white problem; he asserted that this was a social problem: it was everyone's problem. He wrote his essay for *Harper's*, "The Dangerous Road before Martin Luther King." And it was a dangerous road. In "They Can't Turn Back," he wrote of the difficulty faced by black leadership: "trapped in a no man's land between black humiliation and white power."[14] The young, he believed, had started a "moral revolution" and the leaders seemed often somewhere else, with other political goals.

Keenly aware of the responses of Martin Luther King, Medgar Evers, Malcolm X, and other activists to civil rights, James Baldwin wrote essays of celebration, criticism, anger, and indignation. He was to meet Malcolm X on February 23, 1965, shortly before Malcolm X was killed. Later, he spent months on a screenplay about him, *One Day When I Was Lost: A Scenario Based On Alex Haley's The Autobiography of Malcolm X*. Meanwhile, Baldwin saw a miseducation of youth. His novel *Beale Street* (1974) is on inefficiency in the criminal justice system. In his essay "The Evidence of Things Not Seen" (1985) and his preceding essay of that title (1981), he looks at racial struggle in Atlanta. In *Notes of a Native Son*, he recalls how at a diner in New Jersey he tossed water back at the waitress who would not serve his food order.

A storyteller and a mythmaker, Baldwin had to attempt to balance his role as public intellectual with the work of an artist. He knew this well. In his own essay "Everybody's Protest Novel," on Harriet Beecher Stowe's *Uncle Tom's Cabin*, he observed that a work of art must be more than a political tract. One needed genuinely well-rounded characters. Baldwin could be criticized for writing propaganda and for having deflected his commitment to art into the social-political realm. However, it is clear, in hindsight, that the one fed the other. Baldwin was energized by racial tensions. To be black in America, he said, was to be "in a rage almost all the time" and one had to find appropriate channels for this.[15] Art and fiction were one way to do so.

If James Baldwin were alive today, it would be interesting to hear what he would have to say about Quentin Tarantino's *Django* or Steven Spielberg and Tony Kushner's *Lincoln*. A film appearing in 2013, in the age of Obama, will inevitably carry the present concerns of our society. In the perspective of metahistory, proposed by Hayden White, we are engaged in the employment of these dramas of history.[16] History, in this sense, is an act of imagination. It is recalled through narrative means. In this linguistic turn, the process of historical writing is emphasized. White considered how we write history, and we may ask also about how we represent it in film. For example, are we concerned with irony? Do present concerns influence our selection of materials and our focus? White does not hold that the writing of history is no different from the writing of fiction. However, the recognition that historians make use of verbal structures is valuable.

Spielberg's film is, likewise, a filmic creation. This narrative has been invented. The playwright Tony Kushner has worked from Doris Goodwin's *Team of Rivals* and other sources to give us dramatic conflict, and director Spielberg tells a visual story. Their story contrasts the private concerns of the Lincoln family with the vigorous public debate over the Thirteenth Amendment, giving us an intimate look at Mary Lincoln, young Tad Lincoln, and Robert Lincoln's insistence that he be permitted to join the Union army. In *Metahistory*, Hayden White points out, rather than "revealing the true essence of past reality, historical narrative imposes a mythic structure on the events that it purports to describe."[17] That history of culture cannot ignore the impact of myth on people and contemporary consciousness. Even so, we must also ask when we have a functional myth: a story that informs and encourages action and remedies, one we can actualize.

Like the filmmakers Spielberg and Tarantino, a writer like James Baldwin was keenly aware that mythmaking and storytelling were central to his art. He knew that myth circulated throughout America and affected perception. So he created stories; he drew upon life and imagination and hoped to effect change. Baldwin knew that myth is a social practice, an elaboration of archetypes in the mind. One may speak, for instance, of Joseph Campbell's quest for the monomyth across cultures in our sacred stories, our mythos. James Baldwin knew the power of story and that we mythologize America's "heroic" figures.[18]

Myths provide models for behavior, observes Mircea Eliade. They offer a world-view, a cosmology.[19] Myth transmits tradition, or experience, through story, inviting the listener to join in this story. Thus, a myth supports the social order and a person's integration into it, as Joseph Campbell points out. Myth enlivens a person by calling that individual to recognize and realize his or her own psyche, his or her personhood. There is an integral relationship of contemporary film and story making to the ancient Homeric myths. They are ways of speaking of human experience. In part, they are also elaborations upon what may have been historic events. Herodotus suggested this (a *euhemerism*). Myths may be allegories, extended metaphors to transmit values or to help people to understand phenomena in nature; or else they underscore principles of wisdom, arête, courage, and moderation. Myths have symbolic, mythopoetic imaginative qualities. They express our rituals. They are expressive formulations of wonder, awe, and grappling with the unknown. We have our rituals of the singing of the "Star-Spangled Banner" before baseball games, of our inaugurations, and of our weddings.

Films dwell in myth and imagination more than they do in reason. From a nineteenth-century perspective, mythopoetic thinking may seem to be a kind of outmoded thought. After all, from the Comtean positivist perspective, the age of animism has been overcome by positivist scientific reasoning and the acknowledgment of impersonal natural laws. This was the Comtean view of awakening toward the third and highest step of human development: the positivist stage. One would surpass the "primitive." Yet, the reaches of wonder of the subconscious remained. The primal mythmaking persisted. Calling this emotive language, as Bertrand Russell or the logical positivists might, would not do the trick. Nor was it necessary, as some nineteenth-century and early twentieth-century minds believed, to see an irreconcilable clash between science and the mythopoetic.

Metaphor and myth are expressive of a *potential* in the society. They are not only negative images that would lead us astray or keep us bound to "false" myths. One needs to get "at" the myth and how it is operating. And so, it pays for us to ask how the Obama myth is working in American society and to look at these films—*Django Unchained* and *Lincoln*—for what they are telling us about contemporary America. Joseph Campbell once pointed out that in myth, symbols may be presented as "socially maintained rites" or as "observed." The individual may have experiences that he or she seeks to communicate through signs. If this is truly lived and expressed, this "communication will have the force and value of living myth, for those, that is to say, who receive and respond to it of themselves, with recognition uncoerced."[20]

A film like *Lincoln* is a reminder that our dreams are quite alive today in the public sphere of politics, with its practical affairs of legislation, its rituals and debates. To regard myth as obsolete is a premise in itself that is grounded in a myth. It is to assume that a reductionist perspective stands for the whole world. Myth is today a significant part of modern discourse. The images of global communication and news and celebrity deal in myth. Myth is continually present in film and television, not only as our entertainment, but within our discourse and our oral traditions. Humanity has not abandoned myth in film or story or in its politics. Far from it. Though our images may shift from culture to culture, these forms still resonate in the mind. As Carl Gustav Jung recognized, myths are expressions of a society's dreams, its hopes and goals, its sense of itself. Cinema expresses the imaginary of the time. It is a place in which the social imaginary is created. Film is one of our ways of storytelling. Many films arise from the structure of myth.[21]

Spielberg and Kushner's Lincoln likewise arises from myth, as much as from history. Abraham Lincoln, our sixteenth president, has become legendary. The "road of trials" in Lincoln's life has been remarked upon by his biographers. However, Spielberg's film gives us only one last segment of that heroic journey, like Gore Vidal's *Lincoln*, which only gives us the last days, or Doris Goodwin's *Team of Rivals*, which only gives us the presidency. The film *Lincoln* is set in the last year. The film appears to ask: what destiny has Lincoln? On the road of trials can the hero assimilate his opposite, his unsuspected self, his shadow? More broadly, what destiny has America?

Kushner and Spielberg's *Lincoln* is about a war presidency and the Thirteenth Amendment. It does not give any complete view of Lincoln. Nor is it intended to. The amendment was positioned to try to get the South to end the war. In the film, Lincoln first appears as two black soldiers talk about their service in their battalions. Two white soldiers quote the Gettysburg Address. A black soldier completes this as he walks, his back turned in heroic silhouette, away from the camera. Daniel Day-Lewis provides a vivid portrayal of Lincoln as firm in his beliefs, affable in storytelling, and rich in human concern. This is a believable Lincoln. Day-Lewis and the film place Lincoln before us as a fully human individual. He is high-voiced, a legal-political thinker, a moral man, a bit ungainly in his stride. Lewis makes him present to us. In the period after his re-election in 1864, the Thirteenth Amendment is his central goal. In the midst of the war, the debate in Congress goes on. We begin in war, in a muddy battle, and it is ever in the background. Meanwhile, the conflict is cultural and political. Once time period and costume are established, a mythic Lincoln carries this film for two to three hours.

Politics provides much of the tension here. Yet, this is ever balanced by glimpses into the personal life of the Lincoln family. While the youngest Lincoln, Tad, plays on the rug and responds to his father's comforting arms, Mary Todd Lincoln, played by Sally Field, lingers over the loss of her son Willie. The concerns of the family are juxtaposed with the noisy, tangled dialectic in Congress that Kushner's script highlights, with figures like Thaddeus Stevens, played by Tommy Lee Jones. Spielberg gives us portraits, striking images of Lincoln, cuts and sequences, and he keeps slavery at the narrative center. Thus, it is not economics, states' rights, capitalist expansion, Southern whimsy, or the pressures of modernization that foster the war, but it is slavery that is at issue. The plot concerns a compressed juxtaposition of the passing of the Thirteenth Amendment. National needs and negotiations are set alongside the meaning of family: and, by extension, the nation's families.

Day-Lewis's portrayal of Lincoln is one for our time that builds upon a history of representations of the president. In the 1920s America was given Carl Sandburg's *Abraham Lincoln, the Prairie Years* (1926), in two volumes, and *The War Years* (1939), in four volumes. America got its Lincoln via Sandburg—as biography, epic, and myth—for better or worse. The Sandburg volumes led to Robert Sherwood's play *Abe Lincoln in Illinois* (1958). Charles Beard called *The War Years* "a noble monument to literature" and asked what kind of biography it was.[22] We might also ask what Lincoln this was. Sandburg gives us story and a compelling narrative, but he uses evidence uncritically. There was no original research or documentation, despite a list of "sources and acknowledgments" that were all very general. Edmund Wilson called this "poetical" but that was not a compliment. One might be kinder and call it enjoyable sentimental prose-poetry. One might say that Sandburg's Lincoln has what Northrop Frye once called encyclopedic form:

presenting as it does a panorama of culture through Lincoln. Sandburg's Lincoln was a kind of national poem, and it has some lingering effect on how we look at Lincoln.

Lincoln as myth is better treated in Merrill Peterson's *Lincoln in American Memory*. Peterson traces the images of Lincoln as savior of the Union, the emancipator, the common man, the primary American, and the self-made man. Even so, one might ask about the tormented Lincoln or the politician or the public reception that including Lincoln bashing. "Lincoln" is a site of cultural negotiation—and symbolism and construction are at work. This is glaringly obvious in Gore Vidal's *Lincoln* (1984), a book I recall buying as soon as it came out. Vidal offers the narratives of a half-dozen characters: a dialogical play of perspectives on Lincoln. Vidal is quoted as saying, "I set my fictions within history. Imagined characters intersect with historical ones. The history is plainly history. Fiction fiction."[23] However, some reviewers have disagreed. Vidal replied to his critics: "Every now and then the Lincoln priests issue lists of 'errors' that I am supposed to have made in my book—since it follows the progress of the 'actual' Lincoln, so unlike the protean deity whose shape they keep altering to accommodate to changes in our political weather. For the record, Lincoln is identified on the title page as a novel. The story is told in the third person from the point of view of six individuals. An advanced degree in English is not necessary for understanding the book."[24]

That may be so, but the exaggeration of some events, the imaginary staging of other events, the soap-opera-like depictions of Mary Todd Lincoln, and John Hay's dubious night life give pause to some readers. While one critic recognizes that "we have to expect these things in dramatizations of history," Richard Current objects and writes, "Gore Vidal's Lincoln turns into mythic propaganda of the most egregious kind when it becomes a presentation of Edmund Wilson's Lincoln." For Wilson, Lincoln's 1838 Springfield Lyceum speech announced his goal to destroy and remake the Republic. In the TV version of Vidal's *Lincoln*, Stephen Douglas quotes from that speech and refers to this aim. The only good thing is that probably few viewers noticed the problems with this, says Current.[25]

We are faced with the broader issue of how film and fiction affect how we see the American Civil War. The historian's diligent labor and sure documentation are crucial in reconstructions of the past. Yet, the American public responds to film images, cinematography, and story. In *The Civil War in Popular Culture*, Jim Cullen offers the premise that historical interpretation changes across time and affects how we look at the past. He asks if this is not fictive, a social construction, and he starts sounding a bit like Hayden White.[26] When given the historically based film, one has to ask what the film is saying about the present and about cultural values. What are *Django Un-*

chained and *Lincoln* saying about America's racial concerns in the age of Obama?

In *Myths America Lives By*, Richard T. Hughes outlines five myths that he believes are central to American life. These were portrayals of America as: (1) chosen nation, (2) nature's nation, (3) the Christian nation, (4) the millennial nation, (5) the innocent nation.[27] These myths, he asserts, support national identity. This includes the idea of equality, inscribed in the Declaration of Independence. Hughes is critical of these myths and he points to the dissent of W. E. B. DuBois, Martin Luther King, Ida B. Wells, Frederick Douglass, and others regarding race and the American dream. Others, like Richard Slotkin, have written on race and violence and the displacement of the Native American. In Slotkin's fiction, in *The Crater* (1980), *The Return of Henry Starr* (1988), and *The Young Lincoln* (2001), he peered into history, including Lincoln and the Civil War. Here the myth of the hero Lincoln is placed within the circumstances of his life that contributed to creating his character. We follow him on a flatboat journey on the Ohio and Mississippi, in which he sees slavery and the frontier firsthand. This is a tough Lincoln. This Lincoln meets defenders and opponents of slavery. He meets the famous actor Edwin Booth, who is the brother of his future assassin. Slotkin shows racial interaction and portrays Lincoln travelling toward ideas of equality.

The Spielberg film shows us a Lincoln firmly opposed to slavery. Yet there is not time to show the personal history that led him to this. In the Lincoln-Douglas debates of the late 1850s, Stephen Douglas argued for white supremacy. Lincoln countered this. Some might argue that Lincoln made some use of race and the slavery issue to distinguish himself from this candidate. Lincoln was ever conscious of public opinion through the debates of 1858. Lincoln's 1858 Senate campaign focused upon the future of slavery in the nation. The Dred Scott decision and the Kansas-Nebraska Act of 1854 had suggested that slavery was expanding. Lincoln turned attention to the nation's founders, observing that slavery had been seen as a necessary evil but that he wished to reduce and ultimately eliminate slavery. In his address at Peoria in 1854, he said, "The framers of the Constitution intended and expected the ultimate extinction of that institution." Further, while there he asserted, "Let us re-adopt the Declaration of Independence and with it the practices and policy which harmonize with it." Yet he often spoke in general terms. In 1856 in Chicago, he had said, "I think we have an ever growing interest in maintaining the free institutions of our country." In Kalamazoo, Michigan, on August 27, 1856, he said that people must "come to the rescue of this great principle of equality."[28]

It is clear that Lincoln disliked slavery, but he was not an abolitionist. Stephen Douglas may have called Lincoln an extremist, but he was not one. Politically, Lincoln had to be elected by a white Illinois population that had their own issues about race. Lincoln spoke of rights in a nuanced manner and referenced the Declaration of Independence to assert that such rights were natural. Douglas would not call African Americans into the American community. Lincoln, however, opened the forum to let his constituents consider the possibility of recognizing the equality of people of color. Lincoln, like James Baldwin later, likely recognized that the white who enjoyed freedom could not support enslavement in its economic and social forms and believe that their own rights would stay unaffected and secure. To be an American, Lincoln wrote in a letter to Henry L. Pierce, April 6, 1859, "he who would be no slave must have no slave."[29] To secure the rights of others is to also secure the endurance of one's own rights.

The films *Lincoln* and *Django Unchained* may lead us to ask in what ways we today are securing human rights. We may ask how the structural injustice, pointed to by James Baldwin or Martin Luther King, is being addressed. As movies entertain us, filling our lives with story and imagery and sound, in what sense are we lost in illusions? Or are our myths informing us of the work that is yet to be done?

NOTES

1. Jonathan Rieder, "Martin Luther King's Righteous Fury," *New York Times*, Op-Ed, April 16, 2013, A27.
2. "Review of *Django Unchained*," *New Yorker*, January 22, 2013.
3. James Baldwin, "The Artist Struggling for Integrity" (1963), Audio Farum, 2006.
4. James Baldwin, *Notes of a Native Son* (New York: Random House), 1955.
5. James Baldwin, "As Much Truth as One Can Bear," April 29, 1962, in *The Cross of Redemption: Uncollected Writings*, ed. Randall Kenan (New York: Pantheon, 2011).
6. James Baldwin Letter to Desmond Tutu (1985). See *Cross of Redemption*, ed. Kenan.
7. Gwendolyn Brooks, "We Real Cool," *The Bean Eaters* (New York: Harper, 1960).
8. Baldwin, *Notes of a Native Son*.
9. James Baldwin, "A Letter to My Nephew," *Progressive*, December 1962.
10. James Baldwin, "The Uses of the Blues," in *Cross of Redemption*, ed. Kenan, 131.
11. James Baldwin, "What It Means To Be an American," in *Nobody Knows My Name* (New York: Dial Press, 1961), 18.
12. James Baldwin, interview with Studs Terkel, WFMT-Chicago, 1961. See *Conversations with James Baldwin*, ed. Fred L. Standley and Louis H. Pratt (Jackson: University Press of Mississippi, 1989).
13. James Baldwin, *Go Tell It On the Mountain* (New York: Knopf Doubleday, 2013), 14.
14. James Baldwin, "The Dangerous Road before Martin Luther King," in *Cross of Redemption*, ed. Kenan, 260.
15. James Baldwin, "Everybody's Protest Novel," in *Notes of a Native Son*.
16. Hayden White, *Metahistory* (Baltimore: Johns Hopkins University Press), 1973.
17. White, *Metahistory*, 113. Needless to say, many historians have not been particularly happy with Hayden White. White may be viewed as part of the postmodern cultural turn, or the linguistic turn, in approaches to history, in which there is an interest in writing a history of culture.
18. For example, when Merrill D. Peterson studied the reputation of Thomas Jefferson, he followed his name and image across time. See *The Image of Jefferson in the American Mind* (Oxford: Oxford University Press, 1960). Annette Gordon-Reed has looked at the slaveholder who wrote the Declaration of Independence and at his relationship with Sally Hemings. See *Thomas Jefferson and Sally Hemings* (Charlottesville: University Press of Virginia, 1997).

While recognizing Jefferson's achievements, these works add to our understanding of the story of Jefferson, who has, for America, become as much myth as historical record.

19. Mircea Eliade, *Myth and Reality*, trans. Willard Trask (New York: Harper and Row, 1963), 75.

20. Joseph Campbell, *Hero of a Thousand Faces* (Princeton, NJ: Princeton University Press, 1949), 160. Also see *Creative Mythology* (New York: Arkana, 1991), 4; *The Power of Myth* (New York: Doubleday, 1988).

21. A plot sequence is much like the pattern Campbell describes in *The Hero With a Thousand Faces*: calling, departure, initiation, rising tension and obstacles, helper figures, return. In the quest myth, the hero is called to adventure and has to face departure and initiation and overcome a series of tests and threshold experiences. Often this character returns to his society with a gift that is the benefit of that experience. See Campbell, *Hero of a Thousand Faces* (Princeton: Princeton University Press, 1949), 36–38. Films—and the mythic figures within them—are part of our collective cultural expression. Psychologist Carl Gustav Jung has suggested that we share in archetypes: deep figures arising from subconscious forces.

22. Charles Beard, "The Lincoln of Sandburg," *Virginia Quarterly Review* 16 (Winter 1940): 112–16.

23. Gore Vidal, *United States: Essays* (New York: Random House, 1993).

24. Vidal, *United States*.

25. Richard Current in Jim Cullen, *The Civil War in Popular Culture: A Reusable Past* (Washington, D.C.: Smithsonian, 1995); Edmund Wilson, *Patriotic Gore* (New York: Farrar, Straus and Giroux, 1963).

26. Cullen, *The Civil War in Popular Culture*.

27. Richard T. Hughes, *Myths America Lives By* (Urbana: University of Illinois Press, 2004).

28. Abraham Lincoln, address at Peoria, Illinois, 1854; address at Chicago, Illinois, 1854; address at Kalamazoo, Michigan, 1856.

29. Abraham Lincoln, letter to Henry L. Pierce, April 6, 1859.

Chapter Four

The Exceptional N*gger: Redefining African American Identity in *Django Unchained*

Rodney M. D. Fierce

In his essay "Everybody's Protest Novel," James Baldwin mounts a blistering critique of the protest novel, a subset of American literature that exposes the evils of African American oppression by placing its black characters into increasingly horrifying situations in which they are victimized. Employing Harriet Beecher Stowe's *Uncle Tom's Cabin* as his primary model, Baldwin asserts that rather than confronting the evils of racial subjugation, the protest novel does the exact opposite and "reinforces the principles which activate the oppression they decry."[1]

Baldwin's chief grievance against Stowe's novel and others of its ilk is that they mitigate the horrors they supposedly bring to light by "leaving unanswered and unnoticed the only important question: what it was, after all, that moved her people to such deeds."[2] Baldwin charges the novel with the task of revealing hard truths and compelling readers to confront that which they would prefer to ignore, conferring upon it "the power of revelation . . . the journey towards a more vast reality which must take precedence over all claims."[3]

The protest novel, however, does not take up this mantle and instead seeks to whitewash and sanitize African American trauma by fitting it into an aesthetic category that can be consumed safely. This "passion for categorization, life neatly fitted into pegs," Baldwin asserts, "has led to an unforeseen, paradoxical distress; confusion, a breakdown of meaning."[4] The protest novel, after all, is about situation rather than character, generating the horror it seeks to elicit by fashioning characters utterly devoid of agency and placing them in circumstances in which they are brutally victimized. This, more than anything, Baldwin cannot forgive, for if whites are always the evil oppressors, then African Americans become trapped by their own victimhood, lacking identity without their suffering and incapable of ameliorating their situation. In his critique of Stowe's main characters, Baldwin says that "we have only the author's word that they are Negro and they are, in all respects, as white as she can make them."[5] As the essay progresses, Baldwin makes it clear that such novels are incapable of capturing the essence of the African American experience; any attempt to do so results in a bastardization that fetishizes black identity for the white audience, rendering it familiar and entertaining but not authentic.

The sensationalizing of African American suffering, Baldwin determines, undermines the protest novel's most basic function, which is to disturb. Using literary conventions to turn a visceral, horrifying experience into a stylized one divests the protest novel of any ability to shock, rendering it "an accepted and comforting aspect of the American scene, ramifying that framework we believe to be so necessary. Whatever unsettling questions are raised are evanescent, titillating, remote, for this has nothing to do with us."[6] The protest novel, therefore, becomes a safe and even enjoyable experience, marginalizing that which it was meant to expose.

While Baldwin makes some valid claims, his personal investment in matters of African American identity blinds him to the protest novel formula's potential for elucidating the identities of the very characters it marginalizes. Stock characters, devoid of the specificity we associate with identity, are in fact blank canvases upon which the struggle for individuality can be mapped. But by dismissing the protest novel form as an object of meaningless fetish, Baldwin forgets that there is an element of the aesthetic in every artistic depiction of a dilemma and great potential in employing that aesthetic to debate the problems he claims protest novels generally ignore. With the possible exception of documentary, it is impossible to tell any story completely divested of some element of the heightened, the fantasy, the make-believe. The purpose of art, after all, is to engage us critically and sensually, to make us think and also enjoy. The task of the artist is not to perfectly re-create reality (that is mimicry) but to present problems in new frameworks that allow audiences to connect with them and enjoy doing the work necessary to comprehend them. While Baldwin may be correct in proclaiming the limitations of the protest novel, there are other media, such as film, which are able to transcend the confines of literature by employing visual aesthetics to provide more immediate sensory impression. There are critics that claim that film cannot capture the depth of an experience in the way that literature can. That may or may not be true, but film can compel an audience to see and engage with experiences in a direct and relentless manner. You can gloss over words on a page. An image, once seen, cannot be unseen. As David Bordwell and Kristin Thompson note in their book *Film Art*:

> Films offer us ways of seeing and feeling that we find deeply gratifying. They take us through experiences . . . offering a patterned experience that engages our minds and emotions. . . . All the traditions that emerged—telling fictional stories, recording actual events, animating objects or pictures, experimenting with pure form—aimed to give viewers experiences they couldn't get from other media.[7]

Film, as Bordwell and Thompson observe, is uniquely capable of combining various narrative exempla to tell a story, and through this visual medium, even the stock characters of the protest novel can be rendered nuanced and complex. *Django Unchained*, a 2012 film written and directed by Quentin Tarantino, is one of the more recent filmic incarnations of the protest novel to attempt reclamation of African American identity. Set in the antebellum South prior to the Civil War, the film follows the journey of Django Freedman, a former slave who sets out to liberate his wife from Calvin Candie, the sadistic plantation owner who possesses her. While some argue that using highly stylized cinematography fetishizes the black experience in the same way *Uncle Tom's Cabin* does, such a stance ignores the fact that Tarantino's film enables the African American experience to be explored and empowered through fantasy narratives that it has been denied heretofore.

Django accomplishes what *Uncle Tom* fails to, which is to employ the familiar narrative exempla of American Romance, typically inhabited by white characters, and fashion it into a landscape upon which the African American identity can be debated. While retaining the victimized African American characters of the protest novel, Tarantino's fusion of the spaghetti Western and Germanic fairy tale into his characters alters the protest novel formula by affording them almost superhuman agency over their own circumstances. This unique blend of romance and revenge narrative, savagery and soap opera, transforms *Django* into a more effective protest narrative, one that is instructional and watchable and even enjoyable.

Romance, which Toni Morrison notes "was the form in which this uniquely American prophylaxis could be played out,"[8] is a key element in Tarantino's quest to forge an empowered African American identity. In her book chapter "Romancing the Shadow," Morrison seeks to determine what exactly there was in "American romanticism that made it so attractive to Americans as a battle plain on which to fight, engage, and imagine their demons."[9] She determines that Romance, a concept imported from European culture, is ideal for crafting the American identity because it embodied all of the hopes and fears inherent to the founding of a new nation. More to the point, Romance expressed

> Americans' fear of being outcast, of failing, of powerlessness . . . their fear of loneliness, of aggression both external and internal. In short, the terror of human freedom—the thing they coveted most of all. . . . For young America it

had everything; nature as subject matter, a system of symbolism, a thematics of the search for self-valorization and validation.[10]

The creation of Romance fairy tales, stories in which Americans emerged as the conquering heroes, was instrumental in combating powerlessness and establishing a commanding identity, for they provided all of the basic narrative tools of compelling drama: "platforms for moralizing and fabulation, and for the imaginative entertainment of violence, sublime incredibility and terror—and terror's most significant, overweening ingredient: darkness, with all of the connotative value it awakened."[11]

As Morrison notes, the establishment of a white male American hero required a villain against whom the hero could test his mettle. The black slaves, imported by the Americans from Africa, served in the dual capacity of metaphorical villain and literal victim. Their blackness became the receptacle into which the evils of identity could be cast, leaving the white Americans as their masters as well as symbolic superiors. The Africans, within this paradigm, were the sin to the white virtue, the darkness to the white light, ignorance to their master's enlightenment. In defining itself against blackness, the white American identity permanently tied itself to it, for if blacks are the victims and whites the victimizers, blacks the sinners and whites the saints, neither identity can exist without its polar opposite.

This can be seen in the opening of *Django Unchained*, when two white slavers are marching their human merchandise to market. The scene perfectly encapsulates the identities of white victimizer and black victim, as everything in the frame is soaked in darkness and misery. The night is oppressively shadowy, and the slaves chained together are faceless, more like cattle being herded than men. The only discernible characters are those of the two white slavers, and though they are supposedly in control, the fear of the night is evident on their faces. As the slavers look for terrors around every corner, the symbolism begins to merge, and it is evident that they are afraid of the blackness in which they are immersed. By setting the scene at night, Tarantino creates a landscape in which the Africanist victimized identity is challenged from the outset. The darkness of the night, of the terrors the night might be hiding, and of the chained slaves is all interconnected through what Morrison refers to as the inescapable "power of blackness."[12] What the slavers are most terrified of, therefore, is their African victims and the potential that they might rise up and assume the white identity of victimizer.

Morrison observes that because the images of impenetrable whiteness "appear almost always in conjunction with representations of black or Africanist people who are dead, impotent, or under complete control, these images of blinding whiteness seem to function as meditation on the shadow that is a companion to this whiteness."[13] Since the two identities are inextricably linked, there is significant potential for change if the exempla that helped create the ideology are altered. Since the white American identity uses fairy-tale exempla to gain agency and victimize Africans, then that same framework applied to the African characters can empower them to break from victimhood. This is precisely what begins to happen when Dr. King Schultz, a German bounty hunter, encounters the slave Django in this opening scene. Approaching the chain gang of slaves, Schultz proclaims that one of them (Django) has vital information for him, and in doing so pierces Django's status as powerless victim. That Django has information separates him from the other faceless slave victims; he has the potential to become more than a helpless commodity, or as Calvin Candie says, "That one nigger in ten thousand."[14] Tarantino builds a slow and deliberate character arc for Django through which the audience sees him literally emerge from facelessness and victimhood.

In an interview with the *Root*, Tarantino admits that he worried about actor Jamie Foxx trying to play Django as superhuman too soon. Taking him aside, Tarantino drew seven Xs on a piece of paper and linked them together. Circling one of them, he informed Foxx that for the narrative structure to succeed, that X has to be Django upon the audience first meeting him because "he is not Jim Brown. He is not a superhero. You want to be Jim Brown too soon. . . . You gotta grow into the jacket. You have to express a lifetime of slavery. You have to express a lifetime lived on the plantation."[15] The audience must start out with Django as a victim if he is to successfully break with the traditional protest novel formula. He must first be without identity among the other slaves in a chain gang with nothing to distinguish him other than his victimhood. Once Schultz liberates him and Django throws off the cloak he is wearing, the audience sees the muscled black body and the power behind it. As Django rears back his shoulders, the camera moves in slow motion so that the audience watches the covering slowly fall away and a naked man emerge from the chain gang.

First Tarantino gives Django a face, then a body, and now, freed from slavery, Django becomes a blank slate upon which a new identity can be crafted. The darkness, which helped make the slaves faceless, becomes part of Django's power as the great emancipator. He releases his fellow slaves and allows them to kill the white slave owners, and the night, which was hiding their shame, now acts as cover for their revenge. Agency for Django ultimately comes from merging the white man and black man as poles of the same identity, a feat which Tarantino accomplishes by using the framework of the Western to create a student/teacher dynamic between Schultz and Django. After erasing the identity of Django as victim, Tarantino uses the Schultz character to weave two new narratives for Django, that of the revenge-seeking gunslinger and fairy-tale prince.

A trope of Western films, Tarantino notes, is that the young apprentice must learn the craft before he can become the master himself; by pairing

Django and Schultz in a mentor/mentee capacity, Tarantino breaks from the strict racial construct the protest novel form imposes on black and white identity. Morrison notes that American literary history "is permanently allied with another seductive concept, the hierarchy of race,"[16] and while Tarantino's narrative does not ignore race, the use of the Western conventions enables Django's identity to transcend its confines. During a scene in which Django and Schultz are hunting the outlaw Smitty Bacall, they perch side by side on a high cliff, looking down on the Bacall farm. Schultz is using this particular mark to teach Django about killing without emotion, and the shot tightly focuses on the two main characters, allowing the audience to note the similarities in their appearance and demeanor. Their clothing is a similar shade of gray; both men wear suits and fedoras and are crouching in the exact same position while they survey the farm, eyes fixed on the target. Tarantino notes in an interview:

> [In] telling a story like this you have an experienced gunfighter who meets the young cowpoke who has some mission that he has to accomplish, and it's the old, experienced gunfighter who teaches him the tricks of the trade: teaches him how to draw his gun, teaches him how to kill.... There's an older guy teaching the younger guy and sending him on a vengeance journey.[17]

The importance of the bounty-hunting scenes, aside from giving a visual to Django's tutelage, is to show that this mentorship occurs irrespective of the men's races. Schultz always treats Django as an equal, as a partner and not a sidekick or racial subordinate, though Django is the apprentice for the first half of the film. The Smitty Bacall scene is a pivotal point in the fashioning of this relationship because Django has to decide if this is the identity he wants. Schultz has already freed him, so Django can go off and live quietly somewhere, or he can save his wife, get his vengeance, and become someone who defies the victimhood that was foisted upon him. When Django hesitates to kill Smitty Bacall because his son is standing next to him, Schultz explains what being a hunter entails, saying, "You want to save your wife by doing what I do? This is what I do.... Now quit your pussyfooting and shoot him."[18] Django quickly complies, and in doing so assumes the mantle of the hunter. Later, after their kill, both men are greeted by a white sheriff colleague and invited into his home for coffee and birthday cake. The sheriff addresses both men equally, saying, "Dr., Django, how the hell are you?"[19] and in doing so, indicates that Django is fully indoctrinated into his new identity.

Tarantino's use of the Western exemplum not only breaks with the tradition of the protest novel but also that of the Western itself, for as *New York Times* film critic A. O. Scott notes, "Vengeance in the American imagination has been the virtually exclusive prerogative of white men. More than that, the sanctification and romanticization of revenge have been central to the ideology of white supremacy."[20] Tarantino is not only giving Django an identity that is historically the purview of whites, but by inculcating him into the revenge narrative, Tarantino bestows upon Django all of the "autonomy, authority, newness and difference [and] absolute power"[21] white characters claim through the romanticization of the revenge narrative. Citing Richard Slotkin's book *Regeneration Through Violence*, Scott observes that through the Western and the fairy tale, Tarantino fashions Django and his wife, Broomhilda, into "two essential mythic figures: the captive, usually an innocent woman held against her will by ruthless and alien usurpers, and the hunter, who is obsessed with protecting her honor."[22] As with the Western motif, the fairy-tale exemplum is introduced to Django through Schultz, who, upon hearing the name of Django's wife (Broomhilda), immediately sees the parallels between her situation and that of Brunhilde, her namesake from Germanic/Norse mythology. As the two men eat dinner, Schultz recounts the myth of Brunhilde, the daughter of Wotan (Odin), king of the gods, who is saved from imprisonment on a mountain by a hero who knows no fear, and the comparison of Django with Siegfried becomes evident.

> **Schultz**: It's a German legend, there's always going to be a mountain in there somewhere. And [her father] puts a fire-breathing dragon there to guard the mountain, and he surrounds her in a circle of hellfire. And there Brunhilde shall remain unless a hero arises brave enough to save her.
>
> **Django**: Does a fella arise?
>
> **Schultz**: Yes, Django, as a matter of fact he does. A fella named Siegfried.
>
> **Django**: Does Siegfried save her?
>
> **Schultz**: *[nods]* Quite spectacularly so. He scales the mountain because he's not afraid of it. He slays the dragon because he's not afraid of him. And he walks through hellfire because Brunhilde's worth it.
>
> **Django**: I know how he feels.[23]

By drawing so obviously on this myth, Tarantino not only invites the comparison between Django and Siegfried but encourages the audience to review the events of the film so far through this new exemplum. The opening scene, for instance, becomes one in which the prince is betrayed, brought low, and must fight his way back, a tactic that Tarantino employs to link Django with the legacy of similarly mythic film figures ranging from Charlton Heston's Ben-Hur to Russell Crowe's Maximus. When Django throws off the slave cloak at the scene's climax, he is not simply casting off victimhood; he is reclaiming the identity and quest as the savior of the princess. Much like Django, Broomhilda is not a fully nuanced character, nor is she meant to be. Her presence as the princess in the tower in need of rescue serves to define Django as the hero capable of defending her honor, and Calvin Candie/Stephen as the villains who sully it. The audience's conception of Broomhilda is filtered at first entirely through Django's imagination, and at various points she appears in his mind and on screen. Attired in a spotless white dress, carrying a single yellow daisy and sporting a demure yet playful smile, this vision is Broomhilda as the pinnacle of innocence, and for Django's identity to be solidified, he must safeguard this ideal. Tarantino juxtaposes beauty and savagery in *Django* to continually illustrate the titular character's commitment to his heroic identity, and this is never clearer than in the contrasting depictions of Broomhilda. As Django approaches Calvin Candie's plantation, Candyland, he imagines Broomhilda in her white dress beckoning to him to come to find her. The vision comforts him and gives the audience a false sense of security regarding Broomhilda's situation on the plantation. Later, as she is dragged before Django, broken, naked, scarred, and screaming, from a hole in the ground, the fantasy of unsullied Broomhilda is broken, and through Django's silent rage and stony facial expression, the audience sees him recommit to his quest in spite of her not being "perfect."

Though she is more of a caricature than a character, being the focal point of the Germanic fairy tale complicates African American female identity because it "allows the black woman to embrace a fantasy that historically wasn't available to her."[24] When asked about playing the part of Broomhilda, actress Kerry Washington said that while wanting to be rescued from a tower is not exactly feminist, it nonetheless pierces the identity of black victimhood "by allowing the African-American man to do something chivalrous for the African-American woman."[25] In this way, both the African American man and woman are able to transcend their victimhood, for the woman becomes the object worth saving and the man is afforded the agency to do so. Through being the object of Django's fantasy and of the manipulations of Stephen, Candie's African majordomo, Broomhilda becomes a foil against which the African American male identity can be determined. She is not only Django's wife but the film's metaphorical princess, a victim to be safeguarded by the African American man. Choosing to rescue her against all odds, to "walk through hellfire because Brunhilde's worth it"[26] makes Django heroic, just as the willingness to abuse her to help Candie proves Stephen's self-loathing and consummate villainy.

This first scene featuring Candie, Stephen, and Broomhilda also marks the transition from Django-as-sidekick to his position as master, for "over time the traditional roles of white gunslinger and nonwhite sidekick are reversed, as the duo's mission shifts from Schultz's work to the rescue of Django's wife, Broomhilda."[27] To satisfy the requirements of the fairy-tale/Western exempla, Django must defeat a villain, and in the fashioning of Stephen, played by Samuel L. Jackson, Tarantino confronts Baldwin's accusation that the protest novel ignores "the power of revelation . . . the journey towards a more vast reality which must take precedence over all claims."[28] Since *Django* is a story about identity rather than situation, the villain Django must defeat is not the seductively sadistic Calvin Candie, but Stephen, the race traitor whose tyrannical rule over Candyland forces his fellow slaves into perpetual victimhood.

Baldwin asserts that the protest novel formula renders slavery "an accepted and comforting aspect of the American scene,"[29] but in Stephen, Tarantino constructs a character whose victimization is so horrifyingly complete that he loses all sense of African identity. Candie may own the plantation, but Stephen is his enforcer, the arbiter of punishment, suffering, and misery. It is Stephen, after all, who degrades Broomhilda and parades her before Django. When Candie finds out that Broomhilda is in the "hot box"[30] and is being deprived of food and water, Stephen admits that the torture was his idea, to punish her for running away. When Schultz pretends to want to buy Mandingo slaves[31] and Broomhilda as an afterthought, Stephen is the only one who sees through the ruse. Summoning Candie to the library, Stephen tells him of the deception and advises him on how best to punish Schultz for his duplicity. Later, when Django is captured by Candie's men, it is Stephen who devises the most sadistic punishment for him. The white characters simply want to castrate Django and kill him quickly, but Stephen wants to break his pride for getting "above his station" and daring to regard himself as equal to the white characters. To humiliate Django for his uppitiness, Stephen wants to rob Django of his hard-won identity by selling him to a mining company, where he will become a faceless laborer again. Sporting a malevolent smile, Stephen explains that the LeQuint Dickey Mining Company will strip Django of his name and all other identifiable markers save the number they give him and "they gonna work ya, all day every day, till your back give out, then they gonna hitcha in the head with a hammer, throw your ass down the nigger hole. And *that* will be the story of you, Django."[32]

Much like a Stockholm Syndrome victim, Stephen so identifies with his oppressors that he becomes a victimizer of his own people, "an Uncle Tom whose servility has mutated into monstrosity and who represents the symbolic self Django must destroy to assert and maintain his freedom."[33] Far from rendering slavery safe, Tarantino's depiction of Stephen forces white and black audience members to confront the horrors this institution produced. Broomhilda's humiliation is devastating, Django's enslavement is angering, but Stephen, who gleefully becomes a victimizer of his own kind while mistaking this power for freedom, is truly tragic.

The construction of Django and Stephen seems to be in keeping with what Baldwin would want, in that it reclaims slavery as an African American narrative. *Django Unchained* does not ignore the influence that whites have over the creation of African American identity, but within Tarantino's narrative, their most important contributions are the Western and fairy-tale exempla that provide framework for the film's climactic battle. At its core, the slavery dilemma in *Django* is a personal story in which the slave must battle against his own victimization to find and reclaim his manhood. For this battle for identity to take place, Calvin Candie and Schultz, who helped fashion Django and Stephen's identities until this point, must be removed from the picture so that slave and freedman can confront one another. For the African American victim to break from that identity, he must kill the victimizer but, more importantly, must vanquish that part of himself that falls prey to victimhood. When Django dynamites the big house of Candyland (with Stephen trapped inside), he destroys both the symbol of white oppression and the self-loathing that results from a legacy of African American victimhood.

For the film to work as both an ameliorated protest novel and as entertainment, a delicate balance between comedy and seriousness needs to be maintained. The audience must gasp in horror as the slave d'Artagnan is ripped apart by dogs and laugh as the hapless Klansmen struggle to see through the malformed eyeholes in their masks. More importantly, the audience must be able to identify with Django, to want for him to complete his quest, and enabling Django to transcend his identity as race victim is crucial for achieving this objective. The audiences' reactions, Tarantino notes, indicate the success or failure of his venture, for if it is done correctly, "then the audience will burst into applause. They'll clap with Broomhilda. They'll laugh when Django and his horse do the little dance."[34] The fact that audiences did, in fact, applaud in theaters when Django destroyed Candyland is proof that Tarantino's vision succeeded in divesting the protest novel/Western/fairy tale of their racial strictures, transforming Django from a "black hero" into a universally identifiable one.

Tarantino's *Django Unchained* does not, as Baldwin might have wanted, answer the question of "what it was, after all, that moved [white] people to such deeds,"[35] and the story, both as a film and as an incarnation of the protest novel, is better for not engaging with that concern. Every question need not, and should not, be answered through art. Some are posed merely to be discussed. Rather than debate why slavery happened, Tarantino's film accepts the fact of it so that he can engage with the more compelling issue of how slavery complicates, mutates, and defines African American identity.

By employing the Romantic exempla used to fashion white identity to Django, Tarantino pierces the racialized notion of victimization hitherto employed in the protest novel. Since African and white American identity are inextricably linked through history and literary construction, Tarantino asserts that both races can be victim and victimizer, and that the African American can rise above the legacy of oppression imposed upon him. What makes Django that "one nigger in ten thousand"[36] is not that he is the strongest or smartest character in the film, but that he is the first to recognize that he can claim the narrative agency his oppressors do. He is the first one to say enough.

NOTES

1. James Baldwin, *Collected Essays* (New York: Literary Classics of the United States, 1998), 11.
2. Baldwin, *Collected Essays*, 12.
3. Baldwin, *Collected Essays*, 13.
4. Baldwin, *Collected Essays*, 15.
5. Baldwin, *Collected Essays*, 15.
6. Baldwin, *Collected Essays*, 15.
7. David Bordwell and Kristin Marie Thompson, *Film Art: An Introduction* (New York: McGraw-Hill, 2013), 2.
8. Toni Morrison, *Playing in the Dark: Whiteness and the Literary Imagination* (Cambridge: Harvard University Press, 1992), 36.
9. Morrison, *Playing in the Dark*, 37.
10. Morrison, *Playing in the Dark*, 37.
11. Morrison, *Playing in the Dark*, 37.
12. Morrison, *Playing in the Dark*, 37.
13. Morrison, *Playing in the Dark*, 33.
14. Quentin Tarantino, dir., *Django Unchained* (2012; New York: Weinstein Company, 2013), DVD.
15. Henry Louis Gates Jr., "Interview with Quentin Tarantino," The Root, http://www.theroot.com/articles/history/2012/12/django_unchained_trilogy_and_more_tarantino_talks_to_gates.html (accessed December 23, 2012.)
16. Morrison, *Playing in the Dark*, 38.
17. Gates, "Interview with Tarantino," 3.
18. Tarantino, *Django Unchained*.
19. Tarantino, *Django Unchained*.
20. A. O. Scott, "The Black, the White, and the Angry," *New York Times*, December 24, 2012, http://www.nytimes.com/2012/12/25/movies/quentin-tarantinos-django-unchained-stars-jamie-foxx.html?_r=0 (accessed March 4, 2014).
21. Morrison, *Playing in the Dark*, 44.
22. Scott, "The Black, the White, and the Angry," 2.
23. Tarantino, *Django Unchained* .
24. Nicole Sperling, "Django Unchained Was More than a Role for Kerry Washington," *LA Times*, December 31, 2012, http://articles.latimes.com/2012/dec/31/entertainment/la-et-kerry-washington-django-unchained-20130101.
25. Sperling, "More than a Role," 1.
26. Tarantino, *Django Unchained*.
27. Scott, "The Black, the White, and the Angry," 3.
28. Baldwin, *Collected Essays*, 13.
29. Baldwin, *Collected Essays*, 15.
30. A metal box partially submerged in the ground into which recalcitrant slaves were put as a form of punishment. Exposed to the sun, the box heated up throughout the day, slowly cooking the victim trapped inside.
31. Fighting slaves
32. Tarantino, *Django Unchained*.

33. Scott, "The Black, the White, and the Angry," 2.
34. Gates, "Interview with Tarantino," 5.
35. Baldwin, *Collected Essays*, 12.
36. Tarantino, *Django Unchained*.

Chapter Five

Blaxploitation in the Age of Obama: *Black Dynamite, Django Unchained,* Racial Reasoning, and Racial Capitalism

Brian E. Butler

One of the defining moments of Barack Obama's first campaign for the White House was what has become known as his "race speech," "A More Perfect Union," delivered on March 18, 2008, at the National Constitution Center in Philadelphia, Pennsylvania. He made the speech because of a growing controversy over remarks made by the Rev. Jeremiah Wright, the pastor at a church that the Obamas had close ties to. In his speech Obama characterized America as an "improbable experiment in democracy," a wonderful experiment, but one that was ultimately unfinished and "stained by this nation's original sin of slavery."[1] But, Obama continued, the answer to this sin was already written into the Constitution at the start. This answer was the ideal of equal citizenship under law. Therefore, the founders created a union that wasn't perfect, but one that could rather be perfected upon its own internally expressed principles. But, he continued, this task requires vigilance and struggle. He then related this national struggle to his own personal history.

A child of a black Kenyan father and white Kansas mother, Obama was brought up by white grandparents. This, he noted, has provided him with relatives of every race and every hue. Further, his mixed heritage has put him in a position where he has been called both too black and not black enough. He then noted some derogatory characterizations of his candidacy as an exercise in affirmative action or the attempt to purchase race conciliation on the cheap. Further, he noted that the problem of words like Reverend

Wright's is that because of their characterization of white privilege, they actually widen the divide between white and black. All this Obama found regrettable because, he claimed, the United States needs a more perfected union, not more division. He then turned to the example of Wright's Trinity Church, which he described as being like most predominantly black churches in that it is full of all types of voices. This shows, he claimed, that we cannot afford "to simplify and stereotype and amplify the negative to the point that it distorts reality." Instead the real complexity of race in America must be confronted in order for the project of perfection and perfectibility of our nation's union to be effectively engaged. Ultimately he argued that the real principle of perfectibility that the country and its people should live under is "do unto others as others do unto you." He saw this as the only legitimate option rather than to settle for "this is not the time."[2]

Obama's message was one of essential unity and perfectibility between the races. Race discrimination, though the original sin of the union, was remediable under principles internal and therefore original to the union. Somewhat strangely, Obama had to, in the speech, note and attempt to undermine claims that he, his party, or liberals in general were exploiting his identification as black for political gain. This in the face of the obvious fact that every other president, all forty-three, had exploited the fact, without ever having to acknowledge it, of the privilege of whiteness. Indeed, other presidents all seemed not to be questioned as to whether or not they were too white or not white enough; they were always just right white. There is great irony in the fact that white privilege gets to go unquestioned in an election, whereas blackness becomes something that needs to be apologized for.

Of course slavery and Jim Crow show that exploitation of race is not a new phenomenon in America. What is interesting in relation to Obama's campaign is the accusation that being black and using "the race card" was somehow an unfair advantage. It certainly is the case that the election of a black president was momentous and inspired some of the electorate. And black Americans voted almost unanimously for Obama. In this sense, if one wanted to stretch, the first Obama campaign could be accused of engaging in a kind of blaxploitation. But clearly more worrisome is the white privilege playing in the background and determining the debate so strongly that Obama could not call its history out in all its ugliness but had to leave it largely out of the picture and rest in vague generalizations and apologies for black complaints.

Of course the term *blaxploitation* is used predominantly in relationship to a genre of film related to African American issues. Because such films are dealing with the same issues of race and justice, albeit with different senses of urgency and effectiveness and in the rather different area of entertainment, it might be informative to investigate how blaxploitation films treat issues of race in comparison to the Obama speech. This might be especially interesting in relation to films produced during the Obama election and resulting presidency.

Black Dynamite, for instance, is a 2009 spoof of 1970s blaxploitation action films. Set in the 1970s, the plot starts with Black Dynamite's brother, seemingly working as a drug pusher for a drug syndicate, getting killed execution-style by the white bosses of the syndicate. Dynamite vows to avenge his brother's death and clean drugs off of the streets (a common blaxploitation theme). It is learned during his travails that Dynamite had seen military action in Vietnam and is a former CIA agent. The film's plot weaves in further blaxploitation clichés, such as the main character's "love" interest, a pure-hearted, proud, and politically active Black Power woman named Gloria, who for good measure also works at an orphanage where all the children are addicted to smack sold by the drug syndicate. There are also the weak-willed and somewhat inept black revolutionaries and plenty of "bitches" (seemingly the generic term for all attractive young women other than Gloria), colorful pimps, pushers, and whores. Notable is the appearance of both Arsenio Hall and Captain Kangaroo as pimps. Of course the central cliché—one not exclusive to blaxploitation but generally seen in maybe one of its purest forms within it—is the uber-macho male human-yet-superhero main character that exacts justice through kicking ass via kung fu, various types of weaponry (including a very large and phallic gun), and strategic alliances with other lesser representatives of community-based justice (three of the most central to the plot being "Bullhorn," "Cream-Corn," and "Gunsmoke").

Ultimately we learn that Dynamite's brother was killed because he was not a pusher but rather was working undercover for the CIA in the evil drug syndicate. Further, the syndicate is involved in a secret operation entitled "Code Kansas," the details of which are obscure but ominous. In a classic scene from the movie, Dynamite and a number of his cohorts use the available clues and reason in a meandering and esoterically informed manner (including obscure classical references) to the conclusion that "Code Kansas" is a plan to "fix all the niggers" through the doctoring of a shipment of Anaconda Malt Liquor—"The Big Snake"—a government-approved malt liquor that advertises not only that "when you peel the top the panties drop" but that, more importantly, "it gives you Oooooooo." Part of their reasoning leads to the conclusion that the slogan really means that Anaconda Malt Liquor gives whoever drinks it a little dick. The formula that does this, we further learn, was accidentally created by an evil genius, Dr. Wu, while he was working for the American government on a project to create larger dicks. But once it was learned that the formula shrinks dicks, a plan to use it in malt liquor to reduce the dick size of African American men was created. We then revisit a member of the gang that drank some of the Anaconda, Gunsmoke, and learn that he has, indeed, had his penis shrunk. They decide he must be put out of his misery and aim to stop the distribution of the Anaconda Malt Liquor shipment.

After learning that his old partner, O'Leary (not incidentally white), was in on the plan, Dynamite and his cohorts stop him and then travel to Dr. Wu's island to stop him. Finally, Dynamite learns that the orders for "Code Kansas" came from the president of the United States, Richard Nixon. After an extended kung-fu battle with Nixon—"wicked tricky Dick"—in the White House (or, as it is referred to in *Black Dynamite*, the "honkey house") that is ultimately won by Dynamite, but only though the helpful intervention of the ghost of Abraham Lincoln, Nixon promises to look out for Dynamite "and his people" in order to avoid Dynamite's releasing of incriminating S&M photos of the president. The film ends with Black Dynamite pontificating about justice as he stands heroically, gun and nunchucks in hand, with Pat Nixon and Gloria looking up adoringly from the floor on either side.

Clearly racial stereotypes are exploited throughout *Black Dynamite*. From the use of the cliché black male drink—malt liquor—to ideas of sexuality and genital size, to accusations of not being militant enough, racial stereotypes are noted and parodied relentlessly in *Black Dynamite*. And like Obama's trajectory, the film ends up in the White House as well. But the messages are, needless to say, somewhat different. Obama's message in "A More Perfect Union" is one of reconciliation, unity, and mutual interests. It is serious, dignified, and properly restrained. Dignity and restraint are notably lacking in *Black Dynamite*. Instead of a world of unity, the world is portrayed as one of evil white empires, irresistible black sexuality, and the necessity of kicking ass. Hollywood, of course, was constructed on stereotypes. And if one thinks of *Birth of a Nation* (1915) as a foundational moment in Hollywood, racial stereotypes have been central since film's beginnings. What is interesting about the exploitation of racial themes in *Black Dynamite*, though, is that they are largely appropriated by the film in a positive manner for blacks and a negative manner for whites. The most evil figures in the movie are white. And ultimately Dynamite, through all of his ass kicking, breaks down white systems of power in favor of justice to his people. Of course in the film there is no real hope for a perfected unity of black and white (other than between black men and women of all races through Dynamite's sexual desirability and prowess). Indeed, while the form of comedy seems to allow a more direct look at some of the endemic realities of white privilege in America than Obama is allowed in the political arena, *Black Dynamite*'s ultimate solution—kicking ass—seems somewhat more impoverished than Obama's appeal to the rule of law and the principle of "do unto others."

Like *Black Dynamite*, a film released much later in Obama's presidency, 2012's *Django Unchained*, also abounds with references to earlier classics of the blaxploitation genre. For instance, *Django* is greatly informed by knowledge of the earlier classic *Mandingo* (1975). *Django* begins by being set in

Texas in 1858. In the opening scenes Django, a slave punished for trying to escape with his wife from his previous master, is rescued from some slavers in the process of transporting him by Dr. King Schultz, a German bounty hunter in search of the "Brittle brothers." Apparently only Django is able to identify them. Schultz offers Django his future freedom in exchange for his help in this task. In the rescue scene, Schultz kills one of the slavers because he—the slaver—had aimed his gun at him. From this we learn that Schultz is overly dramatic, a fast draw, and anti-slavery.

Soon thereafter Schultz and Django find the Brittle brothers and kill them. Upon finishing the task, Django becomes Schultz's apprentice, approving of a job that entails the killing of white people for money—in a sense cash for flesh, just like slavery—and they set off to find Django's wife, Broomhilda—note the alternative spelling. Upon hearing that her name is Broomhilda, Schultz explained the popular German legend of Siegfried and Brunhilde. In this legend Brunhilde is doomed by her father to isolation on a mountain guarded by a dragon and circled by a ring of hell. Siegfried runs this gauntlet because of his love for Brunhilde and rescues her. Schultz characterizes Django as an actual Siegfried and explains that as a German he is obligated to help Django on his quest to get her back.

Their quest ultimately leads them to "Candyland"—an infamous slave plantation (the mountain of the legend) owned by the ruthless slaveholder "Monsieur" Calvin J. Candie (who appears to be the dragon). Schultz decides that if Candie knows that they are after Broomhilda, he will not sell her, so they set up an elaborate ruse. They will arrive with Schultz disguised as a wealthy German interested in purchasing a Mandingo fighter. Django will act as his "black slaver" and trusted expert on Mandingo stock. (As Django notes, a black slaver is lower than the head house slave and therefore is the lowest of the low.) In the process they would purchase Broomhilda in what would seem an afterthought. Django furthers the ruse by playing the part of a black slaver/mandingo expert so ruthlessly that Candie starts to be intrigued by the prospect that here in fact might be a uniquely special black man, a one in ten thousand "exceptional nigger." The Mandingo ruse, though, is foiled when Stephen, the head house slave, sees through the game and warns Candie. Candie then gives the group a lesson in southern-style phrenology that explains physiologically—at least to his satisfaction—why the blacks that surround him have not revolted and killed all the whites. In effect, the argument is that blacks have a brain constructed for subservience. After this lesson in retrogressive pseudo-science, he forces Schultz to pay twelve thousand for Broomhilda. All seems OK, but just as the transaction is to be completed, Candie requires Schultz (because of Schultz's visible disdain for him) to shake his hand. Instead, Schultz kills Candie with a gun he had hidden in his sleeve. A huge gunfight ensues wherein Schultz is immediately gunned down and Django in turn kills many of the Candyland regulars. The scene ends when Stephen calls out to Django that they have caught Broomhilda and will kill her unless he gives himself up. He does give himself up and walks through a circle of men aiming guns at him (the ring of hell).

In the next scene, Django is shown hanging upside down, nude, and about to be castrated when Stephen intervenes. He explains to Django that when castrated, most slaves bleed out within seven minutes. Instead he has convinced Candie's surviving sister to condemn him to a much worse fate and send him to a brutal mine operation where he will be stripped of identity, worked breaking rocks until crippled, then unceremoniously killed and dumped nameless into a hole. Django avoids this fate by talking his transporters into letting him free and accompanying him in order to get a huge bounty waiting at Candyland. But once they let him free, he immediately kills them and goes back to rescue Broomhilda. After killing all the Candyland whites and letting all the blacks in the house go except Stephen, Django shoots him in the knees. Then as Stephen yells at Django that he is not exceptional and, further, that he can never destroy Candyland, we see that the house has been filled with dynamite. As Django walks out triumphantly wearing Candie's fancy clothes and smoking a cigarette in Candie's fancy cigarette holder, the big house blows up and is reduced to rubble. The film ends with Django at the scene of all the destruction doing tricks with his horse while Broomhilda watches amused.

As with *Black Dynamite*, the underlying theme seems to be that in America, white and black will not get along. The only white in *Django Unchained* that is anti-slavery is Schultz, who is German and who dies because of his allegiance to Django. And Django does not reconcile with whites, he kills them all (and, of course, this is a Hollywood movie so we know they all deserve it). Even more ominously, the last scene has Django victorious and dressed in Candie's dandyish southern master clothes. It almost seems as if there has just been a complete role reversal. Certainly in *Django*, as opposed to normal Hollywood movies, almost all whites (at least all American whites) are shown as evil, bumbling, inbred, inept, and vain, whereas the blacks are more able, successful, and attractive. Both blaxploitation films, though, seem to point away from any possible unity and toward a looming judgment where whites are damned and blacks have privilege and power. One might see this as an ethics of an eye for an eye.

Importantly, and tellingly, both films are probably more accurate and honest as to the effects of white power and privilege than Obama is allowed to be in the political realm. For instance, in *Django* the combination of setting the action before the Civil War, as well as combining elements of the spaghetti Western and the blaxploitation film, allows Tarantino to include harrowing images of the brutality of slavery and southern slave culture. This displacement is analogous to the comedic setting of *Black Dynamite*. And while Mandingo fighting might not have been a reality as it is portrayed in the film, there is no question that southern slavery was a reality and was brutal. That Obama has to play such aspects of the past down, and can only speak in bland generalities, puts to shame any claims that Americans should be worried that Obama's election rested upon exploitation of race.

Sometime before Obama's "A More Perfect Union" speech and either *Black Dynamite* or *Django Unchained* had been made, Cornel West in *Race Matters* argued that Americans need to start their reasoning about race with Ralph Ellison's thought that "whatever else the true American is, he is also somehow black." That is, "the presence and predicaments of black people are neither additions to nor defections from American life, but rather *constitutive elements of that life*." West continued, that in America, "There is no escape from our interracial interdependence, yet enforced racial hierarchy dooms us as a nation to collective paranoia and hysteria—the unmaking of any democratic order."[3] All this seems borne out in the examples of reasoning about race cited above. Obama faced white paranoia about race, including the possibility of a black president, by offering a picture of perfectibility and unity and leaving unstated and quite abstract both the concrete manner through which this would be brought about and the distinct injustices and cruelties of white supremacy. This abstraction in regard to race issues is even more striking when one of the common strategies in Obama speeches when not dealing with race is the appeal to concrete and detailed narration of individual examples of "salt of the earth" Americans. In contrast, *Black Dynamite* and *Django Unchained* offer much more concrete and explicit examples of racial injustice but then offer what are quite obviously non-democratic "Hollywood" solutions of the most simplistic kind—solutions that rest almost exclusively upon the violent destruction of the opposing parties and installation of alternate hierarchies of dominance.

Strikingly, in 1994's *Race Matters*, West also stated, "Without hope there can be no future . . . without meaning there can be no struggle."[4] This, of course, foreshadows Obama's later "hope" and "change" campaign slogan. But somehow between *Race Matters* and the Obama campaign, the meaning was largely eliminated from the change. West, of course, foresaw this type of problem and was worried that political aims in America were being reduced to a politics of profit and commerce where race becomes only useful or analyzed under instances of individual racial mobility. This, in turn, is just a slight variation on another individualistic and naïve Hollywood-based trope. This West labels "Horatio Alger in blackface."[5] This Horatio Alger in blackface is, of course, in the end just another type of largely meaningless hope for the one-in-ten-thousand black saviors rather than the quest to face and change everyday, on-the-ground reality through the systemic actions of normal people.

Worse yet, now that there are, thankfully, pockets of American society that find diversity a good thing, there is another new blaxploitation danger to look out for. This is a manner of exploitation identified by Nancy Leong in her recent article entitled "Racial Capitalism." As she puts it, racial capitalism is "the process of deriving social or economic value from the racial identity of another person."[6] In the United States today white institutions are deriving value and profit from nonwhites; that is, "nonwhiteness is a valued commodity, and commodification means profit." Therefore "diversity" is largely a term that white institutions profit off of. And this, obviously, is just another game of flesh for cash. Among other harms of this type of racial reasoning is that it "demands certain types of identity performance." Further, by requiring proper representation of diversity, racial capitalism "impoverishes our discourse around race, fosters racial resentment by inhibiting the reparative work essential to improved racial relations, and detracts from more meaningful antidiscrimination goals by prioritizing racial representation at its thinnest and most tokenistic."[7] Ironically, according to Leong, legally speaking in America, affirmative action is now pretty much only allowed under the diversity rationale resting upon racial capitalism.[8]

On August 28, 2013, President Obama gave a speech commemorating the fiftieth anniversary of the March on Washington at the Lincoln Memorial. He once again pointed to "a promise made at our founding" and quoted the "all men are created equal" section from the Declaration of Independence. He then related this section to the March on Washington. President Obama noted that in 1963, though this idea was still not a reality and remained just a promise for African Americans, the marchers did not choose hatred and violence; they chose prayer and peaceful protest. And because they marched, Obama proclaimed, "America changed for you and me." He then claimed that to suggest not much has changed would be to dishonor their struggles. But he also continued that to suggest that the struggle is done is to also dishonor them. That is, there has been tremendous improvement, yet problems such as wealth disparity have grown significantly. But, Obama concluded, the March and its results should ultimately teach us that "we are masters of our fate," and the lesson of our past is "that in the face of impossible odds, people who love their country can change it." Reassuring words, but ultimately meaning what? Is this a call for individual saviors, the one-in-ten-thousand exceptional Black Dynamite or Django Freeman? A blackfaced Horatio Alger? Or is the meaning to be found in facing the brutal realities of America's racial past and embracing the slow ground-up creation of community and democratic hope and change that West called for? It seems neither Washington nor Hollywood is ready for that message.

NOTES

1. Barack Obama, "A More Perfect Union," campaign speech, National Constitution Center, Philadelphia, March 18, 2008.

2. Obama, "A More Perfect Union."
3. Cornel West, *Race Matters* (New York: Vintage Books, 1994), 8.
4. West, *Race Matters*, 23.
5. West, *Race Matters*, 21.
6. Nancy Leong, "Racial Capitalism," *Harvard Law Review* 126, no. 8 (2013): 2153.
7. Leong, "Racial Capitalism," 2156.
8. Leong, "Racial Capitalism," 2163.

REFERENCES

Fleischer, Richard, dir. *Mandingo*. Paramount, 1975.
Griffith, D. W., dir. *Birth of a Nation*. Epoch Production Co., 1915.
Leong, Nancy. "Racial Capitalism." *Harvard Law Review* 126, no. 8 (2013): 2151–226.
Obama, Barack. "A More Perfect Union." Campaign speech. National Constitution Center, Philadelphia, March 18, 2008.
———. "50th Anniversary of the March on Washington Commemoration Speech." Lincoln Memorial, Washington, D.C., August 28, 2013.
Sanders, Scott, dir. *Black Dynamite*. Apparition, 2009.
Tarantino, Quentin, dir. *Django Unchained*. Columbia, 2012.
West, Cornel. *Race Matters*. New York: Vintage Books, 1994.

Chapter Six

Between *The Butler* and *Black Dynamite*: Servility, Militancy, and the Meaning of Blaxploitation

Andrew Grossman

It was hardly surprising that the election of America's first nonwhite president resulted in widespread animus and polarization; the only variable, perhaps, was the veiled or semi-veiled forms that animus would assume. Certainly, Bill Clinton's moderately liberal agenda elicited its own reactionary hysteria, from cliques of gun-hoarding, white supremacist militias, to the 1995 bombing of the Oklahoma City federal building at the hands of anti-government "patriots," to the so-called Arkansas Project, a relentless disinformation campaign coordinated by the *American Spectator* and affiliated members of the *derriere garde*. Notably, after Clinton's failure to integrate gays and lesbians into the U.S. military—his first major policy failure—the right increasingly used homophobic rhetoric to portray, in McCarthyist fashion, Clinton's un-American otherness.[1] Obviously, the animus mobilized against Obama, courtesy of Tea Party tribalists, required no pretext or covert conspiracy. While fringe elements hoisted signs portraying the health-care-reforming president as either a voodoo witch doctor or the African reincarnation of Hitler, more mainstream arbiters of conservatism marshalled the deracialized euphemisms of "Marxist" and "socialist," even if most of them likely never opened *The Eighteenth Brumaire of Louis Napoleon*. No matter that the vilified Affordable Care Act, used by rightists to "prove" Obama's socialistic interventions, in fact, coerces consumers into complicity with private corporations. No matter, too, that those whom the ACA would help are, by sheer numbers, predominantly poor, rural white populations hoodwinked into voting for family-values Republicans.

Anarcho-syndicalists, neo-Marxists, and even some authentic libertarians[2] have long understood that corporatist structures fabricate the liberal-conservative polarity to prevent the left and right from realizing their shared economic interests. Though obviously inflamed by Obama's otherness, the Tea Party movement began during the Bush administration, following the 2008 government bailouts of American International Group, General Motors, and Chrysler. With the reality of corporate welfare brazenly exposed, there existed in 2009 and 2010 fleeting, potentially utopian intersections between the anti-corporatism of the Occupy Movement and the populist elements of the Tea Party, even if the mainstream media took every opportunity to stress the movements' racial and generational differences. Unfortunately, the divisive discourse of Obama's racial otherness became a convenient strategy to sabotage any populist alliances between rightist and leftist dissenters. Ideally, members of the white underclass and black underclass should unite against the media-industrial complex, but conservative media too easily exploit race as a wedge issue, dividing and conquering liberals and nonracist conservatives who should collaborate in the class struggle. For that matter, even *racist* Tea Party members would better serve their own economic interests through ad hoc alliances than by seeking succor in the reactionary and delusional aesthetics of white victimhood.

Certainly, we could not expect Obama to foster ties among disparate grassroots movements—no president has ever done that, and Obama is especially a prisoner of facticity and historical exigency, of the objectified fantasies of his electorate and enemies. As president, he has little choice but to embrace electable centrism, downplaying his history of Chicagoan activism and sympathy for liberation theology.[3] Nevertheless, Obama would likely find greater support among his own base if he openly embraced the activist spirit he once harbored. After his tone-deaf vilification of Obama the community organizer at the 2008 Republican National Convention, ex–New York Mayor Rudy Giuliani found himself the target of even centrist pundits: not only did Giuliani's harangue sound like a parody of conservative elitism, it turned out that many Americans actually *liked* community organizing, especially under Giuliani's own regime. It's also important to remember that in individual speeches Obama's true sympathies occasionally do surface. When eliciting "boos" after reminding a crowd at the University of Michigan that Republicans want to scrap the minimum wage, Obama's impromptu response was "Don't boo, organize!"[4] Such moments of leftist revelation remain rare and extemporaneous, however, and Obama generally speaks safely, knowing conservatives will seize upon and demonize any hint of communitarianism.

As a result, Obama cautiously relegates his rhetoric to the economic problems of the middle class. Frank interrogations of race are both taboo and political suicide; any mention of poverty or the lower class, meanwhile, ignites the right's unironic cries of "class warfare," as if class discrepancies arise only when liberals discuss them, as if a deliberately depressed minimum wage were not itself empirical proof of a merciless economic crusade. Denying the realities of race and class in America is at this point the incongruous stuff of comedy, for every denial only reveals alienation or, at best, anachronism. In the ubiquitous arena of media parodies and burlesques, perhaps no one has better satirized Obama's existential predicament than the skit comedians Keegan-Michael Key and Jordan Peele, whose impersonation of a temperate, diplomatic Obama requires an expressly "black" alter ego to translate his bureaucratic lingo into the angry street talk he surely harbors in his heart. The skit's popularity only proved (quite literally) the endurance of the DuBoisian "double consciousness," as Obama self-consciously walks a tightrope between cautious acquiescence and fugitive authenticity, between the dueling expectations of a centrist president and an activist community organizer. But Obama is not an empty vessel like Ellison's Invisible Man, even if he negotiates a surplus of imposed and projected identities. As the object of excessive visibility, Obama becomes more like Hamlet, under constant political surveillance and searching for an authenticity denied by his role as leader and inheritor of a military complex. In fact, Obama is possibly more helpless than Hamlet. Not merely indecisive, Obama is without a master "Mousetrap," and his rightist enemies—most of them ideologically blind—apparently have no guilty consciences to capture.

The fabricated nature of the double-consciousness is surely exacerbated by America's two-party system, which fallaciously presents political identity as a binary choice, the necessary evil of a centrist republic designed to keep extremists from advancing beyond local governance. At the national level of perpetual stalemate, an intransigent two-party ideology inhibits resolving the static double-consciousness with any kind of political syntheses, Marxist or otherwise. Key and Peele's skit is thus ultimately frustrating, as it only reminds audiences that performances of black and white identity remain static and entrenched, as irreconcilable—and hierarchical—as a superego (here painted white) and an id (here painted black). From a postmodernist perspective, in which all identity is presumably performative, we might abandon the very notion of "authentic" identity and DuBois's dualistic notion itself, which only feeds the exclusionary ideology of the nation-state, that of insiders and outsiders. But American political life has hardly arrived at the moment when we can discard authenticity, especially when nearly every politician—regardless of race—gives a performance in bad faith, rehearsing nationalistic platitudes for the cameras.

In imagining the "proper" role of African Americans still torn between cultural resistance and acquiescence, Hollywood has unsurprisingly put forth allegories more prudent than liberatory. It is probably no coincidence that Hollywood's most conspicuous black-centered films of recent years—*The Help* (2011), *The Butler* (2013), and *12 Years a Slave* (2013)—all confront historical narratives of institutional servility without condoning or proposing any revolutionary solutions. Tarantino's *Django Unchained* (2012) is something of an outlier in this group, as it celebrates a revolutionary black outlaw and casts the "house nigger"—as embodied by Samuel L. Jackson's cruel, opportunistic villain—not as a subaltern survivor but as an active collaborator in the system of domination, a traitor who must be kneecapped and detonated. However, *Django* is so mired in Tarantino's trademark genre pastiche that any revolutionary import is impeded—or at least circumscribed—by the film's spaghetti Western trappings and overall narcissism. As a result, the film's racialized discourse is trumped by Tarantino's own auteurist discourse, and the film's final images of revenge are drawn not from a nuanced understanding of class dynamics but from the sentimental fabric of macho genre fantasies.

Whereas *Django Unchained* offers sadistically gratifying, cartoonish images of retribution, films such as Lee Daniels's *The Butler* and Steve McQueen's *12 Years a Slave* offer masochistic spectacles grounded in historical realism. Perhaps it is inevitable that any "realistic" depiction of racial injustice, like many films about the Holocaust,[5] would become a masochistic experience for audiences—arguably, such films should not only anger and frustrate audiences but strategically deny them the easy, action-movie catharses of Tarantino-ism. Yet these films' directors—now privileged auteurs spearheading multimillion-dollar projects—have also intentionally chosen historicized subject matters that excuse them from addressing ongoing injustices. Both *The Butler* and *12 Years* offer vivid images of history without advancing any usable theses or attempting to agitate or transform the audience. Though *12 Years* offers a vital illustration of the statist terrorism that is slavery, mere illustrations of injustice, accomplished with a decadent Hollywood budget, are inadequate replacements for real, explicit activism. Such illustrations are rationalized as centrist or "reasonable" liberalisms, as uncontroversial engagements with history that will not divide audiences along racial or class identities. As a result, these films stop far short of responsibly naming solutions for present-day inequalities, and viewers are left with the kind of *ressentiment* that Nietzsche, in *Beyond Good and Evil*, ascribes to the spiteful, envious servant, who is roused to anger but powerless to transform his future.

On a more superficial level, *The Butler* and *12 Years* are themselves enslaved to the nonconfrontational humanism typical of post-Reaganite Hollywood aesthetics. This is an obvious point, but it's important to stress the gap between the present generation of filmmakers and their countercultural forebears. In the Hollywood of 1970, six of the top sixteen highest-grossing films could be characterized as *overtly* countercultural: *MASH*, *Woodstock*, *Little Big Man*, *Catch-22*, *Joe*, and *Five Easy Pieces* were popular precisely because they critiqued authoritarianism, militarism, and patriarchy, to varying degrees.[6] International cinemas, informed by antiwar rioting and Marxist student movements, witnessed films such as Pontecorvo's *The Battle of Algiers* (1966) and *Queimada* (1969)—or even Lindsay Anderson's *If . . .* (1969)—that not only attempted agitation but turned a profit worldwide. By contrast, in today's transnationalized Hollywood, where homogeneity and blandness inform the desired aesthetic, acclaimed films such as *Jarhead* (2005) and *The Hurt Locker* (2010) try to critique the ineptitude of American foreign policy but nevertheless glorify soldiery and machismo. As Hollywood budgets have escalated into the hundreds of millions, contentious themes—global warming, wealth inequality, the Wall Street bailout, American imperialism—generally have been relegated to lower-budgeted documentaries. This trend only reinforces the binary distinction between "masculine," mythic fictions (which deserve budgets of hundreds of millions) and traitorous, "un-American" progressivism (which must be shuffled off to preachy documentaries). Of course, many big-budget Hollywood films have progressive subtexts,[7] but that only proves the point—contentious themes are shamefully buried in subtext because opportunities for open, textual confrontation decrease as a film's bloated budget accrues greater commercial risk.

Unsurprisingly, the top twenty-five highest-grossing Hollywood films of 2013—led by *Iron Man 3*, *Despicable Me 2*, and *The Hunger Games: Catching Fire*—are predominantly fantasies aimed at children and adolescents. Of these twenty-five, only *The Butler* (at #22) features expressly political subject matter, and even then the film goes to considerable lengths to excuse its docility and centrism. The semi-factual story of the White House's longest-serving African American butler, the film commences with the image of a moonlit American flag waving over a lynched body, as an epigraph from Martin Luther King appears onscreen: "Darkness cannot drive out darkness . . . only light can do that." With its pacifistic bent clarified, the film proper begins in the Georgia cotton fields of 1926, when Forest Whitaker's hero, then a young child, witnesses a white overseer fatally shoot his father after his mother is raped. The elderly plantation owner then tells the traumatized boy, "I'm going to teach you how to be a house nigger"—a metaphorically resonant phrase for liberal audiences who believe Obama too often acquiesces before John Boehner's belligerent House of Representatives. Framing the hero's lifelong subjection as a lingering symptom of childhood trauma, the film rationalizes his social position as a kind of arrested development, a submissive self-concept indelibly internalized at gunpoint. Inevitably, the film's "traumatic" framework both explains and excuses the orphaned protagonist's subsequent lack of political consciousness or agency.

Attempting to historicize its theme of subjection, the film centers on the butler's relationship with his activist son, whose progression from civil disobedience to post-King militancy contrasts with the father's Johnson-era subservience. Because he has learned too well his acquiescent role as modern-day "house nigger," Whitaker's timorous butler is surely meant to frustrate contemporary audiences, especially when a White House bureaucrat belittles his demand for a raise, telling him he shouldn't let that "Martin Luther King shit" go to his head. Yet the film also discourages audience identification with his community-organizing, beret-wearing activist son and his militant girlfriend (replete with Foxy Brown afro). In the film's central moral climax—repeated and strategically re-edited in nearly every advertisement, trailer, and promo for the film—the son dismisses not only Martin Luther King's *satyagraha* but mocks the butler's favorite actor, Sidney Poitier, who was often seen by 1960s radicals as an unthreatening image of blackness advanced by Hollywood. "I'm sorry, Mr. Butler," the son says, "I didn't mean to make fun of your hero." The butler's wife, played by Oprah Winfrey (always an arbiter of middlebrow morality), then slaps him and reprimands him for his ungratefulness: "Everything you are, everything you have, is because of that butler!" This melodramatic moment became the crux of the film's entire television advertising campaign—yet in a re-edited version that removes any mention of Poitier or *In the Heat of the Night* (1967), the movie at issue in this scene. If one had only seen *The Butler*'s trailer or television spots, one couldn't possibly know to which "hero" Winfrey refers—given that the son wears a beret in the scene, the objectionable hero could well be Dr. King, President Johnson, or anyone who signifies some kind of moderation.

In effect, the contextual identity of the "hero" becomes irrelevant: viewers of the television spots only learn that prodigal sons who wear militant berets should be shamed as ingrates in our allegedly "post-racial" age, for black militancy is not only anachronistic but also less productive than working within the system, as do the butler and, in a grander sense, Obama. The film proper is marginally better than the reductionist discourse of its advertising, which gives no hint of the father and son's final reconciliation at an early 1990s anti-apartheid rally. Even this, however, is a convenient solution, as anti-apartheid protests hardly constitute a controversial stance, even for a timid butler. The protagonist's lack of agency is ultimately a symptom of his pseudo-historicized story, which, following the dubious example of *Forrest Gump* (1994), reduces American history to a highlight reel of textbook events, filtered through the standpoint of a spectating everyman, a cipher to whom history merely "happens." In fairness to the film and its advertising, it should be mentioned that one of its mass-produced lobby posters did suggest that Whitaker's character was not merely a submissive bystander. The two most widely used posters emphasized submission before the nation-state, featuring the butler either holding his hands behind his back, passively watching Washington political life from his cloistered window, or (even worse) holding forth a cup of tea while literally clothed in the American flag. One rarer poster, however, openly acknowledged the butler's political double-bind, as his one hand proffers a tea service and the other is thrust upright, fist clenched in defiant protest. This image, however, tends to protest too much, for audiences hoping that Whitaker's character would signify rebellion would only discover that revolutionary consciousness is embodied by the decentered son, not the patriotic hero.

While making history palatable for the masses is standard Hollywood procedure, director Daniels himself has discouraged any revolutionary messages or interpretations. Promoting the film in an MSNBC interview, Daniels insisted that the character of the butler symbolizes "everyone who serves in America" and that audiences should be thankful for those who "died for our country."[8] The baffling claim that Whitaker's butler symbolizes *every* national servant disingenuously elides the class injustices that ostensibly undergird the film, and Daniels's second, nationalistic assertion is totally irrelevant. Furthermore, the notion that *service* is inherently honorable and easily separable from *servility* is at best naïve, as the American caste system represented in the film renders service within a hierarchy anything but voluntary. Though we might assume MSNBC's left-leaning audience would welcome trenchant class analysis, Daniels instead responds in bad faith, preempting any accusations of "class warfare" and subsuming race under the uncontroversial umbrella of nationalism. The obvious implication is that, in an allegedly post-racial America, injustices both past and present must be addressed within a "unified," nationalistic discourse that buries old wrongs for the sake of a greater, deracialized good. Such is the usual limitation of centrism—the film critiques a particular historical evolution but leaves the nation-state blameless in the abstract, much as moderates may reject particular capitalist excesses but not the overall ideology that produces excess, or as enlightened religious folk may reject dogma but still cling to the oppressive hierarchy of organized religion.

Though a far finer film than *The Butler*, *12 Years a Slave* also fell victim to a "doubly conscious" advertising campaign, which at once broadcast the injustices of slavery and exhorted audiences to repudiate activist or militant choices. In a strategy startling only for its banality, the cable TV and pay-per-view ad campaign[9] for *12 Years* replaced the film's synchronized audio track with bromidic excerpts from King's "I Have a Dream" speech, recasting the gruesome history of slavery in the comfortably optimistic terms of mid-twentieth-century morality. A much more trenchant—and relevant—ad would have foregone "I Have a Dream" and instead overdubbed excerpts from the Economic Bill of Rights that was part of King's ill-fated Poor People's Campaign of 1968. Admittedly, such an ad would unsubtly propagandize and provoke, but that is much the point—because allegedly "liberal" mass media, in fact, only propagate spineless centrism, American audiences need reminding of what true provocation looks and sounds like.

12 Years director McQueen likely had little say in the ad campaign, but the exploitative, manipulative nature of the culture industry has extended the discourse of a film well beyond the film proper. The totalized experience of a film now includes all its extra-diegetic appendages and appendices, from ads and posters, to star and director interviews, to newspaper reviews and journalists' fawning blurbs. As such, the "film" acquires a twofold presence within the machinery of the culture industry, existing first as an "authentic," auteurist text and secondly as the sum total of the text and its rampant publicity and media discourse. Though this commercialistic cleaving of a film's identity isn't directly analogous to a DuBoisian doubleness—the latter is an existentialistic problem—each case does engender something of a Cartesian split, as an authentic form (a soul, artwork, or integral mentality) must adopt multiple, embodying masks to perform within the material world.

If these ad campaigns are any yardstick, successful black-themed films like *The Butler* and *12 Years* have yet to reject politically correct masks, especially as Obama's presidency only intensifies the taboo of addressing racism without apology or hedging. Limiting themselves to descriptive—rather than prescriptive—frameworks, Hollywood filmmakers have thus become illustrators, not provocateurs. Gone are the incisive satires of Robert Downey's *Putney Swope* (1969) or Melvin van Peebles's *Watermelon Man* (1970), or even the interrogations of black masculinity that informed John Singleton's *Boyz n the Hood* (1991) and its numerous 1990s knockoffs. *Watermelon Man*, the story of a white bigot magically turned African American, is acutely sociological in its surrealism. A broad parable almost worthy of Mark Twain, the film refuses to reduce a painful history to middlebrow psychological portraiture, in the manner of *The Butler*. The political problem of insufficiently rebellious Obama-era films is thus also an aesthetic problem, for Hollywood's dominant mode of realist humanism always imagines individual subjectivities, not a collective consciousness. To be sure, the ubiquity of bourgeois individualism has been a stumbling block in Hollywood's treatment of race and class for several decades, especially after the blockbuster aesthetics of *Jaws* (1975) and *Star Wars* (1977) superseded Hollywood's flirtations with leftism earlier in the decade. In an interview that included *12 Years* director McQueen, Columbia historian Eric Foner critiqued Hollywood's tendency to reduce the complex threads of history to oversimplified, individual subjectivities:

> The daddy [of this cinematic trend] . . . I suppose, of all this was *Glory*, which came out in the late '80s. *Roots*, of course, comes before that. All of them suffer from what I see as the problem of Hollywood history. Even in [*12 Years a Slave*], there's a tendency toward: You've got to have one hero or one figure. That's why historians tend to be a little skeptical about Hollywood history, because you lose the sense of group or mass.[10]

Foner's critique could also be leveled at the bland history lesson that is Spielberg's *Lincoln* (2012), another prestige picture about elite individual personalities, not collective action. Extending beyond particular characters and plots, the myth of individualism lurks in Hollywood's economics and very style, from the rise of the star system in the 1910s and 1920s to directors' relentless close-ups, a technique that has sabotaged countless films aspiring to leftism (Spike Lee's *Malcolm X* [1991], for instance). While revolutionary directors from Jean-Luc Godard to Ousmane Sembene have rightly refused the bourgeois ideology of the close-up in favor of "collectivistic" long shots, mainstream Hollywood still insists on the facial close-up as a primary means of psychological signification. Beyond the confines of Hollywood, history is reduced to the cult of personality in every primary and secondary school. As James Loewen has argued, standardized textbooks strategically marginalize accounts of collective action, expunge the radical socialism of minority activists (such as Helen Keller or Paul Robeson), and reduce history to a grim fetish of executive branch personalities.[11]

The politics and aesthetics of reluctant centrism are ubiquitous, even when they extend to images of the liberal 1970s. Indeed, many Hollywood films of recent years, from *Boogie Nights* (1997) to *American Hustle* (2013) to facile exercises in the *Anchorman* (2004) vein, have returned to the 1970s not for the inspirations of feminism or black power but as a font of indulgent nostalgia. No doubt much of this wistfulness stems from a narcissistic generation of directors longing for their childhoods; the blaxploitation pastiches popularized by Tarantino and his epigones have only compounded the problem of sentimentality. The result is that 1970s blaxploitation in particular has been misremembered and mischaracterized as a mere "style" or affectation rather than as a movement that, for all its crudity and generic violence, did advance socialist-Marxist themes within the paradoxical frame of commercial cinema. While African American cultural studies have rightly revived interest in what were previously considered disposable films, many analyses are hampered by both sentiment and conservative, individualistic notions of heroism. For instance, in his personalized account of moviegoing, Nelson George waxes nostalgic over the "mesmerizing" and "glamorous" qualities of Ron O'Neil's "Cadillac El Dorado, big-brimmed hats, and lethal sideburns" in *Superfly* (1972).[12] The emphasis on finding empowerment in individualist black heroes also informs Adilifu Nama's short monograph *Super*

Black: American Pop Culture and Black Superheroes (2011) and Yvonne D. Sims's *Women of Blaxploitation* (2006), which makes simplistic claims for violent black heroines' agency within white patriarchy, as if Pam Grier and Tamara Dobson's action-movie gymnastics were adequate representations of political empowerment.[13] In fact, Grier tried to transcend violent stereotypes and once pitched biopics of Josephine Baker and Dorothy Dandridge only to find that white *and* black producers were uninterested in nonviolent, nongeneric heroines.[14] The male blaxploitation hero is even more a caricature than his female counterpart. Though some audiences may see his exaggerated potency as empowering, and though in *Shaft's Big Score* (1972) and *Hit Man* (1972) his eroticized body is unexpectedly subjected to a female gaze, his individualistic superheroism ultimately mimics and confirms the dominant, imperialistic model of the gunslinging cowboy or (white) pioneer.

Blaxploitation remains something of a sentimental embarrassment, much as black power rhetoric is now little more than a stale joke, especially as Obama's presidency has demonstrated that power comes from rising within the system, not from subverting it. Given the hegemonic masculinity embodied by Richard Roundtree (*Shaft*), Fred Williamson (*Black Caesar*), or Jim Brown (*Slaughter*), one cannot entirely blame the NAACP and the Coalition against Blaxploitation (formed by the NAACP, the Urban League, and allied religious groups) for opposing the genre's caricatures. In attempting to exorcise the stereotype of the black stud and redraw more nuanced images of African American masculinity, contemporary filmmakers have advanced storylines about bourgeois professionals, in the manner of Forest Whitaker's *Waiting to Exhale* (1995) or Chris Rock's *I Think I Love My Wife* (2005). In stressing bourgeois, upwardly mobile individuals, however, filmmakers have generally forgotten that blaxploitation did emphasize something that is not a joke and that shouldn't be rejected: community organization, Obama's greatest political sin.

We should therefore consider director Scott Sanders's and writer-star Michael Jai White's Obama-era blaxploitation spoof *Black Dynamite* (2009), which not only perfectly parodies the genre's style but foregrounds the problem of a black superhero who chooses violent individualism (i.e., Americanism) over community identity (i.e., socialism). Indeed, the standard blaxploitation film negotiates the commercial need for an individual superhero and the political need to acknowledge the work of community organizers, whether violent or not. In *Foxy Brown* (1974), a typical example, Pam Grier reluctantly accepts the aid of Black Panther-esque guerillas, but it is she alone who faces the white villainess in the film's finale. If doubly conscious films such as *The Butler* and *12 Years* solve (or fail to solve) their dilemma by putting on nonthreatening faces of centrism, so do most blaxploitation films conservatively privilege individualistic heroes and subordinate the role of community organizers, who are ultimately too political and dogmatic to act as "authentic," unbridled American heroes. There are, however, some notable exceptions, to which we'll return.

Like the titular heroes of *Shaft* and *Slaughter*, *Black Dynamite*'s crimefighting, kung fu superstud straddles law and lawlessness, the system and vigilantism; because the poles of white and black power are equally doctrinaire and rule-bound, it is preferable to remain in the ill-defined interstices. The white hero of nineteenth-century frontier mythology traditionally had to choose between savagery and civilization (as if the two were mutually exclusive!). The blaxploitation hero, a descendant of slaves, confronts an analogous but more complex choice, for he neither abandons individualistic claims to heroism nor capitulates to an alleged "civilization" built upon imperialism, slavery, and genocide. As he skeptically works within a historically oppressive white system to improve and diversify it (as in *Shaft* or *Slaughter*), he remains equally skeptical of organized black power, realizing that any hierarchy is prone to corruption. His individualism, though ostensibly rugged and manly, nevertheless harbors *ressentiment* at its core, for he knows his unique freedom ostracizes him from every community, much as his rampant heterosexuality precludes stable romantic partnerships. Whereas *The Butler*—or Obama himself—negotiates this bitter, "in-between" position with a veneer of centrism, the blaxploitation hero merely appropriates the modus operandi of the rugged individualist, becoming the arbiter of a stock revenge fantasy. Indeed, he easily appeals to white audiences because they can enjoy his rebellions superficially, as bloody retributions against any generic injustice, without the baggage of a defined political allegiance.

Far more knowing than Damon Wayans's scattershot spoof *I'm Gonna Get You Sucka* (1988), *Black Dynamite* relishes every blaxploitation stereotype: the indulgent white police chief, Italian mobsters peddling drugs in the ghetto, neighborhood antidrug crusaders, and, not least, the light-skinned black politician who rallies against the White Power Structure but secretly conspires with white gangsters to exploit his own people. This last element was a common point of (self-)criticism in *Coffy* (1973), *Friday Foster* (1975), and many other blaxploitation films precisely because they needed to demonstrate (however crudely) a Marxian critique of power reproduction at the structural level. Most importantly, *Black Dynamite* seizes upon the individual-versus-collective dynamic, deftly satirizing how the cult of individualism always trumps grassroots collectivism. Early in the film, Black Dynamite returns to the den of an old militant friend, who is now organizing beret-wearing black guerrillas. Knowing that Black Dynamite partly works within the system and is occasionally enabled by a crusty white police chief, one of the younger guerrillas asks the old friend, "You know this Uncle Tom?" Black Dynamite then responds with a harangue that more or less sums up one theory of blaxploitation:

> Listen, sucker, I'm blacker than the Ace of Spades and more militant than your whole damn army put together! While you're out there chanting at rallies and browbeating politicians, I'm taking out any money-grubbing sucker and hummer that gets in my way. When your so-called revolution starts, you call me, and I'll be right down in front showing you how it's done. But until then, you need to shut the fuck up when grown folks is talkin'!

On the surface, the harangue seems like ordinary genre parody, but it perfectly encapsulates the paradoxical double-binds that would-be activists must navigate—and rationalize. Black Dynamite insists he is more "militant" than the entire militant collective, yet his actions are those of a martial arts superhero, not a collective agent. In other words, he mischaracterizes militancy as individualistic acts of violence, not as a political consciousness. He can rationalize his stoic individualism because the "so-called revolution" has yet to begin—but in fact, the revolution will always be a dream deferred, an underground movement that has no credibly heroic spokesman because, paradoxically, Black Dynamite refuses to speak for it. Furthermore, Black Dynamite sees the movement as infantile, as a group of childish play-actors who are impotent without a leader like himself—yet he is an individualist who would never lead the group. The infantilizing language recalls the rhetoric of Rudy Giuliani and other Republicans who relish mocking—or simply demonizing—Obama the Community Organizer, who is surely too naïve to understand how the "real" world of politics works. This is the ideological problem that Black Dynamite, in his confident individualism, internalizes and parodies. Collective movements and *sociological* understandings of reality are branded by conservatives as "childish," while individual subjectivities and *psychological* (or simply religious) understandings of reality are lauded as "mature." Of course, it is the sociological and not the individualistic explanation that is truly sophisticated. By framing individualism as a mark of adulthood, however, the rightist imagination can deem Obama immature and effeminate, as someone who suffers from sinful defects of character, not from cautious diplomacy.

As satire, Black Dynamite's manliness and decisiveness are made ludicrous, yet his masculinity is the same yardstick by which Obama is ludicrously measured. It is thus no accident that *Black Dynamite*'s plot centers on masculinity, as its hero must foil a scheme (by Richard Nixon, no less) to emasculate the black population by spiking a popular brand of malt liquor with a penis-shrinking serum. In the film's climax, Black Dynamite must also confront a gun-wielding Pat Nixon; after violently subduing her, the hero curiously apologizes to her for his unchivalrous violence, at which point she becomes his love slave. Suddenly ashamed and self-conscious of his performance of hegemonic masculinity, Black Dynamite reminds the audience, too, that his masculinity is just a performance, hardly different from a militaristic politician's swagger.

Though *Black Dynamite* understands that the conventional black hero is existentially caught between a cartoonish individuality and an untested, underdefined revolution, its comedy does overlook a rarer current in blaxploitation, one that embraced the organized collective. Juxtaposing a pragmatic, heroic community organizer with a narcissistic black revolutionary, Lee Frost's obscure *The Black Gestapo* (1975) argues that the hubristic individual is more prone to corruption than the prudent (if imperfect) collective. The film begins as the hero, leader of the "People's Army," delivers a speech that rebuffs the timidity of slick Hollywood films like *The Butler*: "Martin Luther King had a dream, and it was blasted into eternity with him. I offer you reality. You've got to stand tall and demand your rights." Nevertheless, he is a pragmatist, working partly within the system but never selling out. "The People's Army was established with a grant given from the white community," he explains, so "blacks [can] help blacks with white money." Though torn by the prospect of receiving white subsidies, he insists they are necessary to establish a self-defense force that will protect the black community from stereotypical Italian mobsters. But the People's Army consists of poorly trained amateurs, and the leader's hubristic lieutenant grows impatient with bromides, inefficacy, and white handouts.

After the bloodthirsty lieutenant threatens a coup, the leader agrees to deputize six additional soldiers, but only for defensive purposes. Of course, the leader's strategy of appeasement backfires, and soon the lieutenant uses the defense force as a vigilante force: in one scene, the "Black Gestapo" breaks into the bathroom of a white rapist, castrates him, and flushes his testicles down the commode. Such crowd-pleasing revenge fantasies become corrupted, however, when the Black Gestapo begins to extort money from black merchants and erects an armed compound, replete with humiliated white servants.[15] Critiquing demagoguery run amok, the film actually fulfills the *ideal* (i.e., noncaricatured) thesis of blaxploitation—that revolutionaries should not become pseudo-colonialist exploiters themselves[16] —without worshipping an individualistic, superstud hero. Indeed, the film's hero, the ethical leader of the original People's Army, is not a cartoonish Black Dynamite but the type of conscientious community organizer Obama presumably was before he conceded to the corruptions of the White House. When the treacherous lieutenant offers the (former) leader funds to feed the poor, he refuses the dirty money and calls the traitor a "jive-ass nigger." Predictably, the climax witnesses the leader, now alone, take up arms and eliminate the Black Gestapo, though he does so reluctantly, and even in the final showdown the hero regrets resorting to violence. In this extremely low-budget, marginal film, we discover a hero slicker films refuse to imagine: a community organizer who advocates nonaggression and yet does not sacrifice his masculinity or sell out to the Man. Although *The Black Gestapo*'s first half exposes the inefficacy of the leader's self-defense force, the film ostensibly argues that temporary inefficacy is preferable to corruption, extremism, and the reproduction of oppression under a different name. Analogously, *The Butler* admits to its hero's timidity and compliance but also insists that his son's beret-wearing, Sidney Poitier–criticizing militancy is far worse. Because the political assumptions of *The Black Gestapo* are far to the left of those of *The Butler*, however, the hero of *The Black Gestapo* can retain his revolutionary consciousness while rejecting militant options that obviously go astray. In the centrist world of *The Butler*, the "radical" choice is merely the son's ordinary, reasonable militancy, and anyone to the son's political right has (according to the film, at least) few valid activist options.

We have already seen how ads and trailers for *The Butler* and *12 Years a Slave* adopted socially acceptable masks of patriotism or centrism to preempt accusations of race-baiting or so-called class warfare. Notably, the theatrical trailer for *The Black Gestapo* engaged in the opposite strategy, *exaggerating* rather than diluting the film's insurrectionary appeal. In its two and a half minutes, the trailer gives no indication that the conscientious leader, not the egomaniacal lieutenant, is the film's centered hero. Rather, after the trailer shows the People's Army thrashed by white gangsters, a voice-over declares (without irony) that "they had to become The Black Gestapo—the New Master Race!" At this point, the trailer cuts to scenes in which the lieutenant, adopting a Nazi posture and uniform, stands before his soldiers while the soundtrack overdubs chants of "Sieg Heil!" Of course, the lieutenant's pseudo-Nazism is supposed to be a sign of decadence in the film proper (even if the power fantasies might appeal to downtrodden audiences), and the Sieg Heil shouts are no more original to this film than "I Have a Dream" was to *12 Years a Slave*. Obviously, I would not suggest that *Black Gestapo*'s meretricious trailer is any more honest than the gutless, nonconfrontational trailers of contemporary Hollywood. Nevertheless, the trailer adopts a mask—for every film trailer constitutes a public face—designed to provoke and agitate, even to the point of ludicrousness.

Certainly, *The Black Gestapo* is not the only blaxploitation film to seriously entertain the value of community organizing, and one can conclude by briefly considering two other films (and their trailers) that explicitly imagine communitarian rebellions unthinkable in today's Hollywood. Ivan Dixon's *The Spook Who Sat by the Door* (1973), after the 1969 novel of the same name, was indeed controversial in its own time, and United Artists thought twice about releasing the film after realizing it had licensed the filmmakers to stage a revolutionary polemic. The film begins with patronizing white politicians devising a scheme to capture the "negro" vote: use affirmative action policies to integrate black agents into the CIA, in the hopes of propagating nationalistic sentiment among black constituencies. In an early scene, the film satirizes affirmative action policies when one black applicant jokingly suggests the best way to pass the entrance exams: "The word today is 'integration.' ... You just have to understand the theory of tokenism. They grade on a curve—if none of us gets too eager, it's a gentleman's C for everybody." One of the recruits, however, is a black nationalist and veteran of Korea who, disheartened by the tokenism, leaves the CIA to teach his new guerrilla skills to inner-city revolutionaries and even some white dissidents.

After spreading propaganda and inciting riots and public discord, the revolutionary hero is confronted by his old friend, a black police officer appalled by the wanton violence in the streets. The hero stands his moral ground, arguing that his militancy has invested black youths with revolutionary purpose and historical consciousness—youths otherwise destined for the prison-industrial complex. In a struggle, the hero kills the old friend and then delivers a speech to his supporters about the necessity of killing black cops and soldiers and other Uncle Toms. The film ends audaciously with a montage of guerrilla warfare in the Chicago streets, as revolutionaries pick off government soldiers from rooftops and a news report announces that spreading insurrections have forced the president to declare a state of national emergency. Given this plot synopsis, the contrast between *The Spook Who Sat by the Door* and a film like *The Butler* could not be starker or more enlightening. One wonders—if only in jest—how Forest Whitaker's butler might have abandoned his servility, joined his bereted son in the militant cause, and taken up arms against the system. But the jest is bittersweet: not only are revolutionary approaches to race now taboo, but contemporary Hollywood has put forth precious few images of black intellectuals of any stripe, revolutionary or otherwise.

The trailer for *The Spook Who Sat by the Door* doesn't mince words, emphasizing street-level chaos meant to strike fear into the heart of the white establishment. A similar strategy informs the trailer for *Black Samson* (1973), whose communitarian hero not only ejects white encroachers but also subdues various wrongdoers with a great Mosaic staff. While *Black Samson*'s action-movie stereotypes are risible, the film's trailer is quite remarkable, showcasing as its climax a race riot. As the voice-over claims, "When the scene gets really heavy, Black Samson and his people come down—with all their weight!" Yet Black Samson is not actually shown in the scene; we only see, in long shots, a rooftop filled with members of the black underclass, righteously raining down washing machines, television sets, and every sort of commercial refuse onto white miscreants below. Whereas contemporary Hollywood trailers typically end with a comforting or reassuring image (dancing, laughing, kissing, epic explosions, athletic victories, and so on), *Black Samson*'s trailer climaxes with a mass insurrection that privileges neither a single hero nor individualistic psychology. In fact, the trailer suggests that the race riot scene is actually the *selling point* of the film, something more or less unimaginable in any corner of today's Hollywood.

The existence of films such as *Black Samson* and *The Spook Who Sat by the Door* reminds us that there was an era, however fleeting, in which commercial films discarded centrist masks and bravely wore insurrection on their sleeves. Moreover, these images of collectivism were not the products of elite auteurs like Pontecorvo or Godard, but were part of a *generic* film movement that entertained Marxist ideas. With the exception of Depression-era social conscience films such as *I Am a Fugitive from a Chain Gang* (1932), *Our Daily Bread* (1934), and *Mr. Deeds Goes to Town* (1936), these "lesser" blaxploitation efforts might mark the only trend in mainstream Hollywood that explicitly advanced socialist philosophy.

Although today's plutocratic power structure may have convinced many Americans—including Democrats—that "community" and "organizing" are dirty words, blaxploitation, in its less commercial moments, reveals that cinema can propose *collective heroisms*. The point is not to make elaborate biopics about individual leftist leaders—like Soderbergh's *Che* (2008)—and then have a stale debate about the accuracy or inaccuracy of their historical representations. Instead, we should reject the cult of biography altogether and put forth films, whether realistic or fantastic, that reimagine heroism as something other than the exclusive domain of extraordinary individuals. Unfortunately, younger generations don't merely see collective heroism as naïve or unrealistic—they don't even recognize it as a possibility. At the risk of being reductive, allow me to relate a revealing anecdote. A short time ago, I was teaching an introductory film class to a small group of eighteen-year-olds. After watching Eisenstein's *Battleship Potemkin* (1925), I asked a seemingly innocuous question: "Who is the film's hero?" After a minute of deliberation, they realized the question had stumped them. Of course, *Battleship Potemkin*, which emphasizes mass scenes and baroquely composed long shots, has no individual hero. But the students had been so indoctrinated by the Hollywood ideology of singular heroes that they didn't recognize "the revolutionaries" as a plurality of heroes. Honestly, I myself can hardly think of a commercial American film that totally dispenses with individually named heroes, apart from social movement documentaries like *Woodstock* or Barbara Kopple's *Harlan County, USA* (1976) and *American Dream* (1989).

Because mythic fictions hold the greatest propagandistic power, however, we cannot rely on progressive documentaries that preach to the converted and that young people will never see. Likewise, we cannot make apologies for middlebrow productions like *The Butler*, whose aesthetics of servility, of supposedly noble service to state masters, directly contradicts Desmond Tutu's famous admonition: "We don't want our chains made more comfortable." Just as we cannot simplistically look to an individual leader like Obama for liberation, progress, or any other idealized goal, so should we resist identifying with Hollywood's cult of individualistic heroes, who only reproduce neoliberal images of masculinized power and authority, regardless of their race or multiculturalist pretense. Instead, Hollywood directors, who until now have only posed as progressives, must become real progressives, forgoing individualistic subjectivities—and, indeed, the fetishized star system itself—for the kind of collective subjectivity blaxploitation (and Eisenstein) all-too-briefly entertained.

While a rise in collectivism may seem improbable, the time is in fact ripe, if we believe conditions must get worse before they get better. The Supreme Court's 2010 *Citizens United* and 2014 *McCutcheon* decisions may temporarily privatize the electoral system, but they are also a call to arms that can unite right and left in new coalitions. Likewise, America's calamitous war on drugs, imperialist misadventures in Iraq and Afghanistan, and unofficial policy of corporate welfare will eventually unite racially disparate members of the underclass. As the richest four hundred Americans now hold as much wealth as the bottom 50 percent of the population combined, and as conservatives repackage trickle-down economics with the sanctimonious euphemism of "job creators," widespread economic discontent will trump the Republican Party's racialized divide-and-conquer strategy. By 2050 white Americans will be a minority population, but we needn't wait for demographic shifts to effect change. Early in *The Communist Manifesto*, Marx reminds us of a historical reality we too easily forget—that the middle class itself was once a revolutionary movement, for in the seventeenth century, the ascendant bourgeoisie had to displace and supplant the prior feudalist system. If early modern merchant classes could displace manorialism, today's movie audiences could certainly refuse the culture industry's hero cults and insist on collectivistic images that rightly reflect the people's economic interests. We only have to heed the advice of Erich Fromm and realize that power itself has a double meaning: the manipulative, dominating power over a thing, and the emancipatory power to do what hasn't yet been done.

NOTES

1. The most notorious instance of homophobia occurred in 1994, when Sen. Jesse Helms warned Clinton to bring bodyguards when visiting military bases, as American soldiers presumably might want to kill the president for proposing LGBT integration. Helms's homophobia is roughly the equivalent of the perceived racism of South Carolina congressman Joe Wilson, now famous for yelling "You lie!" during Obama's 2009 State of the Union address.

2. Given the Republican Party's current libertarian poseurs, who believe in small government only when it suits their pursuits, the qualifier "authentic" seems necessary.

3. Bowing to public pressure in 2008, Obama had to distance himself from the leftism of his former pastor, the liberation theologian Jeremiah Wright. However, most of the arguments in Wright's sermons—which lambasted U.S. policy in Iraq, exposed massacres of Native Americans, and so on—are already commonplaces in college classrooms and on moderately

liberal PBS documentaries. Obama's backpedaling on the Wright "controversy" is arguably the best illustration of his betrayal of activist causes.

4. From a speech given at the University of Michigan, April 2, 2014.

5. Hollywood's black "servility" narratives might be compared to what Norman Finkelstein had derisively called "the Holocaust industry," as each genre exploits histories of suffering for financial and/or nationalistic gain.

6. Admittedly, 1970's highest-grossing film was *Patton*, though its success rested mainly on George C. Scott's larger-than-life performance.

7. Examples are probably unnecessary, but consider *X Men: The Last Stand* (2006), an obvious allegory about nefarious attempts to "cure" queers and other outsiders.

8. From an MSNBC interview with Martin Bashir, aired on August 13, 2013.

9. These short promos were run continuously in early 2014 by Verizon and other cable providers for the film's home video release.

10. Nelson George, "An Essentially American Narrative: A Discussion of Steve McQueen's Film *12 Years a Slave*," *New York Times*, October 11, 2013.

11. The argument against the history of personality is central to Loewen's popular historiography *Lies My Teachers Told Me* (New York: New Press, 1994).

12. Nelson George, *Blackface: Reflections on African-Americans and the Movies* (New York: HarperCollins, 1994), 30.

13. Though blaxploitation did provide work for many underemployed Hollywood actors, many have expressed frustration about their limited roles. For instance, William Marshall insisted that "Blacula" be a former African prince to add dignity to the character written in the original script. Yaphet Kotto, a powerful actor too often consigned to genre roles, has frankly criticized his James Bond villain "Kananga" in *Live and Let Die* (1973): "There were so many problems with that script.... I was too afraid of coming off like Mantan Moreland.... I had to dig deep in my soul and brain and come up with a level of reality that would offset the sea of stereotype crap that [screenwriter] Tom Mankiewicz wrote that had nothing to do with the Black experience or culture." See "The One and Only: An Interview with Yaphet Kotto," *Cult Film Freak*, http://www.cultfilmfreak.com/yaphetkotto (accessed April 29, 2014).

14. Steve Ryfle, "The Accidental Action Heroine," *Bright Lights Film Journal* 69, http://brightlightsfilm.com/69/69ivgrier_ryfle.php#.U19RsfldW5Y (accessed April 29, 2014).

15. The theme of black entrepreneurs and power holders humiliating their white servants and conquests is common in blaxploitation—see, for instance, *Boss Nigger* (1973) and *Black Caesar* (1973), both with Fred Williamson.

16. The theme of power reproduction is also central to *Bucktown* (1975). Here, Fred Williamson's hero must oppose black militants who abuse newfound power after eliminating the racist white police of a small southern town.

Chapter Seven

Rednecks, Racism, and Religion: King and Darabont's Precarious Prophecy of Obama's Coming

Victoria McCollum

> The best horror films serve the same purpose as nightmares—reflecting the deep-rooted fears of the population that creates them. . . . So how do you paint a masterpiece in blood? The answer is: Jackson Pollock style. Let loose, allow an element of fate to direct the storytelling, and some slithering tentacle of reality will emerge from the fog of the subconscious.[1]

Clearly, entering into the realms of allegory and national mythology is second nature to horror cinema as this "meaning machine" genre has the capacity to inherently transfigure the "real into the representational."[2] Of course, it is no longer novel to read the contemporary horror film as serious enough to decipher traumatic and unspeakable histories. Indeed, for notorious American horror novelist Stephen King, superior works of horror are those that trigger "national phobic pressure points."[3] According to King, it is the pressing of these tender "bruises" that gives valuable horror films "a pleasing allegorical feel."[4] Interestingly, this feel, which seems implicitly tied to the genre's cultural and intellectual value, stems back to David Hume's eighteenth-century philosophical discourse on the "uncountable pleasure" that spectators of "well-written tragedy" received.[5]

Wherever there is societal dissatisfaction, it seems, the horror genre can be found cavorting in the political tensions, exploiting and transcoding new anxieties and anger. Although other genres during times of political turmoil tend to consider silence the only "patriotically supportive response" by abstaining from examining the dubious political repercussions,[6] the horror film arguably begins to fluctuate and function as a "rare protected space in which to critique the tone and content of public disclosure."[7] Whether subtle as an amplified death rattle or a faint allegorical ode to the complexities of the era's political climate, the horror genre surely has the ability to illustrate a more frank and blatant reflection on the anxieties of a culture than any other. As Thompson advocates, "[Horror] is one of the most versatile genres out there, a universal solvent of virtually any news issue."[8]

Yet, until now, little has been said on the American horror film's profound reflection of the Barack Obama administration and the events that have defined it thus far. This inspires examination of the now-thriving Obama-era horror film. This cycle of Obama-specific horror imagery began to emerge during the liminal period between the departing of Bush and the coming of Obama and has continued to flourish.

President Obama's positive mantras certainly personify hope and change for America, yet as Derry suggests on the Obama-era horror film, "no similar optimism" has been projected.[9] Very recently, this deep sense of pessimism was noticeable, not only in horror films, but on social networking sites such as Twitter. Users satirically began to imagine horror film titles inspired by the perceived state of his presidency (#ObamaHorrorFilms). Such tweets included: "Count Barackula," "Invasion of the HealthCare Snatchers," "Night of the Living Debt," "President Evil," and "The Taxorcist."[10]

This same droll sense of cynical partisanship dramatically underscores Frank Darabont's supernatural horror film *The Mist* (2007).[11] Yet, this time, the crux of the pessimism seems symbolically directed at the incompetence of the Bush administration as the film eagerly anticipates the coming of an inevitably overwhelmed Obama. The focus of this chapter will center on a discussion of Darabont's film, which appears to illustrate a gory picture of the precarious fate of the Obama presidency, set to inherit a dystopian America of complex national security issues. *The Mist*, between fantasy and near-term cultural prophecy, does trigger a national phobic pressure point in its depiction of an undesirable and institutionally corrupt post-9/11 America. While Darabont's citizens yearn for leadership and legitimacy amid boomerang violence, biblical fundamentalism, and environmental chaos (a milieu highly evocative of the unpopular Bush regime), an understated message of optimism regarding the coming of an Obama seems to resonate most heavily. This is ultimately due to Darabont's treatment of the narrative and, in particular, the role of African American supporting character Brent Norton (Andre Braugher) in *The Mist*.

Clearly, amid the twenty-first century's "real/unreal political universe," where governmental truth hovers around the White House like "an unidentified flying object,"[12] the murky waters of supernatural horror, where racism, rednecks, and religion thrive, could underscore America's ambiguous yearning for change and the beckoning of a new presidential era by giving eerie prophetic voice to a longing for an Obama.

A FOGGY REUNION: FRANK DARABONT AND STEPHEN KING

Renowned for his cinematic storytelling capabilities, Hungarian American director Frank Darabont's signature style is distinctive for its labored pacing, narrative detail, shrewd casting, and climatic scenery.[13] Yet it would be the screenwriter's prosperous brush with horror novelist Stephen King that would put his film career on the map, earning him three nominations for Academy Awards due to the "slightly anachronistic" quality of Darabont's work.[14] Adapting two of King's prison sagas in succession, Darabont wrote and directed his debut, *The Shawshank Redemption* (1994),[15] followed by *The Green Mile* (1999),[16] and has continued to enjoy a long and illustrious film career in America. More recently, he created AMC's post-apocalyptic horror series *The Walking Dead* (2010–present),[17] the most-watched drama series in U.S. cable history.[18] By breaking convention and defying the predictabilities of the genre,[19] Darabont's craft remains intelligent and ambitious even as it has consistently been "fed into the Hollywood meat grinder."[20]

A third major collaboration with King would somewhat surprisingly result in the grocery-store survival saga, *The Mist*. Although generating modest success at the box office, the film would receive small critical acclaim. Of course, this particular undertaking with King wouldn't earn Darabont the same accolades with the academy, as in his own words, "the genre very seldom gets that kind of attention."[21] Nonetheless, the film was lauded for its "real conviction."[22] "Crude but effective,"[23] *The Mist* was regarded as a horror film of "real heart, brains, and courage"[24] and a "gut-kicking" contribution to the post–9/11 genre.[25]

Although Darabont was intent on embracing "a much faster and looser style" than in his earlier works,[26] his signature approach does incessantly seep through *The Mist*. The film's epic length (127 minutes), cinematic nostalgia (including a black-and-white director's cut), and its familiar themes of injustice and racial pairing, all scream Darabont (and King). Judging by his previous work and latest project, TNT's *Mob City* (2014),[27] a television series about cops and gangsters in 1940s L.A., Darabont's creativity seems to stem from an interest in human nature, survival, and, perhaps most glaringly, race.

WE ALL BLEED RED: RACE AND HORROR

The relationship between horror films and race in general remains notoriously uncharted.[28] Indeed, it is due to the "ideological shortcomings" of the horror genre—its predominately white generic milieu[29] —that we perhaps anticipate the inevitable doom of "token" (nonwhite) characters, a trope frequently parodied in Wes Craven's *Scream* franchise (1996–2011).[30] Although it is beyond the limitations of this chapter to explore in any significant detail the genre's perplexing rapport with race, due to the unusual prominence of Darabont's African American character in *The Mist*, a brief discussion on the notoriety of black characters in horror does seem an important reference point.

While "difference" in horror is usually tackled via the fantastical (winged creatures, "freak" monsters, and mutant bodies), due to the nature of the genre's psychoanalytical rootedness, and its preoccupation with human nature and gender,[31] horror of the 1960s, following the African American civil rights movement, did proffer an array of "race-specific imagery."[32] Fortunately, replacing the unenlightened tribalism of monsters such as King Kong, the young and eloquent black character emerged; take George Romero's *Night of the Living Dead* (1968)[33] for example, yet not unproblematically.

With a host of blaxploitation horror films spawned by the 1970s, black characters on one hand metamorphosed monsters into agents of "black pride and black power"[34] yet simultaneously, perhaps a product of a predominantly white film industry,[35] surrendered to the horror genre's often-racist tropes of perpetuating common white stereotypes about black people.[36] Thus, unfortunately, blackness, particularly in American horror, is nearly always an issue and is often negotiated through questionable comedy.[37]

Indeed, it is a tricky business to dissect the representation of any black character in the genre, as perhaps one tends to suspect horror filmmakers of the very worse motives. This rings especially true when considering a Darabont/King collaboration, as although both *The Shawshank Redemption* and *The Green Mile* tell moral tales of respectable black men enlightening dishonorable white men,[38] due to King's habitual use of his polysemic "magical negro" trope,[39] these representations are often considered infantilizing and insulting.[40]

It should also be noted that the racially charged criticism of the "magical negro" label has not been used solely to condemn King's work, but President Obama himself.[41] Whether in the realms of film or politics, the "magical negro" trope refers to black characters who have "fallen victim" to white America's idealized image; thus, these individuals are perceived as bearing no past of injustice, simply appearing to assist the white majority.[42] Does it not then seem highly appropriate, in light of the age of Obama, to consider the new significance of African American characters in this notoriously "white genre"?[43]

Although Darabont boasted of a departure from his earlier prison sagas, from the moment of the film's plot-alerting line, "There's something in the mist. . . . Close the door!" characters do become imprisoned inside the local supermarket. Yet *The Mist*'s positioning of race, religion, and institution in opposition seems less of an endeavor to allegorize post-9/11 irrational fears of the barbaric other, regardless of the alien invader beyond the store, and more of an attempt to parallel contention over leadership change closer to home.

As Hoberman suggests, Obama's "cleaning up Bush's mess [was] . . . hardly great movie material,"[44] yet the anticipation of his coming *was*. As Kellner illuminates, the United States was made ready to consider a president of color during the 2000s due to a plethora of fictional black presidents on Hollywood film and television at the time.[45] Yet unlike these idealized representations that anticipated the coming of an Obama was the horror genre's precarious prophecies concerning the possible doom of the beckoning presidency. Likewise, since the eve of Obama's second term, horror's images have become "more complex, and in some ways blurrier."[46] Furthermore, as Kellner aptly recommends, film can and should be used to analyze and interpret "the events, hopes, fears, discourses, ideologies, and socio-political conflicts" of the Obama era.[47]

Yet certainly the distinctive appeal of the horror genre in particular lies in its capacity to peel back the "ideologically expedient dressings" that other branches of the cultural industry have applied "to the wounds of the period."[48] Films such as Francis Lawrence's *I Am Legend* (2007),[49] for example, surely apply a sticking plaster to the wounds of an era by honoring, celebrating, and normalizing black male protagonists. Perhaps these idealized representations of black characters, who function more as plot devices than actual people, solely existing to assist the white majority, were only to be expected. If Obama admittedly serves as a blank canvas for many different individuals to project their views,[50] then perhaps it is understandable why the majority of black characters in Obama-era fiction would function as stand-ins for transcendent representations of race.

Like the "bringer of peace" and "race unifier"[51] the characters surely symbolize, these unspoiled representations of black authority figures read as one-dimensional utopian visions of an Obama. Yet is it not inevitable for any blank canvas serving a multitude of conflicting artists to become ruined by a hodgepodge of individual strokes? This is the void that *The Mist* fills, by tackling head-on the strikingly ambiguous and chaotic image that the American public had painted in Obama's image. In contrast, Darabont's film undresses the wounds of this period by exposing a turbulent United States, or a nation "of gathering clouds and raging storms" as Obama put it,[52] plus "[the] atmosphere of real hate and obstructionism" that Stephen King, an ardent supporter of Obama, believed has surrounded America's first black president since his arrival on the political scene.[53]

FAILURE TO RISE TO THE APOCALYPTIC OCCASION

> It appears we may have a problem of some magnitude! —Bud, *The Mist*

Thunder sounds ominously over black as *The Mist* opens, forewarning the horrific elements of a freak storm in small-town Maine. The morning after soon attests to the storm's severity as David Drayton (Thomas Jane) and his family gather in their garden among a plethora of dislocated possessions and tattered stars and stripes to assess the damage. Here, Darabont, perhaps as an ode to the post-9/11 era, gives particular prominence to the uprootedness of a pair of fallen trees that the family reminisce over before becoming preoccupied with an unexplained mist suspended in the distance. Early renditions of paranoia begin to breed as the Draytons fantasize on the possibility of a second encounter with the merciless storm as the fog begins to engulf their small town.

Contemporary horror cinema has become particularly occupied with exploiting an extensive range of environmental issues and threats to civilization. These allegories of environmental disaster and social apocalypse are surely the result of the perceived incompetence of the Bush-Cheney administration toward ecological and other critical issues.[54] *The Mist*, being a post-9/11 disaster film, certainly appears to play off these same uncertainties looming large in the public mind at the time. Yet, simultaneously, the film forges another correlation between the real and unreal, as it doesn't just allegorize the fears and anxieties generated by the Bush administration, but subtextually anticipates the longing for, and consequence of, a change of leadership amid disaster. Chiming somewhat in tandem with Obama's core concerns for the nation—recession, war, and climate change—cited in his victorious election speech,[55] *The Mist* cinematically exploits America's evolving predicaments: a deteriorating economy, increasing threats of terrorism, and the onset of global warming.

Effectively evoking the traumatic imagery of the Indian Ocean tsunami (2004) and Hurricane Katrina (2005), Darabont's unapologetically epic elements of water and wind batter and flood the community, leaving a residue of human despair and awe-inspiring scenery. With a potentially devastating mist hanging in the air, David; his son Billy (Nathan Gamble); and his African American neighbor, lawyer, and out-of-towner, Brent Norton, take to the road. Alerted by a convoy of passing armored vehicles and increasing military presence, the neighbors converse over the existence of "Project Arrowhead"—a pseudo-scientific governmental experiment allegedly being performed in the area.

Of course, David and Norton's whispering of governmental scandal is an entirely unsurprising component of the plot considering the period—an era of climate change and failure to rise to the apocalyptic disaster. As schoolteacher Irene Reppler (Frances Sternhagen) laments in *The Mist*: "Government's got better things to spend our money on, like corporate hand-outs and building bombs." Running parallel to Darabont's offering, similar environmental crisis films such as Roland Emmerich's *The Day After Tomorrow* (2004)[56] and Larry Fessenden's *The Last Winter* (2006)[57] transcode prevalent public perceptions of government as inept and disengaged; thus, these films could be read as playing horrific "tribute" to a presidency (Bush/Cheney) "which ignores serious problems."[58] The "culture of paranoia and fear" bred by the Bush administration's framing of terrorism as "the greatest threat facing the nation"[59] is allegorically exploited in *The Mist* by the menace of the barbaric alien invader, which is about to draw deeply opposed mind-sets, separation, cynicism, and instability.

The inevitable is soon exposed—Darabont's military are wholly unprepared and utterly fail to rise to the apocalyptic occasion as ecological crisis and blowback violence ensues. While David, Billy, and Norton become trapped in the supermarket among the other townsfolk hunting for supplies, the building is submerged in a thick band of treacherous fog. Naturally, with the military floundering and the citizens imprisoned in the store, the mood begins to rapidly shift following the alarm of a civil defense siren, a sudden earthquake, and the disconcerting declarations of an irate and bleeding customer from outside the building. Rumors of what the menacing mist might conceal become the order of the day as the patrons develop a strong dose of siege mentality. Disunity, irrationality, and even calls for a human sacrifice all contribute to the townsfolk's yearning for a leader to emerge amid the catastrophe.

This, like the definitive era it encapsulates, is a world that has changed irrevocably. Naturally, the "movie-like" spectacle of the principal event that the post-9/11 disaster film so often aims to allegorize[60] Darabont accomplishes with ease due to the "unbelievable" nature of the scenes, panoramic shots, and handheld cinematography. The cloud of dust-like mist that rolls malevolently over the buildings, pavements, and vehicles, juxtaposed with the spellbound gazes of the citizens, is undoubtedly evocative of 9/11. Not to mention, the Lovecraftian (frighteningly monstrous and otherworldly) "otherness" concealed by the fog that threatens to viciously attack at any minute. *The Mist* may wear its politics lightly, yet we are left in no doubt that Darabont's film is utterly savage and horribly relevant to this tumultuous period. In the director's own words, the film is "an angry cry from the heart of a humanist" toward the complex conditions of a precarious era.[61]

While the genre's allegories of catastrophic disaster may regurgitate and reflect upon the politics of fear browbeaten by the far right—"unregulated market fundamentalism, rampant militarism, Social Darwinism, and fear"[62] —this "most expressive subgenre"[63] surely proffers a quasi-optimistic flipside: the yearning and materialization of new leadership and legitimacy. Darabont's setup in the first two acts of *The Mist* seemingly foreground figuratively the dramatic political climate of the United States at the time and, via his hankering citizens, the longing for change amid a bewildering array of foreign and domestic crises, as symbolized by his supernatural cataclysm. Yet, as *The Mist* seems to proffer prophetically on the longing for an Obama, for some, change is not necessary and survival is not mandatory. The otherworldly monsters that the mist threatens to unleash at any given moment aren't the real problem here, but the people awash with fear.

LONGING FOR LEADERSHIP

> We are experiencing some kind of disaster. I don't know whether it's manmade or natural, but I do know that it's definitely not supernatural. Or biblical.
> —Norton, *The Mist*

Despite the daunting development of a multitude of creatures outside, which due to their ambiguity remain tangible to some and implausible to others, these supernatural reptiles are, undoubtedly, a secondary source of the horror. While the monsters are the catalyst for rapidly growing tension between the townsfolk, the real horror emerges inside the store when an unfathomable competitiveness for survival flourishes, bringing to the surface the true barbaric nature of some of the locals.

God-fearing local Mrs. Carmody (Marcia Gay Harden) is just as shocking and compelling as the enigmatic creatures in the mist. Persistently threatening the trapped citizens, she deems the situation the apocalypse of a vengeful God sending punishment for the townfolk's denial of religion and morality. Possessing a subtle balance of soft-spoken protest while lacing it with just enough charismatic poison to chill and disorient the audience, Carmody exploits the frailty of the "civilized" others as her fundamentalist ideology develops into a deadly and marauding weapon.

It seems that Darabont's film takes on horrible relevance here, in light of the era, as Carmody's bombastic and biblical tone becomes highly reminiscent of the post-9/11 televangelical blame-game, which sought to accuse those damning the nation for bringing on the terrorist attacks.[64] Carmody's self-presentation as a woman of faith during her demonization of difference is surely evocative of the Bush administration's distinctly religious rhetoric post-9/11. Indeed, striking an uncanny likeness with the unanticipated rise of Obama during Bush's brush with fanaticism is the counterproductivity of

Carmody's fear-mongering and polarization of the people, which subsequently paves the way for more open-minded opposition to rapidly win favor within the store.

Ultimately flourishing within the walls of Darabont's supermarket is a metaphorical wave of domestic terrorism, where the surge of zealous loyalty to one side, Carmody's for example, means jeopardizing other perspectives. Naturally, Darabont's "angry cry" could be read as being directed toward excessive patriotism, fear-based allegiances, and the reduction of civil liberties in a post-9/11 era; nonetheless, what appears to resonate most heavily in the second act is some of the community's opposition toward the African American out-of-towner who seems intent on shaking up the leadership dynamics. This is part and parcel of *The Mist*'s attempt to tap into the events, fears, and fantasies of an era, thus, giving cinematic expression to the longing and anticipation of an Obama. Indeed, there are a series of interesting parallels that can be drawn between Obama and African American character Norton's uphill climb to leadership, particularly that of their opposition.

Offering the townsfolk an alternative to Carmody's dictatorship, Norton shrewdly dismantles this religious maverick's agency. Darabont here, by illuminating the barbarity of a fundamentalist who doesn't reflect the fundamentals of her own religion, offers Norton as a beacon of hope and change amid catastrophe. With the same conviction, confidence, and composure perhaps representative of the Obama campaign, Norton, embodying a message of social liberalism, takes to the "stage" holding the attention of the room with Darabont's camera tracking around him as if he were placed on a pedestal.

Advocating his skepticism toward the threat of the monster beyond the store, while constructively criticizing Carmody's formidable fanaticism and polarization of the people, Norton asserts: "You are welcome to join me" as he endeavors not to share fear but courage with the others. Although many of the townsfolk appear aghast at Norton's unanticipated influence, Carmody is first to unleash her opposition: "Take sides!" she warns. "The saved and the damned." Naturally, to Carmody, the seemingly doomed citizens are those who have begun to side with Norton.

In addition, the local "hicks," mechanics Myron (David Jensen) and Jim (William Sadler), while capitalizing on the store's "free" beer, also take issue with Norton's skepticism and increasing superiority. Here, Darabont injects a subtle measure of class prejudice as Myron and Jim, who are ironically considered as unintelligent and provincial throughout, become distinctly more aware of the new leader's foreignness within the town. Yet with Darabont's text furiously calling for a new leader to emerge amid the savagery, Norton's clout increases as he recommends that everyone remain calm. For him, the danger lies not with monsters in the mist, but with the blind paranoia and panic-stricken imaginations of the townsfolk. Certain the locals are either delusional (the reptiles are an illusion) or prank playing, Norton advocates that they turn their attention to the "real problems" within the store—Carmody's call for a human sacrifice being one.

Indeed, Norton's skepticism toward Carmody whipping the supermarket into a biblical frenzy could be interpreted as level-headed agnosticism or militant atheism. Either way, what becomes clear is that those who oppose Norton's leadership do so on the basis of his religious allegiances, race, and lack of enthusiasm for concern and conflict over the exotic outsider. Is this not highly evocative of Obama's hard-fought struggle for leadership and legitimacy amid a complex and difficult post-9/11 world teetering on the edge of an eroding leadership? Indeed, Obama's campaign was partially tarnished by his having trouble convincing the American people that he possessed Christian values,[65] his "anything but post-racial" struggle against presidential prejudice,[66] and his incompatibility as a "peace candidate" to fill the shoes of a "war president."[67]

So, symbolizing an Obama in a nonidealized manner, Norton's innate leadership qualities, his fresh perspective, and the horrific state of current events render him a target of opposition from a variety of skewed perspectives. Nonetheless, he causes a cross-racial collaboration—a fairly surprising feat for the horror genre, if not American politics itself. Thus, via his cinematic exploitation of an African American character, striving for change in a perilous world against the already established "rules of old," as Carmody puts it, Darabont frames a metaphor that anticipates the coming of Obama. Like the coalition-building newcomer that he effectively allegorizes, Norton has handled his difference of opinion rationally and respectfully, not through force but via quiet persuasion. The quasi consensus reached earns him a small following, including most of the minorities in the store.

Norton does seem to represent a shift from the disconcerting and controversial procedures of the other chiefs within the store, particularly due to his questioning the existence of the monsters lurking outside. Clearly, his message of hope and optimism has temporarily supplanted the politics of fear deeply engrained in some of the townsfolk, yet it remains to be seen whether Norton is right and his solution effective. Convinced of his undaunted vision, Norton, much to the disapproval of some of the town's pessimists, whom he dubs the "flat-earthers," signaling their stubborn adherence to their own discredited convictions, leads his people into the mist—their fate remaining unknown.[68]

PROPHESYING OBAMA'S MISSION (IM)POSSIBLE

You don't have much faith in humanity, do you? —Amanda, *The Mist*

If *The Mist* does allegorically anticipate the beckoning of, and longing for, an Obama amid a dystopian America, then surely the precarious fate of the impending administration is implied as Norton leads his group daringly into the abyss. It seems that Norton and his group's ambiguous departure functions as a metaphor for a doomed Obama presidency inevitably overwhelmed as it is set to inherit mayhem. After all, for some viewers, Norton will be deemed delusional and held responsible for leading his people to the slaughter. Surely, there is cynicism and doubt symbolically expressed toward the anticipation of Obama here, yet the primary target of Darabont's critique seems centered on the incompetence of the administration that came before. Indeed, Norton could have led his people to survival, but we simply cannot be sure. It is this flip side and the open-ended nature of post-9/11 horror that allows the film to be received and interpreted in a variety of ways.

Effectively connoting the many flip sides of Obama's perceived character—"a dreamer mugged by reality, a pragmatist confounded by ideology, a radical to some, a sell-out to others"[69] —is Darabont's mystifying depiction of Norton and his mission, which renders him a hero to some, yet a fool to others. From the outset, it is entirely possible that Norton, being an articulate attorney from out of town, would win influence among the more hopeful townsfolk in the thick of disaster. Yet, as Darabont's corrupted institutions—the supermarket, the military, and Carmody's religion—so effectively signify, Norton's mission is an utterly constrained one. His optimism—that no monsters roam beyond the store—seems much like the campaigning of a seemingly "progressive purist" like Obama, who faced a mission "impossible to fulfill" due to his maintaining ideological convictions in an unideological climate.[70]

Interestingly, after Norton and his followers' ambiguous departure and their assumed death by the rest of the townsfolk, all hell breaks loose as the deadly reptiles invade the store. Having escaped, David, his son, and a few of the others take to the road, dodging an abundance of extraterrestrial monsters through the apocalyptic terrain until their vehicle fails. Darabont then executes what could be perceived as the most nihilistic ending of post-9/11 horror cinema as David, seemingly doomed, takes out his gun, and with the silent agreement of his hopeless passengers, he assists their suicide, including shooting his own son. With only four bullets for five passengers, it appears that his only prospect of escape is to will a beckoning reptile to devour him. However, much to David's utter dismay, it is not monsters that emerge from the mist, but military tanks flanked by soldiers. With the government apparently in control of the catastrophe and all creatures seemingly destroyed, David drops to his knees wailing in agony with the cold realization that his killings were wholly unnecessary.

One could make an unconventional argument that as a consequence of Norton's absence, the situation becomes entirely detrimental. In Frank Capra's sentimental *It's a Wonderful Life* (1946),[71] a compassionate yet hopelessly disheartened businessman, George Bailey (James Stewart), catches a glimpse of the future without him, a world of tragedy and ruin. By the same token, what if we imagined *The Mist*'s third act, following Norton's disappearance, as a prophecy of a future devoid of an Obama?

Norton's abilities, akin to those of an adept politician, of simultaneously affirming the conflicting views of many irreconcilable townspeople, thus winning their concurrence, are no longer accessible. In addition, the stark absence of his yin to Carmody's yang seems to cause a tidal wave of hazardous moral certainty and political incompatibility among the townsfolk as in the end they are goaded into sacrificing each other. It seems that the audience's general consensus on Norton's character and undetermined fate is that of a rash and pragmatic fool who led his followers to their demise.[72] Nonetheless, an original observation might deem Norton's anti-supernaturalism as that of a level-headed rationalist who perhaps led his people from danger. The outlandish invaders could have been nothing more than a figment of the townsfolk's startled imagination under Carmody and the military's appalling tenure.

Certainly, there is an air of unnaturalness to the final sequence regardless of the unearthly creatures. Although Darabont made a key omission from the novella by excluding King's fleeting back and forth to David's nightmares, premonitions, and the ambiguity of the monster, it seems that a literary illusion is substituted with a cinematic one.[73] Amanda's (Laurie Holden) suggestion to Billy, "It's just a bad dream," alongside David's fantastical remark to Norton during the storm: "I thought we were gonna take off and head for Oz," to name but a few, all remain inexplicit references to King's dream sequences, which are overlooked in the film.[74] While realism is undoubtedly advocated by Darabont's cinematic terror, some of his sequences do appear to possess a dream-like quality, which further epitomizes the utopianism of anticipation in general. The foreboding apocalyptic landscape following the storm, excessive long shots of the lake, and the single elevated tree that stands poised in it,[75] all attest to the chimerical quality of Darabont's increasingly obscure allegory.

Whether the monsters actually existed or were imagined is much more ambiguous in the novella; nonetheless, perhaps Darabont's subtle homage to King's dream-like imagery implies that the creatures were indeed nonexistent, and thus Norton's skepticism justified. It is Norton's divergence from the intimidating and controlling nature of the two hazardous systems, both religious and governmental, that renders him an ally to the people. Again, if this budding rookie does symbolize the coming of a promising yet inevitably overwhelmed Obama, then perhaps we can consider *The Mist* a quasi-optimistic prophecy, as it condemns the preservation of already established institutions and advocates the risky yet undeniable promise of bracing new leadership.

Norton's precarious disappearance into the mist and the consequential development of further destruction and detriment surely functions as a forewarning of an America in utter jeopardy if devoid of an Obama, even if an utterly overwhelmed savior. According to *The Mist*, a victim of real or unreal catastrophe has but two choices: hail a fresh perspective and stand a chance of survival or become rapidly indoctrinated by the established and corrupt institution. As Stephen King once miserably lamented: "It always comes down to just two choices. Get busy living, or get busy dying."[76]

Like the moment of catharsis that swept across the nation on President Obama's election, purging an abundance of negative sentiments caused by Bush's adversity, the Obama-era horror film offers, via its mastery of metaphors, a kind of cultural catharsis. Naturally, the plethora of allegories that lie beneath the surface of the American horror film can become somewhat obscure as the genre generally mediates between both our fears and our fantasies, thus providing at times a sense of double vision. Yet, reading between the lines, it seems that at the heart of *The Mist*'s pleasing allegorical feel is Darabont's polysemic depiction of Norton, a figure who symbolizes the peril and promise of an improbable leader on the beckoning of a new presidential era.

So how does *The Mist* allegorically anticipate the coming of, and longing for, an Obama? Darabont's first act paints a gory metaphor of a dystopian America amid a crisis of leadership. Adding fuel to Darabont's fire is the paranoia and polarization of the people and a dysfunctional and disengaged military—all rendered utterly incompetent in the thick of environmental chaos. Horribly relevant to the plight of the time, *The Mist* evokes a world irrevocably transformed by terrorism, climate change, and a deteriorating economy. By utilizing imagery of natural and unnatural disaster, alongside the terror and frailty of the townsfolk under the abysmal religious tenure of Carmody and a disengaged military, Darabont seeks to exploit and parallel Bush's United States post-9/11—a world tainted with allegations of dubious leadership, illegitimacy, and failure to rise to the apocalyptic disaster.

This metaphorical wave of domestic terrorism bleeds effectively into Darabont's second act setting up the frantic locals' opposition to an aspiring African American leader, Norton. Ultimately providing an indirect commentary and critique of the social and political context of the time, Darabont's depiction of Norton symbolizes an Obama: a maverick-defeating, coalition-building newcomer. Yet, simultaneously, the film allegorically anticipates the conflict still to come: the uphill struggle for respect and leadership that the beckoning president would inevitably face. By the third act, via its offering of an inconclusive ending regarding the fate of Norton and his followers, the film seems to embody a prophecy on the precarious fate of the overwhelmed Obama administration, as it beckoned to inherit a problematic world.

Again, the tactlessness of the Bush administration appears to be the primary target of the metaphorical criticism, yet the beckoning of Obama doesn't entirely escape Darabont's strong stench of skepticism either as Norton's questionable fate epitomizes. In saying all of this, an underlying message undoubtedly resonates, that in an America devoid of an Obama, all else is lost. Ultimately, Darabont's *The Mist* functioned as a safe and protected space with which to explore the public's fantasies and fears in anticipation of the "impossible": Obama's coming.

NOTES

1. Anthony Breznican, "Today's Fears Emerge in Stephen King Horror Flick 'The Mist,'" *USA Today*, November 20, 2007, http://usatoday30.usatoday.com/life/movies/news/2007-11-19-darabont-mist_N.htm?csp=1.
2. Aviva Briefel and Sam J. Miller. "Introduction," in *Horror after 9/11: World of Fear, Cinema of Terror* (Austin: University of Texas Press, 2011), 2–5.
3. Stephen King, "Danse Macabre," "October 4, 1957," and an "Invitation to Dance," in *Danse Macabre* (New York: Berkley Books, 1981), 4.
4. King, *Danse Macabre*, 5.
5. David Hume, "Of Tragedy" (1757), in *Of the Standard of Taste and Other Essays*, ed. John W. Lenz (Indianapolis: Bobbs-Merrill, 1965), 29.
6. Peter Bradshaw, "9/11 Films: How Did Hollywood Handle The Tragedy?" *Guardian*, September 8, 2011, http://www.guardian.co.uk/film/filmblog/2011/sep/08/9-11-films-hollywood-handle.
7. Briefel and Miller, *Horror after 9/11*, 3.
8. Robert J. Thompson, quoted in Rick Lyman, "Horrors! Time for an Attack of the Metaphors? From Bug Movies to Bioterrorism," *New York Times*, October 23, 2001, http://www.nytimes.com/2001/10/23/movies/horrors-time-for-an-attack-of-the-metaphors-from-bug-movies-to-bioterrorism.html.
9. Charles Derry, "The Horror of Armageddon, Revisited," in *Dark Dreams 2.0: A Psychological History of the Modern Horror Film from the 1950s to the 21st Century* (Jefferson, N.C.: McFarland, 2009), 283.
10. Free Republic, "Tweeted Obama Horror Film Titles (Starring Bella Pelosi)," *Free Republic*, September 9, 2012, http://www.freerepublic.com/focus/f-news/2928560/posts.
11. Frank Darabont, dir., *The Mist* (Burbank, Calif.: Dimension Films and Darkwood Productions, 2007), DVD.
12. Marleen S. Barr, "Fantastic Language/Political Reporting: The Postcolonial Science Fiction Illocutionary Force Is with Us," in *The Postnational Fantasy: Essays on Postcolonialism, Cosmopolitics and Science Fiction*, ed. Masood Ashraf Raja, Jason W. Ellis, and Swaralipi Nandi (Jefferson, N. C.: McFarland, 2011), 192.
13. Martin Flanagan, "Frank Darabont," in *Contemporary North American Film Directors: A Wallflower Critical Guide*, ed. Yoram Allon, Del Cullen, and Hannah Patterson (London: Wallflower Press, 2002), 124.
14. Flanagan, "Frank Darabont," 124.
15. Frank Darabont, dir., *The Shawshank Redemption* (Los Angeles, Calif.: Columbia Pictures, 1994), DVD.
16. Frank Darabont, dir., *The Green Mile* (Burbank, Calif.: Warner Bros. Entertainment Inc., 1999), DVD.
17. Frank Darabont, developer, *The Walking Dead* (New York: AMC Studios, 2010–present), DVD.

18. James Hibberd, "Walking Dead Finale Breaks Series Records," *Inside TV*, April 1, 2013, http://insidetv.ew.com/2013/04/01/walking-dead-finale-ratings-3/.

19. Tim Goodman, "The Walking Dead," *Hollywood Reporter*, October 30, 2010, http://www.hollywoodreporter.com/review/first-hollywood-reporter-review-tim-33846.

20. David J. Skal, afterword, in *A Cultural History of Horror* (New York: Macmillan, 2001), 393.

21. Frank Darabont, quoted in Fred Topel, "Interview with Frank Darabont on The Mist," *About Movies*, November 15, 2007, http://movies.about.com/od/themist/a/themist111507.htm.

22. Tom Charity, "The Mist is Bold and Frightening," *CNN Entertainment*, November 22, 2007, http://edition.cnn.com/2007/SHOWBIZ/Movies/11/22/review.mist/index.html.

23. J. R. Jones, "The Mist," *Chicago Reader*, April 13, 2013, http://www.chicagoreader.com/chicago/the-mist/Film?oid=1066747.

24. Andrew Kasch, "The Mist (2007)," *Dread Central*, November 12, 2007, http://www.dreadcentral.com/reviews/mist-the-2007.

25. Nick Rogers, "Heroes of the Zeroes: Stephen King's The Mist," *Film Yap*, June 11, 2010, http://www.thefilmyap.com/2010/06/11/heroes-of-the-zeroes-stephen-kings-the-mist/.

26. Topel, "Interview with Frank Darabont."

27. Frank Darabont, creator, *Mob City* (Los Angeles, Calif.: Darkwood Productions, 2014).

28. Alan McKee, "White Stores, Black Magic: Australian Horror Films of the Aboriginal," in *Aboriginal Culture and Literature in Australia*, ed. Geoffrey V. Davis and Dieter Riemenschneider (Amsterdam: Rodopi, 1997), 196.

29. Pamela Craig and Martin Fradley, "Teenage Traumata: Youth, Affective Politics, and the Contemporary American Horror Film," in *American Horror Film: The Genre at the Turn of the Millennium*, ed. Steffen Hantke (Jackson: University Press of Mississippi, 2010), 94.

30. Wes Craven, dir., *Scream* (Burbank, Calif.: Dimension Films, 1996–2011), DVD.

31. Craig and Fradley, *American Horror Film*, 196.

32. Peter Hutchings. *The Horror Film* (Essex: Pearson Education Limited, 2004), 112.

33. George A. Romero, dir., *Night of the Living Dead* (New York: Walter Reade Organization, 1968), DVD.

34. Harry M. Benshoff, "Blaxploitation Horror Films: Generic Reappropriation or Reinscription?" *Cinema Journal*, 39, no. 2 (2002): 37.

35. Hutchings, *The Horror Film*, 113.

36. David Skal, *V Is for Vampire: The A-to-Z Guide to Everything Undead* (New York: Penguin Group, 1996), 30.

37. Hutchings, *The Horror Film*, 112.

38. David J. Leonard, "The Ghettocentric Imagination," in *Screens Fade to Black: Contemporary African American Cinema* (Greenwood, Conn.: Praeger Publishers, 2006), 47.

39. Patrick McAleer, "More Than a Matriarch: Tabitha King's Canon," in *The Writing Family of Stephen King* (Jefferson, N.C.: McFarland, 2011), 97.

40. Touré Neblett, "The Magical Negro Falls to Earth," *Time* magazine, September 26, 2012, http://ideas.time.com/2012/09/26/the-magical-negro-falls-to-earth/#ixzz2D93CK53p.

41. David Ehrenstein, "Obama the 'Magic Negro,'" *LA Times*, March 19, 2007, http://www.latimes.com/news/opinion/commentary/la-oe-ehrenstein19mar19,0,3391015.story.

42. Ehrenstein, "Obama the 'Magic Negro.'"

43. Richard Dyer, "White Death," in *White* (London: Routledge, 1997), 210.

44. James Lewis Hoberman, "A New Obama Cinema?" *New York Review*, February 11, 2012, http://www.nybooks.com/blogs/nyrblog/2012/feb/11/new-obama-cinema-clint-eastwood-halftime/.

45. Douglas M. Kellner, "Reading Film Diagnostically: Imagining Obama," in *Cinema Wars: Hollywood Film and Politics in the Bush-Cheney Era* (New York: John Wiley & Sons, 2011), 35.

46. Hoberman, "A New Obama Cinema?"

47. Kellner, *Cinema Wars*, 34.

48. Linne Blake, "From Vietnam to 9/11: The Orientalist Other and the American Poor White," in *The Wounds of Nations: Horror Cinema, Historical Trauma and National Identity* (Manchester: Manchester University Press, 2008), 120.

49. Francis Lawrence, dir., *I Am Legend* (Burbank, Calif.: Warner Bros. Pictures, 2007), DVD.

50. Barack Obama, *The Audacity of Hope: Thoughts on Reclaiming the American Dream* (New York: Crown Publishers, 2007), 11.

51. Cindy Simpson, "The Picture of Barack Obama," *American Thinker*, September 30, 2013, http://www.americanthinker.com/2010/12/the_picture_of_barack_obama.html.

52. Barack Obama, "Transcript: Barack Obama's Inaugural Address," *New York Times*, January 20, 2009, http://www.nytimes.com/2009/01/20/us/politics/20text-obama.html?pagewanted=all.

53. Stephen King, quoted in Scott Whitlock, "Author Stephen King: Right-Wing 'Hate' of Obama Is Like Anger That Led to JFK's Murder," *NewsBusters*, November 12, 2011, http://newsbusters.org/blogs/scott-whitlock/2011/11/11/stephen-king-right-wing-hate-obama-anger-led-jfks-murder.

54. Kellner, *Cinema Wars*, 81.

55. Barack Obama, "Campaign Announcement Speech 2007," BarackObama.com, September 20, 2012, http://www.barackobama.com/press/release/statement-romney-sets-a-new-record-in-desperation/.

56. Roland Emmerich, dir., *The Day after Tomorrow* (Los Angeles, Calif.: 20th Century Fox, 2004), DVD.

57. Larry Fessenden, dir., *The Last Winter* (New York: IFC Films, 2006), DVD.

58. Kellner, *Cinema Wars*, 82.

59. Armando Navarro, "The Restrictionist Nativist Legislative Surge (2004–2007)," in *The Immigration Crisis: Nativism, Armed Vigilantism, and the Rise of a Countervailing Movement* (Lanham, Md.: Altamira, 2008), 281.

60. Geoff King, "Just Like a Movie?: 9/11 and Hollywood Spectacle," in *The Spectacle of the Real: From Hollywood to Reality TV and Beyond* (Portland, Ore.: Intellect, 2005), 47.

61. Frank Darabont, quoted in Blake Hennon, "The Mist: Frank Darabont, Thomas Jane on Angry, Bleak Ending," *LA Times*, May 12, 2013, http://herocomplex.latimes.com/movies/the-mist-frank-darabont-thomas-jane-on-angry-bleak-ending/#/0; "The Mist Advances," in Frank Darabont's *The Mist* (2007), film still, http://images2.wikia.nocookie.net/__cb20110505174525/stephenkingsthemist/images/f/fa/Advancing_Mist.jpg.

62. Kellner, *Cinema Wars*, 91.

63. Derry, *Dark Dreams 2.0*, 283.

64. Jerry Falwell and Pat Robertson, "Falwell and Robertson on The 700 Club after 9/11," YouTube, November 7, 2007, http://www.youtube.com/watch?v=H-CAcdta_8I.

65. Corwin Smidt, Kevin den Dulk, Bryan Froehle, James Penning, Stephen Monsma, and Douglas Koopman, "Religion and the Summer Interlude," in *The Disappearing God Gap? Religion in the 2008 Presidential Election* (New York: Oxford University Press, 2010), 115.

66. Michael Tesler and David O. Sears, "Obama as Post-Racial?" in *Obama's Race: The 2008 Election and the Dream of a Post-Racial America* (Chicago: University of Chicago Press, 2010), 5.

67. Stephen Carter, *The Violence of Peace: America's Wars in the Age of Obama* (Philadelphia: Beast Books, 2011), 70.

68. "Norton Leads," film still from Frank Darabont's *The Mist* (2007), http://images.wikia.com/stephenkingsthemist/images/3/39/Norton_in_the_Mist.jpg

69. Peter Baker, "Obama, Seeking Re-Election, Asks for Patience," *New York Times*, September 6, 2012, http://www.nytimes.com/2012/09/06/us/politics/obama-seeking-re-election-asks-for-patience.html?pagewanted=all.

70. Tim Dickinson, "The Case for Obama," *Rolling Stone*, October 13, 2010, http://www.rollingstone.com/politics/news/the-case-for-obama-20101013.

71. Frank Capra, dir., *It's a Wonderful Life* (New York: RKO Radio Pictures, 1946), DVD.

72. Todd Gilchrist, "Chalk up King and Darabont's Third Collaboration as a Missed Opportunity," *IGN Entertainment*, November 20, 2007, http://www.uk.ign.com/articles/2007/11/20/the-mist-review.

73. Mark Browning, "The Mist (Frank Darabont, 2008)," in *Stephen King on the Small Screen* (Chicago: Intellect, 2011), 94.

74. Browning, "The Mist," 94.
75. Browning, "The Mist," 94.
76. Stephen King, *Different Seasons* (New York: Signet, 1983), 106.

Part II

The Present Is an Eternal Now Connecting Past and Future

Chapter Eight

"I Am Trayvon Martin": Obama and the Black Male in Cinema

Mohanalakshmi Rajakumar and Alisha Saiyed

General consensus, circulated by mainstream media, asserted that the election of a black president would usher in a new epoch in American race relations. From the *Wall Street Journal* to news shows on MSNBC, pundits announced the end of "the old politics of race," a discourse they characterized as "focusing on Black grievance, victimhood, and protest."[1] Obama's election was heralded as the evidence of what Enid Logan describes as "color-blind individualism" or the idea that discrimination against African Americans was "infrequent, unlikely, and overreported." A black president was tangible proof that America had "overcome the scourge of racism."[2] Such a belief is grounded in the hope that the popular vote represents the majority of American opinion and therefore sanctions a racially neutral government, which more accurately represents America's multiethnic composition. This set of assertions overlooks the systematic and long-standing inequities of American society toward African Americans. Since the 2008 election of President Barack Obama, however, race has become an even more vexing topic of public discourse in America. From his middle name, of Arabic origin, to his mixed ethnic heritage, Obama represents the dual taboo specters of Islamic and black identities, which challenge a middle-class white hegemony. The 2008 race, rather than being colorblind, was evidence of the prevalent racial stereotypes in American society and the divisions within contemporary black society. Obama the candidate and eventually president became a symbol of the middle-class African American man whose upward mobility was predicated on hard work that enabled him to embody the American Dream. Less talked about but perhaps even more important in terms of contemporary black culture was his converse, the African American male criminal. While Obama was used as a symbol of a black man making good in the meritocracy, he was vastly outnumbered by his incarcerated counterparts that made up 42 percent of inmates on death row despite only being 12.5 percent of the overall American population.[3] The blind assertion that race had been solved in America could not continue unchallenged against the backdrop of declining status of black men's rights in civil society.

Having a black president did not change the stereotype of young black men as "crime prone, [having] bad values . . . [choosing] to commit crimes."[4] Rather, having a black president highlighted the failure of the promise of the American Dream for millions of African Americans. The disparity between the president and others like him, including popular cultural icons like Oprah Winfrey or rapper Jay-Z, forced race as a topic of national discussion without the vocabulary or training to discuss a previously taboo topic. Being the first black president has forced Obama into a corner in which if he attempts representational politics, he risks alienating white people who voted for him and confirming the suspicions of those who did not vote for him that he will only have black interests at heart. Obama has been trapped in this dichotomy and is prevented from fulfilling his assumed mantle as a role model for young black people. Obama's official stance on racial issues demonstrates the necessity of dual political positioning. In March of 2008, the president delivered a speech entitled "A More Perfect Union"[5] in response to criticism about the comments made by a former pastor with whom he was associated. Although he reprimanded the pastor for the comments, he also defended the African American community by offering perspectives on the context of such opinions. He sought to resolve the two sides: the generation that lives in the past and holds history and discrimination close to their hearts and the one that is moving into the future.

What the election of a black president has ensured is that race has become part of the national conversation. Film has allowed us to more closely examine the relationship between community, identity, and sentiment toward young black men in a way that the American public has not been able to discuss in other forms of media. Obama is a realization of the paradox of the image that was created of black men. On one hand, there were the political activists and achievers that were revered and held in high esteem, and on the other, the slaves and the downtrodden of the community. The paradoxical nature lay in the fact that without the unfortunate ones, there would be no need for the activists and do-gooders. Labeling an entire race of people within two extremes, activist or victim, establishes the precedent for stereotypes and erases any space for racial differentiation. A black president, someone directly connected to the whole country yet who does not fit the mold of the predominant stereotype, forces questions about identity and the role of black men in contemporary American society. In fact, Obama has been subject to racism despite his high office. The members of the Tea Party movement "represented Obama as a figure who lacked the state-authorized long-form birth certificate required to certify his status as a legitimate United States citizen and re-imagined him as a Muslim terrorist."[6] Obama's detractors used familiar tropes of the illegitimate urban black male, at loose in urban landscapes, to discredit his candidacy. Questioning his citizenship raised fundamental assumptions about origin and place in contemporary society—questions that black filmmakers and actors had been exploring since the 1990s in film and music.

Hip-hop culture emerged in the early 1990s as a means of asserting a black urban identity from within the urban spaces of ghettos across America. Originally expressing ideas of race and class through rap, dance, and film, this subculture went mainstream when commercialized by the record industry. Rap, once the voice of the ghetto, speaking out against police brutality, now blared through the speakers of white middle-class suburbia; the connection to the harsh realities of life for urban youth was lost. Films like *New Jack City* (1991), *Boys n the Hood* (1991), and *Menace II Society* (1993) demonstrated the concerns of the life in the ghetto, featuring prominently the ups and downs of life for young black male characters.[7] With the rise of commercial viability of black popular culture, black film moved away from race dramas and toward light-hearted comedies about the working class. These social dramas, including *Waiting to Exhale* (1995) and *The Best Man* (1999), were more palpable for a wider, mixed-race audience. Other offerings like *Barbershop* (2002) and the sequel, *Barbershop 2: Back in Business* (2004), demonstrated the rise of a black entrepreneurial class that self-referentially critiqued the commercialization of ghetto culture and the era of "bling bling" or hyperexpressive consumption and concerns with upward mobility.

The election of a black president, the increasing gaps in black society between the middle and lower classes, and current events meant that these modern dramas could not continue to dominate the film landscape. Once again film became a medium to discuss social, racial, and class issues. The depiction of black people in films like *Fruitvale Station* (2013) explores the stereotypes of black men as dangerous, unemployed agents in American society. The release of the film, based on the true events of the transit authority's detention and shooting of Oscar Grant, coincided with the public trial in Florida of a private citizen, George Zimmerman, who fatally shot an unarmed black teenage boy, Trayvon Martin, while pursuing him through neighborhood streets in 2012. The two shootings of unarmed black males, and the subsequent verdicts, not guilty for Zimmerman and involuntary manslaughter for the shooter of Grant, emphasized how few strides have been made in the perception of male black youth in public spaces, as well as the failure of the legal system to exact justice.

In the tension and outrage that brewed after the Zimmerman hearing, in which Martin's killer was cleared of all charges, the nation waited for the president to comment on race. When he addressed the issue of the shooting, not as a legal or moral issue, but through the invocation of personal comparison, Obama said that the African American community perceived the verdict "through a set of experiences and a history that doesn't go away."[8] According to him, the history of the African American people has become a baggage that they carry around with them and they view everything that goes against them with resistance and a sense of injustice. His comments indirectly addressed the American community at large and the tendency to look at black men with suspicion. In order to show the unfairness of such stereotyping, Obama drew bold parallels between himself and Martin, comparing Trayvon to himself thirty-five years earlier. While Martin came from a very different upbringing and background than Obama, the point was that in any situation in his youth, he could have been as unfortunate as the young Martin. In this regard, Obama could easily have been Oscar Grant or any other young black male who, without the benefit of context, may be seen as a malevolent threat and profiled on a daily basis. His remarks highlighted that even he would not have been exempt from experiencing racism and hinted that the nation is losing much of its potential in the senseless violence directed at purported perpetrators.

In *Fruitvale Station* (2013), the director, Ryan Coogler, takes the tragedy of an unjust shooting of a young man and turns it into a narrative of the last day in the life of Oscar Grant. Coogler's artistic decision mimics Obama's rhetorical approach to separating stereotypes from an individual by going deeply into the personal story of one person. *Fruitvale Station* depicts the final day in the life of Grant, before he was shot by a BART officer in a train station in front of a train full of witnesses. The mundane goings-on of his daily life re-create Grant to be more than just a tragedy on the evening news. In following Grant as a father, brother, lover, and compassionate stranger, the audience must witness his humanity. He becomes a kind of everyman, faced with decisions about whether or not to return to selling drugs, bad behavior that costs him precious time with his mother, and a simmering anger at those who won't help him. Grant becomes someone every viewer can relate to if the audience is feeling generous; he becomes harmless, even if the audience is not. The man who cradles a dog until he dies after a hit and run, taking the body to the dumpster, is not a man you will worry about stealing your car in the gas station. Watching the film reveals Grant to be a son, a father, a civilian, and a human.[9] All of these movements are without any racial connotations and remind us of a shared humanity. Through this very personal story of an individual going through his daily life, Coogler is breaking stereotypes against an entire community. Grant becomes someone that could have been anyone; at the very least he is an average nice guy you do not need to hold your purse more tightly around.

The anger that ensued after the trial of Grant's shooter resulted in peaceful and violent protests; Johannes Mehserle was found guilty of involuntary manslaughter, not second-degree murder or voluntary manslaughter. Coogler chooses to focus on a bigger picture, depicting Grant as the average middle-class black man with aspirations to be a productive member of society. Coogler attempts to give us an idea of what being a young black man is like in America. Through the scenes Oscar spends with his daughter and the effort he puts into his mother's birthday, we see Grant as an everyday Joe instead of a victim or a criminal. He is a guy, in the rhetoric of the 2012 election campaign, who is trying to make it on "Main Street." The character of Grant is depicted as that of a young man making mistakes, yet trying to be the best version of himself. He is a person in progress, trying to make good on the American ideal of hard work when his potential is cut short.

Coogler highlights Oscar Grant's compassion, despite his many deficiencies. Grant is portrayed as a loving father, and we can see that through many of the scenes he shares especially with his daughter. The scene when they have a conversation before Grant goes out for the night (and is later shot) is filmed intimately, with both of their faces in the frame. This is an uncommon technique for a dialogue shot (the more conventional being the over-the-shoulder shot), but it serves to show the nature of their relationship and the care Grant has as he consoles his daughter. The scenes with his daughter—and Grant whispering, "I have a daughter" to his shooter on the train platform—are another way Coogler challenges the negative stereotype of black men as irresponsible or absent parents.

The film reminds us that the authorities that we come in contact with on a daily basis fail us. The scene with the BART officers occurs in the beginning and in the last scenes of the film. When an unarmed, handcuffed black man is shot by a BART (Bay Area Rapid Transit) officer, the audience becomes stand-ins for the real-life witnesses, questioning who the criminals really are. The system that was put in place to protect civilians simultaneously threatens a large part of the population.

The shootings of unarmed Oscar Grant and Trayvon Martin are not the first incidents of their kind, nor, statistics remind us, will they be the last. Whether President Obama, Oscar Grant, or teenager Trayvon Martin, to be a black man in America means that you will be accused of criminality during your lifetime or will be the unwilling victim of violence; "Black men are imprisoned at several times the rate of white men."[10] Black men have a criminalized image in society that is perpetuated through popular culture. This normalized image of the black male as a criminal ensures ready acceptance of the need to arm oneself against him. The response to the Grant and Martin shootings and Obama terrorist accusations is to dismantle the myth of the violent criminal. Films like *Fruitvale Station* and real-life events, like Martin's shooting and the Obama presidency, challenge the circulation of such narrow definitions of black male identity.

NOTES

1. Enid Logan, "We Don't Have to Listen to Al Sharpton Anymore: Obama's Election and Triumphalist Media Narratives of Post-Racial America," in *Getting Real About Race: Hoodies, Mascots, Model Minorities, and Other Conversations*, ed. Stephanie M. McClure and Cherise A. Harris (Los Angeles: Sage Publications, 2014), 211–19.
2. Logan, "We Don't Have to Listen," 213.
3. Logan, "We Don't Have to Listen," 215.
4. Sara Buck Doude, "If Black People Aren't Criminals, Then Why Are So Many of Them in Prison?: Confronting Racial Biases in Perceptions of Crime and Criminals," in *Getting Real About Race: Hoodies, Mascots, Model Minorities, and Other Conversations*, ed. Stephanie M. McClure and Cherise A. Harris (Los Angeles: Sage Publications, 2014), 238.
5. Barack Obama, "A More Perfect Union," campaign speech, National Constitution Center, Philadelphia, March 18, 2008.
6. Gregory D. Smithers, "Barack Obama and Race in the United States: A History of the Future," *Australasian Journal of American Studies* 28 (2009): 1–16.
7. Roopali Mukherjee, "The Ghetto Fabulous Aesthetic in Contemporary Black Culture," *Cultural Studies* 20, no. 6 (2006): 600–602.
8. Barack Obama, Remarks by the President on Trayvon Martin, July 19, 2013, http://www.whitehouse.gov/the-press-office/2013/07/19/remarks-president-trayvon-martin.
9. Wesley Morris, "Strange Fruitvale: The Eerie Intersection of Trayvon Martin and *Fruitvale Station*," *Grantland*, July 25, 2013, http://grantland.com/features/fruitvale-station-trayvon-martin/ (accessed April 7, 2014).
10. Doude, "If Black People Aren't Criminals," 239.

Chapter Nine

Invictus: South Africa as a Post-racial Fantasy in the Age of Obama

Sohinee Roy

The election of Barack Obama, the first African American president of the United States, has piqued Hollywood's interest in African American history and experience as a viable subject for films. Relegated to supporting roles or villains in Hollywood, barring a few exceptions such as Denzel Washington and Halle Berry, African Americans are suddenly protagonists in films featuring black experience such as *The Help*, *Django Unchained*, *The Butler*, *12 Years a Slave*, and *Beasts of the Southern Wild*. Consequently a lot of critical attention has been devoted to this trend in Hollywood. The attention to Hollywood's new African American obsession has overshadowed another sub-trend in Hollywood during the Obama presidency: films on post-apartheid South Africa. So far four films have been commissioned on South Africa in the six years of the Obama presidency. In 2009 two of the films were released—*District 9* and *Invictus*. Of the other two, *A Long Walk to Freedom* is set for release later this year while *Winnie Mandela*, a biopic of Nelson Mandela's second wife, has had limited release. It seems that post-apartheid South Africa speaks powerfully to the American imagination at the historical juncture of its forty-fourth president and first African American president. While the films on African Americans focused on themes of justice, equality, and so forth, the films on South Africa have focused on racial reconciliation.

This is not the first time South Africa has captured the imagination of Hollywood. Rob Nixon points out that from 1987 to 1989 there were a number of films focused on South Africa, such as Richard Attenborough's *Cry Freedom*, Chris Menges's *A World Apart*, and Euzhan Palcy's *A Dry White Season*.[1] This period was followed by a lull in Hollywood's interest in South Africa until the election of President Obama. While the earlier films focused on apartheid, the current crop of films have gravitated toward racial reconciliation because reconciliation fits the optimistic white narrative of a nation that has repaid its historical debts with the election of its first African American president.

Both the earlier and recent Hollywood films on South Africa face the same challenge: how to present post-apartheid South Africa for a U.S. audience? How to convey South Africa's militant struggle and its consequent complex reconciliation policy to a white liberal United States, eager to move into a post-racial future? When a cultural issue is exported to another culture, it is "subject to refraction" because the "needs and concerns of the society in which it arrives becomes a transforming influence, so that the issue shapes itself as a compromise between the prevailing history, preoccupations and ambitions of the society of origin and those of the society with which it intersects."[2] Thus it is important to consider "the ideological transformations and their political ramifications."[3] *Invictus*, released in 2009, highlights the challenges of conveying South Africa's reconciliation discourse to a post-racial United States during the tenure of its first African American president. *Invictus* focuses on reconciliation through the true story of Nelson Mandela's use of the controversial sport rugby as a means of bringing about reconciliation. In the film South Africa is a parallel to the United States during President Obama's tenure and displaces the racial anxieties and fears of a contemporary United States to a foreign land.[4]

Given the cross-cultural transmission involved in *Invictus*, critiquing the film for failing to present a realistic vision of post-apartheid South Africa's first African president, Nelson Mandela, or of South Africa's reconciliation experience is an unfair assessment of the politics involved in transmitting events from one culture to another culture. In *Invictus* the narrative of a sports victory uniting historical racial enemies transforms South African reconciliation discourse to fit the liberal post-racial ideology/fantasy. A sports event as a solution to South Africa's historic race problem betrays commitment to true racial reform and avoids the complex changes necessary to bring about long-term reconciliation. In reality *Invictus* represents the mainstream U.S. dream of moving beyond race. This hope is a white liberal dream. In *Invictus* South Africa and Mandela become a projection of U.S. fears and aspirations during the Obama presidency.

SOUTH AFRICAN RECONCILIATION VS. THE AMERICAN POST-RACIAL DREAM

In post-conflict societies, reconciliation, at least political reconciliation, is a process of integrating the various hostile groups to enable a society to move forward. As a process reconciliation is mired in the power politics of post-conflict societies: questions of who sets the terms of reconciliation, how the reconciliation tackles the effects of the past conflicts, and how inclusive is its aim become critical in the process of reconciliation. Given their long and messy history of racism, both South Africa and the United States have, at points of their history, tackled the thorny issue of racial reconciliation between their white and nonwhite populations. However, their approaches to integrating the hostile groups into a positive relation so that civil society can function have differed greatly. The strong liberal tradition in the United States envisions a nation that has moved beyond race, a United States where racial identity has become invisible and inconsequential. This post-racial ideology that dominates the legal, political, and even religious discourses is a result of the fact that African Americans are a minority in the United States compared to whites. In South Africa, where the nonwhites have always formed the disempowered majority, the much-debated policy of racial reconciliation is less about moving past race and more about accounting for the past and building a future free from violence. The dilemmas of cross-cultural representation between the United States and South Africa relate to their very different approaches to the future of racial relations.

In recent years the United States has adopted a post-racial approach to including African Americans in society. Post-racialism in its current iteration is a twenty-first-century ideology that believes "that due to the significant racial progress that has been made the state need not engage in race based decision-making or adopt race-based remedies, and that civil society can eschew race as a central organizing principle of social action." The goal of post-racial logic is to effectuate a "retreat from race."[5] Post-racialism levels "the discursive playing field, allowing whites to oppose civil rights remedies and advocate for race-neutral policies because society has transcended the racial moment, or the civil rights era."[6] As a result "centuries of apartheid and neo-apartheid are eclipsed by a symbolic big event signifying transcendent racial progress." The central features of post-racialism are a belief in racial progress, in race-neutral universalism, in moral equivalence between racism and racial reference, and in distancing itself from the past.[7]

Post-racial politics perceives race as a simple linear system, so that one event—be it political, economic, or religious—can erase it. But in reality race is a complex and dynamic system of discourses with its own agenda that is separate from those of its foundational discourses. By race as discourse Goldberg means that it includes "descriptive representation of others" and "a set of hypothetical premises about humankind . . . and about the differences between them."[8] The premises, which include ethical choices, institutional policies, and rules of interaction, are "manifestations of power relations vested in between historically located subjects."[9] Race is thus a "socio-discursive praxis in determinate historical circumstances" that is integral to subject formation.[10] The two aspects of race as discourse suggest that changing representation will not change the premises and practices that inform race. The fluid nature of race, its dependence on other factors, and its own goals mean that the practice of race perpetuates and changes its meaning. As an instrument of social formation and naturalization of group relations, race itself is not violent (even though it is not ethical). It becomes violent when it is used by the agents, in particular historical contexts, to violent ends. When race is used for the "exclusion of people in virtue of their being deemed members of different racial groups," it is institutionalized.[11] Thus the practices and fictions of race are sustained and perpetuated by the discursive practices of racism, which is a "product of economies of power, reflected in the interrelation of bodies produced and refined in practice."[12] However, once initiated, "they pass onto the practico-inert, ready to be passed on, inherited, reproduced and reformed."[13] These exclusions include "actual or intended effects or affects of racial and racialized discourse."[14] The discursive nature of racism implies that there is no transcendental racism.

Since race includes representation of subjects and social practices, and is the conceptual basis of racism, racism can be eliminated by attacking its racial foundation. Changes in racial patterns can be effected through "changes within a discourse and changes of a discourse."[15] The former involves "local changes in some constitutive feature or element of the discourse," while the latter refers to "shifts from one discursive formation to another" that involve "changes in whole ways of world making."[16] This means that changes in one strand set off a chain reaction of changes in other strands that, ultimately, reconfigure and reorder racist expression. Thus there is no way of transcending race. But it is, however, possible to create opportunities for new positive dynamics between groups through change in practices. In short, reconciliation can realistically end racism, not race. It can reorder the relations to create positive patterns; it can create a different relation to history. It cannot, however, wipe the slate clean of the past. Racial reconciliation therefore does not have an end point, but is a process of negotiating this power relation across time.

Post-racial ideology has given rise to post-racial liberalism. Post-racial liberalism combines the contradictory trends of race-neutral rhetoric and color-blind public policy.[17] It acknowledges race's declining significance on one hand, and on the other it forces adoption of universal policies and vetoes any policy that offers race-specific solutions to poverty, education, or employment opportunities. The belief in universal policies rather than race-specific solutions for social issues such as poverty, education, health care, and so on ignores the fact that due to the United States' long history of racism, poverty affects blacks differently. For example, black men with college degrees are twice as likely to be unemployed as their white counterparts; on average, blacks are three times more likely than non-Hispanics to be poor and twice as likely to be extremely poor.[18] Ignoring these realities for race-neutral policies is as exclusionary as conventional racism. The result of belief in transcendence of race as a category of classification and reference is its relegation to the private sphere and individual pathology. Thus the solution to racism is individual transformation. This is a solution that Clint Eastwood, the director of *Invictus*, endorses when he claims that "you are never too old to learn and embrace people you did not understand to begin with."[19] Eastwood implies that the solution to the deep history of racism in the United States can be transformed through cultural familiarity. However, this liberal solution to racism prevents examination of the structural aspects of racism or the effects of white supremacy. It prevents discussion of policies to tackle specific effects of racism on class, poverty, and gender. Thus universal policies, while race neutral, prevent addressing the specific consequences of racism and are in the end as exclusionary as racism. Sumi Choo thus appositely describes post-racial ideology as not just an ideology but a racial project along the line of Omni and Winnat's definition of a "racial project" as "one that organizes the distribution of resources by the state according to racialized categories."[20]

Thus, post-racialism is a fantasy rather than reality. Wilbur Rich points out that "an end to racial essentialism does not mean that there is an end to individual acts or favoritism/nepotism and outright public discrimination."[21] It is not surprising that during the Obama presidency income inequality between African Americans and whites has increased. Poverty rates for African Americans increased to 27.4 percent according to the 2010 U.S. census. African American poverty when Obama took office was 12.5 percent. The percentage of African American children in poverty is 38.2 percent.[22] The continuing miserable plight of African Americans during the tenure of the first African American president proves that the "post-racial society does not represent a utopia."[23] An African American in the highest executive office in the United States does not change the circumstances of the majority of African Americans. Despite these statistics, claims of moving beyond race continue because the first African American president plays into the white hegemonic fantasy narrative that the United States has moved beyond race, that the white population has repaid the debt of its racist past. Post-racial ideology consequently "disavows history, overlaying it with an upbeat discourse about how things were never really that bad, are not so bad now, and are only getting better."[24] It is a strategy of avoidance and betrayal. The post-racial discourse with its premise of transcending race and the burden of racist history is a rhetorical sleight of hand rather than the erasure of race. By focusing on superficial aspects of race, post-racialism stops discussion of racism and racial problems such as unequal distribution of resources. As a fantasy, the post-racial project is similar to Manifest Destiny.[25] Insofar as it is exclusionary of target-specific policies to tackle institutional problems created in a society with a long and violent history of racism, post-racialism is racist in its effects.

Reconciliation in the post-racial ideology feeds into the post-racial fantasy because it creates the illusion of a new beginning. Reconciliation as the cessation of hostilities offers the appearance of a new beginning, a beginning that cancels out earlier difficult history. It thus catapults the United States into racial transcendence and frees it from uncomfortable reminders of slavery and Jim Crow. Since the post-racial ideology does not address the structural aspect of racism, reconciliation becomes a single magical event through which the past is cancelled and the racial *other* assimilates into the white body politic. Assimilation necessitates the renunciation of those values that do not tie in with the core values of the "class and culture that had historically become hegemonic."[26] Reconciliation conceived in this way is about fitting into the white paradigm by purging the undesirable qualities. White hegemony calls the shots in the process. Reconciliation thus builds a narrative of progress in racial relations, a progress assessed by the ability to move away from race as an identity category.

In its early formulation, South African reconciliation discourses focused on creating a new pattern of racial interaction that acknowledged the sedimentation of long racial history in racial identities instead of ignoring the messy past. Mandela described reconciliation as "working together to correct past injustice."[27] Mandela's own definition is the opposite of forgetting history. The Truth and Reconciliation Commission (TRC) was conceived to go beyond investigating past abuses in order to create a positive future free of racism.[28] The Truth and Reconciliation Commission tried to achieve this through a two-pronged approach. First, it sought to recover truth by making the possibility of amnesty contingent on public confessions of racist behaviors by perpetrators that were transmitted throughout the country through mass media. The recovery of the past was important because if the past was glibly declared to be over, the resultant "amnesia would have resulted in further victimization of victims by denying their awful experiences."[29] Second, it offered the suggestion in its final report of not just monetary compensation, but the roles of business, education, and church in regeneration of the nonwhite population and the importance of medical, particularly psychological, resources for the victims. The TRC referred to reconciliation as a process "offering a road map to those who wish to travel into our past" but not under any circumstance "the whole story."[30] At best it "provides a perspective on the truth about a past that is more extensive and more complex than any one commission could, in two and a half years, have hoped to capture."[31] As a process the early reconciliation discourses drew attention to the continuation of reconciliation beyond the event of the TRC and the need for active involvement by foundational institutions of society to this process.

The TRC drew attention to the different demands on the perpetrators and victims in the reconciliation process. It requires perpetrators to acknowledge their crimes, their actions, and their effects. It requires victims to give up revenge. It was thus a complex ethical process that involved moral choices. Instead of moving ahead by forgetting the past, the reconciliation policy as conceived in the early years of the post-apartheid era required accounting for the past to build a future where the problems of the past are not repeated. To consider the past dealt with is to ignore its effects on the victims whose material and physical conditions are glaring evidence and testimony of its continuing legacies. This attitude to the future and present as intricately entangled with the past is different from being paralyzed by the past. Instead it recognizes a dynamic relation between the past, present, and future that enables progress to not erase the past, but learn from it. Hope is not seen as a moving away from the past, but as negotiating a relation with the past that moves beyond amnesia and paralysis.

Reconciliation in South Africa, at least as conceived in its initial stage, is different from the post-racial project in the United States. The South African discourse on the subject recognizes reconciliation as a process, a process that is complex, is without telos, and involves structural changes as well as ethical choices. Thus the goal of reconciliation is not integration but an attempt to create an inclusive and positive relation between the hitherto hostile races by accounting for the way history informs and shapes the present. Since reconciliation as conceived by the founding documents of the new South Africa is opposed to the values of post-racialism, in order to fit South African reconciliation discourse to the United States' post-racial ideology in *Invictus*, reconciliation is transformed into a magical event tied to messianic politics.

SPORTS AS RECONCILIATION

The South Africa that is represented in *Invictus* is very similar to the United States Obama inherited. Mandela and Obama both came to power at critical times for their country. Mandela came to power when South Africa was transitioning into multiracial democracy, while Obama came to power in the middle of an economic recession and crisis in the banking sector and a real estate meltdown. In the film *Invictus*, the first African president in South Africa in 1994 is greeted with two contradictory responses. The white community is filled with trepidation while the nonwhites are filled with hope and jubilation. As the cavalcade carrying the just-liberated Mandela passes by, the coach of the rugby team mutters, "Remember this as the day our country went to the dogs," while the white workers in Mandela's office arrive at the first meeting expecting to be fired. On the other hand, the nonwhites are eager to reverse signs of Afrikaner power, starting with the use of the term *springboks* for the rugby team. Post-apartheid South Africa, as the visuals show, is not much different from apartheid South Africa as far as racial relations and economic relations are concerned.

The election of President Obama as the first African American president of the United States is marked by similar contradictory responses. On one hand Obama's victory in 2008 and reelection in 2012 were hailed as the move from the civil rights era to a post-racial era. It was seen as "a triumph of integration."[32] At the same time others regarded his victory with fear. The nascent Tea Party, in 2009, held signs saying, "Obama Plans White Slavery," while Congressman Steve King complained that Obama favors the black person and Glenn Beck called the president's health care plan "reparations."[33] This rhetoric of paranoia and fear has been marked by a simultaneous increase in racial profiling by policemen and civilians as demonstrated by the Trayvon Martin case and the New York City "Stop and Frisk program."[34] These contradictory responses suggest that proclamations of having moved beyond race coexist alongside fear of loss of white privilege. This fear is not based on actual threat since the election and reelection of President Obama has been marked by worsening conditions for African Americans. This paranoia stems from the fear that the first African American president will use his executive power to benefit the black population and exact historical revenge, even as one celebrates transcending race. The parallels between post-apartheid South Africa under Mandela and the United States under President Obama make post-apartheid South Africa a proxy for the United States.

Racial tension and hostility are prevented by Mandela's strategic use of the Rugby World Cup to unite the hitherto historic enemies in cheering for the national rugby team. Rugby as the sport of choice is significant because in a nation where even sports are deeply racialized, rugby was the sport of the Afrikaners and identified with Afrikaner masculinity and identity. Springboks, the rugby team, was the symbol of Afrikaner glory. For this reason, during apartheid, the resistance movement cheered against the Springboks. For the Africans in South Africa, soccer is the sport of choice. The Rugby World Cup is an ideal opportunity to make the Afrikaners, trying to adjust to the new regime, feel included. Mandela in the film and in reality harnessed the "us vs. them" aspect of sporting competition to reterritorialize the Afrikaner vs. Africans divide into South Africans vs. foreign country. In the second half of the film, the affective energy derives from swift cuts between tackles and slow-motion races across the field resulting in erupting cheers. However, sports as the solution to racial hostility is problematic, not the least because it implies that race and other complex issues can be blithely resolved by a simple sporting contest. A sporting victory that has both groups forgetting each other and erupting in joyous cheers may create affective bonhomie; however, it does not tackle the roots of racial inequality that continue despite political change. A rugby victory presents reconciliation as a magical and miraculous event, while the reality is that reconciliation is a complex process without telos.

The rosy picture of reconciliation created by the images of crowds hugging presents the symbolic as the actual. The victory of the Springboks over the New Zealand rugby team results in multiracial crowds in the stadium, bars, and streets breaking out in cheers. The camera pans to the audience and zooms to team captain Francois Pienaar's mother and the household help hugging each other in joy. A similar scene erupts outside, where two Afrikaner policemen embrace a ragpicker they were dismissing earlier. This image of the different racial groups coming together to celebrate a victory presents reconciliation as a fait accompli. While a black servant and white mistress present a moving photograph of racial reconciliation, casting aside differences in the joy of victory does not change the material circumstances of the two characters. The differences in their experience of history, reflected in their very different material circumstances, do not disappear because of a sporting victory. These scenes of reconciliation present brief interludes of camaraderie rather than any actual change in the racial dynamic.

Reconciliation as achieved by an extraordinary event of a sporting victory in *Invictus* suggests that the past can be magically erased. An event disrupts the existing continuity to bring forth a new order. A rugby victory disrupts racial hostility to usher in a new era of racial amity. Time, under the circumstances, is linear and progressive. The election of a nonwhite president and the end of apartheid, according to this narrative, signal improvement. But within the complex and dynamic discursive system of race, political change does not transform the economic and social situation for the nonwhites, who continued to live in dire poverty in the dilapidated slums and townships. It does not account for the tangible and intangible effects of apartheid or racism on the individual and collective psyche. Thus reconciliation, symbolized by the sporting victory, ignores reality to present a progressive narrative of race.

In order to cater to this progressive narrative of reconciliation, the film avoids the deep and complex history of racism in South Africa. It remains silent about the history of colonialism, forced segregation, and land appropriation. It avoids references to the Land Act of 1915, which expropriated land from the Africans and confined them to separate enclosures called Bantustans, and the Bantu Education Act, which created a separate education for nonwhites to create a docile labor class for the white capitalists. The effects of this long history did not end with the end of apartheid or the election of the first black South African president. Without this history, racism becomes a matter of personal prejudice rather than a systemic problem that requires revising the foundational discourses of society. Thus the images of Pienaar's mother and housemaid sitting side by side, hugging in joy, or the black African ragpicker who is embraced by the Afrikaner policemen signal momentary suspension of hostilities in the wake of an extraordinary event.

The vision of reconciliation presented by these images of shared jubilation shifts the responsibility of reconciliation onto the blacks. Mandela's injunction to his African National Congress (ANC) bodyguards when they protest having to work with members of the erstwhile Vlakplaas is to remind them that reconciliation begins at the personal level. He offers the same advice to the sporting authority of South Africa when they want to pass an order banning the Springboks logo. However, unlike the TRC hearings, where victims learned the truth about missing relatives or the cause of death and thus received some closure, there is no corresponding benefit to the victims for sacrificing the human desire for justice in the film. The responsibilities of the whites in the process of reconciliation are never mentioned. To ask for victims to give up the quest for justice is a tremendous demand, especially if equally challenging moral demands are not placed on the perpetrators or a transformation in the material condition of the victims is not guaranteed. In addition, by presenting reconciliation as a personal moral choice blacks must make to integrate with their erstwhile perpetrators of violence, the film elides the macro-level social and institutional transformations necessary for reconciliation. Since the nonwhites were victims of the inhumane racist policies of apartheid, determining their role in the reconciliation politics repeats the violence of apartheid in a different register. If anything, as victims, in the post-apartheid regime they should have the dominant voice in the reconciliation process, especially their role in the process. The representation of reconciliation in the film that absolves whites of all responsibility fits in with the post-racial view of integration that seeks to maintain the power and status quo of the whites.

MESSIANIC POLITICS AND THE RE-CREATION OF NELSON MANDELA

The vision of reconciliation in *Invictus* is not a collective effort but the result of messianic politics centered on the personality of President Mandela. Reconciliation is presented as the vision and accomplishment of President Mandela, a sage and saintly elderly statesman. From the time of his release, the West has portrayed Mandela as messiah. Ted Koppel, reporting on Mandela's release from prison, insisted that "we need a Messiah to lead us out of the wilderness. Maybe Nelson Mandela is the man."[35] Messianic politics centered on a saintly nonwhite leader is an attempt to reframe and reimagine the integration of African Americans into the white body politic without disturbing white supremacy. In this re-creation of the black leader, the frame of reference remains the dominant white population of the United States. Thus, post-apartheid Mandela, rather than the militant Mandela of the apartheid era, is attractive because his mission of reconciliation in post-apartheid

South Africa fits the post-racial narrative of racial integration in the United States.

Mandela is established as the beacon of post-racial reconciliation in *Invictus* through two strategies. First, *Invictus* establishes him as an advocate for forgiveness and reconciliation through a series of swift cuts of Mandela from his release to his inauguration as president. These rapid cuts are paired with random quotes from his speeches after his release to convey ideas that present him as a pacifist committed to reconciliation. These select phrases from his speeches focus only on the post-prison Mandela. The radical Mandela of his pre-prison years, the Mandela who cheered for the opposing team when the Springboks played, is elided. In one of the quotes, Mandela harangues the ANC cadres to "throw the pangas and machetes and guns into the sea." This is an excerpt from his speech in Natal in 1990 when the violence threatened to disrupt the negotiations between the ANC and the National Party (NP).[36] However, by leaving out this context, this quote makes Mandela out as a saint, an African who has triumphed over bitterness and vengeance to achieve a sagacity that the rest of the nation needs to prevent a bloodbath. But Mandela's position on violence is much more complex and nuanced than the film portrays. In a memorandum to P. W. Botha, written at Victor Verster prison, Paarl, South Africa, in June/July 1989, Mandela wrote, "But we consider armed struggle a legitimate form of defense against a morally repugnant system of government which will not allow even peaceful forms of protest."[37] He continues to defend the violent response to a violent regime after his release when, in February 1990, he described violence against apartheid as the last resort because "if we had channels, peaceful channels of communication, we would never have thought of resorting to violence. If there was not the violence of apartheid, there would never have been violence from our side."[38] By reducing Mandela to a few select sound bites about reconciliation and ignoring his radical past, a complex human being is reduced to a one-dimensional stick figure.

Another strategy to distinguish Mandela as a pacifist saint sets him apart from his peers and the rest of black Africa in his allegiance to reconciliation. Mandela's pacifism is contrasted with other characters in the film who are resistant to reconciliation, such as his bodyguards, his advisor Brenda, and the other members of the ANC. Despite resistance from his bodyguards, he hires the Vlakplaas, the apartheid secret police, to protect him and foils attempts of the ANC to ban the Springboks, the Afrikaner symbol for their rugby team. He is thus the lone fighter for reconciliation. His doubters are proved wrong when the nation, particularly the Africans, begin to support the Springboks and unite to cheer and celebrate South Africa's victory in the Rugby World Cup. Thus Mandela proves to be the sage elder statesman who is able to guide his short-sighted group into the path of forgiveness and reconciliation through his own example.

Mandela as the architect of reconciliation is a simplification of the complex process of reconciliation in South Africa, which in the end was a strategic process that involved the ANC and the National Party led by F. W. de Klerk. Reconciliation became a state policy because of the nature of South Africa's journey from apartheid to democracy. The ANC's triumph in the elections was not a victory of the nonwhite faction. Apartheid's inability to protect the economic interest of the whites and the rising militancy of the MK, the militant wing of the ANC, and the Azanian People's Liberation Army (APLA), the militant wing of PAC, split the NP into conservative and reformist factions. The reformist faction gained voice when de Klerk took over. De Klerk granted more power to blacks at the local level. Consequently, the local Afrikaner councilors were replaced by black councilors, who started their own corrupt regime in the townships to line their pockets. But leading nonwhite parties like the ANC and PAC rejected reforms. They wanted democracy, and their militant wings launched guerrilla warfare against the white establishment, targeting security forces and paramilitary forces that terrorized townships. Since the ANC was banned and operated from abroad, it had no control over its young cadres, who went on an unrestrained rampage, attacking not just white power but nonwhites of other ideologies. Black councilors, members of rival nonwhite political organizations, and members from other townships and classes became targets of their wrath. At the same time, tribal chiefs in the various homelands set up vigilante forces to bring the blacks in their territory under their control and fight the APLA and MK. Simon Skosana organized private armies for the independence of Kwa Ndebele, while Mangosuthu Buthelezi, the Zulu chief, distanced himself from the ANC, in an attempt to portray himself as a moderate black.[39] The fractured black identities meant that there was no cohesive nonwhite opposition. It comes as no surprise that the nonwhite resistance was unable to overcome the white establishment.

At this juncture—when the Afrikaner-majority NP government was brought to its knees by the international boycott and the collapse of law and order, but the resistance was not strong enough to capitalize on the moment—negotiations were in order. The NP originally planned to share power, securing minority rights and veto power over major decisions for the Afrikaners. The process of negotiations, initiated in the 1980s through a series of secret meetings between the ANC and the ruling white NP, was carried out through the Groot Schmur Minutes (May 1990) and the Pretoria Minutes (August 1990). The result was the unbanning of the ANC and the release of Nelson Mandela. As exiles returned and many political prisoners gained freedom, there was backlash against whites. The National Peace Accord was formed at the encouragement of the national human rights movement and the South African Council of Churches with the triple aim of (a) eliminating violence, (b) promoting democratization, and (c) reconstruction and development. Side by side, the Convention for a Democratic South Africa (CODESA), the first multiparty organization to discuss South Africa, was formed. Nineteen parties participated. CODESA1 and CODESA2 failed in the face of unabated violence. In fact, the ANC withdrew from CODESA2 because of the Boipotang killings. From this point of no return, negotiations began anew. The NP was forced to agree to a democratic election, while the ANC agreed to an amnesty policy that would provide indemnity from civil or criminal prosecution in return for disclosure of crimes. Finally, in 1994 the elections were held. The historical events preceding the end of apartheid suggest that the post-apartheid era did not end white supremacy: it brought an end to a racist government.

The representation of Mandela as a saintly pacifist continues the presentation of the black characters as either thugs or saints. Mandela's pacifist philosophy is contrasted with his bodyguard, who is eager to engage in a brawl with any Afrikaner, particularly the erstwhile Vlakplaas policemen he is forced to work with at Mandela's insistence. Presentation of blacks in Hollywood films as historical figures and pacifist figures is one of the oldest Hollywood tropes of normalizing black difference. The focus on a historical leader suggests that black characters as ordinary everyday human beings have no value. In fact the camera travels around places of power: presidential offices, TV stations, expensive hotel rooms, rugby stadiums, and player training facilities. The ordinary lives and intimate spaces of blacks as they struggle to survive and perhaps imbibe reconciliation remain out of the narrative. Presenting the discourse of reconciliation through the historical character of Mandela makes it a dogmatic injunction. Whitewashing black personalities to suit the dictates of white hegemony is nothing new. It is why Martin Luther King's "I Have a Dream" speech is celebrated, but the radical King of "Letter from Birmingham Jail" or "Beyond Vietnam" is erased. King's pacifism is easier to manipulate and accept than Malcolm X's radical politics. Similarly Mandela is a more palatable black leader for the U.S. audience than Steve Biko and his "Black Consciousness" movement.

The presentation of Mandela as a saintly elder statesman elides the role of the United States in branding him a terrorist and the CIA's involvement with his arrest. President Reagan placed the ANC on the terrorist watch list, and until 2008 it remained on the terrorist watch list. As a result Mandela needed a special waiver from the secretary of state to visit the United States in 2008. Dick Cheney voted against releasing Mandela in the 1980s. Mandela was labeled a terrorist because of his communist sympathies. During the Cold War, communist sympathies were suspect. Mandela's communist sympathies were guided by the fact that the Communist Party of South Africa was one political organization that did not differentiate according to race. The Soviet Union was one of the ANC's biggest supporters against apartheid, and Fidel Castro helped the ANC in its fight against apartheid.[40] In the Cold War

United States, an African leader who was against the government and advocated the use of violence and had clear communist sympathies was deeply problematic. However, in the post-racial United States, the same man as the elected leader and statesman who advocated reconciliation and a move away from violence embodies the saintly values they deem safe and acceptable in a nonwhite leader. Thus Mandela in the contemporary U.S. imagination has metamorphosed into a saint from a terrorist in keeping with the changing political and ideological climate in the United States.

This messianic construction of Mandela is a U.S. media endeavor that involves glossing his consistent rejection of such a messianic role. "I stand before you," Mandela declared, "not as a prophet, but as a humble servant of you, the people."[41] He describes the end of apartheid as the result of "disciplined mass action" instead of individual heroism.[42] In his first public address, Mandela made a roll call of honor of all the organizations—women's groups, trade unions, community groups, guerrilla fronts, alternative press, and so forth—that made the struggle possible. This litany was a move to shift from the messianic politics to which Mandela was in danger of succumbing.

Mandela as a saintly, forgiving figure sets a standard of black behavior that nullifies white fear and paranoia. Since white fear of loss of power is paranoia, rather than based on any real possibility of threat from blacks, any black demands for rights and protests against the past are seen as threatening. Thus black rage, identified with the civil rights era, is seen as threatening, violent, and irrational because it is a reminder of the uncomfortable history of racism. On the other hand, a saintly figure who preaches forgiveness and magnanimity instead of vengeance presents a kinder, gentler version of blackness. If Mandela presents the new model of black behavior, then his bodyguards and advisors stand for the black anger associated with the civil rights–era leaders such as Jesse Jackson, Al Sharpton, and Cornel West, who are militant about the inequalities of U.S. racist society. Mandela's comfortable blackness is preferable because it can be absorbed into the white body politic without discomfort.

Mandela's pacifism aligns him with Obama's own ameliorative blackness, which presents a black leader as an integrative figure rather than a radical other. Tim Wise points out that in his famous "Race Speech," Obama aligns himself with Lincoln and mainstream white icons, instead of African American leaders such as Frederick Douglass or Booker T. Washington. Tim Wise points out that while Obama acknowledges the contribution of the civil rights movement, he is quick to separate himself from it. He acknowledges that "the disparities that exist in the African American community . . . can be directly traced to the inequalities passed on from an earlier generation that suffered under the brutal legacy of Jim Crow."[43] He also acknowledges the root of black anger in this historical disparity. However, when discussing the solution, he places the burden on the blacks. In a solution that has little connection to the systemic inequality he mentioned earlier, Obama suggests taking "full responsibility for our lives" and "spending more time with our children."[44] Therefore it is no surprise that Obama has strong parallels with post-racial Mandela in the film, a man who not only is pacifist but preaches reconciliation as a personal doctrine of the Africans. The parallel between Obama and Mandela challenges Eastwood's claim that "politicians could learn a lot from Mandela."

Despite the parallels, the focus on an extraordinary and pacifist African leader does not predict empathy or understanding for blacks in the United States or anywhere else. Mandela as a pacifist is depicted as someone who has transcended blackness and moved beyond the anger and bitterness the situation causes. In this representation of the venerable African leader, the focus is still on hegemonic American whiteness, which dictates the acceptable modes of black behavior. Wise describes this trend as "racism 2" or "enlightened exceptionalism," a form that allows for and even celebrates the achievements of individual persons of color, but only because those individuals are seen as different from a less appealing, even pathological black or brown public.[45] In addition, "'transcending blackness' is in and of itself racist, insofar as it presumes, if only by implication, that there is something negative about blackness."[46] In fact the general conclusion that African Americans are lazy, inadequate, or inferior and therefore should not be given handouts suggests that empathy does not arise from acceptance of the success of a few African Americans such as Obama, Cory Booker, Denzel Washington, Beyoncé, and so on. Wise points out that historically a few African Americans have risen above the material conditions. But the rise of such individuals has not given rise to understanding of black struggles in the United States. Instead, the rise of extraordinary figures has been used to label ordinary African Americans as inadequate, in an effort to deny the systemic nature of racism.

Setting up a pacifist Mandela as the ideal of black leadership sets up these values as aspirational standards for the black leadership and community. Failing to live up to these ideals and falling back on anger and bitterness is implicitly regarded as a lack of a superior moral compass, as individual moral failure to transcend race, to improve their situation. Presenting emotions such as anger, bitterness, and mistrust toward the white population in the black community as individual failures dismisses these emotions. The dismissal of black emotions other than forgiveness may absolve the paranoid white Americans from understanding the roots of that anger and confronting their complicity in the racist society, but by dismissing uncomfortable black emotions, the film still upholds white values as the central pivot.

Even then, Mandela's saintliness is presented through the mediating white presence of the rugby captain Pienaar. While Mandela's own party has little sympathy for reconciliation, his unlikely ally in the reconciliation endeavor is Francois Pienaar. Pienaar, whose life was centered on rugby and who had iconic status among Afrikaners as the captain of their favorite sport, ventures into the townships to popularize rugby among the township children, to hold rugby camps and fund-raise for the townships' welfare. He also takes on the task of educating his less-than-eager teammates, including arranging for a visit to Robben Island, including Mandela's cell. Thus he becomes the audience's guide for the journeys into townships, into Robben Island, instead of a black character, whether it is Mandela or Chester (the only black player on the team). The presentation of the townships through the eyes of the naïve Afrikaner, the white character, makes "third world politics adventurous and manageable."[47] The white outsider, here embodied by Pienaar, mediates the black spaces and ideologies, making them less threatening, less ominous. But this politics is not without ideological ramifications.

Even though at the narrative level *Invictus* presents an optimistic narrative of a black man and a white man working together to heal a nation, Pienaar's transformation dominates the screen time. Pienaar's mediating white presence transforms a film about Mandela's vision of reconciliation to a film about Pienaar's racial education. Once Pienaar enters the picture, the focus shifts from Mandela to rugby, Pienaar's education, and the Rugby World Cup Finals. The rugby final takes at least twenty minutes of the second half. This shift in focus from Mandela to Pienaar is corroborated by the film's poster, which presents Matt Damon (playing Francois Pienaar) and Morgan Freeman (playing Nelson Mandela) with their backs against each other as two faces of reconciliation. Yet Freeman has his back to the camera so that only a sliver of his face is visible, while Damon faces the camera. This composition makes it appear as if Freeman's back is the backdrop for a smiling, jubilant Damon. It appears as if Pienaar's journey into the township, to Robben Island, educates him about the anti-apartheid struggle and Mandela's life. The result is a deeper understanding of his fellow nonwhite countrymen and empathy for them. He no longer shares his father's racist views. In an unprecedented move, he secures a ticket for the finals for the family help. Pienaar's pivotal role in the success of Mandela's vision of reconciliation replays the paternalist white trope of the white man as the savior of the black man against other black men. Also, Pienaar's education through his involvement with Mandela's mission reduces Mandela's reconciliation goal to that of reinvigoration of the white man and his community. The plight of the nonwhites remains out of consideration. Pienaar's transformation makes eradication of racism a multicultural project. A multicultural project "emphasizes the need to respect cultural diversity . . . often at the expense of confronting directly histories of racial domination and structured social inequality."[48]

POST-RACIAL VS. POST-RACIST POLITICS

Invictus ends with the country euphoric with the World Cup victory and Mandela a man proven right in his belief in reconciliation. The images of a nation forgetting differences and hostility in the joy of victory suggest that reconciliation has been accomplished. Since the film presents South Africa as a substitute for the United States, this happy ending may be read as hope that President Obama's election to office marks the end of racial hostilities in the United States. However, this is a fantasy rather than reality. It presents a vision of a superficial momentary cessation of hostilities as racial reconciliation, completely eliding the structural aspect of racism, without which reconciliation cannot happen. Its hope is, thus, little more than illusion, an illusion of an unfettered and unburdened present. By presenting this post-racial dream, the film perpetuates a fantasy rather than a hope. In perpetuating this fantasy, instead of critiquing it, the film itself participates in the racial project of post-racialism. It distracts attention, reconstructs history to erase the past, and adjusts the contemporary situation to deny historical and contemporary reality. The wide reach of films and the clout of the director Clint Eastwood and actor Matt Damon ensures that this post-racial fantasy will circulate as reality.

This does not mean that reconciliation is impossible. However, to realize reconciliation as a complex project of structural and ethical change, it is necessary to switch from dreaming of moving beyond race to focusing on moving beyond racism. This means moving from the dream of the United States as a post-racial state to the United States as a post-racist state. A post-racist state is "vigorous both in refusing racist practice and in public representation of the unacceptability of all forms of discriminatory expression."[49] This requires more than personal reformation.

In a *GQ* interview Eastwood loads *Invictus* with a moral purpose. He claims "politicians could learn a lot from Mandela . . . about racial relationships" because the nation was making a mistake in "calling everyone racist."[50] Eastwood perceives in Mandela's personal ethics "what Christ would be like if he existed: a guy who would forgive." Eastwood contrasts Mandela's forgiving spirit with President Obama, whom he claims "sided with Gates instead of the policeman."[51] In Eastwood's world silence about race is desirable and transformation of the racially naïve characters makes them heroes. In reality, these post-racial liberal values side with political complacency and apathy instead of social reform. Despite charging the film with moral purpose and making Mandela an aspirational figure, *Invictus* does not present America with an alternative model to racism. Instead, it uses the smoking mirror of post-racialism to manipulate history and avoid confronting reality. In the end *Invictus* is an enactment of white paranoia that is distanced by being displaced to a different country and historical context. It is a feel-good fantasy that caters to the dominant white hegemony of the United States, instead of shedding light on the reality of race.

NOTES

1. Rob Nixon, *Homelands, Harlem and Hollywood: South African Culture and the World Beyond* (New York: Routledge, 1994), 77–97.
2. Nixon, *Homelands, Harlem, and Hollywood*, 78.
3. Nixon, *Homelands, Harlem, and Hollywood*, 78.
4. In South Africa the racial categories are a little different from those in the United States. In the United States, according to the "one-drop rule," anyone with only a drop of non-Caucasian blood is considered "colored." In South Africa "colored" refers to those born of miscegenation between the European (British and Dutch) colonials and Africans. The Europeans of British and Dutch descent are considered whites (English South Afrikaners and Afrikaners) and the descendants of indigenous African tribes are called blacks or Africans. In addition there are the Cape Malays who are of South Asian descent. In this essay when referring to African Americans, I have used the terms *blacks* and *African Americans* interchangeably. In the case of South Africa I have used the term *nonwhites* as a blanket term for all the different groups who were not counted as European and therefore at the receiving end of apartheid racism in varying degrees.
5. Sumi Choo, "Post-Racialism," *Iowa Law Review* 94 (2009): 1594.
6. Choo, "Post-Racialism," 1595.
7. Choo, "Post-Racialism," 1600.
8. David Goldberg, *Racist Culture: Philosophy and the Politics of Meaning* (Cambridge: Blackwell, 1993), 47.
9. Goldberg, *Racist Culture*, 48.
10. Goldberg, *Racist Culture*, 59.
11. Goldberg, *Racist Culture*, 98.
12. Goldberg, *Racist Culture*, 2.
13. Goldberg, *Racist Culture*, 57.
14. Goldberg, *Racist Culture*, 2.
15. Goldberg, *Racist Culture*, 10.
16. Goldberg, *Racist Culture*, 10.
17. Tim Wise, *Colorblind: The Rise of Post-racial Politics and the Retreat from Racial Equality* (San Francisco: City Lights Books, 2010), 16.
18. Wise, *Colorblind*, 64–70.
19. Michael Hainey, "Icon: Clint Eastwood," *GQ*, December 2009, http://www.gq.com/entertainment/men-of-the-year/2009/badass/clint-eastwood-legend-invictus-director.
20. Choo, "Post-racialism," 1594.
21. Wilbur C. Rich, *The Post-Racial Society: Recognition, Critics and the Nation State* (New York: Routledge, 2013), 3.
22. "Poverty in the United States," National Poverty Center, http://www.npc.umich.edu/poverty/.
23. Rich, *The Post-Racial Society*, 3.
24. Kent Ono, "Post Racism: A Theory of 'Post' as a Political Strategy," *Journal of Communication Inquiry* 34, no. 3: 227.
25. Ono, "Post Racism," 227.
26. Goldberg, *Racist Culture*, 218.
27. Nelson Mandela, *Nelson Mandela by Himself: Authorized Book of Quotations*, ed. Sello Hatang and Sahn Venter (Johannesburg: Pan Macmillan, 2011), 220.
28. John W. De Gruchy, *Reconciliation: Restoring Justice* (Minneapolis: Front Press, 2002), 12.

29. Truth and Reconciliation Commission, *Truth and Reconciliation Commission of South Africa Final Report*, vol. 1 (Johannesburg: Government of South Africa, 2009), 7, http://www.justice.gov.za/trc/report/index.htm.
30. Truth and Reconciliation Commission, *Truth and Reconciliation Commission of South Africa Final Report*, vol. 1, 2.
31. Truth and Reconciliation Commission, *Truth and Reconciliation Commission of South Africa Final Report*, vol. 1, 2.
32. Coates, Ta-Nehisi, "Fear of a Black President" *Atlantic*, November 27, 2013, 9, http://www.theatlantic.com/magazine/archive/2012/09/fear-of-a-black-president/309064/.
33. Coates, "Fear of a Black President," 9.
34. New York City's Stop and Frisk program was in place before Obama's presidency. However, there has been increasing protest against it as the program targets African Americans and Hispanics. According to the New York City Civil Liberties Union, nine of the ten people stopped by this program have been innocent without any indication of criminal activity.
35. Nixon, *Homelands, Harlem and Hollywood*, 179.
36. Nixon, *Homelands, Harlem and Hollywood*, 180.
37. Mandela, *Nelson Mandela by Himself*, 268.
38. Mandela, *Nelson Mandela by Himself*, 269.
39. For more information on the history of the transition to apartheid, see William Beinart, *Twentieth Century South Africa* (Oxford: Oxford University Press, 2001), 254–85.
40. See Peter Beinart, "Don't Sanitize Nelson Mandela: He Was Honored But He Was Also Hated," *Daily Beast*, December 5, 2013, http://www.thedailybeast.com/articles/2013/12/05/don-t-sanitize-nelson-mandela-he-s-honored-now-but-was-hated-then.html.
41. Nixon, *Homelands, Harlem, and Hollywood*, 183.
42. Nixon, *Homelands, Harlem, and Hollywood*, 183.
43. Wise, *Colorblind*, 49.
44. Wise, *Colorblind*, 53.
45. Tim Wise, *Between Barack and a Hard Place: Racism and White Denial in the Age of Obama* (San Francisco: City Lights Books, 2010), 9.
46. Wise, *Between Barack*, 86.
47. Nixon, *Homelands, Harlem, and Hollywood*, 83.
48. Bruce Baum, "Hollywood on Race in the Age of Obama: *Invictus*, *Precious* and *Avatar*," *New Political Science* 32, no. 4 (December 2010), 628.
49. David Goldberg, *The Racial State* (Cambridge: Blackwell, 2002), 248.
50. Hainey, "Icon: Clint Eastwood."
51. Hainey, "Icon: Clint Eastwood."

REFERENCES

Baum, Bruce. "Hollywood on Race in the Age of Obama: *Invictus*, *Precious* and *Avatar*." *New Political Science* 32, no. 4 (December 2010): 627–36.
Beinart, Peter. "Don't Sanitize Nelson Mandela: He Was Honored But He Was Also Hated." *Daily Beast*, December 5, 2013.http://www.thedailybeast.com/articles/2013/12/05/don-t-sanitize-nelson-mandela-he-s-honored-now-but-was-hated-then.html.
Beinart, William. *Twentieth Century South Africa*. Oxford: Oxford University Press, 2001.
Coates, Ta-Nehisi. "Fear of a Black President." *Atlantic*, November 27, 2013, 1–17. http://www.theatlantic.com/magazine/archive/2012/09/fear-of-a-black-president/309064/.
Choo, Sumi. "Post-Racialism." *Iowa Law Review* 94 (2009): 1589–649.
De Gruchy, John W. *Reconciliation: Restoring Justice*. Minneapolis: Front Press, 2002.
Goldberg, David Theo. *Racist Culture: Philosophy and the Politics of Meaning*. Cambridge: Blackwell, 1993.
———. *The Racial State*. Cambridge: Blackwell, 2002.
Hainey, Michael. "Icon: Clint Eastwood." *GQ*, December 2009. http://www.gq.com/entertainment/men-of-the-year/2009/badass/clint-eastwood-legend-invictus-director.

Mandela, Nelson. *Nelson Mandela by Himself: Authorized Book of Quotations*. Ed. Sello Hatang and Sahn Venter. Johannesburg: Pan Macmillan, 2011.
Nixon, Rob. *Homelands, Harlem and Hollywood: South African Culture and the World Beyond*. New York: Routledge, 1994.
Ono, Kent. "Post Racism: A Theory of 'Post' as Political Strategy." *Journal of Communication Inquiry* 34, no. 3: 227–33.
"Poverty in the United States." National Poverty Center. http://www.npc.umich.edu/poverty/.
Rich, Wilbur C. *The Post-racial Society: Recognition, Critics and the Nation State*. New York: Routledge, 2013.
Truth and Reconciliation Commission. *Truth and Reconciliation Commission Final Report*, vol. 1. Johannesburg: Government of South Africa, 2009. http://www.justice.gov.za/trc/report/index.htm.
Wise, Tim. *Between Barack and a Hard Place: Racism and White Denial in the Age of Obama*. San Francisco: City Lights Books, 2010.
———. *Colorblind: The Rise of Post-racial Politics and the Retreat from Racial Equality*. San Francisco: City Lights Books, 2010.

Chapter Ten

"Mama, I Think I Broke Something": Thinking about the Environment in Benh Zeitlin's *Beasts of the Southern Wild*

Irina Negrea

Beasts of the Southern Wild, directed by Benh Zeitlin (2012), illustrates the classical tale of a film completed on a shoestring budget that in the end exceeds all expectations. Indeed, it received numerous accolades in the United States and in Europe: the Grand Jury Prize at the Sundance Film Festival in 2012, the Camera D'Or at the Cannes Film Festival, the Audience Award and Best Narrative Feature at the Los Angeles Film Festival, the Best Film and the Revelations Prize at the Deauville Film Festival, the NAACP Image Award 2013 in the categories of Outstanding Independent Motion Picture and Outstanding Director, and the list continues.[1] It was also nominated for four Academy Awards in the categories Best Motion Picture of the Year, Best Performance by an Actress in a Leading Role, Best Achievement in Directing, and Best Writing (Adapted Screenplay).[2] The film's critical reception was also overwhelmingly positive. *Beasts* has been called a "paean to childhood perception and human resilience,"[3] a "mixed race Utopia,"[4] "hauntingly beautiful,"[5] "a film about a child's sense of causality,"[6] the "year's little film that could,"[7] a "remarkable creation,"[8] a film about "the unsentimental necessity of survival,"[9] and an "allegorical coming of ager, a cross between *Where the Wild Things Are* and *The Tempest*."[10]

Given the success of the film—a success that was unexpected even to its creator, Zeitlin[11] —one has to wonder exactly what the film "is about." Is there a subtext that speaks to all (or most of) us on a level that resonates with our fears, our ideals, our expectations? Is the film a cautionary tale that is trying to compel us to change the way we think about the world around us in order to avoid the potential catastrophic effects of our actions? Is it trying to (re)direct our attention away from consumerism and toward issues that truly matter (or should matter) most? The answer to all these questions is a resounding yes, but they do merit more qualified responses. This essay is attempting to do just that: to go beyond the yes to the "yes, but . . ." and "yes, and . . . " type of answers and to explore the intersections of *Beasts* with "the real world," particularly with what this collection aptly names "the age of Obama." To be more specific, the essay is analyzing how Zeitlin is challenging his audiences to reframe their way of thinking about the environment and the world, to refocus their attention and energy on issues that go beyond consumerism and partisan politics, and even to contemplate a bleak future if changes are not put into effect soon. The film resonates mostly with two of the buzzwords often heard during the "age of Obama:" "sustainability" and "renewable." The latter features heavily in President Obama's remarks on climate change, made at Georgetown University on June 25, 2013, a year and a half after *Beasts* emerged on the film landscape of the world. The film is also part of a preoccupation with climate change that seems to have taken over the arts worldwide, including a summer-long art festival at MOMA in New York in 2013, the Berlin-based "Anthropocene Project" that focuses on the impact of humans on nature, the Carbon 14 art exhibition at the Toronto Royal Art Museum, and the British-based Cape Farewell organization that involves artists and scientists going on expeditions throughout the world to observe the effects of climate change, among other events.[12]

The relationship between art and society and/or "reality" is one that has been studied and argued ad infinitum. It is not the scope of this essay to dwell on such an argument. Suffice it to say that Bertolt Brecht's saying "Art is not a mirror to hold up to society, but a hammer with which to shape it,"[13] seems to be very apt when analyzing *Beasts of the Southern Wild*. One other similar assertion was made by bell hooks, whose reading of the film goes completely against the overwhelmingly positive reception it received: "Movies do not just mirror the culture of any given time; they also create it."[14] In light of these two statements, one sees that the intersections between *Beasts* and reality are multiple: the film reflects the general conversation about climate change that intensified during the "age of Obama." These intersections are evident not only in the discourse of the film, but also in the way it was made, the way the screenplay was completed, the construction of the sets, the casting process, and the actors themselves. It seems at least puzzling that a film that was labeled as "mythic" and "magical-realist"[15] by several critics is so rooted in reality. Contrary to what Agnes Woolley discusses in her article "The Politics of Myth Making: *Beasts of the Southern Wild*,"[16] Zeitlin uses myth not to obscure important questions and issues, but to (re)focus our attention on these issues—one of them being the potentially devastating effects of climate change, which is what President Obama mentions in both his inaugural addresses, in 2009 and 2013. In order to discuss these intersections with the environmental politics in the age of Obama, one must first discuss the discourse of the film and how it proposes a different way of thinking about the world that surrounds us.

The very first frames of the film set up nature as a main character in it: the sky is overcast, gray; it is windy—so windy that one can hear the wind on the sound track, and the camera itself is moving, transposing the viewer into the bayou in the first minutes of the film. As bell hooks argues, "Nature is the most compelling force in the world of the Bathtub."[17] In the next scene, the camera focuses on a mound of dirt that Hushpuppy (still off-camera) has made; it has a hole in it, in which she pours water, only her hands being visible. The scene is meant to remind the viewer of the way in which the bayou is renewed every year, of the close interdependence between the water and the earth—a fragile equilibrium that humans have upset by building levees, Zeitlin later implies in the film. The viewer finally sees the little girl in the next frame; she is listening to a chick, and the bird's heartbeat is heard on the sound track of the scene. Hushpuppy places the chick on the fresh mound of wet dirt that she has just created, and the chick stays there, seemingly content. This particular scene suggests that the protagonist is a creator, not a destroyer. She is already queen of the Bathtub. The next scene has Hushpuppy outside, apparently checking on all the animals; it is very windy—so windy, that at one point, she almost loses her balance when walking. The sound track with the heartbeat can be heard again when she touches the pig, and finally when she picks up another chick and holds it to her ear like a telephone. This particular image was present as a still in numerous articles about the film. It is an arresting image, and it resonates with what Hushpuppy is about to say as a narrator: "All of the time, everywhere, everything's heart is beatin' and' squirtin' and talkin' to each other in a way that I can't understand. Most of the times they probably be sayin,' 'I'm hungry; I gotta poop,' but sometimes they be talking in codes."[18] There is a sense here that this child has (partial) access to a world that is completely closed to adults, that somehow she intuits that every living thing is connected to the next, and that the connection is something that humans have lost and/or are gradually losing—she understands some of the communication, especially the one that refers to basic needs, but she also has the sense that as a growing human, she is losing the key to a code that perhaps used to be familiar to humans in times immemorial. The scene in which she seems to be using the chick as a telephone is extremely compelling, as it speaks to her attempt to recapture that code. hooks aptly argues, "Hushpuppy finds solace in natural wildness, listening to the heartbeat of animals, envisioning her connection to a primordial world. . . . Hushpuppy has visions of a natural world humans are destroying."[19] The fact that this particular scene opens the film leaves no doubt about Zeitlin's message to his viewers: we all need to recapture that type of thinking, especially in dealing with nature.

The scene is interrupted by Wink, Hushpuppy's father, whose presence is (aptly) announced by a bottle that he pushes through a hole in the wall of his trailer. We do not see Wink yet; we only see the bottle and hear it land among other (perhaps many) bottles, and then we hear, "Get out the way!" Since later in the film, the viewer sees a dog in Wink's trailer, it can be assumed that he is talking to it. The scene is in sharp contrast to Hushpuppy's actions of creation, nurture, and attempt to understand the language of nature. It is safe to assume that Wink is the intruder in this scene, even this world, and that if he once had Hushpuppy's world vision, he has lost it, as an adult. The second sentence that he utters is addressed to his daughter: "Put your pants on, man!" At this point in the film, the viewer is not completely certain of Hushpuppy's gender.[20] hooks also mentions the "transgendered casting of Hushpuppy as sometimes representing maleness and sometimes femaleness," but hooks also reads the opening scene, when Hushpuppy appears wearing only orange underwear and a dirty white vest as "pornographically eroticizing" the body of a little girl.[21] One can respectfully disagree with hooks's reading of the opening scene. Zeitlin offers us a view of Hushpuppy's world and a view into her way of thinking. The protagonist is five years old and living in a place that is isolated from mainstream America, or "the dry world," as she calls it.[22] Even though gender may be taught in the form of patterns of behavior to a lot of children that age in American society, the Bathtub is a place where these rules do not apply. Hushpuppy is not taught to behave "like a girl." One proof in point is that Wink calls her "man" in his first line in the film.

Insofar as Hushpuppy and her way of thinking are concerned, living in the Bathtub, away from mainstream American society, race, class, and gender are not relevant, or at least not to the extent to which they are in the "dry world." Hushpuppy is preoccupied with completely different issues, and her view of the world does not encompass these artificially created differences. According to Roger Ebert,

> This is only an illustration of the way small children think, translating the mysteries of an unfolding world into her own terms. . . . We understand how literally her mind deals with the world when she tries to hide from the fire [that she started] inside a cardboard box—as if she will be safe if the flames can't see her.[23]

In the grand scheme of things, when they are trying to make sense of the big world around them, small children do not care about what they are wearing: underwear, vest, and rubber boots are OK for Hushpuppy because in the world that she inhabits, possessions do not define people and social status is irrelevant. Zeitlin's choice of clothes for Hushpuppy does not belie a desire to eroticize the body of a young girl. It is what Hushpuppy would have picked herself before running outside to check on her animals.

Juxtaposed with the first scene of the film is the scene where all the inhabitants are forcibly taken to the evacuation center after the levee is blown up by Wink. We see a Hushpuppy who is wearing a dress and shoes and whose hair is combed, and we hear her description of the "dry world": "It didn't look like a prison; it looked more like a fish tank with no water."[24] Her vision of the world on the other side of the levee aptly describes not only a world that is artificial, but one that is likely to kill its inhabitants. She knows that she cannot survive in this world, and we see her putting up a fierce fight and refusing to leave Wink behind when she is put on a bus with other evacuees. She even translates medical care into her own terms: "When an animal gets sick here, they plug it into the wall."[25] She tries to apply her thinking in this world as well, as we see her listening to the heart of a patient in a coma, just like she listened to the hearts of the other animals in the beginning of the film.

In her article "No Love in the Wild," bell hooks argues, "That Hushpuppy has this advanced state of cosmic consciousness is one of the fanciful and irritating aspects of the film."[26] Again, one can disagree with hooks and argue that Zeitlin's intention was to merely (re)acquaint the viewer with the way a six-year-old's mind works. The "cosmic consciousness" moments are interspersed with moments of clearly immature judgment, such as the time when the protagonist sets fire to her trailer and hides *inside* the trailer, in a cardboard box, thinking that the fire will not reach her. We are not offered the picture of a very precocious child who has the means to articulate the tenets of an environmentalist policy. The wisdom that she has is more instinctual than anything else. There is a basic, innate goodness in the protagonist, and what we are offered through Hushpuppy is, in Zeitlin's words, "a moral compass for behavior."[27]

Later in the film, Hushpuppy narrates, "The whole universe depends on everything fitting together just right." At this point, the image the viewers see is one of worms teeming on a tree branch, and then there is a cut to glaciers melting. Hushpuppy's voice is heard again: "If one piece busts—even the smallest piece—the entire universe will get busted."[28] The image of the glaciers falling gives way to one where big pieces of ice are floating on the ocean, and when the camera pans to one of them, the viewer realizes that the aurochs, the mythical beasts that Hushpuppy learned about, are frozen in those giant chunks of ice that are floating and about to melt. What the viewer gathers also is that Hushpuppy thinks that this is her fault. In a previous scene, she hits her father, and the enormity of her act is emphasized by Zeitlin in the sound that is heard and reverberates (in her mind) "far too deep and loud for a six-year-old fist hitting flesh and bone,"[29] while the scene cuts to the image of icebergs melting and falling into the ocean in an apocalyptic image. The sound track also contains ominous thunder noises that scare Hushpuppy even more, to the point where she runs to the edge of the water and yells, "Mama, I think I broke something."[30] Wink seems to be having a heart attack, fallen on the ground, and in the next scene we see Hushpuppy running among a crowd that is already evacuating the Bathtub because of the impending storm. She is running against the crowd, and the hand-held, mobile camera that follows her, along with the sound track that contains the noise of the wind and the loud sounds of panicked people and honking cars leaving the Bathtub, give the viewer an idea of the terror that the little girl must feel, especially since she clearly thinks that she caused all this by hitting her father. As Rebecca Harkins-Cross aptly notes, the film is about "a child's sense of causality. At this age we believe we are the center of the universe, where each one of our actions has some larger effect on the world around us. For Hushpuppy, the impending death of her father is akin to the entire universe falling apart,"[31] as she believes that she upset the equilibrium of the universe.

After she asks for help from Ms. Batsheba and receives some roots and herbs to give to her father,[32] Hushpuppy returns to where she left Wink on the ground, and when she does not find him, she assumes that her father has turned into a tree. She buries the medicine jar in a tree trunk, and she thinks that this act will heal her father, and by extension, the world that she thinks she "broke." In an interview with Charlie Rose, Zeitlin relates a discussion that he had with Quvenzhané Wallis, who at the time of the filming was five years old:

> I asked her, you know, 'If you were to break the world, what would you do?' And she said, 'I would have to—I would have to fix it.' And I said, 'Well, what does it mean to you to fix it? How would you go about it?' And she said, 'Well, I would go to bed on time. I would always listen to my mom. I would do my homework.' And I realize, you know, this specific thing about being a kid is that you feel like your actions, even if there isn't a tangible connection, that the quality of your actions can actually affect the world. And that—and that became sort of the principle on which the film works.[33]

Hushpuppy's type of thinking and her world vision is something that Zeitlin is asking the viewer to embrace in order to save the world from the devastating effects of climate change, brought about by human action. It is one of the main messages of the film. Hushpuppy thinks that she is saving the world if she cures her father. Conversely, she also thinks that burying the medicine in a tree will save her father and the world. Zeitlin is suggesting that even the smallest actions may have huge consequences in the natural world. In her critique of the film, Woolley aptly argues that "this vision of interdependency quite rightly suggests the re-evaluation of anthropocentrism necessary for a sustainable future."[34] Zeitlin suggests that we have to rethink the idea that nature exists for our benefit only and that we can use it (and abuse it) as we see fit. Rather, we should regard ourselves as part of it, and as such, we need to be aware that all our actions, no matter how small or insignificant, have consequences on the level of the environment, sometimes akin to losing a parent on the human level. In his interview with Charlie Rose, Zeitlin specifies that he intentionally drew the parallel between "the loss of a parent and the loss of a place"[35] in *Beasts*, to give the viewer some perspective on the magnitude of the event: "Living here, you don't feel there is a way to fight off this oncoming environmental catastrophe. The same way there's inevitability to the fact that your parents will die one day, there's inevitability to the fact that this place is going to go under water."[36]

Even though Wink chooses not to share the details of his mysterious disease with his daughter, Hushpuppy senses that she is losing her father long before he tells her so, and she also senses that her world is about to collapse. What Wink is trying to do throughout the film, albeit using questionable methods and taking actions that take the viewers out of their comfort zone when it comes to fatherhood and "tough love," is teach Hushpuppy to survive without him and to become, in his words, "king of the Bathtub." Critics such as hooks, Woolley, and Dunn note that in the film, "Wink's model of toughness is clearly gendered masculine,"[37] that "when the effects of climate change begin to re-shape our world . . . the most valuable qualities will be those traditionally associated with masculinity,"[38] and that "ultimately it is patriarchal masculinity that rules."[39] While it is true that Wink as the undisputed leader of the Bathtub seems to promote that survival is connected with traits that are coded as masculine (which is definitely problematic, but beyond the scope of this essay), the viewer has to note that even though Hushpuppy ends up acquiring some of these traits, she never loses the traits that were emphasized by the very first scene of the film: those of a creator of life, a nurturer, and a "fixer" of the world—traits that are traditionally associated with femininity. She is the one that nurtures Wink in his last moments, by feeding him from her hand, and when she bends down to listen to her father's last heartbeats, the viewer is reminded of the first scenes of the film when Hushpuppy is listening to her animals' hearts. If gender is relevant for the viewer, it is not relevant in her way of thinking.

The community's undisputed leader dies, and he leaves behind not a king, but a queen. Hushpuppy is hailed in the chant that the community uses to send Wink floating away on his funeral pyre: "Here *she* comes." The chant continues after a cut to a close-up of Hushpuppy's face: "And that is dying/ Here she comes!"[40] The next scene is that of the ragtag community of survivors toasting Wink and Hushpuppy in a kind of "the king is dead; long live the queen" salute. In the final scene of the movie, we see what was left of the fierce community of the Bathtub being clearly led by Hushpuppy down a pier that is either slowly being submerged by the invading water or is emerging out of water, attesting to the uncertainty of the future, while we hear her voice-over: "I see that I'm a little piece of a big, big universe. And that makes things right. When I die, the scientists of the future, they're going to find it all. They're going to know, once, there was a Hushpuppy, and she lived with her daddy in the Bathtub."[41] The new queen of the Bathtub has the right way of thinking to lead her people to safety, Zeitlin seems to suggest.

Gender is not the only issue that numerous critics have remarked on; it is impossible to ignore the fact that race is irrelevant in the Bathtub community, and that, as hooks remarks, "no race talk, no racial discourse disturbs the peace."[42] Other critics, such as Woolley, remark that the film "seems to studiously ignore the deep-rooted racial and social stratifications revealed by [Hurricane Katrina]."[43] In his book *The Audacity of Hope*, President Obama discusses the disparities brought to light by the hurricane: "It was obvious that many of Katrina's survivors had been abandoned long before the hurricane struck. They were the faces of any inner-city neighborhood in any American city: the faces of black poverty."[44] It is true that the aftermath of Katrina revealed what America already knew and "studiously ignored": the huge racial and class disparities present in our society. However, this truth applies to the "dry world," not the world that is on the other side of the levee. The Bathtub residents have much more to contend with than to be embroiled in the artificial categories of mainstream society: they have to figure out how to survive in a place that may be obliterated off the map at any second. In spite of all the representational issues that the critics remarked on, Wink is the undisputed leader of the Bathtub and *is* African American. A discussion of how the movie itself affects African American representational issues in culture is a good subject for another essay.

Zeitlin himself addresses race and class in his film in one of his interviews:

> Lena Dunham is getting a lot of shit for being a privileged white person who only has privileged white people in her show. I assume I'll take shit for being a privileged white person who doesn't have white people [in my movie]. We're so obsessed about race and class in this country. The film doesn't have anything to say about being a poor black person. To me, the Bathtub is a different society where money doesn't exist.[45]

What the director wants to capture in this film is how people find the indomitable will to survive after their world falls apart time and time again, and how they find the resources to stay and continue living in this world because they want to, because "the Bathtub's got more holidays than the rest of the world,"[46] and because they are deeply attached to this part of the world that "the dry world" separated itself from by "a wall."[47] This kind of life cannot include artificially created categories. The film shows, indeed, "a mixed race

Utopia uncorrupted by politics, religion or consumerism,"[48] and the director aptly remarks that "the residents give up the comforts of modern civilization, and what they gain is a freedom and unity that would be impossible on the other side of the wall."[49] Zeitlin is perfectly aware that this Utopia would be impossible to achieve and/or represent in other conditions than the specific ones of the Bathtub. However, as a member of a racially mixed family, this author can attest that this Utopia is tangible in mainstream American society in certain circumstances. In his book, President Obama discusses his own family:

> As the child of a black man and a white woman, . . . with a sister who's half Indonesian . . . and a brother-in-law and niece of Chinese descent, with some blood relatives who resemble Margaret Thatcher and others who could pass for Bernie Mac, so that family get-togethers over Christmas take on the appearance of a UN General Assembly meeting, I've never had the option of restricting my loyalties on the basis of race, or measuring my worth on the basis of tribe.[50]

The residents of the Bathtub do not have the option of racial loyalty because of their lifestyle, but Zeitlin is, of course, proposing to the viewer an America where these artificial categories cease to be relevant. In a way, he is urging his viewers to make the same move that the president is explaining in his book: "To think clearly about race, then, requires us to see the world on a split screen—to maintain in our sights the kind of America that we want while looking squarely at America as it is, to acknowledge the sins of our past and the challenges of the present without becoming trapped in cynicism or despair."[51] It is a mix of realism and idealism that can be the starting point of (yet another) discussion about race in America. The viewers are compelled to compare the "race-free" world of the Bathtub to the world they live in, and they will inevitably find mainstream America lacking.

It is also impossible to watch the film and not make a parallel between Zeitlin's apocalyptic storm and Katrina, which was one of the most mediatized natural disasters that hit Louisiana. Causing at least 1,833 deaths and $108 billion in damage, Katrina was followed by Gustav in 2008, which caused $6.6 billion in damage and so far the largest evacuation in the country's history: 3 million people.[52] Zeitlin also remarks that the storm in the film is representative of several hurricanes that hit Louisiana between 2005 and 2008: Katrina, Rita, Gustav, and Ike, and that the film is also about "living in a constant state of hurricanes . . . in a place that is going to get torn off the map."[53] There is a correlation that Zeitlin alludes to in the film, and clearly makes in interviews, between climate change and the increasing severity of the storms that are hitting Louisiana.

Speaking about climate change, President Obama stated in his 2013 inauguration address: "Some may still deny the overwhelming judgment of science, but none can avoid the devastating impact of raging fires and crippling droughts and more powerful storms."[54] Climate change, affected by the actions of humans, also affects weather patterns, which causes storms to be more powerful and to grow in number. In his 2009 inauguration address, the president remarked, "The ways we use energy . . . threaten our planet,"[55] drawing a clear line between our actions and the changes in weather. In discussing environmental issues, Zeitlin remarks, "I could never begin to confront this problem as a politician or as a call to action. . . . My interest in this story was much more, 'How do you emotionally survive inevitability?'"[56] However, by making the viewer think about the environment and how it is affected, by focusing the viewer's attention on a part of America that is off the grid and that lives every day with the consequences of our actions on the environment, and finally by giving us Hushpuppy's world view as a model to follow in order to be kinder to nature, Zeitlin is definitely political.

In several of his interviews, the director discusses at length what challenges are created for the people in south Louisiana by the actions taken in "the dry world":

> As you drive south in Louisiana, there's basically an environmental apocalypse moving from the Gulf of Mexico inland, with the salt water infusion, the rising water, and the barrier islands falling apart.[57]

> The canals that have been cut for oil drilling are allowing salt water in, the trees are being killed by salt water, the fish are being killed by salt water. . . . The levees that have been put around the Mississippi are not allowing the land to replenish itself with silt.[58]

One of the first scenes of the film has Wink and Hushpuppy in their boat near the bridge that still connects the Bathtub to the rest of the world. They are both looking at the heavily industrialized zone beyond the levee, which seems to loom over the Bathtub as ominously as the smoke coming out of the stacks of the oil refineries. Wink says, "Ain't that ugly over there? We got the prettiest place on earth."[59] He is clearly situating himself in an "us vs. them" mentality, which becomes more evident as the film unfolds.

As if the levees and the storms were not enough, reality also intruded while the crew was filming in south Louisiana: the BP Deepwater Horizon spill happened in April 2010 and continued for three months. The crew was not aware of the spill in the beginning, but then Zeitlin recalls that when they were in Montegut, Louisiana, "there was a real sense this could be the end of the town. One day, there was even an announcement that they were going to close fishing for 10 years, which would have been a death sentence."[60] As another consequence of the oil spill, the crew had to fight in order to be able to film in certain locations because the Army took some of them over in the effort to contain the damage caused by the spill. Ray Tintori, special effects director on the film, remarks: "Suddenly it didn't feel histrionic to be making a film about the apocalypse when the world was very aggressively disintegrating around us."[61] The damage caused to the ecosystem by the oil spill is extensive. According to NOAA, "the oil spill and plume covered almost 360 square miles with the most severe reduction of biological abundance and biodiversity impacting an area about 9 square miles around the wellhead, and moderate effects seen 57 square miles around the wellhead."[62] As this essay was being completed, one of the former BP drilling engineers was found guilty of hiding information about the spill by deleting text messages from his phone and interfering with the evidence.[63]

The intersections of the film with reality are multiple, and one cannot ignore the way the screenplay was completed. Inspired by a play that Zeitlin's co-writer Lucy Alibar wrote in order to come to terms with the loss of her father,[64] the screenplay for *Beasts* was, according to Zeitlin, completed and rewritten as the film was being shot. "Zeitlin didn't so much make *Beasts* as mine it," Lidz notes, "generating material with his cast, then working with each actor individually. 'The narrative changed and adapted to whatever was going on,' he says. 'We tested it against the actual people and places that are in it.'"[65] Traditionally, the script is completed before shooting begins, but Zeitlin managed to create a democratic enterprise where the crew members were asked for input and the script was completed in an organic approach: "It wasn't like we locked the script and went down there and executed it. We had a very fluid plan responding to the world that we were discovering as we did our research."[66]

In keeping with the organic approach and with the idea of sustainability, the sets for the film were built out of materials found on site. The boat that Hushpuppy and Wink use in the bayou was made out of Zeitlin's old truck: "It was a blue Chevy that I got for $500, and it was basically dead when I bought it."[67] After the truck caught fire and seemed to have run its usefulness, it was turned into part of the set. When the film opens, the sight of the shacks in which the two protagonists live is arresting: they are made of leftover wood planks and metal sheets, and surrounded by old tires, wheels, parts of engines, rusty gas tanks, and rusty metal pans. Within the discourse of the film, the viewer understands that all these objects were repurposed presumably by Wink, but when one looks at the way the film was made, the same repurposing took place: "The world of this movie is all about scrapping together whatever's nearby and making something useful and beautiful," Alex DiGerlando, the production designer, remarks.[68] What is more, the sets doubled as bedrooms for some of the crew: "Benh's sister stayed in Wink's house.... And someone else slept in the school boat we built."[69] In making the film, Zeitlin also proposes a way to do so that is based on repurposing and being environmentally aware.

The casting of the film took the same organic approach. Instead of hiring actors, Zeitlin and his crew decided to use locals: "Everybody who is in the film is from south Louisiana."[70] In searching for Hushpuppy and Wink, the director and his team posted fliers in New Orleans and "held grass-roots meetings in community centers and schools, a strategy they had learned while working on Barack Obama's first presidential campaign."[71] The fact that part of the movie crew was connected with and worked on President Obama's first campaign should not surprise anyone by now, as the film itself espouses many of his views on race in America and the environment.

Speaking about the casting of locals, Dunn aptly remarks:

> [The film] doesn't merely indulge in mythologizing the moral dignity of poverty but rather wants to suggest the very real resilience of the human and cultural spirit of people in the midst of suffering and who are unapologetically proud of being folks whose identity is inextricable from their Louisiana, hurricane-ridden, homeland, and who would rather die than abandon that tie. The casting of non-actors from Louisiana helps to convey that genuine ethos.[72]

Dwight Henry, the now-famous New Orleans baker who plays Wink, is a hurricane survivor himself and did not evacuate during Katrina.[73] He weathered his first hurricane (Betsy) when he was two years old.[74] He also states in an interview that "I really felt some of the things that we were doing in the film; I felt it in real life."[75] Henry owns the Buttermilk Drop Bakery and Café in New Orleans. When offered the role of Wink, he refused it because he did not want to put his business in jeopardy. When he finally agreed, they had to rehearse in the bakery at night, while he was preparing the food for the next day. Zeitlin remarks: "One of the things that made me know he was right for the role is I saw that he cared as much about his bakery as I cared about the film and as much as Wink, the character, he cares about his town."[76]

The story around casting Quvenzhané Wallis in the role of Hushpuppy is by now the stuff of legend: initially, four thousand little girls were auditioned for the role.[77] Of the twenty little girls that were called back, half were white.[78] Finally, Zeitlin explained why he decided to give Wallis the role even though she was five, not six: she was what he was looking for, "somebody who was fearless."[79] On her acting in the film, Wallis has this to say: "I didn't even know about acting. That was just me. Bored. Happy. Sad. Mad. Angry. Everything just popped out of me."[80] Zeitlin's move proved to be very inspired, as Quvenzhané ended up being the youngest nominee for an Academy Award in the Best Actress category and "the 10th African American in 85 years to get a best actress nod. Halle Berry remains the only winner in this category."[81]

As one can see, the intersections of *Beasts* with reality are multiple. The "age of Obama" did not bring only race to the forefront as a topic of discussion, but also the environment, among other issues. The film is part of a conversation on climate change and consequences of human choices that affect the environment and the planet in general that was started by the president in his first inaugural address and that continues to this day. There are a lot of dissenting voices (Al Gore's, among others) that point out that so far, the president's environmental agenda is a failure. However, starting with the first year of President Obama's first term, and continuing into his second term, carbon dioxide emissions in the United States have decreased by 12 percent, which is very close to the 17 percent pledged by the United States in 2009.[82] Green energy was subsidized to the tune of $90 billion through the American Recovery and Reinvestment Act—a fact that gave a boost not only to new industry, but to the research connected to it. Finally, Jonathan Chait aptly notes that "the administration has also carried out an ambitious program of regulation, having imposed or announced higher standards for gas mileage in cars, fuel cleanliness, energy efficiency in appliances, and emissions from new power plants. In aggregate, they amount to a major assault on climate change."[83] In his remarks on climate change at Georgetown University, the president announced a new national climate action plan that included acknowledging that our actions affect our planet in a drastic way: "Our planet is changing in ways that will have profound impacts on all of humankind. . . . The 12 warmest years in recorded history have all come in the last 15 years. Last year, . . . ice in the Arctic shrank to its smallest size on record—faster than most models had predicted it would."[84] Ice in the Arctic and its apocalyptic sounds as it melts and falls in the ocean are both part of the *Beasts* discourse, and the haunting images and sounds keep coming up every time Hushpuppy thinks she did "something bad" that affects her whole universe. In Roger Ebert's words, Hushpuppy is the "new generation put forward in desperate times by the human race."[85] Zeitlin offers us a way of thinking that involves the awareness that all our actions impact the planet, if not now, then in the near future. The future is bleak, in terms of the environment: "The planet will slowly keep warming for some time to come. The seas will slowly keep rising and storms will get more severe, based on the science. . . . You and your children, and your children's children, will have to live with the consequences of our decisions,"[86] the president says, and in offering solutions, he urges the youth to "spread the word: Understand this is not a job only for politicians. So I'm going to need all of you to educate your classmates, your colleagues, your parents, your friends. Tell them what's at stake. Speak up at town halls, church groups, PTA meetings. Push back on misinformation. Speak up for the facts."[87] It is this type of grassroots initiative that will work, coupled with decisive political action, the president says, and will help us preserve what we still have of the environment.

Zeitlin's film seems to be part of this grassroots initiative to remind the public that we need to focus on our environment. It proposes a way of thinking and looking at the world that would push us into action to protect our planet and save it from an ecological disaster, which is in line with President Obama's initiatives on the environment. What Zeitlin is urging us to take from the Bathtub and its undisputed queen, Hushpuppy, is the incredible passion for the land, the joy of living every moment to the fullest, and the awareness that we need to see ourselves "a little piece of a big, big universe,"[88] a fact which hopefully will shape our responses to the consequences of climate change, and a fact which, in Hushpuppy's words, "makes things right."[89]

NOTES

1. IMDb.com.
2. IMDb.com.
3. Franz Lidz, "Light and Magic," *Smithsonian* 43, no. 8 (2012).
4. Lidz, "Light and Magic."
5. Manohla Dargis, quoted in Lidz, "Light and Magic."
6. Rebecca Harkins-Cross, "Surviving Life in the Bathtub: Beasts of the Southern Wild," *Screen Education* 68 (2013): 19–27.
7. Stephane Dunn, "Into the 'Wild': The Arresting Poetry of *Beasts of the Southern Wild*," *NewBlackMan*, January 13, 2013.
8. Roger Ebert, Review of *Beasts of the Southern Wild*, RogerEbert.com, July 4, 2012.
9. Derek Daschke, Review of *Beasts of the Southern Wild*, *Journal of Religion and Film* 16, no. 1 (2012), 4.
10. Peter Howell, "'Beasting It' with Benh Zeitlin," *Toronto Star* (Canada), July 13, 2012.
11. "I was focused on trying to get the movie to a version I could live with. But it's been an amazing experience to see the film travel this far. It was just such a ragtag little film when we were making it. I don't think anybody ever imagined that the movie would be so big while we were doing it" ("Personal Quotes," IMDb.com).
12. "Chilling: Art about Climate Change," *Economist* 408, no. 8845 (2013): 72.
13. "Chilling," 72.
14. bell hooks, "No Love in the Wild," *NewBlackMan*, September 5, 2012.
15. Agnes Woolley, "The Politics of Myth Making: *Beasts of the Southern Wild*," *Open Democracy: Free Thinking for the World*, October 29, 2012, http://www.opendemocracy.net/5050/agnes-woolley/politics-of-myth-making-beasts-of-southern-wild.
16. "[The film's] mythic, magical-realist form not only occludes a troubling representational politics, but also permits its director to evade questions surrounding changing social and political relations in the era of climate change." Woolley, "The Politics of Myth Making."
17. hooks, "No Love in the Wild."
18. Benh Zeitlin, dir., *Beasts of the Southern Wild* (Los Angeles: Fox Searchlight, 2012), DVD.
19. hooks, "No Love in the Wild."
20. As an aside, and also to anchor this argument into reality, as I was watching *Beasts* again, my daughters (nine and seven) saw the first few frames of the film, and the first question they asked me was, "Mommy, is that a boy or a girl?"
21. hooks, "No Love in the Wild."
22. Zeitlin, *Beasts of the Southern Wild*.
23. Ebert, Review of *Beasts of the Southern Wild*.
24. Zeitlin, *Beasts of the Southern Wild*.
25. Zeitlin, *Beasts of the Southern Wild*.
26. hooks, "No Love in the Wild."

27. Charlie Rose, "Conversation with Benh Zeitlin; Conversation with Allen Pizzey." *Charlie Rose Show* (MSNBC), February 7, 2013.
28. Zeitlin, *Beasts of the Southern Wild*.
29. David Larsen, "Four Shades of Angry," *Metro* (NZ) 369 (2012): 112.
30. Zeitlin, *Beasts of the Southern Wild*.
31. Harkins-Cross, "Surviving Life in the Bathtub."
32. Note also that when she gets to Batsheba, Hushpuppy only tells her that Wink "fell down," even though she believes that she "broke" him. She is afraid to admit to another adult the enormity of what she has done, so she uses a euphemism, which is also symptomatic of the way a young child behaves and thinks.
33. Rose, "Conversation with Benh Zeitlin."
34. Woolley, "The Politics of Myth Making."
35. Rose, "Conversation with Benh Zeitlin."
36. Larsen, "Four Shades of Angry."
37. Dunn, "Into the 'Wild.'"
38. Woolley, "The Politics of Myth Making."
39. hooks, "No Love in the Wild."
40. Zeitlin, *Beasts of the Southern Wild*.
41. Zeitlin, *Beasts of the Southern Wild*.
42. hooks, "No Love in the Wild."
43. Woolley, "The Politics of Myth Making."
44. Barack Obama, *The Audacity of Hope* (New York: Vintage Books, 2008), 271.
45. Jada Yuan, "Born on the Bayou: How *Beasts of the Southern Wild* (and Its 8-Year-Old Star) Became a Film-Fest Phenomenon," *New York Magazine*, June 25, 2012, 122.
46. Zeitlin, *Beasts of the Southern Wild*.
47. Zeitlin, *Beasts of the Southern Wild*.
48. Lidz, "Light and Magic."
49. Zeitlin, quoted in Lidz, "Light and Magic."
50. Obama, *The Audacity of Hope*, 274.
51. Obama, *The Audacity of Hope*, 276.
52. Harkins-Cross, "Surviving Life in the Bathtub."
53. Howell, "'Beasting It' with Benh Zeitlin."
54. "Inaugural Address by President Obama," WhiteHouse.gov, January 21, 2013, http://www.whitehouse.gov/the-press-office/2013/01/21/inaugural-address-president-barack-obama.
55. "President Barack Obama's Inaugural Address," WhiteHouse.gov, January 20, 2009, http://www.whitehouse.gov/blog/inaugural-address/.
56. Zeitlin, quoted in Harkins-Cross, "Surviving Life in the Bathtub."
57. Zeitlin, quoted in Peter Debruge, "Benh Zeitlin: *Beasts of the Southern Wild*," *Variety*, December 13, 2012.
58. Zeitlin, quoted in Harkins-Cross, "Surviving Life in the Bathtub."
59. Zeitlin, *Beasts of the Southern Wild*.
60. Stephen Galloway, "Making of *Beasts of the Southern Wild*," *Hollywood Reporter* 40 (2012): 108.
61. Yuan, "Born on the Bayou."
62. "Deep Sea Ecosystem May Take Decades to Recover from Deepwater Horizon Spill," *NOAA*, September 25, 2013.
63. Michael Kunzelman, "Former BP Engineer Kurt Mix Convicted on Obstruction Charge for Destroying Gulf Spill Evidence." *Huffington Post*, December 26, 2013.
64. Lidz, "Light and Magic."
65. Lidz, "Light and Magic."
66. Peter Debruge, "Benh Zeitlin."
67. Zeitlin, quoted in Galloway, "Making of *Beasts of the Southern Wild*."
68. Christopher Ross, "The Backstory: Inside This Month's Eye-Popping Film," *Details* 30, no. 8 (2012).
69. Producer Penn, quoted in Galloway, "Making of *Beasts of the Southern Wild*."
70. Zeitlin, quoted in Rose, "Conversation with Benh Zeitlin."

71. Galloway, "Making of *Beasts of the Southern Wild*."
72. Dunn, "Into the 'Wild.'"
73. Roy Blount, "Beasts of the Southern Wild," *Smithsonian* 44, no. 3 (2013): 66.
74. Steven Zeitchick, "*Beasts of the Southern Wild*: A Conversation with the Cast and the Crew," The Envelope Screening Series by the *Los Angeles Times*, 2013.
75. Zeitchick, "*Beasts of the Southern Wild*."
76. Zeitlin, quoted in Rose, "Conversation with Benh Zeitlin."
77. Rose, "Conversation with Benh Zeitlin."
78. Lidz, "Light and Magic."
79. Zeitlin, quoted in Rose, "Conversation with Benh Zeitlin."
80. Yuan, "Born on the Bayou."
81. Miki Turner, "Hollywood's New 'It Girl' Keeps It Real," *Root*, January 19, 2013.
82. Jonathan Chait, "Obama Might Actually Be the Environmental President," *New York Magazine*, May 5, 2013.
83. Chait, "Obama Might Actually Be the Environmental President."
84. Chait, "Obama Might Actually Be the Environmental President."
85. Ebert, Review of *Beasts of the Southern Wild*.
86. "Remarks by the President on Climate Change," WhiteHouse.gov, June 25, 2012, http://www.whitehouse.gov/the-press-office/2013/06/25/remarks-president-climate-change (accessed February 12, 2014).
87. "Remarks by the President on Climate Change."
88. Zeitlin, *Beasts of the Southern Wild*.
89. Zeitlin, *Beasts of the Southern Wild*.

REFERENCES

Blount, Roy. "Beasts of the Southern Wild." *Smithsonian* 44, no. 3 (2013): 66.
Chait, Jonathan. "Obama Might Actually Be the Environmental President." *New York Magazine*, May 5, 2013.
"Chilling: Art about Climate Change." *Economist* 408, no. 8845 (2013): 72–73.
Debruge, Peter. "Benh Zeitlin: *Beasts of the Southern Wild*." *Variety*, December 13, 2012.
"Deep Sea Ecosystem May Take Decades to Recover from Deepwater Horizon Spill." *NOAA*, September 25, 2013.
Dunn, Stephane. "Into the 'Wild': The Arresting Poetry of *Beasts of the Southern Wild*." *NewBlackMan*, January 13, 2013.
Ebert, Roger. Review of *Beasts of the Southern Wild*. RogerEbert.com, July 4, 2012.
Galloway, Stephen. "Making of *Beasts of the Southern Wild*." *Hollywood Reporter* 40 (2012): 108.
Harkins-Cross, Rebecca. "Surviving Life in the Bathtub: Beasts of the Southern Wild." *Screen Education* 68 (2013): 19–27.
hooks, bell. "No Love in the Wild." *NewBlackMan*, September 5, 2012.
Howell, Peter. "'Beasting It' with Benh Zeitlin." *Toronto Star* (Canada), July 13, 2012.
"Inaugural Address by President Obama." WhiteHouse.gov, January 21, 2013. http://www.whitehouse.gov/the-press-office/2013/01/21/inaugural-address-president-barack-obama.
Kunzelman, Michael. "Former BP Engineer Kurt Mix Convicted on Obstruction Charge for Destroying Gulf Spill Evidence." *Huffington Post*, December 26, 2013.
Larsen, David. "Four Shades of Angry." *Metro* (NZ) 369 (2012): 112.
Lidz, Franz. "Light and Magic." *Smithsonian* 43, no. 8 (2012).
Obama, Barack. *The Audacity of Hope*. New York: Vintage Books, 2008.
"President Barack Obama's Inaugural Address." WhiteHouse.gov, January 20, 2009. http://www.whitehouse.gov/blog/inaugural-address/.
"Remarks by the President on Climate Change." WhiteHouse.gov, June 25 2013. http://www.whitehouse.gov/the-press-office/2013/06/25/remarks-president-climate-change.
Rose, Charlie. "Conversation with Benh Zeitlin; Conversation with Allen Pizzey." *Charlie Rose Show* (MSNBC), February 7, 2013.

Ross, Christopher. "The Backstory: Inside This Month's Eye-Popping Film." *Details* 30, no. 8 (2012).
Turner, Miki. "Hollywood's New 'It Girl' Keeps It Real." *Root*, January 19, 2013.
Woolley, Agnes. "The Politics of Myth Making: *Beasts of the Southern Wild*." *Open Democracy: Free Thinking for the World*, October 29, 2012. http://www.opendemocracy.net/5050/agnes-woolley/politics-of-myth-making-beasts-of-southern-wild.
Yuan, Jada. "Born on the Bayou: How *Beasts of the Southern Wild* (and Its 8-Year-Old Star) Became a Film-Fest Phenomenon." *New York Magazine*, June 25, 2012.
Zeitchick, Steven. "*Beasts of the Southern Wild*: A Conversation with the Cast and the Crew." The Envelope Screening Series by the *Los Angeles Times*, 2013.
Zeitlin, Benh, dir. *Beasts of the Southern Wild*. Los Angeles: Fox Searchlight, 2012, DVD.

Chapter Eleven

It's Not a Wonderful Life: The Financial Crisis on Film and the Limits of Hollywood Liberalism

Peter Grosvenor

The science-fiction action thriller *Elysium* (2013) is set in the year 2154. A small hyper-wealthy elite lives a luxurious existence on the Elysium space station, while the mass of humankind struggles against poverty and disease among the ruins of an overpopulated and environmentally devastated Earth that is policed by robots. It is an explicitly political film that condemns economic exploitation and unambiguously calls for restored civil liberties, open borders, and universal health care. The film is South African writer/director Neill Blomkamp's second venture into progressive science fiction, having enjoyed unexpected success with his *District 9* (2009)—an allegory on racism, apartheid, and post-apartheid inequality.

The star of *Elysium* is Matt Damon, one of Hollywood's leading actor-activists. In promoting the film on Black Entertainment Television (BET), Damon regretted that he and President Obama had gone their separate ways politically—"He broke up with me," as he put it.[1] In that BET interview, Damon pointed to drone strikes and to the pursuit of National Security Agency whistleblower Edward Snowden as his most recent disagreements with the president. He even cited former president Jimmy Carter's recent assertion that "America does not have a functioning democracy at this point in time."[2]

Damon had been an early and vocal supporter of then-Senator Obama in the 2008 Democratic primaries, but he has since become one of the most severe celebrity critics on the president's left. Obama even used the 2011 White House Correspondents' Dinner to reply to an earlier Damon criticism: "Matt Damon said he was disappointed in my performance. Well, Matt, I just saw *The Adjustment Bureau*, so right back atcha, buddy!"[3]

Hollywood liberals appear to be replicating with President Obama their earlier relationship of infatuation and disappointment with Bill Clinton. It would be easy to dismiss this replication as an indicator of the political naïveté, fickleness, and short attention spans of movie types, and no doubt that is part of the explanation in some cases. But that would be to miss a much larger point: the frustrations of Hollywood liberalism are intimately connected to a crisis in American liberalism itself—and perhaps, as Carter indicated, to a crisis in American democracy itself. That crisis is the inability of civic institutions to hold private economic power to account—a failure that subverts the central assumptions of political liberalism and thwarts Hollywood liberalism in what can be argued to be its core mission: to restore America to its ideals. The conjoined on-screen and off-screen crises of liberalism are nowhere better illustrated than in cinema's response to the financial crisis of 2008 and the Great Recession.

The terms of American political debate have been fundamentally altered twice in the past ten years. Americans faced the new millennium with a confident expectation of a second American century. The 1989 fall of the Berlin Wall, followed by the sustained economic growth and technological innovation of the 1990s, appeared to support the claim by political scientist Francis Fukuyama that history itself had come to an end, at least if history is interpreted as a conflict of ideologies.[4]

The decade of economic buoyancy accelerated the trend, first identified in the 1970s by political sociologist Ronald Inglehart, toward "post-material" politics.[5] Traditional preoccupations with material issues such as employment, wages, and housing receded as environmentalism and identity politics moved forward. Although the 1990s saw the emergence of an amorphous and inchoate left-wing critique of, and movement against, corporatization and globalization, the decade's political discourse remained dominated by a *Kulturkampf* over social issues such as abortion, contraception, civil unions, gay marriage, and affirmative action.[6]

The first change in the tenor of American politics came, of course, with the collapse of the Twin Towers in the terrorist attacks of September 11, 2001, after which Samuel Huntington's "clash of civilizations" thesis supplanted the "end of history" in America's sense of itself and its place in the world.[7] National security, warfare, and civil liberties came to the forefront of political debate. The second change came with the collapse of Lehman Brothers, and the crisis in the subprime lending market, in 2008. This was the most serious financial emergency since the Great Depression of the 1930s, and it turned the economic slowdown that had begun the year before into the Great Recession. Suddenly, material issues of job security, home ownership, living standards, and health care came back to the fore.

These transformations in American political discourse were registered in cinema. The preoccupation with the destabilization of traditional identities was a major theme of 1990s American cinema.[8] But those issues seemed to lose something of their immediacy following 9/11, and the debate over the so-called War on Terror came to prominence on the screen.[9] During both these periods, issues of economic inequality and injustice were relatively—though by no means entirely—neglected by American filmmakers, or else were explored as subordinate themes in films concerned with environmental or identity politics. The effect of the financial crisis was to stimulate cinematic interest in economic justice to an extent that had not been seen since the 1970s, which produced films such as *Bound for Glory* (1976), *Blue Collar* (1978), *F.I.S.T* (1978), and, most notably, the powerfully pro-union *Norma Rae* (1979).

Even before the crisis, twenty-first-century cinema had engaged with concerns over globalization and corporate power. Stephanie Black's compelling 2001 documentary *Life and Debt* excoriates the International Monetary Fund (IMF) and the World Bank for the consequences of their structural adjustment policies in Jamaica. The collapse of the Enron Corporation, and the criminal trials of some of its leading executives, was the subject of *Enron: The Smartest Guys in the Room* (2005), a documentary from director Alex Gibney. Based on the book by financial journalists Bethany Maclean and Peter Elkind, the film is narrated by veteran left-wing actor Peter Coyote.

The protests that disrupted the World Trade Organization (WTO) summit meeting in 1999 were brought to the screen by first-time director Stuart Townsend in *The Battle in Seattle* (2007). The film clearly aligns itself with the critique of the labor and environmental practices of corporations operating in the developing world. At the same time, it thoughtfully examines the conflicts not only between the police and the protesting crowds but also between the peaceful and violent protesters. The late Roger Ebert loosely compared it with Haskell Wexler's landmark *Medium Cool* (1969), a film about the demonstrations outside the 1968 Democratic National Convention in Chicago.[10]

There were also less pointedly political treatments of working life in the "new economy." *Office Space* (1999), from director Mike Judge, is a satire set among the alienated employees of a software company. Jason Reitman's *Thank You for Smoking* (2005) lampooned corporate ethics, focusing on Hollywood's favorite incarnation of evil, the tobacco industry. And in John Jeffcoat's romantic comedy *Outsourced* (2006), a Seattle-based employee in the call center of an American novelty products firm is sent to India to train his own replacement. Toward the end of the film, the jobs of the Indian call center workers are in turn outsourced to China. The film gave rise to an NBC spin-off television series in 2010–2011.

Post–financial crisis, however, cinema's engagement with economic justice issues has become more serious and sustained, most notably in documentary form, but also in drama. As Terry Christensen and Peter J. Haas have noted, "the improbable ascent of the documentary film" has been one of the most notable developments in late twentieth-/early twenty-first-century popular cinema: eight of the top ten most commercially successful nonmusical documentaries of all time were produced after the year 2000.[11] The efforts of documentary filmmakers to explain the financial crisis, to analyze its causes, and to illustrate its human effects have been considerable.

Obviously, conservative political ideas can find effective expression in documentary form, as in the case of Davis Guggenheim's *Waiting for Superman* (2010), which aggressively promoted the case for charter schools. Significantly, however, there have been no post-crash documentaries seeking to affirm America's contemporary economic structures or to defend Wall Street. But two radical documentaries appeared in 2009: *The Shock Doctrine* and *Capitalism: A Love Story*. *The Shock Doctrine*, from British filmmakers Michael Winterbottom and Mat Whitecross, and narrated by Kieran O'Brien, had its U.S. premiere at the Sundance Film Festival. It has been widely shown across the United States, especially on college campuses, and has become part of the American debate over the relationship between economic and political power in the new millennium. Winterbottom is an eclectic director whose earlier expressly political films include *Welcome to Sarajevo* (1997) and *The Road to Guantanamo* (2006), the latter also co-directed with Whitecross.

The Shock Doctrine is based on the 2007 book of the same name by the Canadian journalist and political activist Naomi Klein. In partnership with Alfonso Cuarón, Klein made a six-minute short film promoting the book. Klein has sought to return the left to a more materialist analysis of economic globalization and the social stratification to which it gives rise. Following her anti-corporate polemic *No Logo* (1999), published shortly after the Seattle WTO protests, Klein emerged as an intellectual leader of the so-called alter-globalization movement, which seeks to harness greater connectivity for the cause of economic and social justice. In 2004, Klein herself made a radical documentary, in collaboration with Avi Lewis, which told the story of Argentinean workers who took over and ran a closed-down factory.

Winterbottom and Whitecross vividly illustrate *The Shock Doctrine*'s disturbing connection between psychiatric electric shock treatment, economic shock therapy, and "shock-and-awe" military strategy. One reviewer of the book cleverly anticipated its film potential when he remarked that it was "as though *One Flew Over the Cuckoo's Nest* had been mixed with *The Quiet American*."[12]

Klein's starting point is Dr. Ewan Cameron, a psychiatrist who conducted electric shock experiments on patients at McGill University during the 1950s. It was later revealed that Cameron was part of a CIA research program. Cameron's aim was to use electric shocks to break down psychiatric patients as a prelude to rebuilding their personalities. This process was known as "depatterning," and it is chillingly illustrated by Winterbottom and Whitecross's use of actual footage of patients receiving this treatment. The film also contains a poignant interview with one of the victims of this experiment.

At the same time that Cameron was conducting his experiments in Montreal, Milton Friedman was developing his neoliberal theories of economics at the University of Chicago. In Klein's analysis, there is a close parallel between psychiatric depatterning and the imposition of neoliberal privatization, marketization, and deregulation on countries that have experienced "shocks" such as wars, coups d'état, and natural disasters that undermine, or even sweep away, previous economic institutions. In fact, "shock treatment" appears to have been coined as an economic term by Friedman in an April 1975 letter to Chilean dictator Augusto Pinochet, to whom he acted as an adviser.[13]

Clearly, Thatcher and Reagan advanced neoliberalism through the ballot box, but equally clearly, both looked to Pinochet's Chile as an economic model. In 1973, the democratically elected socialist government of Salvador Allende was overthrown in a CIA-backed coup, and Chile became the laboratory of neoliberal economic reform.[14] Klein uses the term "disaster capitalism" to describe neoliberalism's progress around the world in the wake of "shocks." Her examples include development of turbo-capitalism, and massive economic inequality, in Yeltsin's Russia, the Sri Lankan government's opportunistic use of the 2004 tsunami to force fishermen off beachfronts to make way for hotel developers, and the replacement of the previous public education structure of New Orleans with a voucher system in the wake of Hurricane Katrina. The left-wing British commentator Owen Jones has extrapolated Klein's argument to explain the dismantling of European welfare states in the name of bond market–imposed deficit reduction.[15]

Jones is using the Klein thesis in its most radical form: the contention that neoliberalism exports itself through the actual induction of the "shocks" that clear the ground for it—as Klein herself argues was the case with the Bush administration's "shock-and-awe" invasion of Iraq. From this perspective, the Iraq War and its aftermath were globalization by force: conveniently, de-Baathification was also neoliberalization, and the principal beneficiaries were Western, primarily American, contractors and developers. In Klein's terms, the Green Zone in Baghdad was created as a model neoliberal city-state. Iraq is the culmination of the film's argument, according to which there is a discernible line of progression from Dr. Cameron's laboratory, through to Pinochet's torture chambers and on to Abu Ghraib.

Klein's location of the Iraq War's true motivations in the economic interests of U.S. elites was anticipated by veteran left-wing documentary polemicist Michael Moore in his 2004 film *Fahrenheit 9/11*. Moore has been an unabashed class warrior on behalf of America's blue-collar workers for over two decades. In 1989, he broke new ground in documentary filmmaking with *Roger and Me*. Throughout that film, Moore's efforts to personally confront General Motors (GM) CEO Roger Smith over the downsizing of GM plants in Moore's hometown of Flint, Michigan, serve as a metaphor for the unaccountability of private economic power in contemporary America. The film's principal device is comedy, which it blends powerfully with a pathos that it achieves by its documenting the hardships of Flint residents—hardships that are emblematic of an American middle class in decline. The same economic analysis informs *Fahrenheit 9/11*. The film aims to expose the Bush administration's entire case for the war in Iraq as an elaborate fraud from which crony capitalism was the true beneficiary, and its chosen device is the unsparing comic manipulation of media images of key administration officials, including Bush himself.

Before public support for the war collapsed in 2006, this was dangerous territory. In the buildup to the war in 2003, Natalie Maines, the lead vocalist with the country music band the Dixie Chicks, said from a London stage that she and her two fellow band members were ashamed that Bush was from their home state of Texas. What followed were demonstrations outside their concert venues, boycotts of their music by radio stations, and even death threats. In 2006, directors Barbara Kopple and Cecelia Peck cataloged all this in the documentary *Shut Up and Sing*, which follows the band's ordeal through to the release of their defiant single "Not Ready to Make Nice." Against the background of such a reaction to a singer's on-stage remark, it is unsurprising that Moore's detailed and fundamental attack on the Bush administration's foreign policy would prove to be the most controversial American documentary of the new millennium.

By contrast, it is a significant indicator of the change in America's political climate that *Capitalism: A Love Story*—so far, Moore's only major work in the Obama era—seems to have drawn just the predictable opprobrium of the political right. *Capitalism* may be no more sympathetic to its subject than is *The Shock Doctrine*, but Moore's analysis is not Klein's neo-Marxism; rather, it is a root-and-branch excoriation of the ethics on which Moore believes the contemporary capitalist system to be based: "giving and taking, mainly taking." Moore believes that the nature of American capitalism was fundamentally transformed in the Reagan era, and that in its deregulated, finance-dominated form, it ceaselessly undermines earlier American values and promotes individualism, selfishness, greed, and venality. He even gives an approving nod to Jimmy Carter's badly received address to the nation in July 1979, in which the president lamented the consumerism that had engulfed American culture.

The film opens with video footage of actual bank robberies, and later gives voice to victims of foreclosure who feel themselves moved close to physical violence by their experiences. It progresses to a comedic comparison between the contemporary United States and a Roman empire in decay. But the film really begins where Moore himself began, in Flint, Michigan. Moore was born in 1954 to a blue-collar family that shared in the prosperity of post-WWII, and we are treated to home-movie footage of his childhood.

In *Roger and Me*, Moore was concerned with the rusting of American industrial capitalism and its effects on the community with which he has never ceased to identify. But in *Capitalism*, the focus switches to financial capitalism and its domination of the real economy. The visual Moore selects is footage of Donald Regan standing next to President Reagan at the New York Stock Exchange. From 1971 to 1980, Regan was chairman and CEO of Merrill Lynch; for Moore, his appointment first as Reagan's treasury secretary, and then as White House chief of staff, symbolizes the financial takeover not only of the American economy but of American politics. Henry Paulson, formerly of Goldman Sachs, is Moore's symbol of financial dominance for the Bush era.

Central to the film's analysis is the case of Citigroup's leaked "plutonomy memos." Plutonomy is a form of political economy characterized by an upward flow of wealth—the opposite of "trickle-down" Reaganomics—and Citigroup approvingly identified the United States as the prime example of such an economy. A recurring Moore technique is to allow his targets to condemn themselves in their own words, and there is a remarkably large supply of volunteers to provide the necessary self-incrimination. *Wall Street Journal* editorial board member Stephen Moore, for example, un-self-consciously states to the camera that "I think capitalism is more important than democracy. I'm not even a big fan of democracy."

Moore's central point is that concentrations of wealth lead to concentrations of power that are ultimately undemocratic. He holds that the Bush administration's $700 billion bailout of the banks in 2008, for which he indicts Democrats as well as Republicans, was nothing short of a financial coup d'état—and he gets Ohio Democratic congresswoman Marcy Kaptur to agree with him. What follows is the signature Moore device pioneered in *Roger and Me*: a comic series of thwarted efforts to "speak truth to power," in the academic cliché, by visiting financial institutions to get the taxpayers' money back and to place the directors under citizen's arrest.

But Moore is clearly in earnest in his conclusion that America has effectively become a post-democratic society—a plutonomy, in fact. He tells his audience that "capitalism is an evil, and you cannot regulate evil. You have to eliminate it, and replace it with something that is good for all the people . . . " This sounds unambiguously socialist. Indeed, the film's play-out music is "The Internationale." But it is an ironic show tunes version, by lounge singer Tony Babino. Moore concludes his sentence with " . . . and that something is called democracy." His appeal, ultimately, is not to socialism but to Jeffersonian democracy, and to the New Deal that he believes saved democracy in the 1930s. His footage of the National Guard's deployment to defend the sit-down strikers against strikebreakers at the GM plant in Flint in 1937 is his vision of the proper relationship between politics and capital. What he wants is the Second Bill of Rights proposed by Franklin Roosevelt in his 1944 state of the union address—a guarantee of the economic pluralism that is the necessary precondition of political pluralism.

Close to the end of his film, Moore says, "I refuse to live in a country like this, and I'm not leaving." He calls upon his audience to help him restore American democracy. The problem is that, apart from a favorable nod to workers' co-operatives of the kind also supported by Klein, he does not tell us what he wants us to do. And that is precisely what also disappoints about the Academy Award–winning documentary *Inside Job* (2010), produced, written, and directed by Charles Ferguson, and narrated by Obama critic Matt Damon. Like Klein and Moore, Ferguson turned his attention to the economy after criticizing the Iraq War: his directorial debut was *No End in Sight* (2007), a documentary about the Bush administration's tragedy of errors during the invasion and occupation.

Unlike *Capitalism*, *Inside Job* makes no use of humor. The film's atmosphere is that of a brisk-paced and enthralling thriller, though not a satisfying one—the villains walk away not only unpunished but generously compensated. But, as good thrillers often do, *Inside Job* has a startling opening that pulls the viewer into what is about to unfold.

The film opens with vistas of Iceland's volcanic topography and tranquil communities, immediately establishing the global nature of the financial crisis—something entirely missing from Moore's more parochially American perspective. We are then presented with three stark Icelandic statistics: population 320,000; gross domestic product $13 billion; bank losses $100 billion. This was the outcome of what Damon's narration describes as "one of the purest experiments in financial deregulation ever conducted." Leading Icelandic novelist and environmentalist Andri Magnason tells Ferguson that until that deregulation in 2000, his country had enjoyed "end of history status." Then, as University of Iceland economist Gylfi Zoega explains, "Finance took over and more or less wrecked the place." Ferguson cuts away from Iceland and brings the film home: the film's opening credits run over stunning panoramas of New York while Peter Gabriel's "Big Time" (1986) appropriately evokes the Reagan-era origins of financial deregulation.

The film very effectively explains through narration, graphics, and expert testimony the process by which a mutually reinforcing combination of deregulation and technological innovation resulted in the proliferation of increasingly complex derivatives, the development of securitization, the inflation of a real estate bubble, and the implosion of the subprime lending market that threatened to bring leading Wall Street institutions to their knees—indeed, would have done, had they not been "too big to fail."

Through a series of interviews, Ferguson juxtaposes economists, financial journalists, consumer activists, and politicians who foresaw the crash with those who did not. But the juxtaposition is not symmetrical because many of those blamed by Ferguson for complicity or negligence simply refused to participate: former Federal Reserve chairman Alan Greenspan and former treasury secretaries Larry Summers, Tim Geitner, Hank Paulson, and Robert Rubin.

Ferguson's perspective is neither the radicalism of Klein nor the populism of Moore, though like them he is equally condemnatory of both parties. *Capitalism* ended with faint optimism about the early Obama administration, but *Inside Job* is two years on, and the film is dismissive of the 2010 Obama regulatory reforms. There is both a political and a cultural dimension to Ferguson's argument. Politically, Ferguson believes that the crash was the product of bad decisions by government, such as the 1999 repeal of the Glass-Steagall Act (a New Deal–era law preventing banks with consumer deposits from engaging in high-risk investment ventures) and passing the Commodity Futures Modernization Act in 2000, which blocked the regulation of derivatives.

Ferguson's contention that these decisions reflect the revolving door between politics and finance has become a commonplace. But Ferguson extends the argument to indict the financial world for its corruption of intellectual talent. In the film, Chinese financial commentator Andrew Sheng laments the diversion of highly trained minds away from the real economy and into finance, asking, "Why should a financial engineer be paid four times to a hundred times more than a real engineer? A real engineer builds bridges; a financial engineer builds dreams." More specifically, Damon's narration talks about "the corruption of economics," and Ferguson's interviews expose the vested interests that economists at elite American institutions have in promoting deregulation. The economists interviewed are as inept in their denials as any of Moore's willing self-incriminators.

But it is in Ferguson's attack on the culture of Wall Street that the film packs its punch. Ferguson draws a close parallel between hazardous short-term financial speculation and the use of illegal stimulant drugs—one that has the same metaphorical power as Klein's "shock" parallels but is easier to substantiate empirically. A therapist serving Wall Street clients reports, presumably to no one's surprise, that financiers make extensive use of cocaine. Professor Andrew Lo, of the MIT Laboratory for Financial Engineering, tells Ferguson that MRI scans of financiers have revealed that money stimulates the same parts of the brain as cocaine. The stimulant addiction parallel is also indirectly endorsed in the contribution from Lee Hsien Loong, the prime minister of Singapore, who volunteers that "when you start thinking you can create something out of nothing, it is very difficult to resist." Damon even goes so far as to suggest that financiers' recourse to illegal drugs and prostitution "on an industrial scale" could be used by the authorities as leverage with which to extract information on financial wrongdoing.

But that is the limit of the film's prescription. *Inside Job* ends with a shot of the Statue of Liberty and Damon's closing words "Some things are worth fighting for." Up to this point, the film has been muckraking at its very best, but a weaker ending is scarcely imaginable. Perhaps this was inevitable on account of the contradiction that is inherent in the film's message: the title suggests criminality but, as Ferguson himself documents, the law has been changed to legalize the activities that led to the crash. Consequently, the film stirs up anger in its viewers, but leaves them not knowing what to do with it.

By contrast, Robert B. Reich has attempted to use film for the expressly liberal purpose of demonstrating that the institutions of government can reform American capitalism toward social justice through greater economic equality. Reich's book *Aftershock: The Next Economy and America's Future* is an unlikely candidate for a film version, but he has brought it to the big screen as *Inequality for All: A Passionate Argument on Behalf of the Middle Class* (2013), made in collaboration with director Jacob Kornbluth. *Inequality for All* is film's most in-depth and intellectually rigorous contribution to the debate over the Great Recession and the financial crisis, and so engaging is Reich's presentation that he is likely to send a sympathetic audience away with a liberal spring in its step.

Reich is currently a professor of public policy at the University of California, but his place in the national debate over America's economic future is in large part secured by his four years of service as labor secretary in the first Clinton administration. The best known and most influential of his fifteen books is his Keynesian interventionist text *The Work of Nations* (1991), which he and his long-standing friend Bill Clinton intended to be the theoretical framework for progressive labor policy in the global economy. But the administration early on took a neoliberal turn, which led to Reich's stepping down after the presidential election of 1996.

Inequality for All was released in September 2013, exactly five years after the collapse of Lehman Brothers, and two years after the launch of Occupy Wall Street in Zuccotti Park. The transposition of the book to the screen is justified by its effectiveness in conveying the biographical origins of Reich's political and intellectual interests, by its use of dynamic computer graphics to illustrate the economic trends Reich describes, and by the opportunity it provides to ordinary Americans to tell their own stories, in their own words.

As Reich states in the film, "Of all developed nations, the United States has the most unequal distribution of income, and we're surging towards even greater inequality." Reich contends that American economic history exhibits a pendulum swing between periods in which the benefits of economic growth are widely dispersed, and periods in which those benefits are narrowly concentrated. And the narrowness of concentration in our time is staggering. As

Reich explains, in 1978 the typical male worker made $48,302, whereas a typical member of what we now call the One Percent made more than eight times as much—$393,682. By 2010, however, that average male worker's wages were down to $33,751, while the One Percenter earns thirty-two times as much, or $1.1 million.

In classically Keynesian terms, Reich believes that dire economic consequences, including both the Great Depression and the Great Recession, have flowed from concentrations of income and wealth at the top. Such concentration saps the overall level of demand in the U.S. economy because the rich simply do not spend as much of their money as does the middle class. This drop in the level of demand then causes unemployment and wage suppression, which drop demand further. Reich and Kornbluth find a very plausible ally in Nick Hanauer, a Seattle-based multimillionaire CEO of a pillow-making company, who illustrates Reich's case by pointing out that "even the richest people only sleep on one or two pillows."

Reich tells us that he is frequently asked which country's model of political economy he would recommend in order to improve the living standards of ordinary Americans. It is never advisable for American politicians, or public intellectuals, to argue that the United States should emulate other nations, so Reich nominates a period of American history within living memory for millions of Americans—a period he terms in the original book the "Great Prosperity" from 1947 to 1975.

The Great Prosperity, Reich argues, was the result of public policy. His argument relies heavily on Keynes's "paradox of thrift": the perceived threat of unemployment causes consumers to save rather than to spend, thereby sucking demand out of the economy and increasing the risk of unemployment that the saving was intended to insure against. An understanding of this paradox underlay the expansionary policies of Franklin Roosevelt, though Reich concedes it was the extraordinary stimulus of WWII that ended the Great Depression in America.

Keynesian demand management became a bipartisan economic orthodoxy in the postwar decades. This was not achieved through the redistributive fiscal policies, or nationalization, characteristic of European social democracy. Instead, public policy in the United States created the conditions in which the middle class could share in the benefits of its own increased productivity: employers were required to pay overtime, which gave employers an incentive to hire new workers, rather than sweat current ones, when demand was expanding; the federal government introduced a minimum wage and provided unemployment benefits that usually extended until laid-off workers found new jobs, thereby propping up demand during a downturn; it created jobs directly through infrastructure projects such as Eisenhower's federal highway construction program; it facilitated home ownership through low-cost mortgages and mortgage interest tax reductions; and workers were guaranteed the right to join unions, which were then able to negotiate better health and retirement benefits. Only with the introduction in 1965 of Medicare and Medicaid did America approach European social democracy.

The argument of *Inequality for All* is that the Great Prosperity came to an end when public policy ceased to underpin the link between pay and output. In contrast to Klein and Moore, Reich insists that it was not a casualty of globalization. He concedes that since the late 1970s, U.S. manufacturing jobs have migrated overseas and that, by the 1990s, even high-paying technology jobs were being outsourced. But he reminds his viewers that free trade also opened new markets to American exports and gave American consumers access to cheaper imports. Reich also denies that the Great Prosperity was a victim of technological innovation, which he recognizes as inevitable. But technology has destroyed high-paying, unionized manufacturing jobs and replaced them with low-paying, nonunionized service sector jobs. Ultimately, what matters is not jobs but pay. Renewed prosperity will require America to generate more high-skill jobs and to educate and train the workers who can do them.

But that is not the direction in which public policy has been headed for the past thirty years. Beginning in the late 1970s, successive Democratic and Republican administrations deregulated and privatized; they halved the top rate of income tax; they altered the tax code to allow the richest Americans to treat their income as capital gains subject to a maximum of 15 percent; and they shrank the inheritance tax so that it applied only to the richest 1.5 percent. At the same time, they introduced restrictions on unemployment benefits, so that by 2007 only 40 percent of the unemployed qualified for it; they abolished Aid to Families with Dependent Children (AFDC); they cut funding for public transportation and education; and they failed to invest in infrastructural renewal, resulting in collapsing bridges and burst levees. The result has been a massive upward redistribution of wealth and an erosion of middle-class living standards.

Michael Moore devotees may ask how what Reich describes differs from plutonomy, and it would be a good question. Reich shares with Michael Moore a nostalgia for the Great Prosperity in which they both grew up, but he does not suggest that the era's economic security, equitable distribution, or social mobility are recoverable in the foreseeable future. Nonetheless, *Inequality for All* reasons that if America's excessive economic inequality is political in its origins, then politics also offers the path to greater equality.

Reich is disappointed in President Obama's record, which he believes peaked with the significant but limited achievements of the Affordable Care Act of 2010. But the film closes in an upbeat mood, showing us the immense student appreciation at the end of Reich's triumphal lecture course. Once again, this is a film that calls upon us to act but, curiously, omits the policy prescriptions set out in the book on which it is based: a reverse income tax, higher marginal rates of tax on the wealthy, an active labor market policy of re-employment, college loans linked to subsequent earnings, and the generalization of Medicare.

While *Inequality for All* appeals to the values of equity and social solidarity that appear to have been in retreat for the past three decades, Lauren Greenfield's documentary *The Queen of Versailles* (2012) is a vivid illustration of the consumerism and conspicuous consumption that have been in the ascendant over the same period. The queen is Jackie Siegel, the third wife of property mogul David Siegel, CEO of the time-share business Westgate Resorts.

At the beginning of this film, the Siegels are building their dream home, inspired by Louis XIV's residence. It is to have thirty bathrooms, a children's wing, a full-size basketball court, a sushi bar, and a movie theater. Asked why he wanted to build it, he replies, "Because I could." Siegel believes that his motivations and the motivations of those who buy his time-shares are the same: as he tells us early on, from his throne-like chair, "Everybody wants to be rich. If you can't be rich, the next best thing is to feel rich. And, if they don't want to feel rich, they're probably dead."

During the two years covered by the film, the credit crunch intervenes. The still-incomplete dream house is sold; the Siegels cannot hold on to their relatively modest 26,000-square-foot mansion in Orlando, Florida; thousands of Westgate staff have been let go; and the Siegel children move from private to public school. Jackie likens the bankers who force them to sell their assets to vultures who circle and wait for people to fail, while Siegel himself reinforces the drug metaphor of *Inside Job*: the bankers are pushers of the easy credit to which he became addicted. Siegel is a man given to regrets: the Iraq War led him to regret what he claims was his decisive role in tipping Florida to George W. Bush in 2000, and he regrets the self-deception that led to his massive financial overextension. Jackie, meanwhile, stoically accepts their diminishing circumstances, but struggles unsuccessfully to restrain her spending.

This is not *Mr. Blandings Builds His Dream House* (1948), and few viewers will sympathize with the Siegels as they appear here. Indeed, Siegel later sued Greenfield. Siegel believes his to be a "riches to rags" story, but this can only mean that he has no real familiarity with rags. Our sympathy is better reserved for the more vulnerable casualties of the crunch. Cinema, television, and the mainstream media all neglect the experience of poverty in America. That is why the HBO documentary *American Winter* (2013), which was also shown in cinemas, is especially valuable. Directed by Joe Gantz, and produced by Joe and Harry Gantz, the film takes us into the lives of eight families in Portland, Oregon, as they struggle to cope with unemployment, eviction, homelessness, hunger, sickness, and, not least, the horrors of out-of-pocket medical expenses that make America an anomaly in the developed world.

America has intergenerational urban poverty that is the result of long-term industrial decline and the economic hollowing out of inner cities, and it disproportionately afflicts ethnic minorities. HBO's multiple award-winning series *The Wire* (2002–2008), set in Baltimore, tackled with unusual insight the social consequences of such endemic poverty. There is also the rural poverty of regions like Appalachia that were never included in the Great Prosperity, as depicted in the FX television series *Justified* (2010–). But the families in *American Winter* live in an affluent city; they are predominantly white; and they have all at some point enjoyed the education, employment, homeownership, marriage, and family that typify the idealized American middle class. The fragility of the American economy and the exposure and vulnerability of the American worker are chillingly revealed. What we learn from this film is that any ordinary, hard-working American could fall out of employment, fall into sickness or homelessness, and fall through the interstices of an inadequate welfare support system.

The most callous of Dickensian villains would find it hard to construct a narrative in which the eight families featured in *American Winter* are architects of their own misfortune. Quite simply, they are not. Even remotely empathic viewers will be in low spirits as the film concludes, though they may be heartened by its tribute to the work performed by homeless shelters and the food bank movement, whose tireless voluntarism does what it can to help those who seem all but disavowed by government at local, state, and federal levels.

All these documentaries about the financial crisis and the Great Recession have come from an ideological perspective critical of American capitalism in its contemporary financialized form. Many successfully expose the sway that finance enjoys over the political process. Some have connected the financial crisis with the response to terrorism. Others have emphasized the addictive quality of the financial system's dynamic. And others still have sought to bring to the wider public the ongoing human costs of the 2008 crash.

But while the documentary may be the best medium in which to tackle an issue of such complexity, dramatic cinema deserves considerable credit for its surprisingly effective efforts to take us inside the world of finance itself. Once again, the perspective is generally critical, but the remarkable achievement of dramatic cinema has been to give us a more nuanced depiction of the undeniably human quality of the financiers' flaws and follies—to articulate their world view and their predicament more clearly and, to a degree, more plausibly and sympathetically than they have themselves been able to do in their documentary interviews.

If cinema was going to attempt to dramatize the financial crisis, it was perhaps inevitable that Oliver Stone would re-enter the fray. Stone, whose father was a Wall Street stockbroker, made a milestone contribution to the treatment of finance on film with *Wall Street* (1987). Coincidentally arriving in theaters two months after the Black Friday stock market crash of October that year, it instantly became an iconic picture of the Reagan era. This was not, however, the director's intent: for Stone, the reactivation of the Cold War and foreign policy scandals such as Iran-Contra were the definitive stories of the 1980s.[16] In that sense, his 1986 film *Salvador* may be a better indicator of his political priorities at the time.

Wall Street earned Michael Douglas an Academy Award for his portrayal of Gordon Gekko, and Gekko's (usually misquoted) line "Greed, for lack of a better word, is good" remains cinema's most succinct and enduring characterization of the era's business ethos. The plot follows ambitious stockbroker Bud Fox (Charlie Sheen) into Gekko's cutthroat financial world and culminates with Fox helping to expose Gekko's insider trading and securities fraud. The film was a commercial success and remains popular, thus reassuring other filmmakers that the world of finance can be interpreted dramatically.

As Stone's sequel *Wall Street: Money Never Sleeps* (2010) opens, Gordon Gekko (once again played by Michael Douglas) is released from an eight-year jail sentence. The film's largely unmemorable plot has Gekko attempting to reconnect with his estranged daughter (Carey Mulligan), via her Wall Street banker fiancé (Shia LaBeouf). In the process, he pursues a business enemy from his own Wall Street past (Josh Brolin) and attempts to reestablish himself in the financial world.

Gekko embarks on a lecture tour to promote his book *Is Greed Good?* In the film's best and most important set piece, he tells a student audience that "someone reminded me the other evening that I once said greed is good. Now, it seems, it's legal." With an unappealing schadenfreude, he tells them that they are the "NINJA generation," with "no income, no jobs and no assets." The cause of their bleak economic prospects, he explains, is a generalization of the greed for which Gekko himself had become notorious:

> It's greed that makes my bartender buy three houses he can't afford, with no money down. And it's greed that makes your parents refinance their $200,000 house for two fifty. And then they take that extra fifty and they go down to the mall. They buy a plasma TV, cell phones, computers, an SUV and, hey, why not a second home? . . . We all know that prices of houses in America always go up, right?

Then, once again, we have the link with the terrorist attacks of 2001:

> And it's greed that makes the government of this country cut the interest rates to 1 percent after 9/11—so we could all go shopping again.

Here, Americans of all classes are implicated in a crassly consumerist distortion of the American Dream. But, via Gekko, Stone tells us that the principal threat to that dream remains Wall Street. Though not as (mis)quotable as "greed is good," Gekko's new message is that "the mother of all evil is speculation." In a dialogue with the fiancé, Gekko warns that high-risk speculation in pursuit of short-term profits now constitutes a genuine threat of financial apocalypse, and that there are no longer the necessary regulations or institutions in place to prevent it. As Gekko puts it, "Nobody knows what to do next except repeat the insanity until the next bubble blows. That'll be the one—the big one."

Stone's perspective, like Michael Moore's, is moral: Gekko remains duplicitous, old-school bankers kill themselves, and LaBeouf's halfway sympathetic character is guilty of serial deceit. This film has the cultural argument of *Inside Job*, but, unlike the original *Wall Street*, it is superficial in its treatment of the inner workings of the financial world.

Not so *Margin Call* (2011), probably the best film ever made about Wall Street. Written and directed by J. C. Chandor, the film is set in the offices of a Manhattan investment bank during a twenty-four-hour period in which financial analysts realize that their firm is overleveraged and laden with toxic assets. The quality of both the script and the performances are such that even reluctant viewers will find themselves acquiring at least some understanding of how the structural dynamics of the financial system, and the workplace psychological pressures they produce, could induce in brilliant people a collective myopia, or even delusion, that would take their firm to the brink of destruction.

The film does not expect us to like its characters. Those who insist on finding a hero will settle on the risk analyst Peter Sullivan, played by Zachary Quinto. Sullivan is a perfect specimen of the problem identified by Andrew Sheng in *Inside Job*: an engineering Ph.D. who moved to financial modeling as a massively more lucrative career. It is Sullivan who discovers the potentially fatal extent of the overleveraging of the firm. Over the course of the film, we watch as the various players come to realize the magnitude of the problem. What alarms us is that they are as incredulous as we are. Gordon Gekko's apocalyptic warning suddenly seems more credible.

Once the problem has been discovered, blame has to be allocated, and the firm has to be extricated from the catastrophic position into which it has put itself. There is much finger-pointing before the ruthless scapegoating. But the crisis is so deep that CEO John Tuld (Jeremy Irons) has to descend ominously from the sky by helicopter in the middle of the night. What Tuld brings to the situation is not intelligence or insight, but ruthlessness. He orders the dumping of the firm's toxic assets, in the full knowledge that this will destroy the personal reputations of the individual traders and cause complete chaos in the market. Tuld is unperturbed and explains to a colleague (Kevin Spacey) over breakfast that this is simply another in a long line of crashes out of which his firm, and many others like it, have ultimately made killings.

At various points in the film, the dominant position of finance is symbolized by shots of investment bankers looking down on the city. In a particularly effective scene, two high-ranking executives (Demi Moore and Simon Baker) talk corporate politics in an elevator, literally over the head of a much smaller woman janitor. But a middle-ranking character, played by Paul Bettany, anticipates the oncoming backlash against Wall Street and defends the financial world as simply an intensified expression of the wider culture. In terms similar to Gekko's in the *Wall Street* sequel, he expounds on the complicity of the general population in the creation of the bubble. It is unlikely that the bankers will be happy with their portrayal in *Margin Call*, but it seems clear it is the best they are going to get.

The HBO film *Too Big to Fail* (2011), directed by Curtis Hanson, is a less-accomplished effort to engage with the details of the financial crisis and to overcome the obstacles to drama that those details pose. The film is based on the authoritative 2009 book of the same name by Andrew Ross Sorkin. Unlike any other dramatization of the crisis, *Too Big to Fail* portrays the real-life players from politics and finance, played by A-list actors: Treasury Secretary Henry Paulson (William Hurt), Federal Reserve Chairman Ben Bernanke (Paul Giamatti), investor Warren Buffett (Ed Asner), and Lehman Brothers CEO Richard S. Fuld (James Woods). In depicting the pressured decision making of the players involved, the film creates the impression that the bailout was less a product of a finance-politics axis than of the absence of alternatives: once Lehman Brothers had gone under, buying the toxic assets of multiple banks was the only way to prevent a complete financial collapse. The rescue package involved bundling banks together, with the result that institutions already too big to fail become bigger still. In contrast to Moore's perspective and Ferguson's, government is not so much corrupt as impotent.

In his generally favorable review of *Too Big to Fail*, Michael Kinsley asked how anyone could make a thriller without blood or corpses and based on a scandal that might as well have been called "Too Complicated to Understand."[17] *Killing Them Softly* (2012), written and directed by Andrew Dominick, is an attempt to answer that. The film is set in a world of drugs, illegal gambling, and contract killing, punctuated by television reports in the background detailing the onset of the financial crisis. The attempt at allegory is cinematically crude and not redeemed when Brad Pitt, as the contract killer, hears Obama's election night victory speech and scoffs that "American isn't a country; it's a business."

Criminality in finance is the catalyst that sets in motion the disturbing downward spiral of events in Woody Allen's *Blue Jasmine* (2013), but the film is perhaps unique in its efforts to present the cross-class effects of financial ruin. In an extraordinary performance, Cate Blanchett plays Jasmine, a New York socialite whose wealth derives from the corrupt practices of her businessman husband (Alec Baldwin). Her life falls apart when he is arrested and sent to jail, where he kills himself. As a last resort, Jasmine moves into the rundown San Francisco apartment of her adoptive sister Ginger (Sally Hawkins). Forced to work at what she sees as the menial job of a dental receptionist, she persists in her snobbery, is clearly delusional, and becomes increasingly reliant on pills and alcohol. Impossible to like, she is also a victim, and her predicament is harrowing. As unlikely as it seems, this attempt at an *American Winter* for socialites actually works.

The leftish liberalism that occasionally informs Allen's films is nowhere in evidence here; indeed, *Blue Jasmine* has no discernible political perspective at all. The influence of Tennessee Williams's *A Streetcar Named Desire* is hard to miss, and Blanchett is probably drawing on her portrayal of Blanche DuBois in Liv Ullman's 2009 stage production. The blue-collar males have a touch of Stanley Kowalski about them, and that is part of the problem with *Blue Jasmine*: it's almost entirely negative depiction of the American working class, the obesity of Ginger's two badly behaved sons being a particularly egregious example of the stereotyping.

Ordinary Americans and the economic hardships they face have never been favored Hollywood subject matter, and some critics believe that the cinematic response to the slump has been seriously inadequate. For journalist Daniel D'Addario, the recent revival of class resentment in America was itself short-lived, and "movies post-crash have barely acknowledged the themes of fundamental inequity expressed in Zuccotti Park." There has been, he acknowledges, "a slow trickle of films about Wall Street" but, he maintains, by 2013 Hollywood had returned to its fascination with the glamorous lifestyles of wealthy financiers. For D'Addario, this is exemplified in Martin Scorsese's *The Wolf of Wall Street* (2013), based on the memoir of the same name by Jordan Belfort, who was indicted for securities fraud and money laundering.[18] Leonardo DiCaprio appears in the leading role, having also recently starred in Baz Luhrmann's screen adaptation of F. Scott Fitzgerald's *The Great Gatsby* (2013).

But it is not clear that the reinjection of class into American political discourse has proven to be ephemeral. The Occupy movement and its supporters have continued to get their story out, including in online films. *Occupy Love* (2012), from Canadian filmmaker Velcrow Ripper, illustrated the broad spectrum of Occupy opinion, from Naomi Klein on the socialist left to "degrowth" activist Charles Eisenstein, and in 2013 Occupy put out its own documentary, made by multiple directors, *99%: The Occupy Wall Street Collaborative Film*. Although the Occupy movement in the United States has unarguably failed to maintain the same momentum exhibited by the European movements that inspired it, such as *los indignados* in austerity-ravaged Spain, it has nonetheless left its mark on American politics: the perception of

Governor Mitt Romney as a candidate of the One Percent appears to have significantly damaged his campaign for the presidency.

Class issues have reclaimed a place even in mainstream politics. The liberal left of the Democratic Party has shown signs of re-energization in its successful opposition to the president's planned appointment of Larry Summers as chairman of the Federal Reserve, in the election of the liberal Bill de Blasio as mayor of New York City, and in the widespread clamor for Massachusetts senator Elizabeth Warren—a long-standing and severe critic of Wall Street—to run for the Democratic presidential nomination in 2016. More significantly, on December 4, 2013, President Obama himself made a landmark speech declaring that government activism to restore America's lost social mobility would be the central focus of his second term. Using an analysis very similar to that of Reich in *Inequality for All*, the president acknowledged "a dangerous and growing inequality and lack of upward mobility that has jeopardized middle-class America's basic bargain—that if you work hard, you have a chance to get ahead."[19]

It is not clear that these developments will satisfy the Matt Damons of this world, or that they should. But a renewed left emphasis on economic justice has demonstrably re-entered American political debate. We cannot measure how much, if anything, cinema has contributed to this. But the financial crisis has undoubtedly been a significant theme of cinema in the age of Obama, and the perspectives taken on that crisis have all come from various vantage points on the left.

In *Hollywood Right and Left* (2011), historian Steven J. Ross has sought to show that a predominantly liberal Hollywood is substantially a myth. He maintains that the Hollywood right has generally been more successful in its political interventions than the Hollywood left. Ross fully acknowledges that left-wing filmmakers played crucially important roles in highlighting the threat of fascism in the 1930s and 1940s, in supporting the civil rights movement in the 1950s and 1960s, in critiquing the Vietnam War in the 1970s, and in promoting a progressive social agenda. But this has been an issues-based approach, in contrast to the right's formulation of a broader narrative about the nature of America and its place in the world.

From Ross's perspective, conservative Hollywood has more successfully shaped American political culture as a whole through its depiction of "a nostalgic Golden Age of America that never was," whereas for liberal Hollywood "a better America means looking to the future rather than the past."[20] But it is not at all clear that nostalgia is the preserve of right-wing filmmakers. As the British film academic Ian Scott has argued, testing America against its own democratic mythologies and traditions is a defining feature of American political cinema as a whole.[21] Accordingly, so also is the recurring use of American democracy's iconic imagery, such as the Statue of Liberty and the monumental architecture of Washington, D.C. In a very real sense, therefore, liberal Hollywood's political agenda is as restorative as the right's, as Frank Capra's *Mr. Smith Goes to Washington* (1939) illustrates.

During the presidential election of 2012, documentary filmmaker Ken Burns cited Capra's 1946 classic *It's a Wonderful Life* to explain his support for President Obama's re-election campaign. For Burns, Obama is a champion of Bedford Falls's communitarianism, as against the Pottersville plutocracy with which the country is threatened by an increasingly right-wing Republican Party. Revealingly, he credits Obama not only with having brought America back from the brink of economic depression but also with having introduced "better, smarter regulation of those who brought this upon us . . . and a request that the very super rich . . . ,who have taken advantage of loopholes and deductions and off-shore accounts to amass their fortunes, pay their fair share."[22]

Obama's more left-wing critics, of course, deny that he has brought Wall Street under effective control, and some question whether he could if he tried. Perhaps unwittingly, Burns concedes something to these critics when he writes about the president *requesting* that the super-rich pay their taxes. In the companion volume to his 2012 Showtime documentary series *The Untold History of the United States*, Oliver Stone, co-writing with historian Peter Kuznick, unfavorably contrasts Obama with Capra's Mr. Smith: "Obama was much more savvy and, apparently, more cynical than Smith. By knowingly surrounding himself with establishment insiders as domestic and foreign policy advisers, he preemptively closed the door on the kind of bold innovations and breaks with the past that his campaign had promised." In particular, Stone and Kuznick draw attention to Obama's refusal of public campaign financing in 2008 and his reliance on "Wall Street funders with deep pockets," including Goldman Sachs, Citigroup, J.P. Morgan Chase, and Morgan Stanley.[23]

If the financial crisis was the product of irresponsible private economic power, and even liberal presidents are beholden to that power, then there is a crisis of liberalism too. If governmental institutions cannot counteract the economic power elite that are the subject of *Inside Job*, can those same institutions really help the subjects of *American Winter*? Robert Reich's experience as labor secretary in the first Clinton administration suggests not. As he tells us in *Inequality for All*, his persistent advocacy of the middle class and the poor caused the administration's Wall Street contingent to roll their eyes as they pressed on with their own deregulatory agenda.

On screen, liberalism wants the restoration of the ideals it believes have been subverted by neoliberalism, but like its real-life counterpart, it cannot suggest ways forward. From the 1930s through to the 1960s, it could. That is why cinematic liberalism shares with cinematic conservatism a nostalgic yearning for an irrecoverable past. Liberalism cannot plausibly exhibit confidence on screen unless it recovers confidence in the realm of real-world politics. And it is in politics, not in film, that the recovery must first take place. If art could breathe life back into American liberalism, then seven years of Aaron Sorkin's Capra-esque NBC show *The West Wing* (1999–2006) would have done it by now.

NOTES

1. Caitlin McDevitt, "Matt Damon: Obama Broke Up With Me," *Politico*, August 8, 2013, http://www.politico.com/blogs/click/2013/08/matt-damon-obama-broke-up-with-me-170232.html.
2. Nick Wing, "Jimmy Carter Defends Edward Snowden, Says NSA Spying Has Compromised Nation's Democracy," *Huffington Post*, July 18, 2013, http://www.huffingtonpost.com/2013/07/18/jimmy-carter-edward-snowden_n_3616930.html.
3. "Matt Damon Down on President Obama in Elle Interview," December 22, 2011, http://abcnews.go.com/blogs/entertainment/2011/12/matt-damon-down-on-president-obama-in-elle-interview/.
4. Francis Fukuyama, *The End of History and the Last Man* (London: Penguin Books, 1992).
5. Ronald Inglehart, *The Silent Revolution: Changing Values and Political Styles Among Western Publics* (Princeton: Princeton University Press, 1977).
6. See James Davison Hunter, *Culture Wars: the Struggle to Control the Family, Art, Education, the Law, and Politics in America* (New York: Basic Books, 1992). For an alternative view, see Morris P. Fiorina, *Culture War? The Myth of a Polarized America* (New York: Pearson Longman, 2005).
7. Samuel P. Huntington, *The Clash of Civilizations and the Remaking of World Order* (New York: Touchstone, 1996).
8. See Chris Holmlund, ed., *American Cinema of the 1990s: Themes and Variations* (New Brunswick, N.J.: Rutgers University Press, 2008).
9. See Philip Hammond, ed., *Screens of Terror: Representations of War and Terrorism in Film and Television Since 9/11* (Suffolk, U.K.: Abramis, 2011).
10. Roger Ebert, *Battle in Seattle* film review, RogerEbert.com, September 5, 2008, http://www.rogerebert.com/reviews/battle-in-seattle-2008.
11. Terry Christensen and Peter J. Haas, *Projecting Politics: Political Messages in American Films* (New York: M.E. Sharpe, 2005), 228.
12. Nicholas Blincoe, "Every Catastrophe is an Opportunity," *Telegraph*, September 22, 2007, http://www.telegraph.co.uk/culture/books/non_fictionreviews/3668082/Every-catastrophe-is-an-opportunity.html.
13. http://wwww.naomiklein.org/files/resources/pdfs/friedman-pinochet-letters.pdf.
14. This view of the pivotal role of the Chilean coup in the rise of neoliberalism is also supported by more theoretical treatments of the subject. See David Harvey, *A Brief History of Neoliberalism* (Oxford: Oxford University Press, 2005).
15. Owen Jones, "This Austerity Backlash Across Europe Could Transform Britain," *Independent*, May 11 2012, http://www.independent.co.uk/voices/commentators/owen-jones-this-austerity-backlash-across-europe-could-transform-britain-7734670.html.
16. Robert Brent Toplin, ed., *Oliver Stone's America: Film, History, and Controversy* (Lawrence: University Press of Kansas, 2000), 234.
17. Michael Kinsley, "Economic Crisis Unfurls in Hushed Suspense," *New York Times*, May 22, 2011, http://www.nytimes.com/2011/05/23/arts/television/too-big-to-fail-on-hbo-review.html?_r=0.
18. Daniel D'Addario, "Did Hollywood Sleep Through the Financial Crisis?" *Salon*, June 21, 2013, http://www.salon.com/2013/06/21/are_we_ready_to_love_wall_street_again/.
19. "Remarks by the President on Economic Mobility," December 4, 2013, http://www.whitehouse.gov/the-press-office/2013/12/04/remarks-president-economic-mobility.

20. Steven J. Ross, *Hollywood Left and Right: How Movie Stars Shaped American Politics* (New York: Oxford University Press, 2011), 412.

21. Ian Scott, *American Politics in Hollywood Film* (Edinburgh: Edinburgh University Press, 2011), 23–25.

22. Ken Burns, "Why I Am Voting for Barack Obama," *New Hampshire Union Leader*, October 18, 2012, http://www.unionleader.com/article/20121019/OPINION02/710199989.

23. Oliver Stone and Peter Kuznick, *The Untold History of the United States* (New York: Gallery Books, 2012), 551.

Chapter Twelve

Reimagining Barack Obama as Jay Gatsby in Baz Luhrmann's Film Adaptation of *The Great Gatsby*

Cammie Sublette

Our protagonist stares deeply into the eyes of his beloved, while the sweet sounds of Beyoncé covering a song about potentially anguished love serve as backdrop. This describes the scene of the first couple's first dance at Obama's first Inaugural Ball, and it also describes director Baz Luhrmann's new vision of Jay Gatsby and Daisy Buchanan in *The Great Gatsby*. These similarities may seem incidental, but in fact, they highlight a constant reimagining of Barack Obama as Gatsby, for in everything from the sound track, to the incessant reiteration of the word "hope" in connection with Gatsby, to even the core story of self-made American hero, Luhrmann's revisions of Fitzgerald's most enduring literary creation make Gatsby start to resemble President Obama.

This is not to suggest that Gatsby's story is to be read as a literal narration of Obama's life, for these men experience radically different contexts and circumstances. Daisy becomes, for Gatsby, the whole of life, and she is married to another man. Obama appears to be married to the woman whom he adores. However, Daisy has long been read as symbolic of Gatsby's desires: Gatsby imbues Daisy with all of his aspirations. She becomes, if not America, at least an emblem of the American Dream. Daisy will never be able to live up to her idealized position, and she is too flawed to even come close. Still, Gatsby believes deeply in the American Dream, in *his* American Dream. He believes in Daisy. Obama likewise believes deeply in his version of the American Dream; he even subtitled his second book "Thoughts on Reclaiming the American Dream."

In addition, as Luhrmann's Nick narrates, "Gatsby has had a vision for his life since he was a boy."[1] Both of Obama's books illustrate that the same can be said of him, though, like Gatsby, he may not have always known how or where to direct his ambitions. The child of a white woman from Kansas and a black man from Kenya, Barack Obama learned early that his family believed him destined for greatness. Once his father returned to Kenya, his mother and her parents took over Obama's education on issues of race. His mother taught him, "To be black was to be the beneficiary of a great inheritance, a special destiny, glorious burdens that only we were strong enough to bear."[2] And though his mother attempted to shield him from his father's failures and disappointments, by the time that he was ten, he was already aware that his father was a deeply troubled and rather unsuccessful man. He writes, "If my father hadn't exactly disappointed me, he remained something unknown, something volatile and vaguely threatening."[3] He, also like Gatsby, therefore seems intent on achieving all that his father did not. He writes, "Someone once said that every man is trying to live up to his father's expectations or make up for their father's mistakes, and I suppose that may explain my particular malady as well as anything else."[4] Thus, Obama lives a life marginally reminiscent of Gatsby's, something Luhrmann exaggerates and distorts in his adaptation of Fitzgerald's classic novel.

ADAPTING GATSBY IN 2013

One of the more telling commentaries in Fitzgerald's *The Great Gatsby* deals with the careless wastefulness of the wealthy: "They were careless people, Tom and Daisy—they smashed up things and creatures and then retreated back into their money or their vast carelessness, or whatever it was that kept them together, and let other people clean up the mess they had made."[5] This theme is highlighted in Luhrmann's adaptation of *Gatsby*, for Luhrmann's aesthetic of excess for excess's sake overlaps Fitzgerald's plot nicely. The endless glasses of champagne, the live performers, the luxury homes and cars, the flowers, the cakes, the mountains of beautiful shirts: they all point to the emptiness of overconsuming, the waste of American excess.

The question for the cultural studies scholar, though, is why now? Why revisit this trope today rather than, say, at the end of the most recent celebration of excess, the 1980s? Baz Luhrmann has suggested that the film responds to at least two cultural conditions, that of the "moral rubberiness" Americans have experienced post-9/11 and the economic recession.[6] Though Luhrmann does not expand upon his references to these two cultural conditions, it is rather easy to read the consumptive excess of the Buchanans set against the stark conditions lived in the Valley of Ashes as a commentary on the increasing class divide in twenty-first-century America. Likewise, that

Gatsby's means are ambiguously immoral, even as his romantic desires find much sympathy with audiences, can be compared to any number of bad faith pragmatisms in the wake of 9/11, including Americans' acceptance of a large military presence abroad as a supposed means to secure the homeland.

The deeper answer to why Luhrmann's *The Great Gatsby* works well in 2013 lies in the American response to President Obama. As A. O. Scott and Manohla Dargis note in their *New York Times* review of movies, from which this collection takes its name and inspiration, "Politically and personally this president functions as a screen onto which different Americans project their fears and fantasies."[7] Lauri Lyons similarly remarks on the pressures to fix every ill, right every wrong, and please every voter thrust onto Obama, noting that "while interviewing people about their view of Obama, I was struck by the high level of expectations being loaded onto one man's shoulders."[8] This is likewise the case with Fitzgerald's Gatsby, a man about whom hangers-on speculate wildly, even asserting that he likely "killed a man," all the while swilling his champagne and treating his home as their own, glibly accepting Gatsby's extravagant gifts as though he is responsible for their happiness. Luhrmann ramps up the fantasy Gatsby even further, allowing one particularly intoxicated party guest to assert, "You won't find him. Gatsby, that is. This house and everything in it are all part of an elaborate disguise to cover up the fact that Mr. Gatsby doesn't exist."[9] So fantastic has Gatsby become in Luhrmann's adaptation, that even a claim of nonexistence seems rather plausible.

A PHILOSOPHY OF HOPE

Of course, Nick meets Gatsby shortly after he hears the intoxicated guest's assertion of Gatsby's nonexistence, and although it takes him some time to get to know Gatsby, he eventually comes to believe him "the single most hopeful person I've ever met and am ever likely to meet again. There was something about him, a sensitivity. He was like one of those machines that register earthquakes ten thousand miles away."[10]

Likewise, Obama's hopefulness has become his political trademark. One of the most memorable moments of Barack Obama's entrance on the public stage came at the 2004 Democratic National Convention. Given more than seventeen minutes of uninterrupted airtime, the rising star of the Democratic Party encouraged the nation to hope, saying,

> Hope—Hope in the face of difficulty. Hope in the face of uncertainty. The audacity of hope!
> In the end, that is God's greatest gift to us, the bedrock of this nation. A belief in things not seen. A belief that there are better days ahead.

> I believe that we can give our middle class relief and provide working families with a road to opportunity.
>
> I believe we can provide jobs to the jobless, homes to the homeless, and reclaim young people in cities across America from violence and despair.
>
> I believe that we have a righteous wind at our backs and that as we stand on the crossroads of history, we can make the right choices, and meet the challenges that face us.[11]

His message was met with warmth and enthusiasm, even if it failed to carry his party's candidate to victory. However, it was this same message of hope and belief in the American Dream that buttressed Obama's successful bid for the White House in 2008. Over and over, in speech after speech, Obama's message was consistently one of optimism in the face of adversity. Calling it "the promise that has always set our country apart," in his 2008 acceptance of the Democratic presidential nomination and address at the convention,[12] Obama repeatedly invoked the American Dream, and his own success as evidence that the dream was alive and well.

Ultimately, it was this philosophy of hope, as Deborah F. Atwater and others have noted, that characterized Obama's campaigns for political office.[13] His second book, published in 2007 and titled *The Audacity of Hope: Thoughts on Reclaiming the American Dream*, outlines a program for all Americans to achieve the dream, though rather than stargazing, this brand of hope is practically a resistance message, as the title implies. Much less personal in nature than his first book, in *The Audacity of Hope*, Obama spends a good deal of time pointing out the many problems faced by millions of lower-class Americans who, plucky and determined, nonetheless find that hard work alone will not allow them to change their circumstances. Still, this is a book bent on optimism, an optimism that careful, considered, and nuanced policies and politics can and will turn things around. The same messages prevailed in Obama's campaign slogan of 2008, "Change we can believe in," and in the popular Shepard Fairey "Hope" posters widely distributed during the 2008 campaign.[14]

THE 2012 ELECTION AND A NEW RHETORIC OF HOPE

Fast-forward to the 2012 election and many of the same messages appeared in Obama's speeches. Republicans made much of what they deemed a more "subdued" message of hope, implying that Obama had changed his message of hope due to failures during his first four years in office. The truth, however, is that the message changed very little from one campaign to the next, for despite having done battle with Republicans for four years, Obama maintained his stance of optimism and hope for the future. Then, too, Obama's previous message regarding the American Dream was not exactly that all

Americans could achieve Warren Buffet's wealth. No, his interpretation of the American Dream has always been rather modest. As he wrote in *The Audacity of Hope*, most Americans believe:

> That anybody willing to work should be able to find a job that paid a living wage. They figured that people shouldn't have to file for bankruptcy because they got sick. They believed that every child should have a genuinely good education—that it shouldn't be just a bunch of talk—and that those same children should be able to go to college even if their parents weren't rich.[15]

The difference in the 2012 election, then, was not in Obama's message, nor even in his enthusiasm. The difference was twofold, for first was the difference in the American people and their ability or willingness to keep believing along with Obama. This was signified prior to the election, during the Occupy Movement, when Shepard Fairey revised his poster from "Hope" to "Mister President, We *Hope* You're On Our Side," a Guy Fawkes mask appearing over the face of Obama.[16] The aftermath of the election has featured continued unrest in the Middle East; revelations about the NSA's broad policies of wiretapping, record collecting, and general disregard for privacy, whether that privacy be Americans' or our foreign allies' or enemies', and political wrangling that led to a government shutdown.

The second key difference, though, is the one that links Obama and Gatsby closely, for it has to do with how the American hero's meteoric rise and grasp at the American Dream is understood by those who would just as soon see the hero fail. As Alex Koppelman notes,

> [Opponents on the political right] have turned [Obama's] background, which he'd managed, through hard work and some shameless massaging, to mold into an asset, into a weapon to be used against him. They've portrayed him as a product of affirmative action, undeserving of his position—not to mention foreign and anti-American. And now they've successfully linked that back to the dismal economy, and his failure to turn it around.[17]

The same sort of negative spin is true for Gatsby, a man who is rumored to be, simultaneously, a murderer, a bootlegger, and a German spy.[18] Even his service to his country during the war leads one gossip to narrow her eyes and whisper, "I'll bet he killed a man."[19] The thing that most inspires such cruel speculation is Gatsby's apparent success in achieving the American Dream. He is a young man who appears out of nowhere, seemingly, and purchases a massive house and treats his guests with endless generosity, thus earning their suspicions and scorn.

Like Gatsby, Barack Obama had to struggle and work hard to achieve the American Dream. As Koppelman argues, this struggle has often been central to Obama's narrative of personal success and thus to his rhetoric of hope.

Indeed, in this rhetoric of hope, Obama aligns himself with the longest of long shots of American Dream dreamers, noting, time and again, how improbable in his own success. In his 2004 DNC speech, he framed his personal narrative as the evidence that the American Dream is truly open to any citizen who will strive, work hard, and believe. He said, in part,

> Tonight is a particular honor for me because, let's face it, my presence on this stage is pretty unlikely. My father was a foreign student, born and raised in a small village in Kenya. He grew up herding goats, went to school in a tin-roof shack. His father, my grandfather, was a cook, a domestic servant to the British. But my grandfather had larger dreams for his son. Through hard work and perseverance my father got a scholarship to study in a magical place, America, that's shone as a beacon of freedom and opportunity to so many who had come before him. While studying here my father met my mother. She was born in a town on the other side of the world, in Kansas. Her father worked on oil rigs and farms through most of the Depression. . . . And I stand here today grateful for the diversity of my heritage, aware that my parents' dreams live on in my two precious daughters. I stand here knowing that my story is part of the larger American story, that I owe a debt to all of those who came before me, and that in no other country on Earth is my story even possible.[20]

Cast thus as exhibit A in our racially and culturally diverse American Dream landscape, Obama became the proof that nothing, not even America's turbulent racial past, could derail the climb of its citizens. His inauguration was historic not just because he was the first African American president of the United States, but because his election on a platform of hope and change seemed to promise that in this American land of opportunity, anything was possible. This speech, read in proximity to *The Great Gatsby*, ends on an eerily familiar note, for Fitzgerald had used the image of African American economic success to frame the following commentary: "Anything can happen, anything at all—even Gatsby."

THE CRITICS AND BAZ LUHRMANN'S *THE GREAT GATSBY*

Baz Luhrmann's readapted *Gatsby* is a film that has been critiqued for *what it is not* a good deal more than it has been studied for *what it is*. That is, in reviews running the gamut from lukewarm to vicious, the film is panned for failing to remain true to Fitzgerald's vision. In this reading, Luhrmann takes too much artistic license with characters, plot, and sound track, the result a spectacularly botched melodrama. Reviewing the film for *Time* magazine, Richard Corliss writes, "This is not so much the Jazz Age, or even the Pizzazz Age, as the Razzle-Dazzle Baz Age."[21] And *New York Times* reviewer A. O. Scott seems to think that Luhrmann glorifies the culture of excess that Fitzgerald held up for critique: "The result is less a movie adaptation than a splashy, trashy opera, a wayward lavishly theatrical celebration of the emotional and material extravagance that Fitzgerald surveyed with fascinated ambivalence."[22]

Paul Giles, however, sees in Luhrmann's film echoes of Fitzgerald's manuscript Gatsby—Gatsby before he was trimmed and groomed and softlighted and romanticized into our now larger than life hero. That is, Giles sees in Luhrmann's Gatsby an outsider, a man displaced by class, ethnicity, education, and circumstance—a man who, as Fitzgerald once wrote of himself, will always be a parvenu.[23] Luhrmann's casting of Leonardo DiCaprio, writes Giles, relocates Gatsby as an immigrant seeking Americanization, for DiCaprio invokes with him former immigrant characters, among them, the immigrant gangsters he depicted in *Gangs of New York* and *The Departed*.[24] Further, as Giles notes, not only does Luhrmann conjure a more ethnic Gatsby, he likewise investigated the rest of the multiethnic landscape that would have surrounded Gatsby's tale, even writing James L. West III, editor of the Cambridge University Press edition of *The Great Gatsby*, wondering about the likely ethnicities of the servants who would have worked for the Buchanans and "whether or not African Americans would have been invited to Gatsby's parties on Long Island."[25] For Giles, Luhrmann's renewed attention to race and ethnicity in Gatsby is evidence that the director crafted a more authentic adaptation than has thus far been attempted.

RACE AND THE AMERICAN DREAM

Luhrmann's revived focus on race and ethnicity is deeply connected to the twenty-first-century loss of faith in the American Dream. Although Fitzgerald's regular alignment throughout *Gatsby* of race and class has gone largely unnoticed, at least until recently, despite its almost constant refrain, it is hard to miss Luhrmann's regular backdrop of African American faces—mostly entertainers and servants—in connection with Gatsby's climb. As Meredith Goldsmith wrote of Fitzgerald's *Gatsby*, "The scandal of Jay Gatsby's success can only be described, it seems, through a series of ethnic and racial analogies."[26] However, unlike the analogized version of race-class assimilation observed in Fitzgerald's text, Luhrmann seems more inclined to represent African Americans in the film as transcendent, stoic, separate, and apart from this hopeless mass of badly behaving white folks. The fire escape scene is perhaps the most telling, for it is here that we see Nick, our ostensibly innocent narrator who reserves judgment, being tugged into the immoral escapades of Tom Buchanan in a sexual tryst with Myrtle Wilson, her sister, and her class-climbing friends. Shot as an orgy of excess inside the apartment, outside, on a neighboring fire escape, a lone black man plays the saxophone. After musing on his insider-outsider status, Nick peers out the window and into those of the neighbors, most of them African Americans. That black faces provide the jolt required to send Nick into contemplation of his own lack of belonging seems in accord with Fitzgerald's original text. However, that these other lives seem so untouched by Nick's corrupt world—save in the one window depicting a black woman in the act of disrobing for an older and fully clothed white man—speaks to a new understanding of race in Gatsby, and a new understanding of race and the American Dream. Ambiguous though this message remains, it implies that if the American Dream is accessible to all, regardless of race, it is only by getting out of the way of careless whites that minorities will achieve their share of the American Dream. Their grasp on the Dream is thus portrayed as tenuous, fleeting, and insecure.

An overly simplistic interpretation of Obama's rhetoric of hope may assert that such a rhetoric ignores racism—indeed, that Obama believes his own achievements evidence of racism's eradication. This could not be further from the truth, however, for in his books and speeches, Obama acknowledges the continued racism that infects our country (and even deals with the global complexities of racism). For example, while an adolescent living in Hawaii, Obama writes that "a warning sounded whenever a white girl mentioned in the middle of a conversation how much she liked Stevie Wonder; or when a woman in the supermarket asked me if I played basketball; or when the school principal told me I was cool."[27] As a teenager, Obama felt even more uncomfortable navigating the gulf between his white and black worlds, noting that even his own white grandmother, whom he loved like a mother, sometimes thought of black men in stereotypical ways.[28] Of these confusing and frustrating identity politics he had forced upon him, Obama writes, "The only thing you could choose as your own was withdrawal into a smaller and smaller coil of rage, until being black meant only the knowledge of your own powerlessness, of your own defeat."[29]

That he achieved the ultimate American Dream and became president of the United States is not evidence that all racism has evaporated, but it is instead evidence that the American Dream is possible even in a society still plagued by racial inequality and antagonisms. The many racist slurs aimed at Obama from right-wing politicians included even an extended national dialogue about Obama's foreign-seeming-ness and barbed questions regarding his qualifications for the highest office in the land, a dialogue that did not dissipate even after Obama made his birth certificate public record.[30]

LUHRMANN'S SOUND TRACK AND OBAMA

The sound track to Luhrmann's adapted film has been met with a good degree of critical derision, tempered, as is so often the case, with overwhelming audience enthusiasm. Joining Richard Corliss in his befuddlement over the sound track, Peter Travers sarcastically says of the choice to update the music of Fitzgerald's novel: "Nothing like hip-hop to add relevance to a retro classic."[31] But Travers could drop the sarcasm, for hip-hop, along with alternative rock and R&B, *do* add relevance to this classic, though perhaps not alone for the reasons Luhrmann has pointed out. As Ann Powers suggests, Luhrmann wanted the music to lend the "feeling" with which jazz infused Fitzgerald's novel[32]—the feeling, that is, of edgy, steamy, provocative, anything-goes decadence that was jazz in the 1920s. Jazz would have seemed maddeningly obscene to Tom Buchanan when in the company of his wife, Daisy, and would have seemed equally titillating to him when in the company of his mistress, Myrtle Wilson. But how could Luhrmann have suggested as much to audiences who understand jazz as the music of choice for respectable twenty-first-century rich white people? All grown up and defanged now, jazz can hardly *feel* naughty to today's audiences, so Luhrmann enlisted Jay-Z, who wove hip-hop and rock into the sound track.

The other reason that hip-hop adds relevance to this sound track, though, is that this is the music Americans have come to associate with Barack Obama, and Luhrmann's Gatsby is heavily inflected by Obama's legacy. Jay-Z, who is featured on the sound track as well as responsible for scoring it, has performed at political rallies in support of Obama, and the men apparently have a close enough friendship that Obama has offered him parenting advice. When asked to name the artists he is most likely to listen to while working out, Obama names Jay-Z's music alongside that of Stevie Wonder and various classic rockers.[33] Another artist featured on the sound track is Beyoncé, who has performed at both of Obama's inaugurations, her cover of "At Last" during the Obamas' first Inaugural Ball a sentimental testament to the long-awaited election of an African American to the first office. Another of the musicians on the sound track, will.i.am, released his hip-hop collage song—pieced together from Obama's speeches—and accompanying video, "Yes, We Can" during Obama's first presidential campaign. Although the song and video were never officially a part of Obama's campaign, the viral video was closely associated with Obama and his bid for office. Fergie, also featured on the soundtrack in a techno-enhanced jazz number, "A Little Party Never Killed Nobody," has performed at the White House and is friendly with the Obamas. In short, then, even the sound track to Luhrmann's *The Great Gatsby* invokes President Barack Obama.

CONCLUSION: MOURNING THE AMERICAN DREAM IN LUHRMANN'S *GATSBY*

Ultimately, I see Luhrmann's film as funerary spectacle, deeply nostalgic for another Gatsby. It is in Barack Obama that Luhrmann finds his Gatsby, but, short of completely rewriting Fitzgerald's novel, and short also of rewriting Obama's own political struggles, Luhrmann must let the film end in frustrated chaos for our American hero.

Then, too, the reality is that many Americans have lost faith in the American Dream, even if they still believe in Obama himself. According to the most recent *Washington Post*-Miller Center Poll concerning the American Dream, optimism has waned more than ever for individual Americans, almost two-thirds of whom worry about their abilities to cover their families' expenses, up from about one-half forty years ago.[34]

Luhrmann's *Gatsby* ends not only with the death of Gatsby, but also with the alcoholism and institutionalization of Nick, a depressing addendum to Fitzgerald's narrator, who, though jaded at the novel's conclusion, is not so deeply wounded. Luhrmann's film, then, suggests that the American Dream has evaporated, even as our optimistic Gatsby surrogate continues to seek the ideal. The best we can do, suggests Luhrmann's *The Great Gatsby*, is get out of the way and let the rich smash up things, whether it's the environment, racial equality, or any sense of class leveling. Through the use of spectacular excess and destruction, Luhrmann's film illustrates the death of the new American Dream so optimistically outlined in Obama's life and service.

In his second presidential nomination address, Obama reiterated his message of hope, stating that despite the many obstacles and struggles he and the country had faced over the previous four years, "As I stand here tonight, I have never been more hopeful about America. Not because I think I have all the answers. Not because I'm naïve about the magnitude of our challenges. I'm hopeful because of you."[35] Sadly, his hope seems misplaced, for the Americans whom he continues to believe in are not the ones with power. The miracle of Barack Obama's presidency and leadership and meteoric rise remains just that, a miracle, not likely to be repeated or to fantastically change power or race or class relationships in the United States. Swept up in a wave of hope for change during Obama's first election, the American public seems to view Obama's second term with as much ennui and grief as hope. The American Dream, embodied as it is in our president, beckons toward a future of democratic equality and mutual concern for humanity, but the reality seems to be that Obama faces a losing battle, as careless people hold most of the power, most of the resources. Excessive and spectacular, Luhrmann's film seems to be the closest cultural artifact we have to a dirge for our American Dream.

NOTES

1. Baz Luhrmann, dir., *The Great Gatsby* (Burbank, Calif.: Warner Brothers, 2013).
2. Barack Obama, *Dreams from My Father: A Story of Race and Inheritance*, Kindle edition (New York: Crown Publishers, 1995), 51.
3. Obama, *Dreams from My Father*, 62.
4. Barack Obama, *The Audacity of Hope: Thoughts on Reclaiming the American Dream* (New York: Crown Publishers, 2006), 3.
5. F. Scott Fitzgerald, *The Great Gatsby* (New York: Scribner, 1925), 179.
6. Baz Luhrmann, interview by Shahendra Ohneswere, *Life+Times*, April 4, 2013, http://lifeandtimes.com/director-baz-lurhmann-speaks-on-directing-the-great-gatsby (accessed November 1, 2013).
7. A. O. Scott and Manohla Dargis, "Movies in the Age of Obama," *New York Times*, January 16, 2013, AR1, http://www.nytimes.com/2013/01/20/movies/lincoln-django-unchained-and-an-obama-inflected-cinema.html?pagewanted=all&_r=1& (accessed November 1, 2013).
8. Lauri Lyons, "Barack Obama and the American Dream," *Huffington Post*, January 29, 2009, http://www.huffingtonpost.com/lauri-lyons/barack-obama-and-the-amer_b_161016.html (accessed December 1, 2013).
9. Luhrmann, *The Great Gatsby*.
10. Luhrmann, *The Great Gatsby*.
11. Barack Obama, "2004 Democratic National Convention Keynote Address," video file, American Rhetoric Online Speech Bank, http://www.americanrhetoric.com/speeches/convention2004/barackobama2004dnc.htm (accessed November 1, 2013).
12. Barack Obama, "2008 Democratic National Convention Nomination Acceptance Speech," video file, American Rhetoric Online Speech Bank, http://www.americanrhetoric.com/speeches/convention2008/barackobama2008dnc.htm (accessed November 1, 2013).
13. Deborah F. Atwater, "Senator Barack Obama: The Rhetoric of Hope and the American Dream," *Journal of Black Studies* 38, no. 2 (November 2007): 121–29.
14. Shepard Fairey, "Hope," print, 2008, http://www.obeygiant.com/headlines/obama-hope (accessed December 1, 2013).
15. Obama, *The Audacity of Hope*, 7.
16. Shepard Fairey, "Occupy Hope," print, 2011, http://www.obeygiant.com/headlines/occupy-hope (accessed December 1, 2013).
17. Alex Koppelman, "Barack Obama, the Lemonade Stand, and the American Dream," *New Yorker*, Daily Comment, September 4, 2012, http://www.newyorker.com/online/blogs/comment/2012/09/obama-the-lemonade-stand-and-the-american-dream.html (accessed December 1, 2013).
18. Fitzgerald, *The Great Gatsby*, 44.
19. Fitzgerald, *The Great Gatsby*, 44.
20. Obama, 2004 Democratic National Convention Keynote Address.
21. Richard Corliss, "Luhrmann's *The Great Gatsby*: From Jazz Age to Baz Age," *Time Entertainment*, May 9, 2013, http://entertainment.time.com/2013/05/09/luhrmanns-the-great-gatsby-from-jazz-age-to-baz-age/ (accessed November 1, 2013).
22. A. O. Scott, "Shimmying off the Literary Mantle: *The Great Gatsby*, Interpreted by Baz Luhrmann," *New York Times*, May 9, 2013, http://www.nytimes.com/2013/05/10/movies/the-great-gatsby-interpreted-by-baz-luhrmann.html?partner=rss&emc=rss&smid=tw-nytmovies&_r=1& (accessed November 1, 2013).
23. Paul Giles, "A Good Gatsby: Baz Luhrmann Undomesticates Fitzgerald," *Commonweal*, July 12, 2013, 12.
24. Giles, "A Good Gatsby," 13.
25. Giles, "A Good Gatsby," 13.
26. Meredith Goldsmith, "White Skin, White Mask: Passing, Posing, and Performing in *The Great Gatsby*," *Modern Fiction Studies* 49, no. 3 (Fall 2003): 443–68.
27. Obama, *Dreams from My Father*, 81.
28. Obama, *Dreams from My Father*, 87.

29. Obama, *Dreams from My Father*, 85.

30. Alan Silverlieb, "Obama Releases Original Long-Form Birth Certificate," CNN Online, April 27, 2011, http://www.cnn.com/2011/POLITICS/04/27/obama.birth.certificate/index.html (accessed December 1, 2013).

31. Peter Travers, "*The Great Gatsby* Movie Review," *Rolling Stone*, online edition, May 9, 2013, http://www.rollingstone.com/movies/reviews/the-great-gatsby-20130509 (accessed November 1, 2013).

32. Ann Powers, "First Listen: Music from Baz Luhrmann's Film *The Great Gatsby*," NPR, May 2, 2013, http://www.npr.org/2013/04/30/180098344/first-listen-music-from-baz-luhrmanns-film-the-great-gatsby (accessed November 1, 2013).

33. "Obama Workout Playlist: Jay-Z, The Rolling Stones, More," *Huffington Post*, November 1, 2012, http://www.huffingtonpost.com/2012/11/01/obama-workout-playlist_n_2057357.html (accessed December 1, 2013).

34. Carol Morello, Peyton M. Craighill, and Scott Clement, "More People Express Uncertainty in Chance to Achieve the American Dream," *Washington Post*, September 28, 2013, http://www.washingtonpost.com/local/more-people-express-uncertainty-in-chance-to-achieve-the-american-dream/2013/09/28/d8e99084-260e-11e3-ad0d-b7c8d2a594b9_story.html (accessed December 1, 2013).

35. Barack Obama, "Second Democratic Presidential Nomination Acceptance Speech," video file, September 6, 2012, American Rhetoric Online Speech Bank, http://www.americanrhetoric.com/speeches/convention2012/barackobama2012dnc.htm.

Part III

The Present Imagines the Future

Chapter Thirteen

The Hunger Games, Race, and Social Class in Obama's America

Sonya C. Brown

The Hunger Games novels by Suzanne Collins were unsurprising best sellers. Swiftly paced and not too sentimental, the novels focused on a tough female protagonist, Katniss Everdeen, who inspired a revolution to save the masses of a futuristic dystopia, Panem, from the domination of an evil dictator while embroiled in a popular love triangle plot. The first novel, which gave the series its name, was published in September of 2008, and the second and third were published in subsequent years. These novels, described by the author as being partly based on popular culture and foreign wars during George W. Bush's presidency, captured frustrations expressed by many before, during, and after Barack Obama's first presidential term, including exasperation with limited, if any, progress in the wars in Afghanistan and Iraq. Collins's plot also seemed prescient in its prediction of huge gaps between social classes; indeed, the stock market dropped in the very month of its publication, ushering in the economic period now being called the Great Recession or the Global Recession, during which economic disparity increased to nearly unprecedented degrees in America, with the wealthy 1 percent controlling approximately 19 percent of the country's wealth as of September 2013, and the top 10 percent holding more than 40 percent.[1]

Collins's books, although marketed primarily as YA science fiction, blended genres and contained mature enough subject matter to appeal to a wider audience than YA; the blend of the love triangle/romantic angle of the *Twilight* saga, the minor science fiction in the weaponry and devices used by the Gamemakers and stylists of Panem's Capitol, the dystopia and war story, the coming-of-age novel for Katniss Everdeen ("The Girl on Fire"), and the social satire all in one meant the novels encompassed many demographics in the early years of Obama's first presidential term. Sales of the trilogy continue as the films are released in 2012–2015.

The novels and Obama's presidential campaign of 2008 both appealed to an American audience nervous about the nation's future, weary of longstanding social divisions, and dismayed by the previous administration's apparent disregard for the needs of the populace at home and abroad, a disregard epitomized for many in the clumsy efforts at evacuation and assistance surrounding Hurricane Katrina's devastation of the U.S. Gulf Coast in 2005. Premature announcements about the success of war efforts in Afghanistan and Iraq, the more than 750 detainees being held at Guantanamo Bay prison without trial[2] and the possible use of torture there, the length of the conflicts, all exacerbated public belief in many sectors that a regime change was necessary to change America's international policies and global image. To many, Obama's election seemed a victory for those about whose woes the previous administration seemed negligent in some of the ways that the Capitol of Panem was negligent of its Districts: the "Hope and Change" campaign promised to promote social equality, to offer health insurance to all, to close the prison in Guantanamo and end U.S. use of torture, to end the wars abroad, and to ameliorate a potential global perception of the country as a bully. The election of America's first black president also initially seemed, to some, a breakthrough in race relations. The assumption that Obama would want—and be able—to push policies promoting more welfare programs and other socialist programs was the hope of some and the phobia of others.

Of course, very few of the campaign promises have been accomplished, and none so far with resoundingly positive outcomes. For example, the president's effort to close the prison in Guantanamo was blocked by representatives of states to which the administration hoped to relocate the prisoners, and the prison remains open. The recent rollout of the health insurance website was marred by reports of improbably long delays in service on the website and higher costs for insurance than expected by many, as well as struggles over the timing of the policies affecting small businesses and hospitals that gained huge amounts of national attention.

Any hope that race relations might improve as a result of the election also appears dashed. Obama's legitimacy as president has often been challenged on grounds that strike many as racially biased in their origins, with some conservatives, and notably celebrity-investor Donald Trump, questioning the legitimacy and even existence of Obama's Hawaiian birth certificate. This group of so-called birthers argues that, rather than being born in Hawaii, Obama was born in Kenya, his father's homeland, a fact that would of course disqualify him from the presidency. The recent death of the official who released the birth certificate has renewed some of the questions about the legitimacy, despite it being the middle of Obama's second term. The case against George Zimmerman, who shot and killed unarmed teenager Trayvon

Martin under circumstances at best unclear to the general public, but who was not found guilty of any charge related to the incident, also ignited the country's focus on race relations. The Zimmerman trial's outcome suggested to many that a black teenager could legally be pursued and killed by a civilian merely for looking suspicious. Thus, as the films of the novels emerge, the nation has not achieved the effects so desired by Obama's avid supporters in the 2008 campaign.

Meanwhile, the Great Recession continues, and *The Hunger Games*'s dystopian vision has been partly translated to film. At the time of this writing, two of the intended four films based on the three novels have appeared at theaters worldwide, and both have been indisputable box office successes. The films themselves, as well as their marketing and their critical reception, reveal important nuances about America's conflicting attitudes about race and social class during Obama's first and second terms, highlighting a potential increase in awareness of race as a social category and a decrease in attentiveness to social class issues overall during his presidency.

The casting of characters for the first film, 2012's *The Hunger Games* , sparked concern over race both during casting and after the movie's release, demonstrating that rather than initiating an era in which awareness of race diminished and social harmony increased, instead Obama's tenure as president extended and perhaps even heightened racial disunity. By the fall of 2013 during Obama's second term as president, when the second film based on *The Hunger Games* trilogy appeared, several themes of the novels—the satire of the fashionable Capitol citizens and their inconsequential lives; the grim parody of American reality television programming and talk shows as a trivial distraction for the people, inuring them to the brutality of their government's policies—had been defanged. If ever the novels questioned the disproportion of most citizens' attention to America's popular culture versus politics, the films have failed so far to motivate fans to social criticism or even, in many cases, self-reflection. Even as the second film was lauded as being a technical improvement upon its predecessor, the film's marketing included almost self-parodic attempts at fashion and cosmetic sales tie-ins, demonstrating an uncanny lack of awareness of the novel's satire of those very elements of distraction in Panem's Capitol. Ultimately, the film versions of the novels reveal some of the schisms of life in America during Obama's presidency: including an inability to envision a country united across racial and ethnic boundaries and a deep lack of awareness of the novels' criticism of the triviality of American popular culture.

INSPIRATION FOR THE NOVELS: MYTH, WAR, EMPIRE, AND TELEVISION

In *The Hunger Games* trilogy, author Suzanne Collins projects a future in which the United States, through civil war, becomes the country of Panem, with the majority of the nation separated into twelve Districts forced into virtual slavery by the wealthy Capitol ruled over by President Coriolanus Snow.[3] Each District is responsible for a critical function within Panem; Katniss Everdeen's home District 12, for example, provides power, at least partly through mining coal. A thirteenth District, which rose in rebellion against the Capitol seventy-four years before the action of the trilogy, was supposedly crushed into nonexistence, though in *Mockingjay* it is revealed that District 13 has merely gone quite literally underground, waiting for the time when the remaining Districts can be incited to revolution.

Each year, the Capitol celebrates the unity of the remainder of the nation by calling for two "tributes," one male and one female, at random via a drawing called the "reaping," from the adolescents in each District. After the names from the reaping are called, one person of the same sex may volunteer to replace the selected tributes. The tributes are brought to the Capitol to compete to the death in the titular Hunger Games, which are televised throughout the Districts. While extremely popular as entertainment in the Capitol itself, the citizens of the Districts are virtually forced to watch the gruesome games unfold until only one young person survives. Throughout the year, in exchange for adding their names extra times into the lottery, youngsters can receive extra rations and oil for each member of their family. In some Districts, "career" tributes are trained from an early age to compete, whereas in other Districts, no such training is undertaken. The "Careers" unsurprisingly often win the games after volunteering during the reaping.

In interviews, Collins was routinely asked about the inspiration for the saga. She cites the source of the novels as a juxtaposition of an American reality television program and footage of war:

> One night, I was lying in bed, and I was channel surfing between reality TV programs and actual war coverage. On one channel, there's a group of young people competing for I don't even know; and on the next, there's a group of young people fighting in an actual war. I was really tired, and the lines between these stories started to blur in a very unsettling way. That's the moment when Katniss's story came to me.[4]

Tom Henthorne explains in "Real or Not Real?" how the events in the competition are similar to reality programs:

> The Hunger Games very much resemble *Survivor*, arguably the most successful of contemporary reality programs, which also pits players against each

other in an outdoor arena. Although *Survivor* contestants do not engage in hand-to-hand combat and are not placed in deadly situations, they are subjected to various forms of privation and required to participate in physical competitions that sometimes involve violence, such as when contestants must knock each other off of platforms or wrestle over objects. Both games are also at once social and individual since winning typically involves forming alliances that can only be temporary since only one contestant can win.[5]

It is important, however, not to lose sight of the fact that Collins's inspiration came not from reality television alone, but also from the reality of combat footage—combat footage that continues not to be widely aired on U.S. television, despite the fact that the war in Afghanistan has continued unabated since 2001, and the war in Iraq since 2003, resulting in approximately 57,000 U.S. casualties and more than 120,000 civilian deaths.[6] It is easy to see from the comparative lack of interest in broadcasting or viewing war coverage that American popular culture already in some ways reflects the frivolity of the Capitol of Panem. Indeed, news coverage of the war accounted for approximately 4 percent of news airtime in December of 2010, according to the Pew Research Center's Project for Excellence in Journalism.[7] Coverage of the war differs between news networks, but even the highest percentage of time dedicated to coverage of the wars abroad in 2012, on CNN, was 9 percent, or "triple the volume of competitors."[8] Throughout the novels, it is made clear that Katniss is sometimes unaware of what is happening in the Districts because the state controls the media and refuses to allow certain things to be shown. In Panem, then, the state deliberately obstructs public access to information about the oppression, rebellion, and suppression. In this way, perhaps Collins refuses to suggest that the public of Panem is jaded enough not to want to watch the coverage it isn't shown; whereas it seems clear that Americans are not demanding more war coverage in droves, or the media, driven by giving consumers what they want, might oblige.

Katniss's narration during key scenes in the book shows Collins's juxtaposition of the reality programming and the reality of combat beautifully through wordplay. For example, in her first interview with Caesar Flickerman in a pre-Hunger Game talk show, Katniss teasingly avoids telling the smarmy host how she earned a highly lethal rating from the Hunger Games judges. In response, Flickerman says, "You're killing us."[9] Soon afterward, Katniss explains how her nerves during the interview are similar to her nerves while hunting: "I feel an icy rigidity take over my body. My muscles tense as they do before a kill." The meanings of the word *kill*, both metaphorical and literal, are conflated here to demonstrate that the games are all metaphor for Panem's Capitol but very real, and very deadly, for the tributes who entertain the crowds.

Two other sources of inspiration for Collins's trilogy are the Greek myth of Theseus and the Minotaur and Imperial Rome. In the Greek myth, Cretan King Minos's hubris leads to the birth of a monstrous creature that is half man and half bull, the famous minotaur for whom the great inventor Daedalus fashions an imprisoning subterranean labyrinth and for whose nourishment King Minos demands sacrificial children from his subject states. Collins remarked in an interview that "[Crete's] message is, mess with us and we'll do something worse than kill you—we'll kill your children. And the parents sat by apparently powerless to stop it. The cycle doesn't end until Theseus volunteers to go, and he kills the Minotaur. In her own way, Katniss ... is a futuristic Theseus. But I didn't want to do a labyrinth story. So I decided to write basically an updated version of the Roman gladiator games."[10]

It is a commonplace to compare the situation of America in the late twentieth and early twenty-first centuries to that of the Roman Empire, remembered best today perhaps for its fall from dominance after wielding tremendous power over a vast territory for hundreds of years. As Pharr and Clark note in their introduction to *Of Bread, Blood, and the Hunger Games: Critical Essays on the Suzanne Collins Trilogy*, "The Hunger Games reflects the postmodern fears that things are not going well for America and that the United States may eventually fall like the Roman Empire."[11] The chief villain, President Snow, is named after the Roman general Coriolanus, whose rule in Shakespeare's tragedy is shown to be resentful of any sort of popular vote or interference in his leadership. In *Mockingjay*, it is revealed that the name "Panem" is Latin for "bread" and derives from the phrase "panem et circenses"—bread and circuses, or bread and games—a tactic for quelling rebellion used by the Romans and derided by Juvenal for distracting Roman citizens from serious issues and toward entertainment. Several other characters also have names derived from Latin, obviously including Caesar Flickerman, host of the popular talk show on which tributes are encouraged to woo viewers, in part because viewer support can be helpful in the arena, as viewers can work together to pay to send tributes valuable tools and food during the games. The Gamemakers, Seneca Crane and Plutarch Heavensbee, are endowed with names of Latin authors, and Katniss's team of groomers includes hairdresser Flavius, nail artist Octavia, and eyebrow (and other body part) waxer Venia. Cinna, Katniss's stylist who equips her with an ensemble that helps her intrigue the Capitol Hunger Games audience and also helps flare the rebellion, is similarly named for a poet in *Coriolanus*, who shares the family name of the populist Roman leader who assassinated Julius Caesar and who was killed in the confused retaliation.[12]

RACE IN THE CASTING AND POPULAR RECEPTION OF *THE HUNGER GAMES*

Collins envisions a future in which race and ethnicity no longer seem to function as meaningful social categories. Certain Districts seem to have less physically demanding, and much more lucrative, employment opportunities than do the people of Katniss's District 12 or District 11, which is dedicated to agriculture. The first novel opens on the morning of "the reaping," when Katniss slips past the fence surrounding District 12 to hunt with her friend and potential romantic interest, Gale Hawthorne. We learn that there are two classes of people in the District—those from "the Seam," who work primarily as laborers in the mines, and those whose professions are more mercantile. These social classes are readily discernible because those from "the Seam" typically have dark hair, olive skin, and gray eyes, whereas those from the merchant class tend to have blond hair and blue eyes. Both Katniss and Gale, and their deceased fathers, are people of "the Seam," whereas Katniss's mother and sister resemble the merchant class, as does Peeta Mellark, whose family are bakers.

Despite the division within District 12's populace in terms of physical features and social class, no mention is made of traditional American racial or ethnic categories. No one is described, for example, as black/African American or white/Caucasian, nor is ethnic background apparently a significant aspect of identity, as no mention of origins outside of "Panem" is made (such as Irish or Italian or Middle Eastern). Similarly, no mention of religion is made whatsoever; people in the District do not appear to worship or follow any particular faiths, and no mention of faith as it may relate to ethnicity is made.

The films based on these novels, however, were cast and filmed in a society very conscious of race and ethnicity. Thus the casting of Katniss and several other characters was debated by different groups interested in the film's diversity before and after the film's release. For example, prior to the casting of Jennifer Lawrence as Katniss, some people questioned why the casting call requested a Caucasian actress.[13] Collins's narration describes Katniss and Gale as both having an olive complexion and gray eyes, leading many to wonder what was meant by *olive*. A Google image search conducted in December 2013 for "olive complexion" intriguingly brings up a range of primarily female images, including many well-known actresses and celebrities, such as Halle Berry, Kim Kardashian, Jennifer Aniston, Catherine Zeta-Jones, Jessica Alba, Eva Mendez, Jennifer Lopez, and Alexa Chung. This wide variety of skin depth demonstrates that "olive" complexions often cross into people of "mixed" heritage, as well as those of Middle Eastern, Mediterranean, and African descent. According to the Fitzpatrick scale of human skin color, developed in 1975 by Thomas Fitzpatrick, a dermatologist associated with Harvard University, olive tones are in categories III and IV, which include "medium, white to olive" and "olive, moderate brown" skin shades.[14] It is clear, then, that the description *olive* does leave skin color open to a broad range of potential actresses who could play the part. Fan confusion, then, over how to envision Katniss depends in part on their understanding of what "olive" complexions encompass, as well as the dispersion of olive tones across many perceived racial and ethnic types. With the character's description being so vague, one person commented that "[Collins] doesn't seem clear on the ethnicity of her characters" and the website Racebending, which had previously protested casting decisions made for *The Last Airbender*, admitted to being beaten to the punch by E!Online and other sources protesting that the ethnicity of Katniss Everdeen was "purposefully left open to interpretation" in the novels.[15] In short, Collins's attempt at leaving descriptions vague for a futuristic society divided less by race and ethnicity than by social class and District failed dismally among many fans when executed as casting calls that deferred to an apparent preference for a white/Caucasian heroine in an era of racial and ethnic division.

Despite the protests, Jennifer Lawrence was cast as Katniss. Collins, interviewed together with director Gary Ross, defended the choice with assertions that Lawrence and the other white/Caucasian leads cast in the films were excellent actors for the roles. When Collins was asked whether she could identify with some fans' disappointment that Katniss was not to be played by a biracial actor, she replied,

> They were not particularly intended to be biracial. It is a time period when hundreds of years have passed from now. There has been a lot of ethnic mixing. But I think I describe them as having dark hair, grey eyes, and sort of olive skin. You know, we have hair and makeup. But there are some characters in the book that are more specifically described. . . . [Thresh and Rue are] African American.[16]

In the same vein, director Gary Ross brushed aside concerns over the casting of Lawrence without considering any actors other than Caucasians. Jen Yamato, in her article for *Movieline*, suggests fans' disappointment: "Missing the greater point, Ross assuaged fan fears with a laugh. 'I promise all the avid fans of *The Hunger Games* that we can easily deal with Jennifer's hair color.'" Responses to online articles regarding the casting decision were predictably variable, with some lauding the choice of Jennifer Lawrence and praising her "gritty" performances in *Winter's Bone* and *The Burning Plain*; others worried that Lawrence at age twenty was too old to play the teenaged Katniss in films to be shot over the course of several years, and others wondered if Lawrence wasn't too full-figured to play a character described in the novel and casting call as "underfed." Disappointment over her race sparked some heated bickering, as well, with one poster (dcmoviegirl) commenting, "Whatever. I'm tired of Hollywood casting callsheets calling for Caucasians ONLY. This should have gone to the best actress for the part. But because of that racist gaff, we only know for sure that she's the best white actress for the part. Also, Gary, [laughs], hair color wasn't the issue. I'm just tired of Hollywood doing the same exclusionary practices." In a reply to dcmoviegirl, Jesse, who seems to believe only white/Caucasian people may have olive skin, writes, "I know. its a bummer they couldn't find a black person with olive colored skin. theres plenty of them around. are you just stupid [sic]."

Neither the trilogy's author nor the director seem to have engaged with the issue at the heart of fans' discomfort, that while the book suggests a future in which there is little emphasis on race, the casting calls were very specific that the heroine be Caucasian, whereas two other characters, Thresh and Rue, were to be African American. In short, fans were disappointed that the future they had envisioned within the world of the book was envisioned by the moviemakers as a reflection of the present, and with present racial categories all too apparently being considered.

Thresh and Rue are the male and female tributes from District 11 and play key roles in the first novel and hence the film after Katniss arrives in the Capitol. In the novel, Katniss volunteers as the female tribute from District 12 after her younger sister Primrose's name is chosen. Male tribute Peeta Mellark, Capitol representative Effie Trinket, and the District 12 mentor, Haymitch Abernathy, accompany Katniss to the Capitol. During the Hunger Games, it is common for tributes to form alliances to kill other tributes—alliances that break down as the number of living tributes dwindles, until only one survivor remains. As her preparations for the Hunger Games progress, Katniss evaluates the other tributes as potential allies during the games, and during the games she befriends Rue, who reminds her of her sister in stature and who, like Primrose, is named for a yellow flower. Rue is described as having "bright, dark eyes and satiny brown skin."[17] Rue's talents for climbing quietly through trees to observe enemies, for healing with herbs, for scavenging for wild foods, and for imitating the calls of birds as signals make her a useful ally in the Hunger Games for Katniss. Rue's fragility, modesty, and generosity make her lovable to both Katniss and readers.

When the pair decides to destroy the food that is helping to sustain the energy of their enemies, they separate, and in the battle, Rue is killed before Katniss can return to her. Katniss manages to kill Rue's attacker and sings the dying child a song, then wreaths her head with flowers to attempt to retain Rue's beauty and humanity in death, refusing to discard her ally readily to the Gamemakers. This rebellious gesture of love for Rue prompts a gift from District 11's citizens. Later, in *Catching Fire*, citizens of District 11 will signal their respect for Katniss on her victory tour of the Districts, sparking continued rebellion in the Districts. Although a more minor character, Thresh does save Katniss's life, and so both are important to the plot and to Katniss's success as a contender in the games. Rue's characterization is a key to Katniss's success as a sympathetic heroine, within the world of the book and with readers.

The novel does seem clear that most people in District 11 have brown skin and brown eyes and that the District is located in the southeast portion of Panem/the United States. Rue explains to Katniss that the people of District 11 are treated even more like slaves than those in Katniss's District 12 and that there are frequent beatings for failing to fulfill quota and even minor theft. There are even suggestions that aspects of the African American cultural tradition have survived or reemerged in the futuristic District 11: Rue tells Katniss that workers in the fields sing work songs throughout the day, much as slaves in the antebellum South did.[18]

Despite these strong suggestions in *The Hunger Games* novel that residents of District 11 would primarily be the descendants of African Americans, some fans were surprised and disappointed to see that in the film, Rue is played by Amandla Stenberg, a biracial actor who is described as black/African American by most who discussed her race in relation to the film, and Thresh is played by Dayo Okeniyi, a Nigerian-born actor. The role of Cinna, Katniss's chief stylist for the pre-game events, was assigned to Lenny Kravitz, also a biracial star whom many described as black in their comments or posts about the casting decisions. In the novels, Cinna is contrasted with the other stylists for the Hunger Games. Katniss says,

> I'm taken aback by how normal he looks. Most of the stylists they interview on television are so dyed, stenciled, and surgically altered they're grotesque. But Cinna's close-cropped hair appears to be its natural shade of brown. He's in a simple black shirt and pants. The only concession to self-alteration seems to be metallic gold eyeliner that has been applied with a light hand. It brings out the flecks of gold in his green eyes. And . . . I can't help thinking how attractive it looks.[19]

Cinna is not, then, so clearly described in ways currently associated with race as Rue and Thresh, yet nothing in the description suggests he might not be black/African American, or of mixed race like Kravitz.

Reactions to the first film's casting from the novel's teen fans included some surprise and, in several cases that quickly became infamous when reposted via blog and Twitter, disappointment that actors perceived as black/African American had been cast in several key roles. Many of the tweets and posts to other social media made by these dismayed fans were captured by a Canadian fan of the books, who explains in his tumblr account "Hunger Games Tweets" that his motives were to "expose the Hunger Games fans on Twitter who dare to call themselves fans yet don't know a damn thing about the books."[20] The tumblr site went viral. While hundreds of these posts were reposted, several of the most repugnant revealed a deep racism within the books' young fans. As Dodai Stewart comments in a post to the website Jezebel, "The posts go on and on and on. It's not just a coupe [sic] of tweets, it's not just a coincidence. There's an underlying rage, coming out as overt prejudice and plain old racism. Sternberg [sic] is called a 'black bitch,' a 'nigger' and one person writes that though he pictured Rue with 'darker skin,' he 'didn't really take it all the way to black.'"[21] Some of the most reposted comments include: "EWW Rue is black?? I'm not watching," "why did the producer make all the good characters black smh," and "Kk call me racist but when I found out rue was black her death wasn't as sad #ihatemyself."[22] (Perhaps not coincidentally, a recent repost on the tumblr account calls out teenagers who write racist remarks about President Obama.)

Some of the tweets posted on Hunger Games Tweets tumblr, as L.V. Anderson points out on *Slate*, seem to suggest that the people who envisioned Rue as a blond girl were suffering from a reading comprehension issue, exacerbated by Katniss seeing her sister, Primrose, in Rue because both are slight and delicate, or perhaps because of the emphasis on yellow in their namesake flowers and their association with blond hair. Anderson points out that not all of the surprise over the casting of Rue is racist, as expressing surprise is not equivalent with expressing disappointment. Anderson goes on to point out that those who commented on the tumblr account were often vicious in their attacks on the putatively racist remarks, which is not necessarily better or more moral than the racism supposedly under attack, and unlikely to inspire changes of mind within the supposed offenders.[23]

Of course, with every post about *The Hunger Games* being followed by reactions, and then more reactions and conversations within the reactions, the discussion is difficult to map. It is clear, however, that attempting to cast a movie in a futuristic world that ignores race becomes problematic and sparks conversation about the very real racial issues in the casting of Hollywood films in today's America.

DESPAIR, DISPARITY, FASHION, AND *THE HUNGER GAMES: CATCHING FIRE*

Collins's narrator-heroine, Katniss Everdeen, never minces words when it comes to revealing her attitudes toward the grooming rituals and fashions of the Capitol's citizens and those who, like Effie Trinket, mentor her in the ways of fashion and appearance in order to appeal to viewers of the Hunger Games and all the pre-game televised promotional material she is forced to endure. Flavius, Octavia, and Venia, who work with Cinna to prepare Katniss for her debut as a tribute in the Capitol, are treated ironically in *The*

Hunger Games: "[Flavius] gives his orange corkscrew locks a shake and applies a fresh coat of purple lipstick to his mouth. 'If there's one thing we can't stand,' he says approvingly to Katniss, who faces death in the arena but has just finished being waxed from the neck down without an objection, 'It's a whiner. Grease her down!'" Octavia is described as having skin "dyed a pale shade of pea green," and as the three examine their charge, Katniss notes, "I know I should be embarrassed, but they're so unlike people that I'm no more self-conscious than if a trio of oddly colored birds were pecking around my feet."[24] Only Cinna seems aware of how Katniss feels about the Capitol representatives who depilate her and make her up: "I look up and find Cinna's eyes trained on mine. 'How despicable we must seem to you,' he says. Has he seen this in my face or somehow read my thoughts? He's right, though. The whole rotten lot of them is despicable."[25] Later, Katniss connects her upset over the Capitol's obsession with appearance with her own reality in District 12:

> Caesar Flickerman . . . who has hosted the interview for more than forty years, bounces onto the stage. . . . His appearance has been virtually unchanged in all that time. Same face under a coating of pure white makeup. Same hairstyle that he dyes a different color for each Hunger Games. . . . They do surgery in the Capitol, to make people appear younger and thinner. In District 12, looking old is something of an achievement since so many people die early. You see an elderly person, you want to congratulate them on their longevity, ask the secret of survival. A plump person is envied because they aren't scraping by like the majority of us. But here it is different. Wrinkles aren't desirable. A round belly isn't a sign of success.[26]

Katniss's disgust over the stylists and Capitol citizens and celebrities may or may not be part of the novel's satire of reality programming (such as the fashion design competition *Project Runway*), but the satire is clearly a commentary on the pursuit of beauty through artificial procedures to the point of health hazards like that of another reality television performer, Heidi Montag of *The Hills* (she briefly attended fashion design school), whose plastic surgeries have been chronicled in numerous tabloid outlets. Montag is certainly not only pursuing fame through multiple surgeries and numerous appearances on reality programs, which seem sometimes to beget each other. And the irony here is that the obsession with celebrity for its own sake is compounded by the obsession with a particular youthful and lean beauty in America's popular culture that Naomi Wolf argued in *The Beauty Myth* prevented or distracted at least American women from focusing on economic and social issues.[27] Other social scholars note that an obsession with physical appearance and fashion is not relegated solely to women,[28] and it is clear that in Panem, as in America, both men and women are judged at least in part on their "swag" and attractiveness.

Despite her disgust, however, there is no doubt that Cinna's work as her stylist, using a fake "fire" on Katniss's capes and gowns throughout her presentation in the first novel and the same fake fire to burn away a white wedding dress to reveal a glamorous mockingjay ensemble in *Catching Fire*, helps Katniss both catch the attention of the Capitol viewers and foment rebellion in the Districts. Indeed, Cinna's work helps give Katniss her nickname, "The Girl on Fire," and connects Katniss and the rebellion in the title of the second novel and film. Cinna is later revealed to be working with Haymitch (the District 12 mentor), Plutarch Heavensbee (the Gamemaker in *Catching Fire*), and even other tributes in the Quarter Quell Hunger Games, to save Katniss's life and promote the brewing revolution. Katniss herself is ambivalent about the fashion, feeling in some ways that it is silly and takes focus away from the real problems of starving people and social inequity she sees in the Districts. Yet she enjoys wearing the clothes Cinna has designed, something perhaps to be understood in a teenaged heroine: "I do love the [clothes] Cinna makes for me. . . . Flowing black pants made of thick, warm material. A comfortable white shirt. A sweater woven from green and blue and gray strands of kitten-soft wool. Laced leather boots that don't pinch my toes."[29]

Katniss seems primarily to value the comfort of clothing made precisely for her from soft materials. As a person living in a desperate situation in which even her hunting for food beyond the fences of District 12 is a punishable offense, the character has presumably rarely had opportunities to purchase new clothing and must wear clothes even when they are worn out or too small. A reader, then, can empathize with Katniss's enjoyment of wearing clothes tailored to fit her. Her other comments about fashion seem designed to portray her as someone grateful to the Capitol for its largesse to her as victor, as when she tells Caesar Flickerman that she "can't believe" she's wearing such a "gorgeous costume."[30] There, however, Collins's dialogue is clear that her clothes are a costume, not what Katniss would choose for herself but part of the role she is playing as a "reality star" who must woo fans. Her real social class as a citizen of District 12, especially one from the Seam, marks her as almost subhuman in the eyes of Flavius and the others, though Collins is careful not to make the Capitol citizens terrible people, only ignorant ones. For example, Katniss praises them internally for their respect for her mother's ability to braid her hair in a classical style. The point, therefore, is not that the Capitol citizens are bad people, merely people distracted into a faulty set of values, based on their misunderstanding that others have the same creature comforts and leisure time for attending to appearance that they have. Thus Collins's satire is biting and yet not cruel, leaving the citizens room to learn and grow once they move from ignorance into knowledge.

Katniss's ambivalence is not well-preserved in the films, especially *Catching Fire*, in part because the filmmakers sought a synergistic tie-in with fashion and other products. Of course, publicity for the film included the appearance of its star, Jennifer Lawrence. For example, in the September 2013 issue of *Vogue*, Lawrence is featured on the cover and in a ten-page interview/photo spread. Also interviewed for the piece was the director of the film *Catching Fire*, Francis Lawrence, who remarks, "I thought there were amazing opportunities for some great fashion moments in the film."[31] Additional quotes from Trish Summerville, the film's costume designer, suggest her vision: "In the first film, it looked like everyone shopped at the same store. I wanted to show variety. The elite, but from all walks of life. So I did fashion trends: Molded felt hats are all the rage! Plaids are in! That kind of thing!"

At least as reflected in this interview, then, neither the director nor the costume designer seem aware that the novels are critical of too much attention being placed on clothing and other appearance-related pursuits. Neither appears to comment or reflect on how their attention to fashion and potential money-making film tie-ins are at odds with the criticism within the novels of just that type of behavior. Overall, comment on the connection between the glamorization of the bizarre costumes in the film and the novels is lacking. Others, when describing the costumes, perhaps unwittingly connect the film to American popular culture. When describing Effie Trinket's clothing, for example, Jonathan Van Meter compares her to "[Lady] Gaga's Crazy Auntie." In other words, the Capitol citizens look like contemporary American pop stars wearing outré outfits that prompt as much admiration for their originality and attention-grabbing ability as distaste for their excess or, indeed, their minimalism.

Perhaps it is predictable, then, that the merchandizing of *Hunger Games* fashions occurred, just as the use of pop stars to sell fashion and beauty products is rampant in American marketing and advertising today. Summerville produced a fashion line based on creations from *Catching Fire*. Other media outlets, such as the *New York Times* and *Vanity Fair*, featured stories about the clothing used in the film, highlighting the designers, such as Alexander McQueen and Tex Savario, whose work was incorporated into the vision of the Capitol designed by Summerville and her team, and praising Summerville and the looks of the characters in the film.[32]

Clothing was not the only item generating interest and potential sales based on the film. In the same *Vogue* issue as the interview with Lawrence, for example, a five-page, foldout advertisement for CoverGirl makeup related to the film shows models wearing hair, makeup, and clothing inspired by Panem's Districts. In this ad, the Capitol image is shown with blond hair that seems like a cross between a Marie Antoinette–style wig and an Afro, adorned with gold jewels, reflecting an ameliorated picture of Effie Trinket, played by Elizabeth Banks in the films, who comments that her team (including Katniss, Peeta, and herself) will show their solidarity by having a gold token of some sort—for Effie, it's her bizarre bouffant hair and her metallic eye makeup. In the CoverGirl ad, the model's gown and huge jeweled ring are also gold-toned, while her lips and nails are red. All of the makeup items (eye shadow, nail polish, and so on) are displayed on the opposing page as "Inspired by District 1: The Luxury Look." Another model wears iridescent blue, green, and gold; sequins; and gloves that look like fishing nets to represent "District 4: The Fishing Look." On CoverGirl's website, a diverse cast of models portrays hair, makeup, and costumes for all twelve Districts, with all sorts of makeup available for sale in the "Flamed Out Capitol Collection."[33]

Another tumblr account (Capitol Cuties) was set up to critique the irony of the films tie-ins—including the CoverGirl makeup but also other marketing tie-ins like "fiery" sandwiches at the Subway restaurant chain and others.[34] This site, however, did not gain as much traction as the Hunger Games Tweets site. It is notable, however, that a film based on a novel that satirizes the entertainment industry that focuses on appearance and ignores starvation all around it prompted the sale of sandwiches, clothes, and makeup, rather than food drives. The films' focus could have been much more critical of contemporary America, but instead, they endorse the popular culture, aiming at the totalitarianism of the Panem Capitol's government alone.

CONCLUSION

If the novels are about satirizing the way that having "panem et circenses" distracts people from those who do not have their daily bread and other luxuries, the films veer toward praising the circuses. So far, it appears *The Hunger Games* films have done in American popular culture a bit of what the Hunger Games within the novels do for the citizens of Panem's Capitol. Rather than inspiring greater focus on the widening disparity in America's economy or increasing attention to those abroad who continue to remain embroiled in a war Americans themselves frequently seem to have no interest in, the Hunger Games films have instead focused our attention on the imagined heroics in the film, the glamour of Katniss's transformation, the deadly dangers she endures, the deaths in the arenas, the frivolity of the Capitol denizens, and the choices Katniss must make between two potential lovers.

In *Mockingjay*, the last novel, which is to be filmed in two separate installments in an attempt to imitate the commercial success of doing so with the *Twilight* film franchise, Katniss learns that the change of leaders from President Snow to revolutionary President Alma Coin from District 13 does not suggest nearly the type of radical change Katniss and many other revolutionaries may have hoped for, and she ultimately assassinates President Coin in order to prevent that leader from repeating the grasping for power of Snow and the Capitol's former leaders. Also, Katniss's beloved sister, Prim, for whom she volunteered as tribute in the first place, is killed during the revolution, making Katniss's sacrifice personally unfulfilling. In the end, the vision of the novels is that there is no change profound enough to change the fact that power corrupts, and life once lost cannot be regained. It will be intriguing to see if the final installments of this film series attempt more powerfully to critique the ways America is like Panem already, or if the two remaining films will continue to offer the circenses form of entertainment, replete with fashionable Katniss Everdeen footwear and Effie Trinket make-up kits, that revealed its lost sense of satire in *Catching Fire*.

NOTES

1. Paul Wiseman, "Richest One Percent Earn Biggest Share since 20's," *Excite News*, September 10, 2013, http://apnews.excite.com/article/20130910/DA8NN7U02.html (accessed January 7, 2013).

2. U.S. Department of Defense, "List of Individuals Detained by the Department of Defense at Guantanamo Bay, Cuba from January 2002 through May 15, 2006," http://www.dod.mil/pubs/foi/operation_and_plans/Detainee/detaineesFOIArelease15May2006.pdf.

3. Names in the novels are so rife with meaning that a book and several websites are available to analyze them, including Valerie Estelle Frankel's self-published book *Katniss the Cattail: An Unauthorized Guide to Names and Symbols in Suzanne Collins' The Hunger Games* (February 13, 2013) and Miriam Krule, "The Hunger Names," *Slate.com*, November 21, 2013, http://www.slate.com/blogs/browbeat/2013/11/21/hunger_games_catching_fire_names_explained_meaning_of_katniss_everdeen_plutarch.html (accessed January 7, 2014).

4. John A. Sellers, "A Dark Horse Breaks Out: The Buzz Is on for Suzanne Collins's YA Series Debut," PublishersWeekly.com, June 9, 2008, http://www.publishersweekly.com/pw/print/20080609/9915-a-dark-horse-breaks-out.html (accessed December 4, 2013).

5. Tom Henthorne, "'Real or Not Real?': Reality Television and The Hunger Games Trilogy," in *Approaching the Hunger Games Trilogy: A Literary and Cultural Analysis* (Jefferson, N.C.: McFarland, 2012), chap. 5.

6. Actual numbers of casualties are difficult to track, so various organizations provide different data: "The Deaths of Afghans: Civilian fatalities in Afghanistan, 2001–2013," TheNation.com, http://www.thenation.com/afghanistan-database (accessed December 17, 2013); "Documented Civilian Deaths by Violence," Iraq Body Count Database, http://www.iraqbodycount.org/database/ (accessed December 17, 2013).

7. Brian Stelter, "Afghan War Just a Slice of U.S. Coverage," *New York Times*, December 19, 2010, http://www.nytimes.com/2010/12/20/business/media/20coverage.html (accessed December 31, 2013).

8. Mark Jurkowitz, Paul Hitlin, Amy Mitchell, Laura Santhanam, Steve Adams, Monica Anderson, and Nancy Vogt, "The Changing TV News Landscape, The State of the News Media 2013: An Annual Report on American Journalism," The Pew Research Center, http://stateofthemedia.org/2013/special-reports-landing-page/the-changing-tv-news-landscape/ (accessed December 30, 2013).

9. Suzanne Collins, *The Hunger Games* (New York: Scholastic, 2008), 129.

10. Sellers, "A Dark Horse Breaks Out."

11. Mary F. Pharr and Leisa A. Clark, introduction, in *Of Bread, Blood, and the Hunger Games: Critical Essays on the Suzanne Collins Trilogy*, ed. Donald E. Palumbo and C. W. Sullivan III (Jefferson, N.C.: McFarland, 2012), 9.

12. Krule, "The Hunger Names."
13. Marissa Lee, "Jennifer Lawrence Cast as Katniss in "The Hunger Games," Racebending.com, March 19, 2011, http://www.racebending.com/v4/featured/jennifer-lawrence-cast-as-katniss-in-the-hunger-games/ (accessed December 4, 2013); Jen Yamato, "Gary Ross Defends Jennifer Lawrence Casting, Says Hunger Games Author Approves," Movieline.com, March 17, 2011, http://movieline.com/2011/03/17/gary-ross-defends-jennifer-lawrence-casting-says-hunger-games-author-approves/ (accessed December 4, 2013).
14. "Fitzpatrick Scale," Wikipedia.org (accessed December 4, 2013).
15. Lee, "Jennifer Lawrence Cast as Katniss."
16. Karen Valby, "Team 'Hunger Games' Talks: Author Suzanne Collins and Director Gary Ross on Their Allegiance to Each Other, and Their Actors," *Entertainment Weekly Inside Movies*, April 7, 2011, http://insidemovies.ew.com/2011/04/07/hunger-games-suzanne-collins-gary-ross-exclusive/comment-page-2/ (accessed December 4, 2013).
17. Collins, *The Hunger Games*, 98.
18. Collins, *The Hunger Games*, 122–23.
19. Collins, *The Hunger Games*, 63.
20. http://hungergamestweets.tumblr.com/.
21. Dodai Stewart, "Racist Hunger Games Fans Are Very Disappointed," Jezebel.com, March 26, 2012, http://jezebel.com/5896408/racist-hunger-games-fans-dont-care-how-much-money-the-movie-made (accessed December 4, 2013).
22. Users are using "text" language here. *smh* is an abbreviation for "shaking my head"; *kk* is the equivalent of "okay, okay."
23. L. V. Anderson, "Talking to Teens Who Posted Racist Things about Hunger Games," Slate.com, April 11, 2012, http://www.slate.com/blogs/browbeat/2012/04/11/_racist_hunger_games_tweeters_speak_out_deny_being_racist.html (accessed December 31, 2014).
24. Collins, *The Hunger Games*, 62.
25. Suzanne Collins, *Catching Fire* (New York: Scholastic, 2009), 63.
26. Collins, *Catching Fire*, 124–25.
27. Naomi Wolf, *The Beauty Myth: How Images of Beauty Are Used against Women* (New York: Harper Perennial, 2002).
28. For examples, see Harrison G. Pope, Katharine A. Phillips, and Roberto Olivardia, *The Adonis Complex: How to Identify, Treat and Prevent Body Obsession in Men and Boys* (New York: Free Press, 2002); and Susan Bordo, *The Male Body: A New Look at Men in Public and Private* (New York: Farrar, Strauss and Giroux, 2000).
29. Collins, *Catching Fire*, 9.
30. Collins, *Hunger Games*, 128.
31. Jonathan Van Meter, "Star Quality," *Vogue*, September 2013, 793.
32. Kathryn Shattuck, "What the Well-Dressed Warrior Wears: Costume Design in 'The Hunger Games: Catching Fire,'" *New York Times*, November 1, 2013, http://www.nytimes.com/2013/11/03/movies/costume-design-in-the-hunger-games-catching-fire.html?_r=1& (accessed December 31, 2013); Chris Rozvar, "Hunger Games Fashion: Costume Designer Trish Summerville Talks about Her Favorite Looks from Catching Fire," VanityFair.com, November 19, 2013, http://www.vanityfair.com/online/oscars/2013/11/hunger-games-fashion-trish-summerville (accessed January 7, 2014).
33. http://www.covergirl.com/capitolbeautystudio/catching-fire?&utm_source=google&utm_medium=cpc&utm_term=%2Bcovergirl%20%2Bcapitol&utm_campaign=Covergirl_Search_Brand+Awareness.BMM&utm_content=sshPyUUCP_dc|35156419718.
34. http://capitolcuties.tumblr.com/.

Chapter Fourteen

Rise of the Planet of the People: Contradictions and Revolution in *Rise of the Planet of the Apes*

doug morris

And by union what we will,
Can be accomplished still,
Drops of water turn a wheel,
Singly none, singly none . . .
—"Step by Step (The Longest March)"

Apes alone, weak; apes together, strong.
—Caesar (*Rise of the Planet of the Apes*)

A REVOLUTIONARY FILM?

In "the age of Obama," or in any other recent age, it is depressingly rare in the United States to see a Hollywood film that literally promotes identification with resistance, rebellion, and revolution in the context of an anti-capitalist agenda and struggle. It is highly unusual to see a film that promotes solidarity, a rising of the "prisoners of starvation,"[1] and even armed, though mostly nonviolent, struggle against dominant systems of repression and degradation emergent with the regime of capital. It is striking to see a popular Hollywood film taking up multiple notions of alienation, for example, exploring how an ideology and system dominated by exchange value over use value in the production of commodities alienates us from a meaningful and livable relationship with nature (including our own nature). It is stirring to see a Hollywood film persistently interrogate one of the primary contradictions of life under capitalism, the contradiction between appearances and reality. It is odd to see a film that intimates how capitalism contains within its own contradictions the seeds of its own destruction (though in the case of the film under examination below, it must be said, we are left to ponder whether the system of capital is destroyed or if only humanity is destroyed and capital remains to be either governed by or later abolished and replaced by intelligent apes).

It is uncommon to see a film that generates storylines (in a somewhat coded form) about the institutional and human tensions present under hegemonic capitalism's social formations, for example, the tension between rational and moral research pursued for the greater good and immoral and irrational research pursued to maximize profits and market share resulting in the greater harm. It is surprising to see a film that alludes to how capitalism uses racialization, incarceration, surveillance, and violence to control, subdue, and dehumanize the other (in this case, the "other" is represented by apes), and how accumulation through dispossession in both material and ideological forms is central to the expansion of capital's markets and profits. It is noteworthy to witness a film that examines how contradictions under the regime of capital may prove fatal to the future of humanity, as well as to observe a film that reveals the dangers that will result from not looking honestly and critically for the realities behind capital's disguises, for example, not seeing (or not caring to look at) the potentially grave harm and greater problems that rest behind the appearance of an achieved cure or solution. It is strange but satisfying to witness a film that connects problems *in* the system to problems *of* the system of capital, for example, a film that looks at the connection between localized abuse, maltreatment, and dispossession (in different locales) representing problems *in* the system, and connects them to the systemic imperative to accumulate and the structural determination to expand that drive the system of capital to relentlessly pursue, at all costs, the exploitation and abuse of nature and workers on a global scale.

It is chillingly surprising to see a film extend the interrogation and suggest that the problems *of* the system of capital may likely produce problems *in* multiple social and ecological systems to the point where it is beyond our capacity to contend with the crises. It is atypical to see a film that not only reveals the profit motive under capital as a machine of abuse, a vehicle of dispossession, and an engine of destruction but also suggests how emancipation from domination by and subjugation to that rampaging global system will come only through an educated, energized, informed, and inclusive popular movement dedicated to eliminating the relentlessly rapacious beast of capital as the driving mechanism of the social disorder, and returning to an existence more in harmony with the rest of nature.

All of these features are conspicuously, and often metaphorically, present in Rupert Wyatt's compelling and stirringly radical 2011 film *Rise of the Planet of the Apes* (*RPA*). When the main characters are apes, we are compelled to extend the metaphors! It is no accident that the film hit the streets at a time when people in multiple locations around the world were taking to the streets in mass uprisings against injustice, inequality, and indignity, from Africa, to the Middle East, to Latin America, to the United States.[2] And, revealingly, the film went "bananas at the box office,"[3] as the number-one film in the United States, suggesting at least some identification with the revolutionary content, if not intent, of the film, especially among younger U.S. filmgoers (judging from personal interviews), even though 60 percent of audiences were over twenty-five.[4] In conversations with fellow viewers, after three different screenings in the summer of 2011, in three different states (New Mexico, Arizona, Pennslvania), in response to the question "What was it about the film you found most compelling?" the overwhelming answer was along the lines of "When the apes rebelled against the system of mistreatment" or "When the apes rose up and fought back" or "When the apes finally returned to the forest at the end." And in response to the questions "With what character did you most identify?" and "Who was the most despicable character?" the answers in almost every case were "Caesar [the ape revolutionary leader]" for the former question, and "Jacobs [the tyrannical 'personification of capital'[5] and CEO of Gen Sys]" for the latter question. Most of those questioned were under twenty-five, and many were high school students.

The answers tentatively suggest a hopeful and simmering anger at unjust systems and unfair treatment; a recognition, perhaps in coded form, of capital's destructive tendencies and structurally determined failings and the pedagogical power of capital's ideological and cultural enterprise to dehumanize (i.e., a power to direct decent people to carry out indecent actions); a moderate capacity to see beyond the ideological masks and disguises used by capital to legitimate itself and to perpetuate its class domination and power; and a smoldering desire to "produce a different [and better] future to that which capitalism portends."[6]

While one does not want to overstate the case based on limited polling information from a rather narrow field of audiences after only three screenings in three U.S. states, and based on one evocatively revolutionary film, the results suggest a large body of radical people among us, or people on the verge of becoming radicalized, who might, given the construction of "political instruments that facilitate processes whereby people can transform society and themselves,"[7] act willingly on their anger and knowledge, and collectively engage in a kind of anti-capitalist political struggle urgently demanded during these perilous times of global crises in "the age of Obama," and beyond.

What those instruments might be and how they should be constructed is one of the tasks left to those of us outside the world of the provocations of *Rise of the Planet of the Apes*. The film leaves us with only weak intimations of what an animated vision of an alternative system might look like but with somewhat clearer indications of what it is we should organize to oppose and overcome. Among other things, an anti-capitalist struggle, of the sort strongly intimated in the film, requires that we follow the lead of the revolutionary ape, Caesar, and allow our outrage to manifest in a collectively rambunctious and rebellious call that says "No!"—i.e., "Enough is enough"—so that we will not take anymore the exploitation, abuse, and destruction consequent with capital's structural imperatives and global expansion. The collective "No!" echoes also the recognition that while it may be true "we have been naught; we shall be all."[8]

In short, the film leaves us with the urgent and compelling task of working to inspire a rise of the planet of the people. Recognizing this means understanding the power of film to function as an educational force and influence machine in the larger society and world.

FILMS AS PUBLIC PEDAGOGY AND THE NEED TO BE CRITICAL

It is surprising to see all of this radical/revolutionary content in a Hollywood film because films function as forms of public pedagogy in the wider culture in that they not only reflect, perpetuate, and reproduce dominant values, beliefs, ideologies, policies, and power systems (far from radical and revolutionary in the United States), but they also construct identities, direct desires, shape values, inculcate beliefs, fuel aspirations, build identifications, and promote attitudes that possess the potential for opening up processes through which people can change themselves and change society. Films can critically take on the contradictions between appearance and reality and can thus help us to both understand the world in which we live and also transform it. In that sense, films can have a revolutionary intention that links knowledge and understanding to agency and transformation. Films can also distort, disguise, and mask reality, and in that sense films serve the interests of dominant systems and ideologies; but they can also, when critical, see into and through the distortions, disguises, and masks, and thus serve the interest of altering perceptions, informing actions, and changing reality when connected to organized collective struggle.

As ideological and material processes and practices enmeshed and operating in, and circulating through, complex social, economic, political, historical, and cultural webs of institutions and people, films inevitably change circumstances and change people. The changes can constrain radical change by promoting the status quo, or the changes can critically spark flames of resistance that can be employed in struggles against the status quo of the sort that arise in *RPA*. In this sense, films must be seen and understood as a human activity, process, and set of relations that always bring with them the potential for revolutionary change, especially when we understand "revolutionary practice" as the "simultaneous changing of circumstances and human activity or self-change."⁹ The change in circumstances changes people and the changes in people changes the circumstances, a dialectical process that works both materially and ideologically. Films are thus always and everywhere political and moral processes, as well as material and ideological sets of relations that can fuel or stifle human agency, human understanding, as well as social transformation. As a moral process, films can reflect and reproduce immoralities present in larger systems, or when critical they can inspire moral actions to oppose injustices. As political processes, films can reflect and reproduce dominant systems and relations of oppressive and hierarchical power, but when critical they can work to reshape the way we think about how we live together with other people in society and therefore lead to social and political transformations along more egalitarian and democratic lines.

Acting productively, creatively, and coherently in the world requires that we see beyond surface-level appearances into what are often harsh institutional realities. As imagination machines, films can help us see into and beyond the masks and disguises that hide the realities beneath. Among other things, this means looking beyond problems *in* the system and into problems *of* the system that produce and perpetuate problems *in* the system. In other words, it means looking beyond symptoms and into root causes of problems, a necessary step if we are to overcome that which is most urgently demanded in terms of structural change and systemic transformations. The contradiction between surface appearances and underlying realities is one we must explore in order to critically address and understand the relationship between causes, agents, and effects, that is, of problems *in* and *of* the system.

NO!

RPA opens with a slow descent into lush jungles in Africa. Birds sing (a sound motif throughout the film indicating freedom). A seemingly carefree community of apes is traversing the forest floor. Humans appear from the shadows and violently assault the apes, capturing/rendering any number of them and placing them into harsh box-like metal containers out of which an ape can look into the world only through a tiny square opening. We soon learn the apes are treated as mere objects to be consumed, contained, and condemned in service to a U.S. (and global) corporate system driven to maximize profits. One of the captured apes is later known as "Bright Eyes" (because of a fierce green glow in her eyes consequent with the introduction of a viral-based drug named ALZ112 into her system as part of an experiment geared toward producing a treatment for Alzheimer's). "Bright Eyes," it turns out, was pregnant at the time of her brutal abduction (unbeknownst to her human keepers) and becomes the mother of the main ape character in the film, the eventual revolutionary, "Caesar."

The film transitions from the jungle to the research lab (a research lab in which the dark jungle of capitalism proves far more barbaric than the dark forests of Africa) where "Bright Eyes" is performing on a "Lucas Tower" (a puzzle involving rods and disks) at a level near perfection, a result of the introduction of the ALZ112 gene therapy. One of the first lines spoken in the film is uttered by the CEO of Gen Sys, Steven Jacobs (David Oyelowo), who tells lead researcher Will Rodman (James Franco), "There is a lot of money riding on this; keep personal emotions out of it." This provides an early indication of how the system in which people are working alienates them in multiple ways, including alienating them from their basic moral emotional attachments. In short, it is an indication of how the system dehumanizes people (and ironically, humanizes apes). Jacobs adds, referring to investors in the ALZ112 research project, "These people invest in results; not dreams." Here we see an indication of how the system driven by money constrains the imagination because at the end of the day it is not innovative dreams that matter but technological innovations that promote profits and perpetuate the dominant and dominating class relations under capital that matter. Benefits that improve the conditions of life are, in the end, incidental. If a technological innovation is produced that would undermine profits and power but improve conditions of life, it would not be pursued, promoted, or supported financially.

Soon thereafter, in a meeting with potential investors in which Will describes the sterling successes of the experiments on apes with ALZ112 and expresses how it will treat a "virtually limitless" range of brain ailments, Jacobs adds that the potential for profits is also virtually limitless, reminding investors and viewers of what matters most. In the background looms a large investment graph promising ten years of escalating profits on the initial investment. Gen Sys is looking for support to extend the experiment into human trials. Just prior to the vote to approve human trials, "Bright Eyes," screaming and wildly gesticulating, crashes through the large investment graph into the room and is immediately shot and killed. Jacobs is offended by the disruption in his plans and the undermining of the potential for years of steadily climbing profits and expanding markets. He therefore orders a research assistant to kill all the remaining apes. When the assistant, Robert Franklin (Tyler Labine), is reluctant to carry out the task, Jacobs condescendingly tells him, "I run a business, not a petting zoo," indicating strongly that in the business system under capital there is no room for care, compassion, tenderness, kindness, or forgiveness, but only room for the ruthless and relentless pursuit of profits and market share. What does not contribute to serving the bottom line is disposable and will be eliminated.

Soon thereafter, Jacobs tells Will, in reference to how investors will respond to data versus real world results, "Will, you know everything about the human brain; except how it works!" In the context of the surrounding scenes with investors and calls for extermination, the intimation is that Will does not understand how the mind is shaped by the system of capital, that is, he does not understand how people are conditioned to make decisions based on the capacity of a commodity to produce a profit in the market place, a capacity that determines whether and in what quantity it will be produced. Whether it is human or environmentally friendly is largely irrelevant (a theme explored with devastating results later in the film). The intimation is that Will brings a moral sense of his humanity into the workplace, and there is no place for that in the corporate facility.

It turns out that "Bright Eyes" was not being aggressive but protective of her young baby, another case in the film in which appearance trumps reality with deadly consequences. In the meantime, Robert has killed all the apes, except for the baby left behind after the shooting of "Bright Eyes." Robert refuses to kill the baby ape and hands Will Rodman the needle to carry out the task. Rodman cannot do it either and ends up taking the baby ape home, where he soon notes the same fierce green light in his eyes.

Rodman lives with and cares for his father, Charles, a former music teacher, who is in the later stages of Alzheimer's (one of the reasons Will is driven to develop ALZ112). Charles names the baby ape "Caesar," after the character from Shakespeare's play *The Tragedy of Julius Caesar*. The film flashes forward several years, and we learn that Caesar has perfected the "Lucas Tower" puzzle, uses sign language to sign up to twenty-four words, plays chess well, and is beyond his human counterparts of the same age in mental dexterity. Will discovers that the ALZ112 was passed genetically from mother, "Bright Eyes," to the baby, "Caesar." Caesar's existence is unknown to the rest of the world outside of Will's house.

When the nurse who attends to Charles's increasingly demanding needs tells Will his father belongs in a home because "this is no way to live," Will decides to purloin a stockpile of ALZ112. He then experimentally administers a dose to his father. The initial results are rather miraculous. Charles not only regains his musical skills, but his mental acuity is enhanced beyond what it was before the Alzheimer's set in. Will is encouraged and relieved by the results; the appearance, however, is not the same as the underlying reality, as proves often the case in the film.

Caesar is feeling trapped; he spends a lot of time gazing out an upper-floor window at the trees just beyond. It is clear he is feeling alienated from his own nature and the nature outside. After seeing several children playing outside, he escapes through an open window into the neighbor's garage and yard. Will's neighbor, an international pilot (a point that later proves disastrous) named Douglas Hunsiker (David Hewlett), attempts to assault Caesar with a baseball bat, but is constrained by Will at the last moment. Hunsiker assumed, not unwisely perhaps, that Caesar is a threatening beast, and he responds defensively (he has young children). The fact is Caesar is by now a much "humanized" ape, who is not a threat. In fact, we later learn, he is possessed of a strong streak of kindness, care, and protective solidarity. But this encounter is another case in which appearances are confused with the reality, and while this initial encounter ends favorably, the next confrontation with Hunsiker does not. In some sense, it is the neighbor's initial hostility that leads, eventually, to a complex series of other hostile relations and to the revolt of the apes (more on that below).

Caesar is injured and requires treatment at the local zoo. It is here that Will meets Dr. Caroline Aranha (Freida Pinto), apparently a veterinarian and paleontologist, who tends to Caesar's wound. Will and Caroline begin a romantic relationship (left cinematically largely undeveloped). She soon warns Will that it is appropriate to be afraid of chimps, a warning that is a precursor to the later revolt of the apes (humanized apes, it should be added).

A trip to the Redwood forest opens with an act of supplication from Caesar. Caesar is released into the trees and he climbs to the top and looks out over the San Francisco Bay and Golden Gate Bridge (in a foreshadowing of the end of the film proper) and the film flashes forward several years. In returning to the car, with Caesar on a leash, there is an encounter with a barking German Shepherd, also on a leash. Caesar reacts angrily and ferociously, not only because of the barking dog (who poses no real threat) but because he sees himself as also a pet on a leash (a greater threat to his sense of self and well-being). He is insulted at this diminishment and humiliation. The scene ends with an act of defiance from Caesar when he refuses to sit in the back of the station wagon, but instead moves forward into a seat (a subtle reference to Rosa Parks and her 1955 act of defiance that helped fuel the spread of the civil rights movements in the United States).

Soon thereafter, Will explains to Caesar what happened to Caesar's mother and how he has come to be endowed with advanced mental tools and skills beyond that of the normal ape and, in some sense, beyond that of the normal human. Will's father, Charles, soon begins reverting to a state of dementia as his body forms antibodies that attack the ALZ112 viral drug. In a hyper-confused state, he enters the neighbor's prized car and with little control over his mental or motor functions drives the car forward and backward into other cars. This elicits a maniacal response from the neighbor who clearly values his much-prized possession above valuing his neighbor who is suffering from a debilitating illness and in need of much care and not an assault. It is Charles who needs care and protection, much more than the car (and appearance again hides a deeper and more important reality). Caesar witnesses the assault on Charles, and in response he attacks Hunsiker in order to protect and care for Charles. Caesar demonstrates a strong identification with the victim, seeing himself too as a constrained and contained victim at this point. His anger is rooted in his love for Charles, and he seems to understand that when we subdue our anger in the face of injustices, we also subdue our love for the victims of the injustice, and in that sense, he expresses an opposition to forces of dehumanization.

As a consequence of Caesar's assault on Hunsiker, Caesar is removed to the "San Bruno Primate Shelter," an Abu Ghraib–style torture center for apes. The torture facility is run by John Landon (Brian Cox), a corrupt and vile manager, and the primary "caretaker" is his son, Dodge Landon (Tom Felton), a sadistic and vicious brute who regularly assaults the apes. He shouts at one point, in describing the facility to some visiting friends: "It's a madhouse; it's a madhouse." In the context of the larger film, it is clearly a reference to more than just the animal shelter.

When Will tells Jacobs that through the use of ALZ112 his father not only reversed the dementia caused by Alzheimer's but also registered significant cognitive improvement beyond the norm, Jacobs is intrigued. Dollar signs flash (a different green flashes in his eyes). Will tells Jacobs about the antibody response, and he orders new research along with needed funding. That leads to the new and improved ALZ113, administered in gaseous form (a shift that later proves catastrophic).

Conditions in the animal shelter continue to worsen, and the abuse and degradation intensify. Caesar longs for freedom and an escape from the alienating conditions under which he is suffering. There are several confrontations with other apes in the facility, but he eventually gains a comrade (an orangutan) who learned how to sign as a circus animal. Meanwhile, Will's father continues to deteriorate. When Will offers him the new and seemingly improved ALZ113, he refuses. He prefers death to the unpredictable technological innovation, and that evening he dies.

During an initial test of ALZ113, the ape on which the experiment is being conducted, Koba (Christopher Gordon), an elderly, clearly abused, lifelong inmate of research labs who harbors much ill will against humans, rips off the hose administering the gaseous form of ALZ113, leaking the gas into the room. Research assistant Franklin's mask was jarred loose, and he ingests the gas. When Will next meets Jacobs he is told, in reference to ALZ113, "We are dealing with a drug worth more than everything else we are doing combined." And Jacobs shares with Will a haunting admonition, "You make history; I make money." The brutal reality is that the drive to make money is a drive that eliminates history. Will offers a warning, dismissed by Jacobs who is blinded by the possibility of untold profits, "You don't know what kind of damage it could do to people!" It is not so much that he does not know, but, as the personification of capital, he necessarily does not care. The immediacy of bottom-line growth trumps the issue of potential long-term problems and harmful externalities. Franklin soon becomes ill. He goes to Will's house seeking help and to share with him that something is potentially wrong with ALZ113. Franklin is confronted by Hunsiker. Franklin coughs blood onto Hunsiker (we soon learn Franklin is infected with an extremely virulent virus that can be transmitted through the air).

Will visits Caesar in prison with the intention of freeing him from "the madhouse." Caesar refuses to leave . . . much to Will's surprise. Caesar feels alienated from Will and the world of humans he represents, and he has built bonds of solidarity with his fellow apes. Maurice (Karen Konoval), the circus orangutan who also knows sign language, meets with Caesar in the "exercise yard" of the prison. Caesar holds a single stick and breaks it, telling Maurice, "Apes alone, weak." Caesar then holds a bundle of sticks together and they are unbreakable. He says, "Apes together, strong." The history of what is necessary for popular struggle, that is, organized people working in solidarity and support, is covered in one short scene. Caesar then escapes from the facility after constructing a key from a pocket knife he stole from a human visitor to the prison. Just outside the horrendous conditions of the prison, he passes an amusement park, another strong indication in the film of how appearances can hide much harsher realities just beyond the surface. Caesar visits Will's house and steals a number of cylinders of ALZ113. He returns to the animal shelter and releases the gaseous form of ALZ113 into the prison. Overnight, the intelligence of every ape is hyper-magnified. The presence of a heightened consciousness is revealed in the fierce green fire present in the eyes of every ape. The apes meet in the exercise yard. Caesar leads the meeting. There are unified grunts of solidarity and support.

Soon thereafter, Dodge confronts Caesar, shocks him with an electric prod, and attempts to brutalize him. Caesar grabs his arm and stops him, then emphatically shouts, "No!" He then moves through the facility shouting repeatedly and vociferously, "No!" "No!" "No!" Dodge is sprayed with water while holding the electric prod and is killed. The apes then liberate themselves from the horror chamber, go to Gen Sys where they free their ape comrades, and also carry out a good deal of violence against property, before moving on to the zoo where they free more comrades. The rebellion is under way. The apes are hoping to cross the Golden Gate in order to get to the Redwood forest. The police have established position on the bridge and a confrontation ensues. A helicopter in which Jacobs is a passenger, and a sort of commander ordering the mass killing of apes on the bridge, is taken down by the large gorilla (and close comrade of Caesar) named Buck (Richard Ridings), who leaps from the bridge onto the landing rails of the copter, forcing it to crash onto the bridge where it is left dangling over the edge above the bay below. Jacobs, stuck in the dangling copter, pleads for help. Caesar directs Koba to push the copter into the bay. Jacobs, the personification of capital, is killed in the process. The apes overcome the police blockade and make their way to the forest. Will follows. He confronts Caesar and advises him to "come home" because the police will hunt down the apes and kill them. Caesar pulls Will close and whispers in his ear, "Caesar is home." Will appears to understand. Caesar and the other apes then climb to the tops of the trees, and the film proper ends with Caesar gazing heroically over the bay and the wreckage left on the bridge, and into the future. Credits roll.

An epilogue appears. Hunsiker, the pilot, leaves his house and makes his way to the airport. He is coughing blood and blood drips onto the floor. He is infected with the deadly virus and is about to pilot an international flight. We see the incoming/outgoing flight board and then a slowly spinning globe that is methodically encircled by a growing array of flights indicating how quickly and easily the catastrophic virus will spread across the planet. We are left to ponder the contradiction of how the humanizing of the apes, that is, the raising of their consciousness through the use of ALZ112 and ALZ113, apparently a good thing, will lead to the extermination of humans, the reality of a bad thing.

CONTRADICTIONS: APPEARANCE AND REALITY IN *RPA*

Films such as *RPA*, and films in general at their best, can shift and broaden our comprehension of the conflicts and tensions between appearances and realities and serve as a tool for diagnosing social problems we must address and overcome in order to live into a better and sustainable future. When the appearance, as in the case of *RPA*, is one in which technological innovations are pursued to cure disease, but the reality is a roomful of investors deciding how best to invest in order to ensure a steady upsurge in profits over a ten-year period, with little concern for possible externalities, we learn the importance of looking behind the mask of appearances if we wish to participate in meaningful ways in shaping both the reality in which we live and also our interactions with other people and the rest of nature.

David Harvey shares with us what he calls "perhaps the most important contradiction of all: that between reality and appearance in the world in which we live."[10] Because appearances are not often the same as reality, critically understanding reality (to the extent that is possible) requires careful, informed, and persistent interrogations that go beneath appearances. Acting in meaningfully productive ways in the world calls for activities that assist us in seeing beyond the surface appearances. Films themselves present an interesting contradiction in that they are both an appearance and a reality; that is, their appearance (fictional) is their reality and their reality is their appearance (fictional). Failing to look honestly and critically can too often result in catastrophes, as is the case in *RPA*, a film that swims continuously through the contradictions between appearance and reality, from beginning to end. The film thus serves as a pedagogical instrument that promotes processes by which we can develop interrogative tools and skills to work through contradictions and thus unmask what might really be occurring in the world inside and outside cinema.

As noted, *RPA* opens with the appearance of a tranquil forest setting through which moves an apparently content community of apes moving happily through their jungle enclave. The appearance masks the reality of a forest occupied by pernicious poachers out to kidnap the apes (in an act reminiscent of CIA renditions), in order to transport them to a medical research facility in the United States. The act of "rendition" is but a symptom (the level of appearance) of an underlying cause/reality that drives the dispossession of the apes. The effect of the operation is that the apes are dispossessed and abducted; the agents of abduction/dispossession are the poachers; but the cause, in the end, is a pharmaceutical company operating within a larger global economic system that demands constant expansion of markets and accumulation of profits. That demand requires expanding the spheres of exploitation (in this case it is expanded into the jungles of Africa).

When the film transitions to the Gen Sys research facility, the appearance is one of a happy ape experiencing heightened intelligence consequent with the application of an experimental viral drug called ALZ112. The appearance is also one of caring workers, intrigued by the success of the experiments thus far. Beyond the appearance are harsher realities, including the abuse of apes and the treatment of apes as expendable when they can no longer serve the profit-maximizing interests of the corporation. The violent outbreak by the ape called "Bright Eyes" is confused as an act of aggression when the reality is that it is an act of protection; she is protecting a baby ape of which the humans are unaware. The humans only see the appearance of aggressive behavior but not the reality of a need to protect that stimulates the contentious outbreak. The confusion between aggression and protection plays out later in the scene during which Caesar protects Charles from assault by Hunsiker, as well as in the final confrontation between apes and the police on the Golden Gate.

The appearance of a roomful of seemingly contented investors reveling in the promise of ten years of steadily climbing profits generated by the new drug, ALZ112, and its apparently successful test results on apes, is shattered by "Bright Eyes" crashing into the room, thrashing and screaming. The thrashing and screaming appears to the humans as a threat so the ape is immediately shot and killed, when in fact the reality was the ape simply wanted to protect the baby and may have been using the impertinent behavior as a distraction (i.e., using appearance to mask and distract from the reality).

Understanding the difference between appearances and reality requires work and often patience, and it is not always the case that the immediate circumstances allow for patience and reflection. Nevertheless, to the extent possible, we should work to understand the realities that underlie the surface appearances, in other words, work to understand causes, agents, and effects. The appearance of belligerent and violent apes driven out of control by the experimental drug leads to the extermination of all the apes at the facility, save one, the baby (a sort of Christ-like episode). Again, it is a case of confusing appearances with realities. The drug did not cause the aggression; it was only the ape's fear of humans assaulting or abducting the baby. The drug was actually working mental miracles on the apes—mental miracles that eventually lead to a much-heightened political and revolutionary consciousness.

The baby ape in question is "Caesar," the eventual "savior" of the apes. Afterward, he is taken to the home of researcher Will Rodman. Will only sees the surface appearance of a happy and thriving ape, but the reality is that Caesar feels increasingly imprisoned and alienated from the world and from his own now complicated nature. When Caesar attacks Will's neighbor, it appears as though the ape is simply out of control, but the reality is the ape is in possession of a profound moral and rational sense, and he is really defending Will's helpless and demented father who was under assault by the neighbor. The interpretation by humans is one based in only looking at the symptoms, not the causes of the behavior, and that undermines the potential for seeing beyond the mystifications and understanding the realities of what is happening. As a consequence of the confusion, Caesar is sent to the San Bruno Primate Shelter. The welcoming title "Shelter" gives the appearance of "protection" and "nurturing," but it disguises the reality that the "Shelter" is really a torture and abuse prison run by fascistic sadists, themselves victims of a harsher larger reality of a global system grounded in abuse, exploitation, and destruction, a system in which decent people are regularly compelled to carry out indecent actions in order to serve the ravaging and rapacious imperatives of the dominant system. And beneath that harsh cinematic reality of imprisonment and torture is a lurking question: what right do we have to abuse, exploit, and condemn fellow creatures? It is a question that must be extended to: what right does anyone have to abuse, exploit, and condemn fellow humans in order to satisfy the imperatives of the dominant systems?

Following on the notion of sadists being victims of a larger sadistic system, we can say that, outside of pathology, the same sadist, if raised under different social conditions and institutional imperatives, might easily become a caring, nurturing, and loving human being, and thus more in line with fundamental and necessary features of our human nature.

Will appears to believe that if he removes Caesar from the "Shelter," he will be offering him freedom, but the leash in his hand points to a different reality, one which Caesar understands but Will does not. It is a crucial lesson. If we want to understand oppression, exploitation, and abuse, we should ask the victims and not the victimizers. The victimizers are often content with the mystifications that hide the harsher realities, a point that runs through most forms of racism, sexism, colonialism, classism, and imperialism. When the apes rebel and free themselves from the torturous prison, the humans respond by mobilizing the forces of violence. The humans only see the appearance of out-of-control apes running rampant through the city and destroying property, when the reality is the apes have developed a moral consciousness and intelligence that led them to rebel against harsh conditions of repression and abuse. Furthermore, they rebelled in order to return to a more harmonious relationship with the rest of nature, in other words, a relationship not grounded in exploitation, humiliation, and abuse, but one rooted in community, solidarity, and care. Rather than the humans stepping back and asking, "What might we learn here?" the only response is to try to kill off the rebellious apes. The apes' response is mostly nonviolent.

Beneath the appearance of a simply out-of-control band of rampaging apes is a reality that the apes are looking for an exit not only from the prison but from the larger system that has dispossessed them, abused them, and killed them. If the humans could step back and see beyond the appearances of their own lives, they would see that they too are living in a world dominated by ideologies and institutions that promote dispossession, exploitation, abuse, and destruction. Upon seeing the harsh reality underpinning the mystifying appearances, humans too might seek an exit from the dominant systems. That is one reason why it seems plausible to argue for *RPA*'s revolutionary intent. In looking for an exit, the apes also recognize they can use tools provided by the system of abuse and exploitation to liberate themselves from that system, tools both ideological and symbolic (as seen in the form of raised revolutionary consciousness and raised fists) and material (as seen in the form of apes using the constraining bars of zoo pens as weapons of emancipation).

These are only a few of the contradictions between appearance and reality present in the film. Virtually every scene can be analyzed as an exercise in working through such contradictions. To take one more example, in the epilogue of the film we see the power and usefulness of global transportation systems represented by an incoming and outgoing flight board at the San Francisco airport. In other words, we see a representation of one of the great technological achievements of humans (air travel and transportation) that is also reflective of capital's structural imperative to always expand and always create new markets and customers in order to sell commodities for profit. A harsher reality is soon revealed because that grand system of international transport and trade will become the vehicle through which a global infectious-disease pandemic will spread and apparently eradicate humans.

One of the key lessons we can learn from working through the contradictions between appearance and reality in *RPA* and in our realities beyond the film is that we must guard against inaccurate and misguided readings and explanations of the world because that will almost surely lead to spurious and unsound political projects and processes that will heighten rather than resolve the multiple economic and ecological crises we now face. When we listen to and discuss the film's lesson about returning to a more harmonious relationship with the rest of nature (and that includes our human nature), we can think beyond the appearance of nature as simply trees and forests and recognize ourselves as material beings that are part of nature, material beings that will suffer increasing misery, hardship, despair, and turmoil if we do not carefully address the foreboding realities that lie just beneath the shiny surface of commodity culture. It means working collectively and in solidarity, as happens with the apes in *RPA*, to overcome the systems of exploitation and destruction, and working to create conditions that nurture and nourish the full range of our creative, caring, loving, convivial, and imaginative human nature. That means developing a raised consciousness about problems and solutions, again following the example set forth in *RPA*.

The film's overall warning points to how there is little time remaining for humans to successfully address the compounding difficulties arising from the interpenetrations between capitalism and nature, that is, the difficulties arising from the ecology of capital that work to serve the interests of capital rather than the interests of humanity and the rest of nature. Faulty policies emerging from false interpretations of surface appearances rather than honest and critical understandings of underlying realities will only intensify the social, economic, and environmental horrors and disturbances we are facing. *RPA* leaves us with an appearance of revolution against the brutalizing system of capital that ultimately is the underlying reality behind the abuse and suffering that permeates the film. The mobilization of resistance that leads to rebellion that foments revolution requires a raised political consciousness among the apes (the result of ingesting the gaseous ALZ113). The cinematic appearance of revolution can provide inspiration to foment struggles and stimulate the raising of political consciousness, but missing in *RPA* is a well-articulated and animated set of ideas and practices around which long-term mobilizations might arise. And there is no magic drug that will provide the necessary revolutionary consciousness; it must be constructed through collective work and struggle.

The reality of revolution is much different than the imagined revolution; cinematic rebellion is much different than rebellion in the streets. The film reveals the power and necessity of individual desire for and dedication to the task of revolutionary struggle while crucially linking that individual commitment (Caesar representing the most visible manifestation) to a robust and awakened collective political movement.

At the core of the rebellion in *RPA* (a point extendable into "the age of Obama") is the recognition that the commercialization and privatization of nature (in the film's case, this includes the apes themselves) has reduced the apes to an exchange value, an expendable object of exploitation in a commodity-driven system. This alienation from nature and the desire to dis-alienate the relationship in order to return to a more palatable relationship drives forward the rebellion. In seeking our own rebellions and revolutions, we must work to identify the sources of alienation in our individual and collective lives and work toward forms of dis-alienation, a necessary step in creating more substantively democratic administrative and organization forms in the political and economic arenas.

The film provides a strong indication of what it is we should oppose and offers a very general sense of the importance of overcoming the system of capital and living in harmony with nature rather than living within and through an exploitative and destructive relationship with other humans and with the rest of nature. We are left with the notion that what is required is an animated vision of an alternative that works dialectically with an oppositional/constructive movement, where the vision informs and inhabits the movement and the movement informs and inhabits the vision. In *RPA* Caesar, at least metaphorically, provides the vision, and that vision is linked to the rebellious movement of the newly informed, inclusive, and energized apes. Having an idea of what we should oppose, as suggested in the film, is not the same as having a vision of the alternative we should work to construct. That is another site in which the hard work of linking understanding to transformation arises, but we can say that if we are committed to both understanding the world and changing it, our ideas and actions should always contain some form of revolutionary intent. It is a reality that comes to light in Caesar's awakening. It will not make us popular with systems of power or with the defenders of those systems, but it may open possibilities for saving a future under serious threat and building better alternatives from what might soon be the ruins.

Understanding the vision is crucial to building the movement. Films such as *RPA* can fuel the development of visions and movements, if we recognize such films as political instruments that can assist in promoting processes through which people can construct new social and economic forms while also transforming themselves as agents of history in the processes. But the questions must be asked, the alternative vision constructed, the movements formed and nurtured . . . in short, the work must be done.

The continuing and expanding suffering in "the age of Obama" under capital's politics of domination and subjugation strongly alluded to in *RPA* calls for the urgent recognition that "so great is the epochal crisis of our time, encompassing both the economic and ecological crises, that nothing but a world revolution is likely to save humanity (and countless others among the earth's species) from a worsening series of catastrophes."[11] That the revolution must be global is strongly implied in the epilogue of *RPA* when we discover that the drive to profit from marketing a nontested drug, ALZ113 in a gaseous form, will prove deadly for humans on a global scale. The implication we are left with from the epilogue is that the forces of global capital are moving rapidly across the planet in ways that are producing a visible and tangible threat to humanity's existence, and along the way there will be increased suffering, misery, and despair.

Beyond the appearance of the spread of the global pandemic is the reality of the root cause in the now globalized system of capital and the more challenging and urgent reality of constructing an oppositional/constructive movement linked to an animated vision of what kind of an alternative is needed. We are also left with the haunting possibility that while capital might survive its contradictions, we will not. When films function as modes of critical public pedagogy, drawing connections between knowledge and action, they open up possibilities for using the films as a political vehicle for individual and social understanding and transformation.

Again linking surfaces to depths, we can say films that function as a form of critical public pedagogy help us see beyond surface-level symptoms of problems and into the underlying root causes. In *RPA*, alluding to the larger system of corporate America, we are confronted with a surface-level appearance of a shiny, well-functioning, high-tech research facility filled with dedicated and innovative workers laboring intensively to produce drugs that will address and, it is hoped, cure brain disorders. Beneath a seemingly benevolent and service-oriented arrangement, there are malevolent and corrupt forces at work as well as a complex history of eco-destruction, abuse, and exploitation; profit seeking at all costs; torture; accumulation by dispossession; and an ideology of greed, domination, and subjugation that in the end puts the future of humanity at risk. And herein is another radical lesson provided by the film about the contradictions between appearances and realities; that is, behind any product, whether it is on the grocery store shelf or the pharmacy shelf and so on, there are questions beyond just "Do we have enough money in our pocket to purchase the product?" We can always ask questions about the history of the product and that means asking: where does it come from; what were the conditions of production; by whom and under what relationships of power was the item produced; why was it produced; who are the winners and losers in the processes and relations of production; what are the immediate and, crucially, longer-term consequences of the production processes and relations; are there conditions of injustice and indignity associated with the production (as is typically the case), and what can we do to ensure production is carried out in ways that are just and dignified; are the production processes ecologically rational and human friendly, and if not (as is typically the case), what can we do to ensure that production is carried forth in ways that are ecologically and human friendly? Prisons are a form of social production and reproduction, and here we can ask a similar series of questions. *RPA*, with its emphasis on the barbaric conditions in the animal shelter/torture/prison facility, suggests we reflect on those processes and relations and seek something other than the current sadistic and fascistic approach to containment and control. In short, the film is again directing us to seek processes and relations that are not dehumanizing, but rather processes and relations that are liberating.

As suggested earlier, because of the pedagogical impact of film as a moral and political process, films must be taken seriously as what Henry Giroux calls "teaching machines"[12]; in other words, films function as a cultural and political educational force that is both reflective and directive. They are also, as noted, imagination machines that can nurture new ways of thinking about the present and future. *RPA*, for example, reflects harsh and burdensome social, political, economic, corporate, and environmental realities in "the age of Obama" and, as noted, directs audiences to say "No!" and "Ya, Basta!" That is, *RPA* advises audiences to say, "Enough is enough," to raise our political consciousness, to organize in support and solidarity with others, to mobilize our political forces, to rebel against the forces of oppression and domination, and to launch a revolutionary struggle. When "Caesar" the revolutionary finally speaks, his noteworthy first word is a shouted "No!" in the face of a long line of abuses, humiliations, and assaults. It is *RPA*'s "I'm mad as hell and I'm not going to take it anymore"[13] moment—and we will do well to listen. In a sense, we can argue that the shout of a speaking ape is otherworldly, but it must be understood in the context of a film that is calling for a different sense of otherworldliness, one in which people should struggle to create a different and better world than the one in which we presently struggle. To avoid thinking about and acting toward this kind of "otherworldliness" is to avoid looking at and recognizing the grim reality behind the distorting mask of appearances.[14]

AND ALIENATION

Caesar's revolt is a revolt against multiple conditions of alienation suffered directly at the hands of workers in the detention facility (reminiscent too of Guantanamo in its torturous horrors). The workers in the facility are themselves alienated from their basic humanity as well as from a basic human understanding of dignity and respect. In the context of the interactions with the apes in the dungeon-like facility, there is the strong intimation that the workers are also alienated from the rest of nature. They thus fail to see nature as an integral component in our human bio-cultural-social-economic lifeworld and humans as material beings in relation with the earth. The multiple forms of alienation are reflective of the values and imperatives of the larger and dominant system of capital (of which Gen Sys is the corporate face and CEO Jacobs the personification) that permeates all corners of life in the film.

Caesar suffers alienated and alienating feelings of sorrow and anguish when he comes to see beneath the appearance of his relationship with Will and into the reality where he is mostly just a pet on a leash. The misery and turmoil of alienation intensifies when he is initially placed in the animal detention and abuse facility. The malaise is the consequence of a profound experience of emptiness that cannot be filled, an experience all too normal for all too many people living under the alienating regime of capital. *RPA* moves from the passive form of alienation to an activated form of psychological alienation, and it is here that it teaches one of its most valuable lessons. The experience of alienation—i.e., dispossession, humiliation, and oppression—needn't only be internalized in destructive and containing ways, but can erupt into outrage and an oppositional awakening that fuels human agency. There is a telling moment in the film when Will returns to the "Bruno" facility to remove Caesar, but Caesar refuses to leave. He refuses for two reasons: (1) he sees the leash in Will's hand and understands that if he leaves he will simply be moving from one zone of hierarchical repression and subjugation, one zone of alienation, to another and that is no longer tolerable given Caesar's raised consciousness regarding the need for freedom from oppressive hierarchies and systemic domination (for Caesar Will is now seen as another personification of that system of authority and control); (2) Caesar is establishing relationships of dependence and solidarity inside the prison and he is beginning to recognize the need for collective struggle in any authentic battle for emancipation. It is an especially telling moment because of how Caesar connects the forces of oppression and domination with the forces of struggle and liberation. He sacrifices a short-term limited freedom from the torture facility in order to stay and struggle for the longer-term, more full-fledged freedom that can only come through struggle against the larger forces of alienation and violence.

FILMS AND SPHERES OF ACTIVITY

Films thus represent and reflect a complex array of social and cultural processes and relationships that can and do produce, perpetuate, inform, shape, and reproduce mental concepts, social relations, daily life, organizational arrangements, institutional imperatives, labor relations, relations with the natural world, technological understanding and innovations, and so forth. These are also revolutionary spheres of activity, to borrow a concept from Marx, and the film, sometimes directly and other times indirectly, explores the force of these spheres of activity as well as their dialectical relationships. It is another valuable lesson we can take from *RPA*.

In brief, Caesar's releasing of the technological innovation ALZ113 to his comrades in the context of their repressive daily life experiences shifts their mental conceptions toward a revolutionary consciousness for liberation in the context of new social relations of solidarity that also bolster a warrior mentality around liberation. This leads to a new form of organization among the apes, now rooted in comradeship and support rather than hostility and divisiveness, new self-directed administrative procedures now grounded in group meetings rather than imposed alienation suffered in isolated cells, and new labor relations that divide tasks in ways that allow for victory in the struggle to create new and harmonious relations with nature. In each case, the sphere of activity works dialectically with the other spheres. Through the revolutionary struggle all spheres of activity are liberated from control and domination by the repressive systems under which they were suffering. We can imagine the impact on all spheres of activity once they have achieved the more harmonious relationship with nature they longed for and thus liberated themselves from the conditions of alienation suffered in the labs and prisons under the larger regime of capital. Such exercises in thinking through revolutionary spheres of activity are useful in developing visions and movements for understanding and transformation in our world outside of cinematic representations. Borrowing the apes' desire for a harmonious relationship with nature in the context of a community in struggle, we might work through how a community organic garden/farm could positively impact all of the revolutionary spheres of activity in our own lives. For example, what might it mean to spend an hour a day after work working in the community garden? How would that begin to transform the spheres of activity? One way to start the thought-experiment is to consider how that hour spent in the community garden working with others would free one from a daily life and mental conceptions dominated from morning until night by the ideological and material forces of capital, and go on from there.

So, in a strong sense, *RPA* reflects a critical and revolutionary pedagogy and struggle, a point that alludes to the unusual nature of the film mentioned above. Films can train us to accept how things are, but they can also educate us to challenge how things are, and the two are not necessarily in conflict. If a film reflects a reality that is all too harsh, the cinematic representation of the harshness may awaken people to challenge the status quo. Some films assist us in escaping from our turmoil, some assist us in understanding our turmoil, some help us link an understanding of our troubles to struggles necessary to overcome those troubles, and some, such as *RPA*, combine all three. In all cases, films are functioning as contradiction-laced pedagogical influence machines that function in the interface between what films bring to audiences and what audiences bring to films. Films typically scan the present in order to reproduce and perpetuate current systems of power and domination while also providing a scan of the present that opens up new and better possibilities for the future. We must be alert to the revolutionary potential present in filmic processes and relations, potentials often buried beneath surface-level appearances.

Films then are contradictory processes containing both reproductive and revolutionary potentials. On the one hand, films train people to be passive observers of action, but on the other hand, films can inspire actions to overcome passivity; the same is true of repressive and degrading conditions, as witnessed in *RPA*. Films thus offer competing demands, and films can never disconnect what happens inside the film from what happens outside the film; similarly audiences can never separate their lives outside the theater from their lives inside the theater. The seeds of revolutionary struggle planted by *RPA* require nurturing and nourishment outside of the cinema. How people respond to the ever-present contradictions films offer will vary depending on a complex array of social, political, economic, personal, and historical factors. Any film must be recognized not as a thing but as a process, part of a complex and ever changing world, informed by multiple relations, not least of which are relations of economic, historical, and political power, regardless of "the age" in which the film circulates and the audiences view it.

To watch and think through a film as a set of processes and relations in "the age of Obama" is to be aware that we are viewing a film produced and consumed in an age of continuing and escalating crises, economic, military, social, environmental, and political. The crises are witnessed in the increasing imposition of austerity measures; the privatization and commercialism of all levels of education; the growth in public political futility and the marginalization, if not repression, of progressive alternative visions, radical social formations, and substantive modes of democracy; growing forms of tyranny and authoritarianism in every sphere; cascading forms of global hunger and poverty, and the consequent suffering; the growing inequalities in wealth, income, privilege, and power; the expansion of a police-state repression and surveillance apparatus; the expansion of the prison population and the harsh conditions therein; the commitment to bail out and protect banks and bankers while people's living standards and hopes for a better future plummet; the widening power of a billionaires club constitutive of an increasingly dominating domestic and global plutocracy; the continuing threat of nuclear catastrophes; and ongoing acts of international violence and aggression accompanied by bloated Pentagon and intelligence budgets.

In this age of multiple crises, the arguably most pressing and historically foreboding crises, however, are those multiple perils associated with global climate chaos and catastrophe. And with talk of a "sixth extinction,"[15] the climate crises now threaten the future of numerous species, including humans. The climate chaos and catastrophes do not present an example of a revolt of nature, as many would have it, but an example of the interpenetrating relationships and contradictions between capital and nature, relationships revealed jarringly in *RPA*. Under the regime of capital, it must be understood that exploiting and destroying the natural world is not seen as a setback or an error but as a measure of success, an inevitable consequence of the imperative to constantly expand and accumulate in order to maximize profits and market share.[16] Our lives, we might say, are no less about capital than they are about nature, and no less about nature than they are about capital. In the battle between capital and nature, one will have to go, and it will not be nature. The more pressing question is: will capital go before we do? With capital's ecology now wrecking, if not eliminating, conditions for a decent human future as strongly suggested in *RPA*, we must ask questions and develop new thinking about how we can exit from these destructive relationships in order to build new and better social, political, and economic systems. These relationships and contradictions between capital and nature are at the core of *RPA*, and a crucial reason to take seriously the lessons of the film.

NOTES

1. P. De Geyter and E. Pottier, "The Internationale," 1888. The song is probably the most widely sung revolutionary song in the world. Lyrics online at: http://www.marxists.org/history/ussr/sounds/lyrics/international.htm.

2. See, for example, N. Chomsky, "Challenging Empire," *UTNE Reader*, February 4, 2013, http://www.utne.com/politics/challenging-empire.aspx#axzz30PC16Nfb>.

3. J. Kay, "Rise of the Planet of the Apes Goes Box Office Bananas in First Weekend," *Guardian*, August 8, 2011, http://www.theguardian.com/film/2011/aug/08/hollywood-report-rise-planet-apes.

4. C. Brodesser-Akner, "*Rise of the Planet of the Apes* Does Excellent Monkey Business," *Vulture*, August 2011, http://www.vulture.com/2011/08/your_box_office_explained_rise.html.

5. K. Marx, *Capital*, vol. III, part VII, ch. 54, 1894, Marxists.org, http://www.marxists.org/archive/marx/works/1894-c3/ch51.htm.

6. D. Harvey, *The Enigma of Capital* (London: Oxford University Press, 2011), 259.

7. M. Lebowitz, *The Socialist Alternative* (New York: Monthly Review Press, 2010), 163.

8. "The Internationale."

9. Lebowitz, *The Socialist Alternative*, 49.

10. D. Harvey, *Seventeen Contradictions and the End of Capitalism*. (London: Oxford University Press, 2014), 4.

11. J. D. Foster and M. Yates, "Notes from the Editors," *Monthly Review*, May 2014.

12. H. Giroux, "Animating Youth: The Disnification of Children's Culture," *Socialist Review* (1994), http://www.henryagiroux.com/online_articles/animating_youth.htm.

13. See Sidney Lumet's 1976 film *Network*.

14. T. Eagleton, *Why Marx was Right* (New Haven: Yale University Press, 2011), 159.

15. J. Feffer, "Earth: Game Over?" *Common Dreams*, April 24, 2014, https://www.commondreams.org/view/2014/04/24.

16. E. Meiskins-Wood, *Democracy Against Capitalism* (London: Cambridge University Press, 1995), 255.

Part IV

2013 Academy Award for Best Picture: *12 Years a Slave*

Chapter Fifteen

"Under the Floorboards of This Nation": Trauma, Representation, and the Stain of History in *12 Years a Slave*

Ed Cameron and Linda Belau

Henry Louis Gates Jr. has argued that *12 Years a Slave* is "the most realistic account of slavery in a feature film."[1] The principal reason for this claim lies in the fact that, unlike its progenitors, *12 Years a Slave* is adapted from a firsthand autobiographical account. *Birth of a Nation* was adapted from a Confederate romance, *Gone with the Wind* was adapted from a plantation novel, and *Django Unchained* was adapted intertextually from the Italian Western. These films not only tend to sentimentalize or romanticize, to use Gates's words,[2] slavery, but they also tend to situate slavery into a larger drama that minimizes the cruel impact the peculiar institution has on the audience, making slavery little more than "a sideshow, a springboard for spectacle, melodrama, and revenge fantasy."[3] Based on historical events, films like *Amistad* and *Glory* deliver a more realistic account of the experience of slaves, but they lack the up-close, personal account provided by the adaptation of a slave narrative, an account that narrates the day-to-day existence under bondage. Gates claims that, with *12 Years a Slave*, Steve McQueen has managed to reappropriate slavery from the fabulists.[4] Just as the authors of slave narratives themselves, who were "intent upon refuting the rosy depictions of slavery,"[5] McQueen created a cinematic adaptation that does not ignore the traumatic nature of American slavery. In the words of his female lead, Lupita Nyong'o, McQueen's film affects the spectator by "taking a flashlight and shining it under the floorboards of this nation and reminding us what it is we stand on" like no other film chronicling slavery.[6] *12 Years a Slave* shines a light on that most traumatic and avoided aspect of American history precisely because it is adapted from an actual slave narrative, which itself points to the indirect manner in which the trauma of slavery can be portrayed.[7]

In McQueen's adaptation, as is always the case in the transference from written text to film, imagery is foregrounded at the expense of the symbolic coordinates of a written narrative. From a Lacanian psychoanalytic account, film functions primarily as an imaginary supplement to the symbolic realm of writing. Writing is symbolic in nature because the written word produces a symbolic representation. This is in fact one of the primary purposes of the more than one hundred slave narratives penned before the Emancipation Proclamation. Slave narratives were written not only in support of the abolitionist movement but also as a means to critique "statutes forbidding literacy training among black slaves" and to create an opening in the socio-symbolic space for ex-slaves, especially since the "equation of the rights of man with the ability to write" was indirectly enacted through these autobiographical narratives.[8] This is aptly illustrated right from the beginning of the film. McQueen's opening sequence begins in medias res with the only scene that repeats in the story. While hired out to a neighboring sugar cane plantation owner, Solomon (Chiwetel Ejiofor) is shown turning blackberry juice into a makeshift ink that is desperately needed to write a letter notifying authorities in New York of his abduction. When Solomon's experiment fails, his frustration signifies in a number of telling ways. Dramatically, it postpones Solomon's freedom from bondage. Symbolically, it manifests the connection between literacy and symbolic sovereignty, as with bondage comes both the denial of subjectivity and the inability to write one's own story. Conceptually, it connects the film formally to the written trauma memoir that it adapts, the historical Solomon Northup's narrative account, since it evokes an impossible act of writing, a certain failure in the field of representation.

Solomon's inability to write is clearly a privileged moment in the film since it is the only scene that is repeated in the entire feature. While, at first glance, it appears to be just another of Solomon's experiences in slavery, a quiet, almost peaceful moment free of the more harrowing brutalities of a slave's existence, this scene of writing that the film represents so prominently directly figures the experience of trauma that is central to both the written narrative and the cinematic adaptation: in the same way that our cinematic protagonist suffers the impossibility of writing an account of his experience (due to the lack of proper instruments), the actual Solomon Northup—the survivor of a profoundly traumatic experience that essentially shattered both his identity and his subjectivity—is unable to directly articulate the trauma of his harrowing experience in his own autobiographical writing. McQueen's doubling of this scene conveys both the practical inability Solomon encounters while on the plantation and the inescapable condition all survivors of trauma face when it comes to providing a full account of their traumatic experience in memoir form. Thus, McQueen's film seems to indirectly recognize the survivor's inability to fully account for (or represent) the traumatic experience, an inability that has been frequently described in the discourse of trauma studies as an impossibility.

This inability is a recurrent characteristic of the trauma survivor's experience and one that creates the most difficulties for understanding the force of trauma since it is, seemingly, the autobiographical narrative that would offer the most reliable access to traumatic experience. Because it is the autobiographical witness account that attempts to retell the trauma, to describe the traumatic event, and to make sense of the injury, it would seem, on the surface, that such a narrative does represent the experience of trauma. Traditional autobiographical narratives, however, do not begin to do justice to the survivor's relation to the event. Responding to a radical disruption of meaning, the survivor is suspended in an experience that cannot be addressed directly in the realm of representation. While most survivors feel a compelling need to communicate their experience of the event in the aftermath of trauma, the autobiographical account of catastrophe is both an exposure to and recoiling from the traumatic real, which also figures as a void in or negation of the symbolic field. The experience itself—its traumatic core—remains inaccessible in the realm of symbolic exchange, and the written word can only fail to adequately represent the full contours of the experience. As the author of the trauma narrative addresses his need to recount the impossible event to the Other, to make the event meaningful in a broader symbolic register, a demand for coherence is expressed. Such coherence, it is presumed, would close the void in the symbolic—the real dimension of the shattering experience—that the subject of trauma encounters. Given the nature of trauma and its resistance to representational form, however, one cannot expect a symbolic intervention to positivize the impossibility that constitutes the radical negativity that is traumatic experience. Thus, the exigency involved in trauma testimony bears on something much more distressing than the inability to make an accurate account: it both reflects and inaugurates the shattering of the subject. Despite the survivor's best attempts to situate the trauma through his testimonial practice, a written account of the event remains impossible. And while this inability, more than anything else, can account for the survivor's failed narrative, it also engenders the very need to write, to make sense of the trauma that the narrative was initially intended to address. This is traumatic repetition, and it finds its most dramatic form in the testimonial account.

One could argue that Northup's written narrative is characterized in and through the same impossibility, this same movement of traumatic repetition. While it is clear that Northup published the work to support the abolitionist cause, it is also evident that he wrote his story in order to attempt to reassert his place as a symbolic subject, a status that was taken from him when he was thrown into the abyss of the slave's existence. Telling his story, circulating it in the wider symbolic economy, was his means of reentering his symbolic community and reestablishing his identity as a sovereign subject. On the surface, Northup's narrative is very much the typical kind of slave narrative that was circulated in the northern states as a means to further the politics of emancipation. The structure of the text is similar to numerous slave narratives in that it is grounded, as it were, in the editorial framing devices that were an elemental part of slave narrative conventions. In Northup's text, for example, his co-writer, David Wilson, adds a brief preface that attests to the veracity of the details. At the close of Northup's narrative, the reader will find a number of appendixes that establish the symbolic validity of the text and, in this case, that show the actual legal documentation that testifies to his status as a freeman. Also true to convention, the text is constituted by a number of recollections that take on a strongly didactic function. Northup, in fact, opens his text by explaining his reasons for writing: "It has been suggested that an account of my life and fortunes would not be uninteresting to the public."[9] Also characteristic of the typical slave narrative, Northup's account often reads in the tradition of the travel narrative, and he takes extra effort to inform his readers about the customs of places in the South that they may never visit. There are, in fact, entire chapters devoted to explaining agricultural practices on both the cotton and sugar cane plantations. The text, then, presumably has a symbolic purpose, and it is further presumed that it will fulfill its symbolic role as a purveyor of enlightenment. Northup also often exclaims in his text how one should not give way to despair, something that is clearly carried over into McQueen's film, and, in so doing, is careful to make an ongoing statement about the moral value of overcoming difficult experiences, another lesson to be learned from the slave's experience.

However, while the narrative appears to be another abolitionist piece of propaganda, the story here is resoundingly different: Northup was a sovereign subject who was kidnapped and thrown into an experience that truly was beyond the pale of comprehension for him. He had never lived as a slave. His wife had never lived as a slave. And his children had never experienced the cruelty of that peculiar institution. Northup's entire identity was negated—shattered—in the void of this experience. It is precisely this difference that will ultimately hinder Northup's narrative as a means to symbolic reintegration. Unlike other slave narratives, written by emancipated slaves who had usually managed to escape from slavery, Northup's text circles around the experience as something that is essentially unspeakable, beyond the parameters of his subjective understanding. Numerous times in his narrative he exclaims how "language can convey but an inadequate impression of the lamentations" of the broken slave.[10] In the text where he tells of his fight with Tibeats and then waits in fear for the repercussions (a pivotal scene, incidentally, that is well captured in the film), Northup expresses the essential poverty of language in the face of his profoundly traumatizing experience:

> An unfriended, helpless slave—what could I do, what could I say, to justify, in the remotest manner, the heinous act I had committed, of resenting a white man's contumely and abuse. I tried to pray—I tried to beseech my Heavenly Father to sustain me in my sore extremity, but emotion choked my utterance, and I could only bow my head upon my hands and weep.[11]

In his moment of greatest suffering, Northup's most sustaining symbolic anchor—the Heavenly Father—fails to guarantee his place as a subject of language. While well-known slave narratives such as Harriet Jacobs's *Incidents in the Life of a Slave Girl* or Frederick Douglass's *Narrative of the Life of Frederick Douglass, An American Slave* function to articulate a new subjectivity for the author,[12] Northup's narrative—and story—circles traumatically around the loss of subjectivity, due both to the actual denial of his juridical rights as a free human being and as a result of the symbolically shattering experience of trauma. In this sense, his narrative is as much about the events recollected as it is about the events that resist recollection, the traumatic experiences that stain the symbolic landscape and render his narrative impossible.

Perhaps one of the most significant things about Northup's text is that he actually, despite being literate, did not write the narrative himself. We are unable to know the reasons for this: his writing skills may not have been developed enough to be up to the task, though he was known to be quite eloquent in his written and spoken word, or he may have been forced to take second seat and defer to the authority of Wilson, a lawyer who was already somewhat known as a writer. Regardless, it is telling that, in the end, Northup literally was not able to write his own narrative. As with other survivors of traumatic experience, he was not able to directly represent the hard kernel of this experience since the scene of writing the trauma necessarily takes him beyond this inscription to the limit of symbolic representation, the traumatic void in the symbolic, where he encounters an impossibility that, Jacques Lacan says, "doesn't stop not being written."[13] Thus, Northup's inability to write works against his survivor's demand that an account be written, that impossibility be articulated. And this goes a long way toward understanding the oddly indifferent tone that often characterizes much of Northup's narrative, especially as he endeavors to create an accurate account that will function as both a travel narrative and as an example of moral instruction. Despite the didactic nature of Northup's text, however, the survivor subject's narrative circles restlessly around the traumatic stain that cannot be epistemically captured, at least not in writing. It would take a more imaginary vehicle—the cinema—to finally, if indirectly, express the trauma of Northup's shattering experience within the symbolic horizon.

McQueen begins his adaptation of *12 Years a Slave* with Solomon immersed in the impossible scene of writing that both characterizes and constitutes Northup's memoir, and the director later repeats it when the flashback chronicle catches up with this point in the narrative, as if to suggest that his film circulates around the same kind of unsignifiable trauma that persists in Northup's narrative. The film, however, elevates this experience of and encounter with trauma from a more or less ontogenetic—or individual—level to the space of a collective and ultimately historical engagement. In this sense, the film functions as an aesthetic means of shining a light on the traumatic stain of slavery that never stops not writing itself both in Northup's narrative and, to this day, in American history.

On one level, the imaginary overlay that film tends to force onto the historical record could easily lead to the type of romanticizing and sentimentalizing of slavery that is produced by *Birth of a Nation* and *Gone with the Wind*, leading to a domestication of the traumatic kernel of American history. On another level, however, the imaginary's supplemental nature can be utilized to indirectly testify to the necessary gap in the symbolic representation of slavery, especially pointing out its inability to convey the true depth of the traumatic nature of slavery. Where romantic Hollywood films like *Birth of a Nation* and *Gone with the Wind* use imagery to make history imaginary, a film like *12 Years a Slave* deploys its artistic potential and use of imagery to bring the viewer closer to the true traumatic stain on American history. Some critics have argued that McQueen's use of violence within his film borders on the gratuitous and that his film ultimately leads to a sort of aestheticizing of torment. Countering this position, Gates responds that McQueen "showed remarkable restraint" and that the film "just hints at how violent slavery was."[14] But since film is an image-based medium, it lends itself quite readily to aesthetic effects in the traditional sense. Therefore, McQueen's depictions of violence and suffering should not be viewed as a form of stylistic exploitation, as a stylistically artistic rendering of the depredations of slavery. Nor should it be argued that McQueen's film capitalizes artistically on the inhumanity of slavery. Rather, the film's depictions and representation of the harrowing conditions of slavery should be understood in the manner in which they affect the viewer, how they make something distant immediate and, thereby, bring the viewer into the scenes viewed, making the viewer part of the history depicted. For better or worse, film has the aesthetic ability to bridge the distance between spectator and artwork in a number of ways that the textual narrative simply cannot. Using his art to exploit this intimacy is ultimately the way that McQueen is able to move beyond an individual instance of trauma—as articulated in Northup's narrative—to an expression of a collective trauma that forces one to overcome the cultural forgetting that oftentimes veils our apprehension of the profoundly savage dimension of slavery.

McQueen is able to conjure the repetitious nature of the trauma at the heart of American history at moments in the film when the viewer realizes he or she is not an innocent bystander catching a surreptitious glance at some spectacle that is indifferent to him or her. Traumatic repetition emerges when the viewer realizes that the depicted events are strategically staged for the audience's gaze. In this manner, through certain aesthetic and filmic techniques, McQueen is able to, in a way that Northup's symbolic narrative cannot, implicate the viewer into the traumatic history. According to Slavoj Žižek, "It is by means of the . . . spot that the observed picture is subjectivized: this paradoxical point undermines our position as 'neutral,' 'objective' observer, pinning us to the observed object itself." This pinning, he concludes, "is the point at which the observer is already included, inscribed, in the observed scene—in a way, it is the point from which the picture itself looks back at us."[15]

Lacan formulated his notion of the gaze as the object cause of desire in the visual field through an examination of Hans Holbein's sixteenth-century painting *The Ambassadors*.[16] In Holbein's painting, the field of representation depicting the figures of the two ambassadors is undercut by an unidentifiable object hovering near the bottom center of the image. The mysterious object remains unidentifiable as long as the spectator focuses directly on the represented image. But as soon as the viewer looks indirectly at the image, looks back at the image when leaving the gallery room, for example, the unidentifiable object morphs into an elongated skull. For Lacan, the anamorphic skull marks the stain in the field of representation, that point within the image that shows the visual field's own limit. Once the skull is recognized, the represented image of the ambassadors loses its reality effect because its coherence relies on the repression of the unidentifiable object (what Lacan calls the object cause of desire) within the visual field. This object cause of desire can also be figured as the frame itself. Once the frame— or, in the case of cinema, the form—noticeably enters the field of representation, there appears an excess that indirectly marks a traumatic excess to the narrated representation. The skull in Holbein's painting is important in this regard because the artist's name translates as "hollow bone," making the anamorphic object a stand-in for Holbein's artistic signature. By objectifying his name in this manner, Holbein manages to allow what should remain repressed and marginalized within his image to emerge in the same field but on a different plane. This is why Lacan maintains that the anamorphosis implicates the spectator and exposes the truth that his or her desire plays a role in the visual field.

Likewise, McQueen's signature manifests itself in various ways throughout the film. As a director who began as a video artist, McQueen is known more for his compositions than as a fine storyteller. This aspect of his talent definitely emerges in his first two features, *Hunger* (2008) and *Shame* (2011). However, since *12 Years* adapts a chronological narrative, McQueen's usual practice of close composition would appear to take a backseat to the importance of remaining faithful to Northup's narrative. Indeed, part of the popularity of McQueen's third feature has to be aligned with its following the classical standards of narrative cinema. Nonetheless, McQueen's own particular style—his signature, if you will—manages to emerge in ways that benefit the impact of Northup's story while providing some indirect comments of the director's own. Part of the Lacanian argument above indicates that when the viewer notices the style of the artist, of the filmmaker in this case, there emerges a stain in the field of representation; the story being represented is marked by the gaze of the Other. This stain signifies the blind spot in the visual field, how the visual field's own space is curved by a traumatic void, by what is in excess of the field of representation. The stain marks that which is impossible to impart to the viewer; in this case, it marks the unrepresentable dimension of Solomon Northup's and every historical slave's experience. It is in this manner that McQueen's film exceeds previous films about the peculiar institution. As Mladen Dolar says about the stain in the field of the visual, it "shatters an everyday idyllic life, a customary order; it emerges as a foreign body, a counter natural element in a natural pattern. It estranges and perverts its orderly background, which suddenly becomes filled with uncanny possibilities."[17] What makes McQueen's film so compelling and also so unique is that the stain in his film is almost ubiquitous.[18]

Usually the stain in the visual field appears sporadically or even only a single time in a film's visual field, but since McQueen's film is focused on the institution of slavery—the stain on American history—it seems almost appropriate that the stain should be almost co-present with Northup's narrative and Ridley's screenplay. Several film critics have commented on the limited reprieves McQueen's camera provides the spectator by showing tangential views of the beautiful Louisiana setting. Occasionally, within the film, the spectator is greeted with seemingly idyllic and isolated images of Spanish moss swaying from the trees, as it does in much of the southeastern United States. However, since one of the first times this tranquil, repeated imagery appears is immediately after Solomon's aborted runaway attempt when he unexpectedly encounters a posse lynching two other runaway slaves, the beautiful image takes on an uncanny dimension. Because the cinematic framing shows the lynching taking place behind Solomon's back (he only hears the event), the immediate image of the seemingly placid swaying Spanish moss becomes associated with so much strange fruit cultivated by the peculiar institution. In another scene, Solomon and a number of his fellow slaves have been loaned out by Master Epps (Michael Fassbender) to another plantation owner (Bryan Batt) because Epps's cotton fields have been overcome by an insect infestation. This infestation furthers the narrative and shows how it is that Solomon was able to earn some of his own money, used later in his failed bribery of a white indentured servant. But the close-up image of the caterpillar calls attention to itself as saying something beyond the narrative at large. Not only does McQueen's close-up shot of the caterpillar symbolize the confined nature and hope of inevitable freedom/flight of Solomon and other slaves, it also references the curse of the pharaohs that Mistress Shaw (Alfre Woodard) claims "is a poor example compared to what awaits the plantation class." Even the noted anachronisms in the film bear an excessive purpose. The use of synthetic violin strings, the term *terraform*, and the images of aquatic hyacinth may, on one level, signify simple unimportant production errors, but through anachronisms, the film is indirectly, accidentally, and perhaps unconsciously implicating the future into Northup's story, indicating the long-term repercussions of the institution of slavery on American culture, and thereby taking the film viewer into account.[19] Since the institution of slavery stained the historical reality of those who were its victims, that reality is subtly portrayed by the film as something other, as bearing an anamorphotic trace that distorts its realism, especially when looked at awry. Thus, the film demonstrates how the institution of slavery curved the space of reality, distorted and damaged it for all those involved. McQueen even shows the devastating effects slavery had on the white plantation class, especially in the depicted relations between Epps and his wife.[20] Even when Ridley's screenplay and McQueen's film deviate from the details of Northup's narrative account—the knifing of the captured freedman on the slave ship instead of a small pox death, the attempted rape of Eliza (Adepero Oduye), the actual rape of Patsey (Lupita Nyong'o)—the film introduces historical atrocities of slavery that, while Northup himself may never have experienced them, many slaves did, thus making Northup's narrative a synecdoche, a stand-in, for slavery itself. The film is obviously a condensation of one slave narrative, necessary for fitting the narrative into the length of a feature film, but it also functions as a condensation of the history of slavery, never quite comfortable documenting just one exceptional slave story.

There are three particular aspects of McQueen's style, which are in one way or another constantly present throughout the film, that carry ramifications beyond the narrative itself and curve the space of representation: the poetic use of the close-up and extreme close-up shot, the ubiquitous use of shallow focus, and the intermittent use of the long take, especially reserved for the most harrowing scenes. After the initial opening, the film transitions to the past to fill in the story of Solomon Northup. This "flashback" is at first a bit disorienting, as McQueen uses an extreme close-up shot of what the viewer soon learns is Solomon stringing a violin. Later, after Solomon's kidnapping and incarceration, McQueen utilizes an extreme close-up shot of

Solomon between the fragmentary memory flashbacks that only partially reveal what has happened to him. Appearing immediately after Solomon recalls being put to bed by Brown (Scoot McNairy) and Hamilton (Taran Killam), McQueen's extreme close-up shot of our protagonist brings the viewer into proximity with Solomon's own bewilderment, as if he himself is too close to the unfolding events to make sense of his situation. These early extreme close-ups prefigure the use of others throughout the film. On one level, these shots are indicative of McQueen's style, of his penchant for composition over story. But, on another level, the use of extreme close-up in these shots and throughout the film indicates, at least figuratively, the director's intention to bring the spectator closer to the content, closer to the traumatic experience of the institution of slavery than narrative will allow, even when the narrative is a first-person testimonial account. With this stylistic technique, McQueen suggests that beneath the symbolic narrative, beneath Northup's attempt to provide a rational narrative to his otherwise harrowing experience of abduction and enforced bondage, there is a content to his experience that has been obscured by the desire to make sense of the experience, by the desire to render his experience meaningful. This use of close-ups by McQueen implies an emphasis with scale as much as with proximity, with the magnitude of the stain of slavery as much as with the haunting nearness of this traumatic aspect of American history. These extreme close-up shots demarcate moments in the film when the scene itself marks a surpassing of the limits of the narrative, an opening onto something that cannot be directly signified. The opening extreme close-up initially disorients the viewer because the viewer is more or less familiar with the general history of American slavery but not with the traumatic actuality beneath the historical narrative. It is McQueen's means of informing the film's spectators that they are entering an uncanny realm, a realm where everything is turned upside down, where the return of the traumatic past that would rather be forgotten is inescapable. In this sense, McQueen's film is able to convey the trauma of Solomon's experience and the slave's experience in general, not just at the level of representation but also through distortions in the visual field.

This idea of getting the spectator closer to the content of Solomon's experience, of providing the spectator a glimpse of what lies beyond the limits of Northup's narrative and of historical narratives themselves, is also figured in McQueen's stylistic decision to shoot virtually the entire film in shallow focus. McQueen is no Wellesian, no huge fan of the deep-focus shot. By using primarily shallow focus, which at appropriate times morphs into selective focusing, McQueen again highlights the particular over the background, bringing the viewer closer to the real as these shots often lift the content and character out of the context into an immediacy that often appears unmediated.[21] Early after Solomon's abduction, for example, when he confronts his kidnappers with the truth about his freeman status, McQueen shoots him in the foreground, out of focus. McQueen saves the focused middle ground of the mise-en-scène for Solomon's captor. By doing so, McQueen emphasizes the lack of belief in Solomon's story by the abductors. Solomon is out of focus as if to indicate the lack of subjectivity that comes with being a "Georgia runaway," as his abductor repeatedly calls him. Later, when Master Ford attempts to negotiate the sale of Eliza's daughter with Freeman (Paul Giamatti) at the auction house in New Orleans, McQueen keeps the focus tight on Ford (Benedict Cumberbatch) and Freeman, keeping the pleading Eliza blurred in the background. In this scene, McQueen strategically keeps Eliza out of focus, testifying to Freeman's inhumane decision to keep Eliza's concerns out of his focus. More significantly, McQueen's decision to use shallow focus throughout the film brings the spectator into an intimacy with Solomon and his fellow slaves in a manner that simply cannot be conveyed in a textual medium. Shallow focus creates a blurred background throughout, not only to draw the spectator to the immediacy of the experience of the characters but also to literally blur the background story, to get to the immediate trauma as a constant pressure.

Lastly, McQueen resorts to long takes in the film, especially for the harrowing, gruesome, and traumatic depictions of the brutality that was part of the slave's experience. The first long take occurs shortly after Solomon's abduction. In the scene where Solomon wakes to find himself chained and locked up after being drugged by Hamilton and Brown, he is shown being beaten by one of the slave bootleggers. In this scene, McQueen combines the long take with shallow focus, keeping the focus squarely on Solomon in the foreground, allowing the spectator an intimacy with the hero's anguish. Through this technique, McQueen isolates the viewer with Solomon, bringing the spectator into the picture in a manner that would not be the same if McQueen had relied on a deep-focus shot or if he had edited the scene back and forth with rapid cutting between the batterer and Solomon. Throughout the film, McQueen utilizes the long take for these traumatic scenes as a relentless means of transfixing the viewer's attention to the scene's immediacy, a capturing that could not work with the reprieve that editing offers. This strategic use of the long take is repeated later in the scene depicting the aborted lynching of Solomon by Tibeats (Paul Dano). In a nearly two-minute take, Solomon is shown dangling from a rope with the tips of his toes barely touching the ground while the film pictures the everyday routine of the plantation roll by in the background. McQueen could have cut this scene numerous times, showing the sky turn darker as the day passes, indicating the length that Solomon had to endure his punishment. But, by providing a single long take, by forcing the audience to watch this unbearable scene without the reprieve and artificiality associated with editing, the film blurs the line between representation and reality and, thereby, allows something traumatic to emerge on a plane outside of or along the side of representation. The longest take of the film occurs near the end during Patsey's whipping. In an almost five-minute take, McQueen dramatizes the most brutal and painful scene of the film. Unlike the other long takes, McQueen here uses a moving camera to capture the intricacy of the action without having to rely on edits. The lack of editing in this brutal scene makes it unbearable and relentless. A five-minute shot in a film seems three times as long to an audience used to the rapid cutting of much commercial cinema, and in this case, the extended scene forces its own measure of anguish onto the viewer. This imposed self-awareness onto the spectator showcases how the film has already incorporated the audience into the story and, by connection, to the larger history.

And it is this connection to a larger history, a history that is grounded in a particular instance of traumatic experience, that sets McQueen's film apart. The film certainly does not cave in to the general American audience's demand for pleasing entertainment, and it equally resists the temptation to romanticize Northup's overcoming of his ordeal. Additionally, the film does not simply show the viewer what most other films about slavery fail or refuse to show. More significantly, the film evokes cinematically what cannot be shown: how the peculiar institution of slavery imposes a traumatic experience that cannot necessarily be readily articulated, how traumatic experience is constituted in a failure of representation or an impossibility of understanding. McQueen's film is not content to leave the traumatic experience and history of slavery to the failure of a specific articulation, however. Instead, *12 Years a Slave* inaugurates a sort of collective working through as it engages aesthetically and compositionally with the impasse in understanding that characterizes Northup's narrative. In re-presenting his story, the film both draws in and elevates the spectator's engagement with Solomon's particular trauma and ultimately conveys the collective dimension of our nation's shattered past, a past that has left its traumatic stain on American history, a stain that shall remain until the trauma is properly worked through. Because of McQueen's compositional techniques—extreme close-up photography, ubiquitous shallow focus, agonizing long takes—his film reveals the essential strength of the cinema: its ability to suggest things that are not expressible in words and, thereby, its ability to shine a light under the floorboards of this nation. In doing so, *12 Years a Slave* intimates precisely what never stops not writing itself within the saga of American history.

NOTES

1. Elaine Dockterman, "Henry Louis Gates, Jr. Talks *12 Years a Slave* and *The African Americans*," *Time*, October 22, 2013, http://entertainment.time/2013/10/22/henry-louis-gates-jr.com.
2. Dockterman, "Henry Louis Gates, Jr. Talks."
3. Thomas Doherty, "Bringing the Slave Narrative to Screen: Steve McQueen and John Ridley's Searing Depiction of America's 'Peculiar Institution,'" *Cineaste* 39, no. 1 (2013): 8.

4. Dockterman, "Henry Louis Gates, Jr. Talks."

5. Henry Louis Gates Jr. foreword, *Unchained Memories: Readings from the Slave Narratives*, ed. Spencer Crew, Cynthia Goodman, and Henry Louis Gates Jr. (Boston: Bullfinch Press, 2002), 9.

6. Lupita Nyong'o, "SAG Award Acceptance Speech." January 18, 2014, http://www.youtube.com/watch?v=EG7LJLDTANQ.

7. Gates observes: "Americans tend to have amnesia about historical events in general, but this is particularly true about the Civil War. And it is obvious why—it was the most traumatic episode in American history. . . . Deep trauma there." Quoted in Dockterman, "Henry Louis Gates, Jr. Talks."

8. Charles T. Davis and Henry Louis Gates Jr. "Introduction: The Language of Slavery," *The Slave's Narrative* (Oxford: Oxford University Press, 1985), xxviii, xxix.

9. Solomon Northup, *Twelve Years a Slave*, ed. Sue Eakin and Joseph Logsdon (Baton Rouge: Louisiana State University Press, 1968), 3.

10. Northup, *Twelve Years a Slave*, 30.

11. Northup, *Twelve Years a Slave*, 86.

12. See Hazel V. Carby, *Representing Womanhood: The Emergence of the Afro-American Woman Novelist* (Oxford: Oxford University Press, 1987); and Teresa A. Goddu and Craig V. Smith, "Scenes of Writing in Frederick Douglass's Narrative: Autobiography and the Creation of the Self," *Southern Review* 25, no. 4 (1989): 822–40, for excellent critical explorations of both Jacobs's and Douglass's slave narratives as vehicles for writing their authors into subjectivity.

13. Jacques Lacan, *The Seminar of Jacques Lacan, Book XX: Encore*, trans. Bruce Fink (New York: W. W. Norton, 1998), 59.

14. Dockterman, "Henry Louis Gates, Jr. Talks."

15. Slavoj Žižek, *Looking Awry: An Introduction to Jacques Lacan through Popular Culture* (Cambridge: MIT Press, 1991), 91.

16. Jacques Lacan, *The Seminar of Jacques Lacan: The Four Fundamental Concepts of Psychoanalysis*, trans. Alan Sheridan (New York: W. W. Norton, 1998), 85–92.

17. Mladen Dolar, "The Spectator Who Knew Too Much," in *Everything You Always Wanted to Know About Lacan (But Were Afraid to Ask Hitchcock)*, ed. Slavoj Žižek (London: Verso, 1992), 133.

18. Lacan maintains that "if the function of the stain is recognized in its autonomy and identified with that of the gaze, we can see its track, its thread, its trace, at every stage of the construction of the world, in the scopic field. We will then realize that the function of the stain and of the gaze is both that which governs the gaze most secretly and that which always escapes from the grasp of that form of vision that is satisfied with itself in imagining itself as consciousness," Jacques Lacan, *The Four Fundamental Concepts*, 74. At one level, McQueen's film attempts to separate the viewer from his or her place of indifferent spectatorship and implicate the viewer into the shared history of slavery.

19. For the anachronisms in the film, see the *12 Years a Slave* IMDb page, http://www.imdb.com/title/tt2024544/?ref_=nv_sr_1.

20. Gates has commented that "one of the most amazing and successful things the film does is show the way that slavery dehumanizes the master as well as the slave," in Dockterman, "Henry Louis Gates, Jr. Talks."

21. Actor Michael K. Williams had an emotional breakdown on the set after the first take of a particularly grueling scene.

Chapter Sixteen

162 Years after *12 Years a Slave*: A Viewing through Double-Consciousness

Salvador Murguia

When *12 Years a Slave* director Steve McQueen won the coveted Oscar for Best Picture at the 2014 Academy Awards, his acceptance speech could not have been more appropriate or humbling. In front of an estimated forty-three million viewers globally, McQueen closed his speech with:

> The last word: everyone deserves not just to survive, but to live. This is the most important legacy of Solomon Northup. I dedicate this award to all the people who have endured slavery. And the twenty-one million people who still suffer slavery today.[1]

In almost complete anticipation, audiences expected McQueen to make mention of the true tragedies that undergirded the film's success. It was, after all, the pain and suffering endured by some twelve million enslaved Africans brought to the Americas between the sixteenth and nineteenth centuries that bolstered the film's powerful impact.

The film is a remarkable work of cinema that retells the true story of Solomon Northup (played by Chiwetel Ejiofor), a "free" African American that was kidnapped and sold into slavery in 1841. After bearing the brunt of twelve years as an enslaved laborer, Northup is liberated and eventually goes on to compose his memoirs—a publication upon which McQueen bases his film.

Of *12 Years a Slave*, film critic for the *New York Times* Manohla Dargis wrote that the film's genius is its "insistence on banal evil, and on terror, that seeped into souls, bound bodies and reaped an enduring, terrible price."[2] In less abstract, though no less complimentary, terms, the *Guardian*'s Mark Kermode noted that it's "pitched pretty near perfectly in terms of sheer narrative craftsmanship. This is an important story, told with passion, conviction and grace."[3] In addition to these snippets from full reviews, it would be difficult to find any major news outlet that reviews the arts posting any negative criticism about the film.

Yet, in a peculiar and almost ironic twist, the actual aftermath of this film may have revealed something rather telling about race and movies in an age that seems to be popularly tied to an America in which Barack Obama is the president, potentially reaching deep into the politics of race relations. The reason for this rests not necessarily in the content of the film itself, but instead in the uncritical exploration of its reception. In other words, the film does a fine job across the board for all that it intends to convey, yet how people received it and the dynamics through which both positive and sparse negative critiques emerged were highly politicized. For example, it wasn't long after the Academy Awards when conservative radio talk show host Rush Limbaugh decided to comment on the film, remarking:

> If it was the only thing that movie won, it was gonna win Best Picture. There was no way. It didn't matter if it was good or bad. I haven't seen it. It was going to win. It had the magic word in the title, "slave."[4]

Of course, like most reactionary banter, Limbaugh's *facts* were simply not factual, as no other movie in the history of the Academy that had this so-called magic word in its title had ever won an Oscar, much less been nominated for one.

Despite bearing no statistical significance whatsoever, thoughts and ideas similar to Limbaugh's remarks were definitely in circulation—especially those in the market to capitalize on the moment for their own professional motives. Take, for example, the host for the Academy Awards evening, Ellen DeGeneres, and her joke that set the tone for the night when she cracked that the awards could only end in one of two ways: "Possibility number one: *12 Years a Slave* wins best picture. Possibility number two: You're all racists!" And as the roar of laughter followed, it became eerily clear that DeGeneres, however smug or tasteless, was onto something.

Taking up the joke in his MSNBC opinion piece, Adam Serwer noted,

> The uncomfortable truth of DeGeneres's joke is that the Oscars can be as much about what the overwhelmingly white film industry wants to say about itself as it is about the quality of the films themselves. The film industry is a place where the stories of people of color are still rarely told through narratives they themselves create.[5]

Perhaps not the only one thinking it, but certainly one of the few that would articulate it, Serwer's comments are incredibly germane to the film's reception. What may be truly poignant within Serwer's remark is not that the film was somehow created and propped up by the "white film industry," as it was not; yet, instead, how this white-dominated industry makes sense of its own feelings about race within this context and how, by extension, black audiences must then view themselves in light of these terms. That's not to say that the film's reception can be couched in one single interpretation of some universal reception, but conversely, to ignore that in many instances this was the case is to ignore something incredibly important about race in America.

How, one might ask, could the film's reception prompt such an involved interpretation of racial dynamics within the film industry? Of course, once a film of this magnitude has been released, it becomes somewhat of a juggernaut and one can't expect its creators to rescue it from any ill or highly opinionated reception. The realist notions of its existence remain, and as an item of popular culture, it's vulnerable to any number of unintended consequences. To begin, the popularity of the film conjures up a particular image of slavery and people of color—both in their historical and subsequential states—that may, in the long run, become a part of conventional thinking, serving to maintain established perspectives on race and racism. This, of course, begs the question as to why this would be considered problematic. Quite frankly, it may not be, except for the fact that audiences—particularly those people of color that the film represents—will view it quite differently in terms of how they see themselves through the eyes of others. White audiences may feel guilt, embarrassment, absolution, perhaps even indifference. Some audiences of color may view themselves as objects of pure entertainment or even objectification; while others may see themselves as objects of resentment, and still others as somehow deserving of unsolicited sympathy. This suggests not that audiences will universally fall into one of these loosely derived categories, but instead that the range of perceptions about how one may experience viewing oneself through the depictions of others is not limited to mere approval and the celebrations that may ensue during a subsequent awards ceremony.

Despite the fanfare and positive acclaim surrounding the film, all of which is well deserved, the film becomes socially significant in such a way that viewers form meaning from its contents. That is, audiences gaze upon the film and arrive at various conclusions; some of which reinforce old stereotypes and conventional imagery, while others simply cultivate something new altogether. To ignore that such gazes exist or suggest that one may be reading too much into the actions of viewership is to venture into a state of social naïveté; just as the tensions surrounding class, gender, sex, sexuality, and age all figure into one's perception of motion picture, race is no exception and is equally present.

The argument herein rests squarely on the work of the sociologist W. E. B. DuBois (1868–1963), as it was DuBois who raised the issue of what it means to negotiate a person of color's image in light of another's perception. In his seminal 1903 book titled *The Souls of Black Folk*, DuBois notes,

> It is a peculiar sensation, this double-consciousness, this sense of always looking at one's self through the eyes of others, of measuring one's soul by the tape of a world that looks on in amused contempt and pity. One ever feels his twoness,—an American, a Negro; two souls, two thoughts, two unreconciled strivings; two warring ideals in one dark body, whose dogged strength alone keeps it from being torn asunder.
>
> The history of the American Negro is the history of this strife—this longing to attain self-conscious manhood, to merge his double self into a better and truer self. In this merging he wishes neither of the older selves to be lost. He does not wish to Africanize America, for America has too much to teach the world and Africa. He wouldn't bleach his Negro blood in a flood of white Americanism, for he knows that Negro blood has a message for the world. He simply wishes to make it possible for a man to be both a Negro and an American without being cursed and spit upon by his fellows, without having the doors of opportunity closed roughly in his face.[6]

This reasoning is based upon unequal power dynamics that are often swept under the rug, so to speak, when it comes to discussions of race—largely because of the uncomfortable feelings and debates they evoke. DuBois's interpretation, however, skirts none of the realities associated with this discussion. The duality of the self-perception among people of color is qualitatively inseparable from images, symbols, and ideals bound to popular culture, and DuBois's notion of a "double-consciousness" serves to shed light on this often ignored subject of unequal power dynamics.

Viewing the reception of *12 Years a Slave* as a medium through which African Americans view themselves places emphasis on how DuBois's perspective functions. Focusing on the section in which DuBois made mention of "amused contempt and pity," one may better see how this double-consciousness operates in tandem with the reception of this film.

The transatlantic slave trade, the exoticism of the *other* that lent itself to it, and the brutal victimization of millions of enslaved peoples are all strong historical evidence enough for this existence of amused contempt. Yet that the release of *12 Years a Slave* that garnered so much positive attention for its attempt to render a more holistic view of slavery would also invoke such amused contempt seems backward at best. Still, there were some critiques that revolved around this type of disdain.

Some were rather blatant in this regard. Christian Toto, a Breitbart.com critic, criticized the film's production studio, Fox Searchlight, for marketing the two-word phrase "It's time," in what he saw as an ad campaign to evoke guilt and win recognition:

> The implications are many. It's time to honor a film that reminds the nation anew of its slavery sins. . . . The issue of guilt, or more specifically white guilt, isn't a topic suddenly tied to the film. . . . Saying "it's time" for the movie to win a major prize actually dulls the glory it has every right to receive.[7]

Others took a much more explanatory approach, qualifying their remarks in such a way that smacked of a post-racial society. Like the opinion piece published by *Guardian* contributor Orville Lloyd Douglas, wherein he commented,

> I'm convinced these black race films are created for a white, liberal film audience to engender white guilt and make them feel bad about themselves. Regardless of your race, these films are unlikely to teach you anything you don't already know. Frankly, why can't black people get over slavery? Or, at least, why doesn't anyone want to see more contemporary portrayals of black lives?[8]

In spite of what may be viewed as a real disregard for the lessons of history, Douglas, a black Canadian, may have in part characterized how the film was actually received. Similarly to Limbaugh's aforementioned remarks—though in a much more factual context—the guilt associated with historical aggressions that propagated slavery can surface and serve to inform the reception of this type of art. Just days after the film won Best Picture, reports circulated about how the film's success may have been a forgone conclusion, based presumably on how the political correctness of its production necessitated social reparations. As John Horn of the *Los Angeles Times* reported, individuals with voting rights within the Academy actually cast their votes in favor of the film for Best Picture without ever viewing it. According to Horn:

> Two Oscar voters privately admitted that they didn't see "12 Years a Slave," thinking it would be upsetting. But they said they voted for it anyway because, given the film's social relevance, they felt obligated to do so.[9]

While there is no evidence that these anonymous individuals were from a white viewership, Horn's report nonetheless demonstrates the presence of this sentiment just the same—the mere notion of what slavery represents, regardless of the medium through which it is depicted, invokes feelings that, in an Althusserian sense, interpellate social interaction and establish the circumstances for which voting for the film is the only option.

This sentiment that undergirds the type of amused contempt, emerging after the film was released, exemplifies only one feature of DuBois's thesis. Such amused contempt accompanied by pity is equally revealing. It is that unwarranted sympathy, after all, that forces the discussion in which people of color are viewed as somehow "begging" for reparations.

If ever this type of pity was clearer for students of race and racism, it was the reaction to the performance of Lupita Nyong'o, the Kenyan actress that portrayed "Patsey," a young enslaved woman that is sexually exploited and held as a mistress of one of the slave masters. Nyong'o's performance was certainly praiseworthy, and for it she won the Oscar for Best Supporting Actress; however, the hyper-reaction to Nyong'o's achievement really was, perhaps, also a result of subconscious voter obligation.

Charish, a blogger for the *Motley News* website, may have hit the nail on the head when she delineated this seemingly contrived outpouring of acclaim. In her piece titled "The Fetishization of Lupita Nyong'o," Charish delivered a scathing but nevertheless decisive interpretation of the implications associated with this type of reaction:

> Black and white people, alike, are enamored with Nyong'o for, what I believe, are different reasons. Blacks are proud that Nyong'o crushed it in her portrayal of Patsey and I'm personally excited that we've got another black woman winning major acting awards. Whites seems to be most preoccupied with Nyong'o's exotic look and I think that's something we, as a society, probably need to address. . . .
>
> I'm also weirded out by the onslaught of white people who are just plain gob-smacked by her exquisiteness. I've received an enormous amount of trending Facebook articles from various fashion sources that seem *almost amazed* by how beautiful Lupita is. It irks me that people don't find it ironic how Nyong'o has performed one of the most gut-wrenching representations of an enslaved black woman. Her character, Patsey, shows the reality of an enslaved body; this body is allowed to be ogled, worked to death, beaten, and raped. This body does not belong to Patsey and for some reason, it feels as though Nyong'o's body doesn't belong to her either.[10]

Charish goes on to list other black actresses and the accolades they received in context for their parts as something both novel and characteristically different from predetermined notions about people of color. What's revealing about her list is that it demonstrates just how different, if not exotic, one must be perceived to be in order to break through the color barrier and receive due respect on the other side of this artistic forum in which racial divisions are so prevalent. Notably, there was Gabourey Sidibe's performance in *Precious* (2009), in which critics showcased her obesity above her talents, and Halle Berry's Oscar for Best Actress in *Monster's Ball* (2002), in which critics essentially overlooked her true acting skills and emphasized the erotic and sexually objectifying scenes she performed with Billy Bob Thornton.

What's at the center of Charish's argument is that this type of praise can be chalked up to disingenuous pity where merits go unheeded and the accomplishment of the person of color somehow fills a void created by regret and misgivings tied to the evils of history. It is the way in which something *seen before* can be instantaneously *never-seen-before* merely because it makes one feel as if one has done one's pious duty in seeing something so mundane in a different and now sacred light. Never knowing Nyong'o, much less her faults, audiences began to relate to her acting, her look, her story, her history, and so on and so on.

I was shocked to see this firsthand through social media interactions. One friend rambled on about how his daughter had attended the same school as Nyong'o, and although she never actually met Nyong'o, the loose association was license to post about how Nyong'o was an inspiration, a role model, and, strangely enough, a friend.

Another acquaintance went on to rant and rave about how she wished she could be "half as interesting and elegant" as Nyong'o. This eventually led to a barrage of complimenting posts that effectively obscured Nyong'o's slice of personality that we all saw at the Academy Awards and cast light on this other individual's character—the created Nyong'o—as if she had won the Oscar. By the end of the posting thread, almost all traces of the original post had been virtually forgotten, as it was now the celebration about the kindness and self-worth of the individual that originally posted her wishes to be like Nyong'o.

In the closing of Charish's blog post, she strikes yet another chord that further fleshes out the dynamics of this disingenuousness. Making mention of Cate Blanchett's performance that earned her the Best Actress Oscar, Charish notes how the merits of Blanchett's performance, not the novelty of her nor the rare frequency in which people of her skin color are honored, are what legitimizes the notion of success in this context. Of Blanchett, Charish wrote:

> I'm sure she did an excellent job, she's a great actress! But did she have to prove anything or teach black people a valuable lesson in history or humanity to get her award? Was she involved in a "teachable moment?"
>
> Just as Blanchett is *classically* beautiful in, I don't know . . . a kind of timeless way, I'm still hoping for the next great black actress to be beautiful in the same way. Not in an exotic, noble, new-car smelling way.[11]

Unfortunately for Nyong'o, if the disingenuousness embodied in the fanfare surrounding her accomplishments is any indication of what audiences want in the next great black actress, perhaps audiences are still not ready to be fans, but instead arbiters of how they should cast their own pities.

How this "amused contempt and pity" that DuBois writes of materializes is intimately tied to how people of color view themselves. Through the interplay of these two unsolicited components, a field of perspective is formed in which one is beholden to the larger view of oneself through the gazes of others. For people of color, viewing the tragedies of slavery within cinema is daunting enough, but to see oneself feigningly perceived in the aftermath of a successful artistic endeavor is simply humiliating.

Though not directly related to *12 Years a Slave*, Quentin Tarantino's 2012 controversial film, *Django Unchained*, became a hot-button topic that epitomized this notion of portrayal. In reaction to Tarantino's movie, celebrated actor, director, and producer Spike Lee took exception to the film altogether, announcing that he simply wouldn't see it. For Lee, it was the genre that Tarantino employed to tell a story about slavery that was insulting. According to his December 22, 2012, tweet, Lee wrote: "American Slavery Was Not A Sergio Leone Spaghetti Western. It Was A Holocaust. My Ancestors Are Slaves. Stolen From Africa. I Will Honor Them."[12] Surprisingly enough, Lee received criticism—some of which came from people of color—for his remarks in what appears to have been a show of the popularity of Tarantino's edgy style, trumping Lee and his remarkable record of incredible filmmaking that has always been honored as art in the trenches of race relations.

This disagreement, however unrelated to the discussion of *12 Years a Slave* it may appear, may in fact be more telling in terms of a double-consciousness than one might think. To explain, like the characterization of people of color that Tarantino so often popularizes with no-nonsense, violent, and intimidating features in his films, audiences also form similar characterizations of people of color—derived from these images. Yet these characterizations do not merely dissolve into the motion picture and disassociate from the actors and actresses that perform within these roles; rather, typecasting begins to set in and audiences allow this to inform their perceptions to a greater extent than one might assume. The popularity of Tarantino's quirky and often rebellious depictions simply appeal to a wider audience than, say, a character of modest or even righteous demeanor—perhaps even those characters that may contribute to a more positive image of people of color.

12 Years a Slave is certainly not a film in which the character portrayals push back against the strides for equality achieved by subsequent generations of civil rights activists. Yet, when people of color are given such a limited and often impoverished set of images from popular culture to which to relate, it seems almost degrading that they must choose between the likes of the Tarantino depictions and those more aligned with the tragic histories presented by directors like Lee or McQueen. That is, although there may be a variety of roles people of color play on the big screen, these roles are certainly limited and this viewership is thus provided with few options of how they may actually see themselves depicted. Regardless of how important it is to see, understand, and appreciate the history of slavery through art—in this case cinema—it is nonetheless a simultaneous reminder of how one's dignity, humanity, and sense of self can be reduced to a set of demeaning and unflattering images. Viewing oneself as both an American in real time, as well as a descendent of all that America exploited historically, is to view oneself through this double-consciousness; the achievement of artistic expression and the successes of the artists that bring us the movies cannot shelter us from this.

It is not the intention here to defile the tragic history of the millions of enslaved people that endured such misery, any more than it is to besmirch the accomplishments of this film. Instead, the position is to scratch the surface of the obvious message this film presents and bring awareness to the sociological factors that may be at play. A critical viewing, even in the aftermath of the film's reception, is vital. After all, what service would people of color be doing themselves to view the implications of such a film uncritically? That is, casting aside the lenses of hermeneutics and joining a celebration, as if the celebrants are of all colors and backgrounds, may appear to some as simply buying into what Stuart Hall called the "dominant/hegemonic" position. In resisting this decoding, it may be important to make attempts at revealing any unintended consequences—specifically those that push back against the strides the filmmakers and actors intended.

For people of color to find no value in such an endeavor implies ever so slightly that one simply embrace all of the facets of a film that was, in many ways, intended to encourage audiences to do the very opposite through historical inquiry, research, self-reflection, and critical thinking. Additionally, it is not the intention in this essay to make claims about how the works of DuBois should be applied—whether appropriately or inappropriately. Yet the visual medium and one's ability to view and *re*view its content multiple times cannot but invite some form of criticism. *12 Years a Slave* is a work of art, a masterpiece, a form of entertainment, a historical rendering of facts—all of which must be open to critique and not simply left to the arbiters of popular film such as the adjudication process of the Academy Awards. This film put into motion the account of one man who may very well have perceived his experience as a painful one that stripped him of his dignity. However, would the reception of his story today have jibed with his initial intentions that were at play when he composed his memoirs, knowing full well that audiences could consume the contents of his story through the gaze of what DuBois might have characterized as "amused contempt and pity"?[13]

Perhaps there are few other modern mediums that can capture and deliver as much imagery that reflects human interaction as film. Through McQueen's direction, the skilled use of technologies by cinematographers, and the exceptional performances by the cast, *12 Years a Slave* did an incredible job of capturing and delivering imagery as such; yet how onlookers receive the film—inclusive of how they see themselves through it—will eventually establish its socio-political impact.

NOTES

1. Steve McQueen, "The Last Word," acceptance speech for Best Picture, Academy Awards, Hollywood, Calif., March 3, 2014.
2. Manohla Dargis, "The Blood and Tears, Not the Magnolias," *New York Times*, October 17, 2013, http://www.nytimes.com/2013/10/18/movies/12-years-a-slave-holds-nothing-back-in-show-of-suffering.html.
3. Mark Kermode, "12 Years a Slave—a Review," *Guardian*, March 5, 2014, http://www.theguardian.com/film/2014/jan/12/12-years-a-slave-review.
4. Jason Linkins, "Let's Help Rush Limbaugh with This Whole Movies with The Word 'Slave' in the Title Thing," *Huffington Post*, March 8, 2014, http://www.huffingtonpost.com/2014/03/07/rush-limbaugh-12-years-a-slave_n_4922052.html.
5. Adam Serwer, "Uncomfortable Truth in the Oscars' '12 Years a Slave' Joke," *MSNBC*, March 3, 2014, http://www.msnbc.com/msnbc/oscars-2014-best-picture-12-years-slave-lupita-nyongo.
6. W. E. B. DuBois, *The Souls of Black Folk* (Rockville, Md: Arc Manor, 2008 [1903]), 12–13.
7. Christian Toto, "Is '12 Years a Slave's' Oscar Campaign Playing White Guilt Card," Breitbart.com, February 20, 2014, http://www.breitbart.com/Big-Hollywood/2014/02/20/slave-plays-guilt-card-oscar-push.
8. Orville Lloyd Douglas, "Why I Won't Be Watching *The Butler* and *12 Years a Slave*," *Guardian*, September 12, 2013, http://www.theguardian.com/commentisfree/2013/sep/12/why-im-not-watching-the-butler-12-years-a-slave.
9. John Horn, "Twelve Years a Slave Puts Spotlight on Hollywood's Approach to Race," *Los Angeles Times*, March 4, 2014, http://www.latimes.com/entertainment/envelope/moviesnow/la-et-mn-oscar-race-20140304,0,2619113.story#axzz2v1iGPZM9.
10. Charish, "The Fetishization of Lupita Nyong'o," *Motley News*, March 3, 2014, http://www.themotleynews.com/2014/03/the-fetishization-of-lupita-nyongo.html.
11. Charish, "The Fetishization of Lupita Nyong'o."
12. Spike Lee, "American Slavery Was Not . . . ," Twitter, December 22, 2012.
13. DuBois, *The Souls of Black Folk*, 12.

Chapter Seventeen

Revoking the Privilege of Forgetting: White Supremacy Interrogated in *12 Years a Slave*

David M. Jones

Spirits of the dead, lingering spirits of the dead, rise up and claim your stories.
—Ghostly narrator from *Sankofa* (1993), directed by Halie Gerima[1]

Steve McQueen, you charge everything you fashion with a breath of your own spirit. . . . I'm certain that the dead are standing about you and watching and they are grateful and so am I.
—Lupita Nyong'o, acceptance speech, Best Supporting Actress, *12 Years a Slave*[2]

If ever in slavery's 250-year history in North America there were a kind master or a contented slave, as in the nature of things there must have been, here and there, we may be sure that Mr. McQueen does not want us to hear about it. This, in turn, surely means that his view of the history of the American South is as partial and one-sided as that of the hated Gone with the Wind.
—Review of *12 Years a Slave* by James Bowman, "Propaganda Is Not 'Reality' or 'Truth,'" *American Spectator* Online[3]

The resistance to terror is what makes the world habitable: the protest against violence will not be forgotten and this insistent memory renders life possible in communal situations.
—Carolyn Forché, introduction to *Against Forgetting*[4]

BLACK SELVES, BLACK FAMILIES, AND
WHITE SUPREMACIST REPRESSION IN THREE SCENES

The memory of legal human slavery lingers as a presence in the twenty-first century, coming to the surface in prominent artistic projects that seek to narrate the human trauma of those years. Awareness of white supremacy should most certainly be prominent in how antebellum human slavery is remembered, particularly since white supremacy endures in both covert and overt forms nearly 150 years after a Civil War and legislative action led to the official abolition of most forms of legal human slavery in the United States. Defined in relation to its global and enduring impacts on public and intimate human spaces, white supremacy remains

> an historically based, institutionally perpetuated system of exploitation and oppression of continents, nations, and peoples classified as "non-Whites" by continents, nations, and people who, by virtue of their white (light) skin pigmentation and/or ancestral origin from Europe, classify themselves as "White."[5]

Working from the history and culture of the United States, particularly the 1853 nonfiction slave narrative of Solomon Northup, director Steve McQueen's 2013 film *12 Years a Slave* presents highly relevant and provocative observations on how human slavery and white supremacy continue to haunt humanity in the age of President Obama, encouraging us to reexamine current-day cultural nostalgia for life in the antebellum South.

My analysis begins with a concise reading of two scenes in Steve McQueen's film that call attention to larger themes of antebellum nostalgia and white supremacy in the age of Obama. In scene 4, the film's protagonist, Solomon Northup (played by Chiwetel Ejiofor), begins to recognize the nightmarish reality that he is being kidnapped, imprisoned, and sold into slavery, no longer a nominally free African American citizen, husband, and father on northern soil. McQueen's depiction of the scene emphasizes that in the context of white supremacy, one of the worst offenses is to resist servility and to assert one's human worth. In the scene, after being drugged by his kidnappers, Merrill Brown (played by Scott McNairy) and Abram Hamilton (played by Taran Killam), Solomon awakens in a dungeon, fully chained. Confronted by jailers, he insists that he is a free man from Saratoga, New York, with a family and full human rights. He is unshaken initially by the jailer's insistence that "you're just a runaway nigger from Georgia," before being yanked from his feet by his chains and beaten with full physical force using a wooden paddle until it splinters. In a film that depicts repeated physical punishments with shocking intensity and realism, the link becomes unmistakable between white supremacy, physical subjugation, and the threat to the system represented by assertions of personhood by African Americans.

A second emotionally resonant scene in the early part of the film depicts the suffering of black women and families under enslavement, suffering that is of no significant note within a white supremacist world view. In scene 8, a slave auction is depicted, with white enslavers eagerly examining enslaved African Americans, including several women who are stripped, with music and refreshments being provided. As conversation proceeds between potential enslavers as to the human sale, one enslaved woman (Eliza, played by Adepero Oduye) pleads that she not be separated from her children. White enslavers attempt to ignore her, talk over her, and, despite her insistence and pleading, do not grant her request to keep her children together.

Scene 11 depicts Eliza's continuous crying after being permanently separated from her children, leading to a confrontation between Solomon and Eliza. Solomon insists that she not fall into despair, but his words provide no comfort for Eliza in this moment of unspeakable sorrow. Eliza then repudiates Solomon's defense of their enslaver, William Ford, as being essentially a good man. In her words from the scene:

> You think he does not know that you're more than you suggest? But he does nothing for you! Nothing! You are no better than prize livestock!

Eventually in the film (and in the historical record), William Ford would mortgage Northup's *chattel value* under the enslavement system to borrow money for the construction of plantation buildings. Subsequent events would land Northup on the Epps plantation, a site of unrelenting suffering and cruelty for enslaved people, for the remainder of his twelve years of enslavement.

Historicizing these incidents is a complex task as we imagine a functioning multiracial democracy where the full human story of African American enslavement and the motivations of white enslavers are discussed openly and fully. Along these lines, one notes that even in the immediate wake of the astoundingly moving film version of Northup's narrative, plans are in process in Richmond, Virginia, to build a baseball stadium on the site where Northup was jailed after his kidnapping, a plan being fought by Solomon Northup's descendants.[6] This example illustrates that within white supremacist logic, a willingness endures not only to celebrate portions of antebellum history that produced mass physical and spiritual death among African Americans, but also to minimize or erase collective public memory of African American mass enslavement. *12 Years a Slave* invites us to resist nostalgia, collectively, by revering the memory of the enslaved.

INTERROGATING WHITE SUPREMACY IN A "POST-RACIAL" ERA: *12 YEARS A SLAVE* AS ARTISTIC STATEMENT

As the notion of a post-racial society is embraced by various segments of U.S. political and public opinion, it remains challenging to imagine how a broad-based conversation about race will emerge that honestly probes the complex discourse and human consequences of white supremacy. Such a conversation is sorely needed, even in the age of the Obama presidency that is widely seen as a significant step toward the end of racial inequality. The Obama age has also been characterized by Sundiata Keita Cha-Ju as "the new Nadir"[7] and by Michelle Alexander as an era of "the New Jim Crow,"[8] underscoring trends toward excessive incarceration, concentrated poverty, and limited educational opportunity for African Americans. Such conditions call on justice-minded and empathic citizens to rethink our notions of racial identity and its social impacts, if we are indeed committed to creating a fully functional multiracial democracy. Another formidable task before us is to identify and challenge white supremacy in an era where resistance to the idea of identify politics is manifest among many in the United States' white majority population.

This leads us to the realm of art—particularly mass market art, where potential remains for incisive and visionary projects that probe and challenge the logic of white supremacy and motivate anti-racist action. Such art can encourage a reverent response to racial atrocities to help us move forward with a deeper respect for the historical and ancestral journeys of all human communities. The opening quotations in this essay from the Halie Gerima film *Sankofa*, from actress Lupita Nyong'o, and from poet Carolyn Forché all emphasize the importance of witnessing injustice, protesting inhumanity, and continually opening spaces for collective healing. It is unfortunate that in so many post-genocidal contexts, silence and denial are chosen as a way to avoid collective accountability for injustice—what I call the *privilege of forgetting*. James Bowman, also quoted on the opening page, indulges this privilege in his assertion that the kind master and contented slave are represented somewhere, "here and there," in the antebellum South, demonstrating an unfortunate cultural habit of investing antebellum imagery with pleasure and nostalgia, while falling silent about human suffering and justice-seeking resistance that was emblematic of this era's history. Wherever there is willful silence or selective amnesia surrounding crimes against humanity—there is where art, argument, and imagery are all needed to touch our hearts, our imaginations, and our intellects, encouraging us to grieve breakdowns in civil order and to remember the human costs of such breakdowns.

Into this context enters director Steve McQueen's 2013 feature film, *12 Years a Slave*, which makes a spectacular contribution toward historicizing the institution of slavery and, in doing so, seeks to revoke the *privilege of forgetting* that forestalls any sustained, collective, public repudiation of white supremacy in the name of anti-racism. With its close attention to the personal and intimate ways that human trafficking impacts human health and wholeness across entire communities, *12 Years a Slave* raises provocative questions about cultural ways of imagining the antebellum South. It may prove to be a signature accomplishment of McQueen's film to reopen contentious questions about how the so-called peculiar institution[9] is to be historicized. McQueen's film builds on genre conventions of the neo-slave narrative that have emerged in literature and feature film, drawing actively from historical sources to create a compelling first-person narrative about the experiences of enslaved people and their enslavers. Rather quickly, the film has generated a highly contentious, emotional, and productive debate through its graphic dramatization of white supremacy in the context of African American enslavement, and this public controversy is relevant and timely for a nation whose continuing economic and social viability depends on fuller inclusion of all communities in national life. Unthinking white supremacy requires public acknowledgment of its presence, followed by consistent, deliberate efforts to identify and disassemble its discursive components, and McQueen's film provides a useful platform for informing this work.

To its artistic credit, *12 Years a Slave* consciously avoids some major limitations of its predecessors in treating the subject of human atrocity under U.S. slavery. There is little trace of a pattern described by Elizabeth Bingell as "Burbanking," where Hollywood logic associates injustice with "individual villainy that would likely succumb to individual heroism,"[10] elements of sentimentality and heightened presences of sympathetic white characters paternalistically shaping film ideology. Instead, white supremacy is presented in serial manifestations—as systematic, as calculated for social control, and as capricious due to individual actions, far beyond individual villainy, never as a textual joke (as in recent auteur films *Django Unchained* and *O Brother, Where Art Thou?*). As a result, the human consequences of white supremacist repression are meted out institutionally in *12 Years a Slave*—a horrendous result of the caveat originating in Virginia colonial law ("Negro women's children to serve according to the condition of the mother"[11]) sanctioning serial rape of African American women and enslavement of their children, enforcing a code of inferiority in social relations through physical brutality and psychological abuse, traumatizing whole communities through white vigilantism, and ensuring that African American witnesses to atrocity have no power to intervene and that white witnesses to atrocity choose a path of least resistance by assenting to white solidarity.

It is probably reasonable to say that McQueen's directorial style in *12 Years a Slave* does not value aesthetic subtlety (at least as that term is conventionally understood) over the intensified dramatization of human cruelty, a stylistic and ideological choice that produced a mini-backlash among several major film critics whose inattention to many of the film's textual features is striking in their reviews. The film's well-deserved earning of Oscar Awards drew greater attention to stellar performances by Chiwetel Ejiofor as Solomon Northup; Lupita Nyong'o as Patsey, a long-suffering young mother who is victimized by slavery's worst atrocities; and the chilling performance of Sarah Paulson, a slaveholding wife at the Epps plantation whose sadistic treatment of Patsey is riveting and heart-wrenching in the film.

In contrast to other notable moving-picture narratives on American slavery and its aftermath, *12 Years a Slave* tells a compact, even claustrophobic story of human cruelty, suffering, and resistance. The film's deliberate pace; its persistent examination of sadism and torture as meted out by white slave owners and overseers in interpersonal, marketplace, and plantation contexts; and its central narrative focus on Solomon Northup's enslavement (rather than his early life or his pursuit of justice) invite audiences to understand American slavery more intimately than is characteristic in mass market film. Moving beyond established filmic vocabularies of the neo-slave narrative, *12 Years a Slave* unflinchingly depicts multiple settings where inhuman acts are perpetrated against enslaved people. The film's depictions of violence represent a distinctive break from the most recent landmark Hollywood film exploring the issue of slavery, *Django Unchained* (2012), a narrative in which graphic violence consistently appears cartoonish in a spaghetti Western context and little space is left for an earnest presentation of character.[12] In the aftermath of *Django Unchained*'s presence at the 2012 Oscars, *12 Years a Slave* will most certainly earn more enduring artistic distinction as an interpretation of the history of human slavery in the United States.

In its uses of sympathetic characterization to tap into audience empathy, McQueen's film has much in common with *The Autobiography of Miss Jane Pittman* (1976), a film adapted from an Ernest Gaines novel that develops the story of one unbowed woman, Jane Pittman, who survived antebellum human slavery and the Nadir, becoming a witness and an activist during the civil rights era (Cicely Tyson's performance as Miss Jane Pittman is truly one for the ages). *12 Years a Slave* expresses similar determination to break silences about the dialectic of racist ideology and acts of sadism under enslavement that also made the television production *Roots* distinctive and timely as a justice-minded production. And yet, because its primary historical source is an autobiographical account of enslavement written before abolition by an ex-slave (Solomon Northup), *12 Years a Slave* has a strong case for preeminence among neo-slave narratives in film. Another successful predecessor in this genre would be *Beloved* (a film adapted from Toni Morrison's rigorously research-based fictional account of horrific events in the life of enslaved woman Margaret Garner), but there is no extant literary narrative where Garner spoke extensively in her own words, nor is the film as consistently strong in its acting and writing for the screen compared to *12 Years a*

Slave. The earlier filmic interpretation of Northup's slave narrative, *Solomon Northup's Odyssey*,[13] also achieved artistic success as a neo-slave narrative, though its fidelity to a television code that restricts nudity, graphic violence, and intensity in characterization prevents it from achieving the heightened realism of McQueen's production. As a filmic dramatization of a first-person, individual account of life under slavery, *12 Years a Slave* is without peer, blending details from Northup's text, imagined sequences, and other sources with striking visual images and characterizations.

A blend of fiction and nonfictional elements and methods is customary for a historical film, given that beyond material artifacts, much of what we know as *history* is unrecoverable in a precise form, and thus core themes are constructed for audiences through argument and narrative. Viewed in terms of its argument, the film's most important contribution may lie in its effort to inscribe antebellum white supremacy as an unspeakable human horror on the level of the Holocaust in the twentieth century, an occurrence to be regarded reverently and regretfully, with mindfulness toward prevention of any future occurrence. In the aftermath of the Holocaust, there is still a neo-Nazi presence in the United States, but a broad public consensus demands that references to the Holocaust should be respectful, and the display of Nazi symbols is widely seen as an expression of hatred, albeit a legal speech act. In contrast to this, significant portions of the U.S. population regard antebellum life and culture with nostalgia or even disassociate antebellum life from white supremacy. *12 Years a Slave* enters into this discursive space and time of both Confederate nostalgia and the reelection of President Barack Obama, which is often interpreted as evidence that racism no longer exists. In such a context, McQueen's film uses literary elements of the slave narrative and film elements of the imaginative documentary to assert that white supremacy is central to U.S. antebellum experience, which should be remembered in relation to its human cost; and trivializing or forgetting of the horror should be rejected by a justice-minded public.

FILMIC FACTS AND HISTORICAL ARGUMENT: *12 YEARS A SLAVE* AS IMAGINATIVE DOCUMENTARY

In addition to the genre of neo-slave narrative, *12 Years a Slave* can be described as an *imaginative documentary*, in that the film draws extensively from historical artifacts but also presents detailed dramatic characterizations and a visual rendering of events where none existed previously. I find the term *filmic fact* helpful for characterizing a common technique in fictionalized historical film and nonfiction documentaries, whereby events that are originally sourced as verbal texts are dramatized visually when no documentary film records exist, and other events are invented for dramatic effect.

Consequently, even when feature films rely heavily on documented fact, what we encounter as a viewer is *"reel truth"* as opposed to real truth:[14] the visual spectacle we encounter is a production, a dramatization that is dependent on the skill of the filmmaker for effective execution and on the audience to suspend disbelief conditionally. When a film such as *12 Years a Slave* enters highly charged territories of collective social values and national myths—in this case, by calling out collusions between white supremacist ideology and grave inhumanity in the antebellum context—some audiences will demand that dramatizations be precisely aligned with documentary facts, but this is never the case with historical feature films. Routinely in fact, we rely on historical films (or in my vernacular, *imaginative documentaries*) to supplement artifacts and primary sources in developing collective historical memory.

In an essay that discusses common ground between documentary and feature films as methods of consciousness raising, film critic Octavio Getino explains the potential usefulness of film dramatization as a means of imagining history:

> Fictional recreation or imagination does not preclude the testimonial vision of a reality; on the contrary, these can often be enriching elements. The use of characters, of re-created sequences, of "fictional" situations, remains relevant so long as their use serves a larger objective which is to use abstractions and fictions to illuminate through documentary a concrete historical situation or political situation. Moreover, in our judgment, this is the best means of liberating the imagination, truly and not fictionally.[15]

Getino's view echoes my own as a spectator for the film *12 Years a Slave*. I allowed suspension of disbelief to serve its specific and limited role during an initial viewing, before reassessing the arguments constructed through *filmic facts* in several key scenes: scene 31, with its the graphic depiction of injuries caused by the whipping of Patsey during excruciating years as a house servant on the Epps plantation, a scene that is distinctive from other representations of sexual sadism among slave owners due to its visual detail and its horrendous treatment of a sympathetic character; scene 13, including the turn in emotion when the character Solomon Northup draws determination from his past as a free man and rebels physically against a cruel overseer, Carpenter John Tidbeats (played by Paul Dano), only to receive retribution by a near-hanging that lasts excruciatingly long from a film spectator's perspective and illustrates the deep entrenchment of inhumanity in a white supremacist social order. There are other scenes in *12 Years a Slave* that are essentially narrative inventions, unsupported by documentary evidence, including two especially poignant and intense moments: Patsey's dramatic plea for Northup to kill her in scene 22, and scene 1 where, in Northup's presence, an enslaved woman pleasures herself sexually in an effort to "take control over her own body," in McQueen's words.[16] Beyond this, the filmic facts in *12 Years a Slave* are predominantly grounded in documented historical facts.

Thinking of these scenes as *filmic facts* within an *imaginative documentary* encourages an understanding of film logic in *12 Years a Slave* as rooted in historical sources, but with the caveat that feature films—biopics, neo-slave narratives, and dramatic epics alike—serve as historical arguments, not historical artifacts. As an argument, this film encourages us to examine historical sources, to empathize with human suffering as it has been perpetrated historically and racially in the U.S. social system, and to reflect on individual and collective value sets in relation to racial identity and social justice. While I am a skeptical critic when it comes to making claims about a film's revolutionary potential (in fact, I think the idea of "revolutionary potential" in a film often becomes a cliché), I would certainly say that the distinctive artistry of this film positions it well to engage broad audiences in assessing the magnitude of slavery's impact. At the same time, however, other reactions to *12 Years a Slave* reveal that some audiences prefer specific and narrow interpretations of the antebellum period, where human slavery and its cruelties are placed at the margins of how the antebellum South is historicized.

WHITE SUPREMACY AND THE PRIVILEGE OF FORGETTING: ANTEBELLUM NOSTALGIA AND POST-RACIAL NOTIONS IN THE OBAMA AGE

> *It's like writing history with lightning. And my only regret is that it is all terribly true.*
> —quotation attributed to President Woodrow Wilson after a private screening of *Birth of a Nation*, a 1915 feature film celebrating the rise of the Ku Klux Klan and embodying white resistance to multiracial democracy [17]

> *I'm proud of where I'm from (If you don't judge my gold chains)*
> *But not everything we've done (I'll forget the iron chains)*
> —lyrics quoted from Brad Paisley and LL Cool J, "Accidental Racist" [18]

12 Years a Slave has opened up a discursive space for anti-racist historicism, reminding us that African American enslavement, white supremacy, and the meanings of antebellum and Confederate experience are far from settled issues of a distant historical time. Even in contemporary public politics, not all voices in U.S. culture are willing to acknowledge the genocidal policies directed at African Americans; myths of gentility and honor in rebellion are also well lodged in the southern and Confederate imaginary and practice. This is illustrated by the song "Accidental Racist," which alludes to tensions over the legacy of antebellum human slavery but imagines that these issues be framed as a dialogue among rough equals. Repeatedly, over decades and even centuries of time and leadership transitions, from the enshrinement of human slavery in the U.S. Constitution to the still-incomplete attempts to ban the practice, from the era of President Bill Clinton to the age of President Barack Obama, white supremacy—the ideological and social foundation of human enslavement within national discourse—is reflected continually and defies direct repudiation.

This section specifically examines the Confederate contribution to white supremacist ideology and its enduring nostalgic power for many audiences. The notion of "states' rights" continues to inform nostalgic views of the Confederate uprising as heroic cause, but my argument (and McQueen's) is that white supremacy and enslavement were so central to the Confederate enterprise that they cannot be separated without engaging in the privilege of forgetting. One can document through artifacts that the Confederacy came into being in order to defend inextricably connected principles of white supremacy and human slavery; recognizing this connection enables us to repudiate white supremacy publicly and historically as a part of a move toward collective national healing and functioning multiracial democracy.

Writing in the *American Spectator*, James Bowman's assertion that there must be a "kind master" somewhere exemplifies the counterproductive logic of antebellum nostalgia. Beyond its sentimental conception of human slavery, the idea of a "kind master" is broadly akin to the notion of "allyship," where persons of conscience within a privileged group reject their privilege and risk personal harm in order to bring about greater justice for those who are oppressed. Conceptually, antebellum nostalgia imagines that white southern enslavers could exist in a relation of allyship despite claiming to own people as property, a notion that echoes paternalistic justifications for slavery in the antebellum period (as stated earlier, enslaved and bereaved mother Eliza energetically and convincingly rejects the idea that any slave master is kind in scene 11). These filmic arguments respond to the historical Solomon Northup's assessment of William Ford as a kindly *man* (as opposed to a kindly *enslaver*). In his narrative, Northup characterizes William Ford's personal character and willingness to enslave African Americans:

> It is but simple justice to him when I say, in my opinion, there never was a more kind, noble, candid, Christian man than William Ford. The influences and associations that had always surrounded him, blinded him to the inherent wrong at the bottom of the system of slavery.[19]

The historical Northup observes a presence of Christian kindliness in Ford's character, but Northup also observes ideological blindness in Ford, a result of the systematic influence of white supremacist ideas in his world view. Incorporating this core portrait of William Ford into his film, Steve McQueen depicts the extremely limited possibilities for white allyship with enslaved people in the face of an entire system of white supremacy, even though individual actions may have profound symbolic or rhetorical power. Scene 12 of the film develops this characterization of Ford (played by Benedict Cumberbatch), when he finds tentative human connections with Northup, expresses an appreciation of his work skills, and incurs the jealousy of a white overseer, Tidbeats (played by Paul Dano). After being verbally demeaned and threatened by Tidbeats, Northup is driven to confront him physically (scene 12) and is nearly hung by white vigilantes in a scene that lasts for an excruciating three and a half minutes. Subsequently, Ford opts for a path of least resistance; being unable to prevent the attempted lynching, he yields to the systematic pressure to enforce the code of white supremacy, knowing that resisting this code entails extreme personal risk. The practical limits of individual white heroism and the virtual absence of committed white allies in the film clarify how a system of white supremacy functions when there is no significant public opposition, a condition that held in the South for much of the antebellum period.

In this way, *12 Years a Slave* demonstrates why a conscious-driven repudiation of antebellum nostalgia remains necessary in the age of Obama. It has now been five decades since the waning of the modern civil rights movement, often called the Second Reconstruction and probably the most purposeful national attempt to expand human rights to all U.S. citizens. And yet, with the passing of time, collective historical memory of these vitally important justice-seeking movements can no longer be just a function of living people; it must be remembered through cultural narratives such as film, public history, and public education models. Active anti-racism is also needed to interrupt continuing internalization of established white supremacist scripts. To intentionally compartmentalize the rise of the Confederacy, the Civil War, human enslavement, and the philosophical design of the U.S. republic as distinct enterprises reinforces white supremacy, by encouraging the privilege of forgetting the human suffering of African Americans who were politically and socially marginalized through this era.

Examining a few key points in the history of enslavement in this country can help clarify what is revealed when enslavement becomes more prominent in public memories of antebellum life. From an anti-racist standpoint, we can productively reassess moments where legislation to limit or abolish slavery emerged from the national government, only to be challenged in grand scale by southern states and the Confederacy. To name two instances of anti-slavery actions by the national government, the United States outlawed the international slave trade by legislative action and a signature by President Thomas Jefferson on March 3, 1807, and on December 18, 1865, the Thirteenth Amendment to the U.S. Constitution outlawing slavery became standing law.[20] These legislative actions in mind, the enduring impact becomes clearer of sectional conflicts that raged from the colonial period through the

Civil War, during which thirteen Confederate states asserted their commitments to continuing human slavery on southern soil and in future U.S. territories, by force as necessary. By the time of the Civil War, a white-dominated social order had firmly established human slavery as a condition limited to persons of African descent, with state laws in place asserting white supremacy and holding that even a small amount of "black blood" was a mark of defilement that could support the status of enslavement for life.

Declarations of secession ratified by Confederate states in the Civil War era hold a high value as primary documents that illustrate the centrality of white supremacy to the political, legal, economic, and social order of the Confederacy. The declarations were ratified by statehouse elites that actually represented a white minority population in two of the thirteen seceding states (South Carolina and Mississippi) and white majority populations elsewhere in the Confederacy. Needless to say, black populations that ranged from about 26 percent of Tennessee residents to nearly 60 percent of South Carolina[21] residents had no voice in deciding how their state's interests were represented in these declarations. Specific language from the declarations ratified by Texas and Mississippi are presented below, providing a reminder of the white supremacist framework embedded in Confederate political, economic, and legal reasoning during Solomon Northup's lifetime.

> She [Texas] was received [into the Union] as a commonwealth holding, maintaining and protecting the institution known as negro slavery—the servitude of the African to the white race within her limits—a relation that had existed from the first settlement of her wilderness by the white race, and which her people intended should exist in all future time.[22]

> Our position is thoroughly identified with the institution of slavery—the greatest material interest of the world. Its labor supplies the product, which constitutes by far the largest and most important portions of commerce of the earth. These products are peculiar to the climate verging on the tropical regions, and by an imperious law of nature, none but the black race can bear exposure to the tropical sun. These products have become necessities of the world, and a blow at slavery is a blow at commerce and civilization.[23]

The language from the Texas declaration emphasizes an unending commitment to white superiority and "African" servility, leaving no question as to the relevance of human slavery to the intention to break from the union. Similarly, the Mississippi declaration connects cotton production, human slavery, and civilization in grand terms, asserting that the "black race" is suited for forced labor in semi-tropical conditions.

As a whole, the declarations of secession remind us that the crimes against humanity perpetrated under American slavery were legally sanctioned by multilayered articulations of white supremacy across the U.S. social landscape, including legal support in the U.S. Constitution. The human slavery–friendly political foundations of the early U.S. republic have had a clear and enduring impact on the economic, political, and emotional lives of Americans all across so-called color lines; and while this fact is easily demonstrable given the subsequent patterns of intense social conflicts rooted in perceived racial differences and unequal access to citizenship rights and economic resources, significant denial exists in public opinion as to *whether the original conception of the United States (or the Confederacy, for that matter) as a slaveholding republic has any enduring impact.* Small wonder, then, that a film project such as *12 Years a Slave*, an *imaginative documentary* presenting one person's experience of enslavement under a white supremacist social order, has generated broad conversation and even intense resistance to its messages.

An ideal function of the film's interrogation of white supremacy would be to reenergize national awareness, conversation, and healing in relation to enslavement and its lingering effects, since even in recent presidential politics, attempts to sustain a discourse on race have not been particularly successful. In 1997, President Bill Clinton considered a national apology about the institution of slavery, perhaps in conjunction with proposals in the U.S. House to take this action. The apology was never made. A broad swath of the U.S. public vociferously objected to the possibility of such an apology (in a June 1997 Gallup Poll, white respondents opposed a national apology by a 67 to 26 percent split; African Americans favored an apology by a similar split, 65 to 28 percent).[24] Reflecting on these results, when given a choice between publicly acknowledging and regretting human enslavement as a crime against humanity and the privilege of forgetting these episodes, a very significant portion of the public opted for the privilege of forgetting. And as a result, opportunities are not taken to heal collectively, to seek remedies, and to claim a present national honor by a simple statement of regret for racially motivated atrocities in the past.

In the wake of this opportunity not taken after many decades since the first Reconstruction (Freedman's Bureau; Thirteenth, Fourteenth, and Fifteenth Amendments) and several decades after the Second Reconstruction (the civil rights movement), it becomes reasonable to wonder if Confederate do-rags and public tributes to Klan figures (Nathan Bedford Forrest) will be a permanent part of the national climate. Refusal to confront white supremacy and public expressions of antebellum nostalgia are unfortunate continuities in popular opinion between the 1910s era of D. W. Griffith and Woodrow Wilson and the 1990s cultural context encountered by President Bill Clinton. Moving forward to the age of President Barack Obama, nearly a century after the release of *Birth of a Nation*—while it is less common to speak literally and publicly about the necessity or benefits of a white supremacist order, nostalgia for cultural texts of the Confederate era remains common.[25] By challenging stereotypes of a cultural landscape marked by colonial architecture, genteel white households, compliant slaves, and righteous Confederate rebellion to preserve states' rights, *12 Years a Slave* reintroduces anti-racist outrage as a public response to atrocities committed against African Americans in the antebellum South. This move toward race-consciousness in historical and policy thinking is directly at odds with a drift during the Obama administration away from acknowledging that racial identity has an impact on life chances—wealth, employment, life expectancy, incarceration, infant mortality, opportunities to marry, and so on.

The current drift away from race-consciousness in social policy was signaled early in the political career of President Obama, even in his first autobiography *Dreams from My Father*, which David Mastey reads as a thinly veiled attempt to "achieve both short- and long-term political success."[26] Such success required black voters to recognize his authentic connections to their communities, without alienating white voters who "expressed skepticism of him as a Black candidate, but who would not automatically disqualify him for this reason."[27] With the encouragement of political advisers David Axelrod and David Plouffe, the strategy adopted by both candidate Obama and President Obama would thus be characterized largely by subsuming topics of race under broader, more populist themes.[28] As highly unequal patterns of incarceration continue to land more African American men in jail than college, and as the Great Recession and urban conditions in cities such as Detroit continue to disproportionately affect African Americans, the Obama White House has persistently avoided addressing these issues directly.

The Obama administration's hesitancy to name racism as a social problem is unfortunately characteristic of the broad social and political climate during the New Nadir, which features conditions of hyper-segregation due to race and class distinctions, disparities in educational access and health outcomes, and entrenched opposition to public policies intended to remedy past discrimination.[29] At the same time, the popular characterization of the current social climate as post-racial helps impede the expression of outrage about racial inequality. Using the term "post-ethnic" in the wake of President Obama's election, David A. Hollinger assesses the appeal of such a trend within social identity:

> A post ethnic social order would encourage individuals to devote as much—or as little—of their energies as they wished to their community of descent, and would discourage public and private agencies from implicitly telling citizens that the most important thing about them was their descent community. Hence to be post-ethnic is not to be anti-ethnic, or even colorblind, but to reject the idea that descent is destiny.[30]

Whether we call the imagined climate post-ethnic or post-racial, it is a reality that racial identity continues to hold significance, as illustrated in multiple ways during Obama's campaign and presidency.

During the first Obama campaign, a political calculus emerged that Thomas Edge calls Southern Strategy 2.0. Conservative pundits and politicians commenting on Obama's campaign described him as an "affirmative action candidate," engaged in racist song ("Barack the Magic Negro"[31]), and egged on supporters at rallies for Republican candidates John McCain and Sarah Palin by repeating

> accusations of Obama's associations with radicals and his questionable citizenship status, while occasionally passing along new stories that were even too radical for the mainstream conservative media . . . questioning his sexual orientation, accusing him of changing his birth certificate, even attributing "violent terrorist bombings" in the 1980s to Obama.[32]

Eventually, several of these stories would be treated by the mainstream media, most notoriously the "birther" controversy over the validity of Obama's birth certificate (the president himself attempted to quash the rumor of a foreign birth when he released an official copy of his birth certificate on April 25, 2011). Following the 2008 campaign, after multiple public attempts to deride candidate Obama with racial slurs (some of which came from fellow Democrats, such as the "hardworking Americans, white Americans" line attributed to Hillary Clinton in a campaign speech), triumphant declarations of the end of racism dominated the news cycle. In Thomas Edge's words:

> The use of affirmative action and other racial markers as stigmatizing tools against the Obama campaign served as a forerunner to the swift about-face performed by conservatives in the immediate aftermath of the election. Often, the same voices that criticized Obama as unpatriotic or questioned his very citizenship were quick to use his election to demonstrate how far America had come in race relations. Suddenly, the "closet Muslim" that associated with "radicals" and threatened to undermine American security was appropriated by right-wing pundits to argue for an end to affirmative action policies and other forms of race-based redress. For conservatives, Obama's election signaled a long-awaited opportunity: a clear advance in race relations that the Right could use to attack the legal legacies and protections of the civil rights movement.[33]

Under these conditions, where the civic and moral rationale for remedying discrimination is under continuous assault, and where with the passing of time, one can no longer rely on civil rights titans to argue the public case for anti-racism, *12 Years a Slave*'s interrogation of white supremacy becomes ever timelier as a move against forgetting. It is highly consequential that this film has intervened in how the antebellum South is collectively imagined, as we move through 150-year anniversaries of the commencing and official ending of the U.S. Civil War. Writing in the *Nation*, Eric Foner draws from fellow historian David Blight a discussion of two contested visions of the Civil War's purposes and legacy, visions that have been debated continually in U.S. public culture, starting in the nineteenth century:

> an "emancipationist" vision that emphasized black freedom and equality as essential to the war's meaning, and a "reconciliationist" narrative that saw both sides as fighting for noble causes—the Union, on the part of the North; local rights and individual liberty, on the part of the South.[34]

This reminder of the nineteenth-century debate over the meaning of the Civil War clarifies an additional deep-seated reason why *12 Years a Slave* touches sensitive national nerves: it is more than some audiences can take to suggest that the Confederate war effort was no just cause, that willful blindness and denial are still pervasive when it comes to the enslavement and other atrocities committed against African Americans during and after this period, and that antebellum whiteness, the Confederacy, and the institution of slavery commiserated in support of a racist social structure and a regime abetted by terror. Through its willingness to challenge *the privilege of forgetting*, McQueen's film makes a provocative argument in favor of anti-racist thought and action, encouraging recognition and public acknowledgment of American slavery as an intolerable crime against humanity.

RESPONDING TO *12 YEARS A SLAVE* AND ITS CRITICAL RECEPTION AS A RESISTING SPECTATOR: DEPICTING UNSPEAKABLE HUMAN TRAUMA AND THE DIGNITY OF RESISTANCE

The film *12 Years a Slave* is a uniquely challenging film to write about due to the weightiness of its subject, from graphic detail that is nearly stomach-turning in its realism, to my own emotional journey as I wonder how I can possibly respond to the ugliness of race hatred and the heart-rending personal stories presented in the film with a productive and even inclusive emotional tone. I would typically describe myself as a resisting spectator as described enduringly by Manthia Diawara in *Black American Cinema*: "Whenever blacks are represented in Hollywood, and sometimes when Hollywood omits blacks from its films altogether, there are spectators who denounce the result and refuse to suspend their disbelief."[35] My habits as a resisting spectator lead me toward impatience and outright rejection of film that oversimplifies African American subjectivity and treats antebellum race relations with anything less than the earnestness that ought to accompany a serious examination of traumatic episodes in human history.

At the same time, I have southern roots myself with two parents born in Arkansas. In fact, my mother's family hails from Forrest City (named of course for Confederate general and Ku Klux Klan founder Nathan Bedford Forrest). I take a great deal of spiritual and artistic sustenance from my family's story of persistence and survival in this region, through difficult periods of the Great Depression, racial segregation, and in-country migration. In many a contemplative moment, my music listening habits reflect a personal fondness for country music from this region, music of a bygone era (George Jones, Jerry Lee Lewis, Patsy Cline); I revere the common artistic roots of American popular music across so-called color lines.[36] So for me, being willing to challenge white supremacy as expressed culturally through Confederate symbols is consistent with appreciating artistic and cultural production contributed by all southern communities. Nevertheless, I find that denying the human cost of antebellum enslavement is offensive and counterproductive, and I am greatly appreciative of *12 Years a Slave* for asserting the need to remember the suffering of the enslaved.

Given this critical orientation, I am fascinated but not surprised that a film such as *12 Years a Slave* has been resisted not only from audiences who indulge in unreflective nostalgia for the antebellum South, but also audiences who object to violent realism in the film's depiction of human slavery. In this vein, prominent film critic Armond White panned this film upon its release as belonging "to the torture porn genre with *Hostel*, *The Human Centipede*, and the *Saw* franchise"[37] (White's alleged heckling of the director McQueen at a New York Film Critics Circle event in January 2014 led to his dismissal from the critics group). Similarly, Dana Stevens observes in her *Slate* review of the film, "I'm just not sure if I'm down with body horror as a directorial approach for a movie on this subject," suggesting a critical hesitation to confront human consequences of slavery if they are not sweetened by sustained empathic characterization. Stevens specifically mentions in her review that she feels more at home with a scene that features Solomon at "an uncomfortable afternoon tea with a house slave turned mistress played by Alfre Woodard," a scene which "points at a different movie McQueen might have made, one about the hierarchies; rivalries; and tenuous, wary friendships among the enslaved characters themselves."[38] It is probably worth noting here as well that the conversation in this scene is an invention with no equivalent in Northup's narrative, though the character played by Woodard does appear in the narrative.[39]

I strongly support the need to consider how graphic sexual violence may serve justice-oriented aims, including in anti-slavery films (*Django Unchained*, *Sankofa*, and *12 Years a Slave* alike): can African American bodies be depicted visually in a torture context without reinforcing sexual exploitation under patriarchy—without reifying a long-standing pattern of fetishizing the exotic other? Perhaps this is a part of the phenomenon Armond White describes as "torture porn" and Hortense Spillers describes as "pornotropes."[40] While I disagree with the implicit claim of generic or ideological equivalency between anti-slavery protest films and pornography films, I find it essential to consider when, if ever, a film's presentation of sexual sadism can serve ethical purposes. In practice, producing such scenes without any unwitting suggestion of sexual allure is extremely challenging, especially given the ubiquitous presentation of nude female bodies as objects of erotic pleasure in mainstream film and pornography alike. Individual films about the history of U.S. slavery have achieved varying levels of success in dramatizing the sexual violation of women as a systematic atrocity that, nevertheless, must be remembered and repudiated publicly if we are to emerge with a justice-oriented view of human history.

One way to shed light on these issues is to compare the depictions of sexual sadism in the films *Sankofa* and *12 Years a Slave*, then to consider which narrative strategies best illustrate the need for justice for enslaved women, then and now. In the 1993 independent film *Sankofa*, the protagonist Mona (played by Oyafunmike Ogunlano) becomes Shola, with an early transition in the film moving from Mona's position as a sexually charged model posing for a white photographer on an African beach to an enslaved woman subject to capture, branding, and the middle passage. Immediately after her capture by ghostly slavers, she is kidnapped, stripped, taken to the United States, and subjected to serial rape. While she eventually achieves a new agency by physically overcoming and murdering one of her rapists during a slave rebellion, the juxtapositions between enslavement, sexual sadism, and voyeuristic gazes at her nude body are sometimes too closely sequenced to fully emphasize the human cost of subjugation while de-emphasizing eroticism.

By way of contrast, *12 Years a Slave* presents the nude bodies of Patsey and other black women in the contexts of human sale and sexual violence, amid the savage and repeated denials of black humanity through the actions of white supremacists in this marketplace for human flesh. In a more interpersonal way, black women's bodies and spirits are entrapped within the twisted sexual triangles of the Epps family, with Sarah Epps's dramatic characterization emphasizing that denial of personhood and the thirst for human cruelty are systematically distributed to all who collude with white supremacy. In scene 31, when Solomon Northup and Epps whip Patsey in turn, expelling sprays of blood and producing deep bloody ruts in Patsey's flesh, this film moves beyond any previous treatment of slavery in insisting that sexual sadism is far beyond erotic allure. In these ways, the narrative qualities of *12 Years a Slave* discourage any justice-minded audience from concluding that the presentation of nude bodies is intended for sexual allure.

Reflecting further on the review by Dana Stevens, I find it understandable, though not acceptable, that the film's reconstruction of monstrous events in the enslavement of human beings is considered to be excessive, especially when it has become so customary to define U.S. antebellum experience in ways that minimize the human costs of a white supremacy. To this point, I submit Stevens's reaction to a scene where Edwin Epps (played by Michael Fassbender) forces enslaved laborers to recite a scathingly antihuman song/nursery rhyme, "Run Nigger Run." Dana Stevens describes this scene as "the hint of a prurient horror-movie vibe that can feel exploitive";[41] I read this scene as a welcome and authoritative counterpoint to cultural texts from Stephen Foster songs to the Coen Brothers' film *O Brother, Where Art Thou?*—any text where nostalgia and irony serve to deflect attention from the core inhumanity of a white supremacist system, especially in the pre–civil rights South. One is reminded of the dilemmas faced by minstrel performers such as Bert Williams and contemporary comedians such as Dave Chappelle and the Wayans Brothers—that the origins of the "happy darky" imagery are deeply rooted in the antebellum culture of white supremacy.

As I see it, early resistance among film critics to *12 Years a Slave* underscores the stylistic panache and textual complexity that director McQueen brought to the subject of American slavery; the director reinscribes elements of the *unspeakable* into collective historical memory through the real and imaginative dimensions of one primary human story. Deftly and at times subtly, *12 Years a Slave* presents white supremacy as systematic and institutional, a feature of legal, economic, and political ideologies rather than simply individual moral failures. And yet, quite remarkably, the film cogently develops its core points about the systematic nature of white supremacy even though none of it takes place in a courtroom, the halls of Congress, or other settings where learned argument holds forth and day-to-day affairs in the lives of enslaved people are relegated to the background (Steven Spielberg's *Lincoln* is limited by this approach). What makes *12 Years a Slave* distinctive is the amount of time, care, and intensity spent in depicting the atrocities that are enabled by the collusion of white supremacy and human slavery. While the film's depiction of white supremacist brutality is extremely hard to take, it is precisely the contextually situated uses of brutality that make the film extraordinarily effective in building a case against the *privilege of forgetting*. To construct a film narrative around genocide and socially supported sadism is a challenging task in any context, let alone in a national climate in the United States that persistently refuses to fully recognize or repudiate the cumulative and human enduring costs of its white supremacist traditions. That this film takes on these ideological challenges so directly is one of its signature accomplishments.

It is fascinating and instructive to consider this film in dialogue with the cultural politics of the Obama presidency and related developments that impact the public career of racial notions in this time. While I do not know if this film will inspire broad-based anti-racist action, one might reasonably argue that *12 Years* is a militant or politically revolutionary film, at least as argued by Octavio Getino, that such films offer audiences "something recuperable in a particular historical circumstance for the liberation process."[42] I am a bit hesitant, though, to hold that the film is in essence revolutionary in the way that this term is most often understood—in fact, it seems to me that to apply such a term is reductive, in relation to the whole human message contained in the film.

Instead, *12 Years a Slave* recognizes that individual human suffering may not (and most often does not) result in systematic change. The film can even serve as a metaphor for the landmark national achievement of electing an African American president—that despite the very real historical significance of President Obama's election, there is no magic solution to the American dilemma of racism. Understandably then, the film does not illustrate or model any methods of mass rebellion or offer lengthy treatises on fundamental human rights, black revolutionary aspirations, or the inevitable triumph of the proletariat—although, in an understated way, the film's characterizations argue for the essential connectedness of all humanity, especially in relation to suffering and trauma. The film offers a powerful prayer for a recognition of common humanity, expressed by the doomed relationship between the enslaved Solomon and Patsey; the painful cries of the bereaved Eliza at the slave auction, where the desire to keep her family intact fails to hold the day even with the sympathetic white buyer; the disturbing and hollow sexualities among master and slave, slave and slave; the sorrow songs that are richly contextualized in the narrative through their juxtaposition with brutal and forced labor; the biblical references that go as far as any element in the film toward an exegesis on freedom, even as other biblical verses are deployed to justify white supremacy and human slavery. Through these attributes, *12 Years a Slave* serves not only as a protest against racism but also as a prayer for humanity, an assertion that the tools of empathy and individual resistance are valuable human possessions, whether or not such tools are sufficient to bring about a condition of universal human liberty. Avoiding the grandiose statement in favor of the dignity implicit across our human lives—this is a mark of highly accomplished art, a standard that *12 Years a Slave* has most certainly attained.

NOTES

1. Halie Germia, dir., *Sankofa*, 1993 (Washington, D.C.: Myphedu Films, 2003), DVD.
2. Caitlin Dewey, "Transcript: Lupita Nyong'o's Emotional Oscar's Acceptance Speech," *Washington Post*, The Style Blog, March 2, 2014, http://www.washingtonpost.com/blogs/style-blog/wp/2014/03/02/transcript-lupita-nyongos-emotional-oscars-acceptance-speech/.
3. James Bowman, "Propaganda Is Not 'Reality' or 'Truth': *12 Years A Slave* Deserved Better," *American Spectator*, online edition, November 29, 2013, http://spectator.org/articles/56909/propaganda-not-%E2%80%98reality-or-%E2%80%98truth.

4. Carolyn Forché, *Against Forgetting: Twentieth-Century Poetry of Witness* (New York: W. W. Norton, 1993), 46.

5. Yaba Amgborale Blay, "Skin Bleaching and Global White Supremacy: By Way of Introduction," *Journal of Pan-African Studies* 4, no. 4 (June 2011): 4–46.

6. Seth Abramovitch, "Plans to Raze '*12 Years a Slave*' Site for Baseball Stadium Draw Outrage," *Hollywood Reporter*, March 25, 2014, http://www.hollywoodreporter.com/news/plans-raze-12-years-a-691195.

7. Sundiata Keita Cha-Ju, "The New Nadir: the Contemporary Black Racial Formation," *Black Scholar* 40, no 1: 38–58.

8. Michelle Alexander, *The New Jim Crow* (New York: New Press, 2012).

9. Kenneth Stampp's description of human slavery in the U.S. South as a "peculiar institution" (*The Peculiar Institution: Slavery in the Antebellum South* [New York: Vintage, 1956]) continues to generate animated conversation due to the phrase's unconvincing striving for academic neutrality.

10. Elizabeth Bingell, "Burbanking Bigger and Bette the Bitch," *African American Review* 40, no. 3: 475; Tino Balio, *Grand Design: Hollywood as a Modern Business Enterprise, 1930–1939* (Berkeley: University of California Press, 1993), 281. Brad Pitt makes a cameo appearance in *12 Years a Slave* as Canadian workman Samuel Bass, whose willingness to write letters on Solomon Northup's behalf led to his eventual escape from slavery. Unfortunately, to cast Brad Pitt in this role came close to being a Burbanking moment in this film, where Hollywood "star system" logic prevailed over the most effective possible dramatization of Northup's narrative.

11. *Slavery and Indentured Servants*, Act XII, Virginia law, 1662, Law Library of Congress, http://memory.loc.gov/ammem/awhhtml/awlaw3/slavery.html.

12. Director Quentin Tarantino settles repeatedly for comic irony as a film language rather than treating the grave subject of mass enslavement grounded in white supremacy with due seriousness. Responding to the film, Kimberly Ellis's essay "Tarantino Flunks American History" is an on-point editorial response to the ultimately stereotypical approach to racial identity and resistance presented in *Django Unchained* (*Salon*, January 12, 2013, http://www.salon.com/2013/01/12/tarantino_flunks_american_history/).

13. *Solomon Northup's Odyssey* was directed in 1984 by the landmark director Gordon Parks for PBS's *American Playhouse* (the film is now distributed by Monterey Home Video, 1996). Among other accomplishments in his stellar career as an artist and activist, Parks also achieved prominence as the first African American director of a major Hollywood film: *The Learning Tree*, 1969.

14. Glen Man, "Editor's Introduction," *Biography* 21, no. 3 (Winter 2000): vi.

15. Octavio Getino, "The Cinema as Political Fact," *Third Text* 25, no. 1 (January 2011): 47.

16. Forrest Wickman, "How Accurate is *12 Years a Slave?*" *Slate*, October 17, 2013, http://www.slate.com/blogs/browbeat/2013/10/17/_12_years_a_slave_true_story_fact_and_fiction_in_mostly_accurate_movie_about.html.

17. *Rise and Fall of Jim Crow*, PBS.org, http://www.pbs.org/wnet/jimcrow/stories_events_birth.html.

18. Brad Paisley, LL Cool J, and Lee Thomas Miller, "Accidental Racist," *Wheelhouse*, Arista Nashville Records B00AZIFU66, 2013, compact disc.

19. Solomon Northup, *12 Years a Slave: Narrative of Solomon Northup, a Citizen of New York, Kidnapped in Washington City in 1841, and Rescued in 1853, from a Cotton Plantation Near the Red River in Louisiana* (Auburn: Derby and Miller; Buffalo: Orton and Mulligan; London: Sampson Low, Son, and Company, 1853), 90, http://docsouth.unc.edu/fpn/northup/northup.html.

20. Significantly, the Thirteenth Amendment includes an exception to slavery's prohibition, "except as punishment for a crime whereof the party shall have been duly convicted." Michele Alexander in *The New Jim Crow* and many others have demonstrated that a consequence of this exception has been a system of race-based social control where forced African American labor has continued through patterns of excessive incarceration.

21. John C. Willis, "America's Civil War. Tables, Date of Secession Compared to 1860 Black Population," http://www.sewanee.edu/faculty/Willis/Civil_War/tables/dateSecession.html.

22. "Declaration of Causes, February 2, 1861," Texas State Library and Archives Commission, https://www.tsl.texas.gov/ref/abouttx/secession/2feb1861.html.

23. "Mississippi Declaration of Secession," Civil War Home Page, http://www.civil-war.net/pages/mississippi_declaration.asp.

24. Claire Jean Kim, "Managing the Racial Breach: Clinton, Black-White Polarization, and the Race Initiative," *Political Science Quarterly* 117, no. 1: 55.

25. Confederate nostalgia arises in varying degrees from cultural texts and performers such as "Sweet Home Alabama," Confederate flag and clothing displays, Kid Rock, and Lady Antebellum.

26. David Mastey, "Slumming and/as Self-Making in Barack Obama's *Dreams from My Father*," *Journal of Black Studies* 40, no. 3 (January 2010): 485.

27. Mastey, "Slumming and/as Self-Making," 486.

28. Mastey, "Slumming and/as Self-Making," 485–86.

29. Cha-Ju, "The New Nadir," 43–45.

30. David A. Hollinger, "Obama, the Instability of Color Lines, and the Promise of a Postethnic Future," *Callaloo* 31, no 4. (Fall 2008): 1034.

31. Matthew Filipowicz, "Chip 'Barack the Magic Negro' Saltsman's RNC Campaign Ad," *Huffington Post*, January 2, 2009, http://www.huffingtonpost.com/matthew-filipowicz/chip-barack-the-magic-neg_b_154678.html.

32. Thomas Edge, "Southern Strategy 2.0: Conservatives, White Voters, and the Election of Barack Obama," *Journal of Black Studies* 40, no. 3 (January 2010): 434.

33. Edge, "Southern Strategy 2.0," 434–35.

34. Eric Foner, "The Civil War in 'Postracial' America," *Nation* 293, no. 15 (October 10, 2011): 24.

35. Manthia Diawara, "Black Spectatorship: Problems of Identification and Resistance," in *Black American Cinema* (New York: Routledge, 1993), 211.

36. Three songs I like to put into conversation are "I Still Sing the Old Songs" by George Jones, "Come on In" by Patsy Cline, and "We Come From" by 8 Ball and MJG to illustrate competing views of the southern and Confederate imaginaries.

37. Armond White, "Dud of the Week: *12 Years a Slave* reviewed by Armond White for City Arts," *New York Critics Circle*, October 16, 2013, http://www.nyfcc.com/2013/10/3450/.

38. Dana Stevens, "Entry #13: My Problem with *12 Years a Slave*," *Slate*, January 27, 2014, http://www.slate.com/articles/arts/the_movie_club/features/2014/movie_club_2013/_12_years_a_slave_my_problem_with_steve_mcqueen_s_harrowing_film.html.

39. Wickman, "How Accurate is *12 Years a Slave*?"

40. See Alexander Weheliye's discussion of "pornotropes" in *Journal of Visual Culture* 7, no. 1 (2008): 65–81.

41. Stevens, "Entry #13: My Problem with *12 Years a Slave*.

42. Getino, "The Cinema as Political Fact," 42.

REFERENCES

Abramovitch, Seth. "Plans to Raze '*12 Years a Slave*' Site for Baseball Stadium Draw Outrage."*Hollywood Reporter*, March 25, 2014. http://www.hollywoodreporter.com/news/plans-raze-12-years-a-691195.

Alexander, Michelle. *The New Jim Crow*. New York: New Press, 2012.

Amgborale Blay, Yaba. 2011. "Skin Bleaching and Global White Supremacy: By Way of "Introduction." *Journal of Pan-African Studies* 4, no. 4 (June 2011): 4–46.

Balio, Tino. *Grand Design: Hollywood as a Modern Business Enterprise, 1930–1939*. Berkeley: University of California Press, 1993.

Bell, Bernard. "*Beloved*: a Neo-Slave Narrative; or Multivocal Remembrance of Things Past." *African American Review* 26, no. 1 (Spring 1992): 7–15.

Bingell, Elizabeth. "Burbanking Bigger and Bette the Bitch." *African American Review* 40, no. 3: 475–92.

Bonilla, Yarimar. "History Unchained." *Transition* 112 (2013): 68–77.

Bowman, James. "Propaganda Is Not 'Reality' or 'Truth': *12 Years A Slave* Deserved Better." *American Spectator*, online edition, November 29, 2013. http://spectator.org/articles/56909/propaganda-not-%E2%80%98reality-or-%E2%80%98truth.

Cha-Ju, Sundiata Keita. "The New Nadir: the Contemporary Black Racial Formation." *Black Scholar* 40, no 1: 38–58.

"Declaration of Causes, February 2, 1861." Texas State Library and Archives Commission. https://www.tsl.texas.gov/ref/abouttx/secession/2feb1861.html.

Dewey, Caitlin. "Transcript: Lupita Nyong'o's Emotional Oscar's Acceptance Speech." *Washington Post*, The Style Blog, March 2, 2014. http://www.washingtonpost.com/blogs/style-blog/wp/2014/03/02/transcript-lupita-nyongos-emotional-oscars-acceptance-speech/.

Diawara, Manthia. "Black Spectatorship: Problems of Identification and Resistance." In *Black American Cinema*, ed. Manthia Diawara. New York: Routledge, 1993: 211–20.

Doherty, Thomas. "Bringing the Slave Narrative to Screen: Steve McQueen and John Ridley's Searing Depiction of America's 'Peculiar Institution.'" *Cineaste* (Winter 2013): 4–9.

Ebiri, Bilge. "Horrendous Acts in a Beautiful Way: Behind the Scenes of *12 Years a Slave*." Vulture.com, November 13, 2013. http://www.vulture.com/2013/11/behind-the-scenes-of-12-years-a-slave.html.

Edge, Thomas. "Southern Strategy 2.0: Conservatives, White Voters, and the Election of Barack Obama." *Journal of Black Studies* 40, no. 3 (January 2010): 426–44.

Ellis, Kimberly. "Tarantino Flunks American History." *Salon*, January 12, 2013. http://www.salon.com/2013/01/12/tarantino_flunks_american_history/.

Filipowicz, Matthew. "Chip 'Barack the Magic Negro' Saltsman's RNC Campaign Ad." *Huffington Post*, January 2, 2009. http://www.huffingtonpost.com/matthew-filipowicz/chip-barack-the-magic-neg_b_154678.html.

Foner, Eric. "The Civil War in 'Postracial' America." *Nation* 293, no. 15 (October 10, 2011): 24–26.

Forché, Carolyn. *Against Forgetting: Twentieth-Century Poetry of Witness*. New York: W. W. Norton, 1993.

Francis, Terry. "Looking Sharp: Performance, Genre, and Questioning History in *Django Unchained*." *Transition* 112 (2013): 32–45.

Gates, Henry Louis. "An Unfathomable Place: A Conversation with Quentin Tarantino about *Django Unchained*." *Transition* 112 (2013): 47–66.

Gerima, Halie, dir. *Sankofa*. Washington, D.C.: Myphedu Films, 2003 [1993]. DVD.

Getino, Octavio. "The Cinema as Political Fact." *Third Text* 25, no. 1 (January 2011): 41–53.

Hollinger, David A. "Obama, the Instability of Color Lines, and the Promise of a Postethnic Future." *Callaloo* 31, no 4. (Fall 2008): 1033–37.

Horan, David. "Slavery and the Shock of the Old." *America*, December 2, 2013, 32.

Kim, Claire Jean. "Managing the Racial Breach: Clinton, Black-White Polarization, and the Race Initiative." *Political Science Quarterly* 117, no.1: 55–79.

Man, Glen. "Editor's Introduction." *Biography* 23, no. 1 (Winter 2000): v–x.

Martin, Michael T. "Podium for the Truth: Reading Slavery and the Neocolonial Project in the Historical Film: *Queimada (Burn!)* and *Sankofa* in Counterpoint." *Third Text* 23, no. 6 (November 2009): 717–31.

Mastey, David. "Slumming and/as Self-Making in Barack Obama's *Dreams from My Father*." *Journal of Black Studies* 40, no. 3 (January 2010): 484–501.

McQueen, Steve, dir. *12 Years a Slave*. Los Angeles: Regency Pictures, 2014 [2013]. DVD.

"Mississippi Declaration of Secession." Civil War Home Page. http://www.civil-war.net/pages/mississippi_declaration.asp.

Northup, Solomon. *12 Years a Slave: Narrative of Solomon Northup, a Citizen of New York, Kidnapped in Washington City in 1841, and Rescued in 1853, from a Cotton Plantation Near the Red River in Louisiana*. Auburn: Derby and Miller; Buffalo: Orton and Mulligan; London: Sampson Low, Son, and Company, 1853. http://docsouth.unc.edu/fpn/northup/northup.html.

Paisley, Brad, LL Cool J, and Lee Thomas Miller. "Accidental Racist." *Wheelhouse*. Arista Nashville Records B00AZIFU66, 2013. Compact disc.

Parks, Gordon, dir. *Solomon Northup's Odyssey*. Monterey, Calif.: Monterey Home Video, 1996 [1984]. Video recording.

Quinn, Eithne. "Sincere Fictions: The Production Cultures of Whiteness in Late 1960s Hollywood." *Velvet Light Trap* 67 (Spring 2011): 3–13.

———. "'Trying to Get Over': *Super Fly*, Black Politics, and Post-Civil Rights Film Enterprise." *Cinema Journal* 49, no. 2 (Winter 2010): 86–105.

Reich, Elizabeth. "A New Kind of Black Soldier: Performing Revolution in *The Spook Who Sat by the Door*." *African American Review* 45, no. 3 (Fall 2012): 325–39.

Slavery and Indentured Servants. Act XII, Virginia law, 1662. Law Library of Congress. http://memory.loc.gov/ammem/awhhtml/awlaw3/slavery.html.

Stevens, Dana. "Entry #13: My Problem with *12 Years a Slave*." *Slate*, January 17, 2014. http://www.slate.com/articles/arts/the_movie_club/features/2014/movie_club_2013/_12_years_a_slave_my_problem_with_steve_mcqueen_s_harrowing_film.html.

Toplin, Robert. "12 Years a Slave Examines the Old South's Heart of Darkness." Perspectives on History Online, American Historical Association, November 2013. https://www.historians.org/publications-and-directories/perspectives-on-history/january-2014/12-years-a-slave-examines-the-old-south%E2%80%99s-heart-of-darkness.

———. "Making a Slavery Docudrama." *OAH Magazine of History* 1, no. 2 (Fall 1985): 17–19.

Weheliye, Alexander J. "Pornotropes." *Journal of Visual Culture* 7, no. 1 (2008): 65–81.

White, Armond. "Dud of the Week: *12 Years a Slave* reviewed by Armond White for City Arts." *New York Critics Circle*, October 16, 2013. http://www.nyfcc.com/2013/10/3450/.

Wickman, Forrest. "How Accurate is *12 Years a Slave*?" *Slate*, October 17, 2013. http://www.slate.com/blogs/browbeat/2013/10/17/_12_years_a_slave_true_story_fact_and_fiction_in_mostly_accurate_movie_about.html.

Willis, John C. "America's Civil War, Tables, Date of Secession Compared to 1860 Black Population." http://www.sewanee.edu/faculty/Willis/Civil_War/tables/dateSecession.html.

Chapter Eighteen

No, You Can't: Passive Protagonists in *The Blind Side, Django Unchained,* and *12 Years a Slave*

Thomas Britt

As President Barack Obama approaches the halfway point of his second term in office, there is no consensus regarding the status of the United States of America as a post-racial society. Opinions on this issue are influenced by individual and collective experiences, a variety of political aims, and different perspectives and degrees of emphasis on historical paradigms. Linguist John McWhorter interprets the question of America being post-racial as asking "whether America is past racism." Asserting that America is largely "past racism against black people," McWhorter concludes:

> It would be a tragedy if any more than a few professional hotheads took this as an opportunity to continue obsessing over racism, rather than conceiving of ways to help the poor. Many suppose the two are the same, and it is precisely that idea that is outdated.
>
> The point is valid even when the terminology is "societal racism," "institutional racism" or "white privilege." Obsessing over things that cannot be changed and are not the real problem anyway is of no use to anyone.[1]

From another side of the political spectrum, the progressive Opportunity Agenda observes that obstacles to achievement are still pervasive enough to deserve analysis and attention, even in the wake of advances made within law and government:

> Over the past half-century, African Americans have made remarkable progress in toppling legal segregation and discrimination, in accessing economic and educational opportunities, and in participating in our political process, includ-

ing, most notably, as President of the United States. Yet significant barriers remain in countless domains, from high school graduation to employment and wealth, to physical health and the criminal justice system.[2]

Beyond political commentators and persuaders, certain spheres of contemporary popular culture are concerned with this conflict between the freedom of future opportunity and the bondage of the past. Hip-hop and rap music, at times more tuned in than any other popular art form to the intricacies of the race discussion, contain a couple of strong recent examples. Kanye West's vulgar yet zeitgeist-capturing/influencing "New Slaves" outlines the dually discriminatory attitudes of stores and corporations that sell high-end products to black Americans: "You see it's broke . . . racism / That's that 'Don't touch anything in the store' / And it's rich . . . racism / That's that 'Come in, please buy more.'"[3]

In Pusha T's "Hold On," the rapper weighs the history of slavery against his own individual power to shake loose the shackles of generations past: "No reading, no writing, made us savage of men / They praying for jail but I mastered the pen / Descended from kings, we at it again / Just hand me the crown, I'm active again."[4] Kanye concludes that he is a slave and then proceeds to target real and imagined oppressors with threats of violence and sexual violence. Pusha, however, commits his efforts to his own material betterment and the advancement of his community. Whether that commitment will involve his continued participation in selling drugs is a question that runs throughout the narrative he creates as a storyteller.

The trajectories of individual heroes and anti-heroes are easy to identify in rap lyrics because a great many of those lyrics originate from and/or narrate the experiences and ambitions of individual men and women trying to come up in the world or to hold on to existing achievements that were hard won. Often less direct are the aims of black heroes in Hollywood films. When the mainstream American filmmaking community creates, supports, and/or distributes films with aspirational plots involving black protagonists, those films often adhere to narrative designs that sublimate the goals and potential agency of the characters.

Interestingly, such films reinforce the conclusions of both McWhorter and the Opportunity Agenda. On one hand, they often foreground the legacy of institutional restriction to such an extent that messages of purposeful advancement (and present attainment) go missing. On the other hand, the texts sometimes successfully achieve the effect of "oppositional works like the Neo-slave narratives" in "reflecting on the social origins of the problematic they define and circumscribe."[5] Regardless, there is an acute irony to the emergence of several such films since the inauguration of Barack Obama. Following an election won with the slogan "Yes We Can," Hollywood's most successful and notable films with black heroes offer variations on the passive protagonist, for whom *no, you can't* more accurately defines the state of being.

I observed this trend by noting feature films with black protagonists that were nominated for the Academy Award for Best Motion Picture in the years of Obama's presidency. Since the February 2009 ceremony, which was held just more than a month after the first inauguration of President Obama, six films featuring black protagonists have been nominated for the Academy's highest honor. Nominees in this category from the 2010 ceremony included *The Blind Side* and *Precious*. The lone nominee in this category from the 2012 ceremony was *The Help*. The 2013 ceremony featured nominees *Beasts of the Southern Wild* and *Django Unchained*. And in 2014, *12 Years a Slave* was nominated and won the Academy Award for Best Motion Picture.

Though *Precious*, *The Help*, and *Beasts of the Southern Wild* are all worthy of analysis, their plots are primarily about characters' experiences with domestic conflicts of various sorts. Their personal conflicts and relatively restricted fields of dramatic action cause these films to sit slightly outside of the grouping I am interested in exploring; that is, protagonists caught in institutionally bound and indeterminate states of action versus inaction. Thus *The Blind Side*, *Django Unchained*, and *12 Years a Slave* form the group of films I will examine in this chapter of black heroes without claim to their own destinies.

One question fundamental to this examination is: what does a black cinematic hero look like anyway? It would be reductive to attempt to create a formula that best expresses his qualities. After all, one rarely asks what constitutes a white hero in Hollywood films. That the screenwriting manuals call protagonists heroes would seem to denote qualities of self-sacrifice or strength or some other virtue. Heroism so defined needs no condition of ethnicity. Yet there are anecdotes from recent Hollywood history that expose the narrow view of on-screen heroism when the films involve black characters instead of white characters. Peter Biskind recalls the Palme d'Or victory of Steven Soderbergh's *sex, lies, and videotape* over Spike Lee's *Do the Right Thing* at the May 1989 Cannes Film Festival, the jury of which was chaired by Wim Wenders:

> Spike Lee was vocal about his disappointment. He apparently was told that Wenders had said there were no heroes in *Do the Right Thing*. He replied that he had a Louisville Slugger with Wenders' name on it, and added, referring to Spader's self-abusing character, "What so heroic about a guy taping women?" In fact, the triumph of *sex, lies* over *Do the Right Thing* ratified the turn away from the angry, topical strain of the indie movement that had its roots in the 1960s and 1970s toward the milder aesthetic of the slacker era.[6]

If the story is true, then Wenders was shortsighted in his assessment of *Do the Right Thing*, especially in evaluating it less favorably than *sex, lies, and videotape* around issues of heroism. After all, the protagonist of that film is only active in the chutzpah he displays when asking women personal sexual questions for his videotape collection. At least in *Do the Right Thing*, characters are engaging in dialogue and action around the future of a multiethnic community overheating with conflicting perspectives. So much more is at stake in Lee's film, even if the action isn't organized around a single character's goals. That Wenders apparently didn't understand the film's network of self-determined characters and dialectical approach to conflict resolution suggests that *Do the Right Thing* might have been ahead of its time.

Comprehensive means for evaluating the characters of filmic texts would not dictate a desired number of characters or viewpoints being followed by the audience. Rather, it is the combined dimensionalities of characters, dramatic action, and thematic import that contribute to the narrative integrity of a film. In this sense, *Do the Right Thing* succeeds because even those supporting characters that are associated with single traits (such as Radio Raheem and his boom box or Smiley with his photographs of Malcolm X and Martin Luther King Jr.) increase in depth and representative power as the racial conversation of the film intensifies and culminates.

For films that utilize a more traditional single-protagonist approach, there exists a need to maximize the dimensionality of that character in order to affect an audience identifying with him. More than seven decades ago, Lajos Egri identified the three dimensions necessary to building and understanding characters within dramatic literature: "physiology . . . sociology . . . and psychology, [which] is the product of the other two."[7] *The Blind Side*, which is the first film in my analysis, pays so much attention to its supposed central character's physiology that his sociology and psychology are afterthoughts—a narrative imbalance that is also indicative of the fictionalized character's lack of agency and dependence on others for advancement.

Writer/director John Lee Hancock's *The Blind Side* is a well-intentioned but misguided film adapted from Michael Lewis's 2006 book, *The Blind Side: Evolution of a Game*. The second major section of the book is devoted to the story of Michael Oher, presently an offensive tackle for the NFL's Tennessee Titans. Oher's life story is defined by an individual determination to succeed combined with the kindness of others who were in a position to respond to his needs. After a childhood marked by having a drug-addicted mother, being removed from his home and family, and moving around from one foster home to another, Oher gained entry into a private Christian school and was adopted by Leigh Anne and Sean Tuohy, the parents of two students attending the same school. As a result of having a stable home life and constant support from the Tuohys, Oher improved his scholastic performance and became a star athlete, fulfilling the promise he had long shown as a football player.

The film *The Blind Side* is the tale of this extraordinary transformation of circumstances in Oher's life, but it concentrates so much attention on Leigh Anne's role in shaping him that Oher himself is reduced to a supporting player in his own story. Leigh Anne (played in an Academy Award–winning performance by Sandra Bullock) is the first character to address the audience, through voice-over narration. She describes "the ideal left tackle" as "big . . . wide in the butt, and massive in the thighs. He has long arms, giant hands, and feet as quick as a hiccup. This is a rare and expensive combination."

As she says this, an image emerges from the compilation of football game play that has been on-screen. Actor Quinton Aaron is Michael Oher, walking through housing projects on a sunny day. There is happy activity behind him, but he wears a sad expression on his face. Physically, he is the ideal size and shape Leigh Anne outlines, but his melancholy demeanor and the quick intercutting with images of some ill-defined childhood trauma suggest that there is something substantial underneath the surface. Later, as he passes through the gate of the school for the first time, he has the same lumbering, sad physicality that defined him in his opening shot. Before the first half hour of the film is finished, he appears with this exact gait four times, repeated in different locations. But the movie offers little insight or apparent interest in mining his character for motivations or goals. Instead, the script creates emotional identification with Leigh Anne, the character who narrated his first minutes on screen. Thus the introduction of both characters inadvertently establishes the film's one-dimensional approach to characterizing Oher. He's a silent body on screen, and someone else speaks for him.

To be fair to the story being told, Oher's silence is a part of the plot. When he arrives at his new school, teachers talk about his silence. One teacher has rescued his writing from the trash can, and in his poem called "White Walls," he talks of his isolation and disconnectedness. But even when we're teased with this access to his inner psychology, the voice reading us the letter belongs to the teacher and not to Oher. This effort to foreground his lack of communication has the effect of making him exotic and alien. As such, the movie adds to the separation and isolation mentioned in his poem. Although the early sections of the movie frequently put him in situations that are supposed to arouse sympathy (such as his studying biology alone in a grungy late-night laundromat), there is no accompanying evidence that he's capable of doing anything positive for himself. Despite multiple scenes of teachers and educators discussing him, for most of the film's running time, there are no scenes of him articulating his feelings or goals.

Before (and for quite a while after) Oher enters the Tuohys' home, he is referred to as "Big Mike." Leigh Anne recognizes the inherent insult, just as she's able to identify any number of Oher's vulnerabilities. She insists that others call him Michael. She lets him sleep on an expensive couch and then later gives him his first bed and bedroom. She buys him clothes. More than once, she goes to "Hurt Village," which is the name of the housing project where he grew up, to take care of business regarding his guardianship. And while all of these acts are motivated by her good heart and Christian philosophy, the movie overplays the sociology of her existence and how far outside of that world Michael exists.

It is one thing to show an underprivileged black teenager experiencing the comfort of a nice house and stable family for the first time in his life, but it's quite another to pretend as if his introduction to a wealthy white family is as dramatic as a rebirth. *The Blind Side* chooses the latter, infantilizing Michael in scene after scene. On his first day at the private school, he draws what looks like a child's drawing of a boat on the back of a quiz that is otherwise left blank. Later, Leigh Anne reads Munro Leaf's *The Story of Ferdinand* to her young son and Michael. The intention is to fill a void in his life, but the scene reiterates the message that despite being a near-adult, Michael is stuck in boyhood.

Although the benefits of Michael's new existence are many, the movie treats Leigh Anne's transformation as being fulfilling on multiple levels that promote greater emotional engagement with the audience. Michael's presence in her family's life encourages her to turn off the television and eat Thanksgiving dinner at the table. He (and what he represents) allows her to be charitable with her enormous wealth and to try to influence her casually racist friends, family members, and fans of rival schools with a message of being blind to skin color. Michael also gives her children a chance to develop similar values of selflessness and being open-minded to people from different backgrounds. Yet each scene and sequence that bonds the audience to Leigh Anne and her transformation plays like a missed opportunity to become better acquainted with Michael, who stays comparatively unknowable.

This combination, of Leigh Anne's pronounced goodwill and Michael's utter lack of independent ability, situates *The Blind Side* within Cynthia A. Hamilton's discussion of "the Negro Problem":

> Before the Civil War, abolitionists tended to present themselves as the primary agents of liberation. After the Civil War, the "Negro Problem" was defined in terms of the need to elevate a race degraded by slavery. Throughout, the African American was seen as a victim in need of sympathetic benevolence. In this view, the self-reliant efforts of African American communities and individuals were obscured. Independent efforts by African Americans during the Civil War and Reconstruction to husband resources, obtain educational advantages, and use what property and skills they possessed to obtain a livelihood remained relatively invisible, and this invisibility expanded the dimensions of the "Negro Problem" in the popular imagination.[8]

Although Hamilton is exploring the issue within the framework of slave narratives, specifically Frederick Douglass's *The Heroic Slave*, the enhancement of white benevolence and diminishment of black self-reliance in stories about human advancement persists in a variety of narratives, from feature films, to documentaries, to the evening news.

Unsurprisingly, Michael's psychology is conveyed through the same means used to establish his sociology. It is speculated by others and always in relationship to how he could serve someone else's narrative. His football coach laments his lack of violent aggression, observing, "Most kids from bad situations can't wait to be violent, and that comes out on the field. But this kid—he acts like he doesn't want to hit anyone." Leigh Anne responds by calling Michael "Ferdinand the Bull," meaning that he is gentle despite his imposing physicality. It's a plot point that links his prior infantilization with the more privileged characters' current need to shape Michael into an aggressive player. When Leigh Anne suggests to her husband that they should take Michael to a child psychologist, he concludes, "Michael's gift is his ability to forget. He's mad at no one and he really doesn't care what happened in the past." That this viewpoint is accepted without criticism from Leigh Anne or input from Michael is symptomatic of the movie's lack of true concern for the roots of Michael's psychological condition. "The past" has served its purpose to the narrative and the movie must move on to Michael's transformation into an athletic star. Once again, his sociological experiences and psychological needs recede into the background, portrayed as less worthy of investigation/cultivation than his physical ability.

From this point in the narrative, each obstacle Michael faces is expressed as an impediment to playing football at the college level. The dominant sequences and montages are comic in tone, including the youngest Tuohy child teaching Michael the basics of football with kitchen condiments and the college recruitment process featuring celebrated real-life coaches. Michael's grades improve, but apart from a brief (and unengaging) essay he narrates late in the picture, we rarely see him display or articulate his knowledge. His being tutored is regarded as yet another humorous counterpoint to the comparatively higher-stakes business of getting his career in motion. Only when a series of conflicts of interest prompt an NCAA investigation concerning Michael's eventual choice of university and team does Leigh Anne finally ask Michael whether he even wants to play football. This is one of the movie's few conscious recognitions of its character's lack of agency, though, as it occurs in the final act of the film, her question feels more like an obligatory gesture by the filmmakers to create an impression of dimensionality for the film's variation on Michael Oher. The act is unconvincing.

The ultimate proof of *The Blind Side*'s disinterest in creating an active protagonist has come in the form of subsequent statements from the individuals characterized in the film. The Blu-ray release of the film includes bonus features profiling both Oher ("Michael Oher Exclusive") and actor Quinton Aaron ("The Story of Big Quinton"), whose life "has much in common with the football star he portrays."[9] Despite the fact that these featurettes last but a fraction of the feature film's running time, each gives its central figure greater ownership of (and means to articulate) his own rags-to-riches narrative and attest to a variety of experiences, influences, and efforts made individually and collectively. Oher has also written a memoir, *I Beat the Odds: From Homelessness to "The Blind Side" and Beyond*, which is among other things an attempt to take control of the narrative that got away from him in his big-screen representation. In Deirdre Donahue's February 2011 *USA TODAY* story promoting the book, Oher is quoted as saying, "People who see the movie think they know all about me. . . . I have more personality. . . . I'm not dumb, I just wasn't educated."[10] Donahue also compares Leigh Anne and Sean Tuohy's perspective on the film to Oher's, writing, "And like parents everywhere, they remember things a bit differently than their kids. Sean says the film version was 'pretty accurate' in depicting the withdrawn, homeless teenager. He's not surprised Oher disagrees, because one of Oher's gifts is his ability to forget. 'It's a gift,' Sean says."[11] In the end, the enduring problems with the film *The Blind Side* could be summarized by the dynamic on display in Donahue's article: Oher provides a perspective that goes far beyond the movie's characterization of him, while Tuohy merely recycles dialogue from his on-screen counterpart. Where the blind spot exists could hardly be clearer.

The second film of my analysis is writer/director Quentin Tarantino's *Django Unchained*. On the surface, the Tarantino brand, hard-R rating, and explosive marketing campaign make the film appear to be altogether different from *The Blind Side*, which was created and marketed as a family film. However, the film offers variations on several core issues of the earlier film, such as frustrated individual agency, displaced emotional engagement with a privileged protagonist, and institutional training for violence.

Django Unchained opens in 1858, "Two years before the Civil War" and "somewhere in Texas." Although the setting and time period befit those of a traditional literary slave narrative, Tarantino's approach to history is closer to what A. Timothy Spaulding identifies as a "postmodern slave narrative," as the film uses "elements of the fantastic to occupy the past, the present, and, in some cases, the future simultaneously."[12] Indeed, Tarantino frames the narrative arc of a "freed" slave in the American South with the aesthetics of 1960s Italian Western films and a sound track that imposes contemporary rapper Rick Ross's voice as a portent of vengeance. *Independent* critic Jonathan Romney identifies several strains of artistic/aesthetic influence that support a postmodern reading, and in his opinion this mélange distracts from the historical subject: "*Django* is less about American slavery than about the intersection of three movie genres: the spaghetti Western (notably Sergio Corbucci's *Django*, whose star Franco Nero has a cameo here); Seventies blaxploitation; and a somewhat disreputable cycle depicting slavery in a trashily erotic manner, e.g. 1975's *Mandingo*."[13]

As its title announces, *Django Unchained* is intended to be perceived as a story of newfound individual liberty. But the conditions of that liberty are worth investigating for the limits they place on the ostensibly free character who gives the film its title. In the beginning of the movie, Django (Jamie Foxx) is identified and procured by a fiercely intelligent and mannered European dentist called Dr. King Schultz (Christoph Waltz, in an Academy Award–winning performance). The two men make an odd pair as Django conspicuously rides atop a horse alongside Schultz the dentist through the town of Daughtrey, Texas. Spectators cannot believe they are seeing a black man on a horse. At least one of them expresses his shock by using racist language.

Compared with the slavers that Schultz had to kill in order to complete his "transaction" with Django and the mystified onlookers of Daughtrey, Texas, Schultz is a benevolent, if sudden, new presence in Django's life. Schultz reveals to Django that he is a bounty hunter who "deals in corpses. . . . Like slavery it's a flesh for cash business . . . the badder they are, the bigger the reward." Schultz knows Django is in a unique position to help him identify the Brittle Brothers, a group of men he is attempting to track down. He promises Django freedom and seventy-five dollars in exchange for his help. Schultz is keen enough to address the thorny topic of slavery within their business relationship, expressing guilt for letting the "slavery malarkey work to [his] benefit." He says, "On the one hand I despise slavery, on the other I need your help. If you're not in a position to refuse, all the better."

By articulating the realities of the power imbalance between them, Schultz displays a rare sort of honesty. Compare his straightforward sociological treatise with *The Blind Side*, which reached its third act climax with the realization that no one had ever asked Michael what he wanted, and *Django Unchained* seems radical by comparison. Yet Schultz's silver-tongued, audience-friendly, above-the-law shtick is insidious in its capacity for minimizing Django's need to express himself vis-à-vis his own psychological trauma.

Similar to my own reading of *The Blind Side*'s Leigh Anne Tuohy, Romney sees Schultz's constant talking on Django's behalf as a way of stifling the potential of the black hero. He links this narrative element with Tarantino's own role in fashioning the character of Django, writing, "It apparently takes a white movie nerd to make a black screen hero these days, so Django himself is the creation of the urbane European who talks him into being."[14] But the more pressing problem with the Django character is not in his lack of verbalization. Instead it is in his relationship to violence, and the way that Schultz and Tarantino exploit that capacity for violence, that Django joins the ranks of the passive protagonists being considered here.

Django's past trauma has a direct bearing on his present goal. He has been separated from his wife, Broomhilda (Kerry Washington), and he is single-minded in his attempt to get back to her. Throughout the early sections of the film, Tarantino inserts scenes of Django and Broomhilda being tortured, branded, and whipped. Contemporary scenes of humor, in which Schultz talks his way out of situations and a regally dressed Django stands out among the slaves at a plantation, intersect but never interfere with the graveness of the past torture. Thus Tarantino is to be commended for balancing his stylistic flourishes of verbal flair and sight gags with a serious acknowledgment of the evil that fueled the institution of slavery.

Django Unchained is a movie that looks unflinchingly at slavery as being about "flesh for cash." And the depiction of Django and Broomhilda's past abuse—the damage done to their flesh—proves to be merely a prelude to other, more extended horrors such as a forced fight to the death among two slaves and a runaway slave being torn apart by dogs. But Schultz only complicates the level of psychological manipulation already present within the slave system by training Django to be his partner in bounty hunting and then attempting to manage Django's instinct to avenge his wife. His messages to Django have shades of moral difference but are ultimately contradictory and deeply manipulative and damaging in light of Django's recent past as an abused slave, for whom being *acted violently against* was a daily reality.

In one scene, Schultz revives the "corpses for cash" justification in order to convince Django that it is okay to kill a man in front of his young son. In essence, he is saying this is violence that should require no contemplation. Later, however, when Django is working undercover as a black slaver in order to infiltrate the plantation known as Candyland, where his wife is captive, Schultz says, "Don't get so carried away with your retribution. You'll lose sight of why we're here." This is contrary advice that encourages Django to be reflective with his instinct for violence and to keep his eye on the prize of rescuing Broomhilda.

The result of these mixed messages on the subject of violence is that Django is stuck. In one case, he's told to ignore his conscience; in the other, to pacify his righteous anger. Although Tarantino likely didn't intend for Schultz to be another master for the supposedly free Django, the sort of mental captivity Schultz exerts through his conflicting advice is substantial. On a psychological level, Django becomes enmeshed in an even more intricate set of chains. And when Schultz is killed at Candyland, Django's physical reaction is problematic for a number of reasons Tarantino seems not to have considered.

In short, Django kills nearly every person in sight. Schultz the gamesman is allowed to enter, endure, and exit the events of the movie as a man bound to an ethic of violence that is above the law but never meant to be interpreted as lawless. He's classy through and through. Tarantino gives Django no such grace notes. The orgy of blood that constitutes the film's third act is executed (and popularly received) as a wish fulfillment—one that retroactively avenges one and all victims of the institution of American slavery. However, the unintended message is that a black man—especially one who has been told to be passive and stand down—will become a killing machine when he tastes freedom for the first time.

In this sense, *Django Unchained*—by many accounts a movie conceived as a progressive and postmodern corrective against the evils of the past—becomes another example of the type of media that "[uses] black male characters disproportionately to represent both the victims and perpetrators of violence."[15] In a *New Yorker* review of the film, Jelani Cobb concludes, "The primary sin of *Django Unchained* is not the desire to create an alternative history. It's in the idea that an enslaved black man willing to kill in order to protect those he loves could constitute one."[16] Cobb's point is that individual or collective agency exhibited by slaves in the form of violent reaction or uprising continues to be underreported in the popular narrative of slave emancipation.

I argue that *Django Unchained* is insufficient to correct that record because apart from reuniting with Broomhilda, the fruit of Django's freedom is to become little more than an avatar of bloodshed by the film's end. He represents not liberation, but destruction. He has far more blood on his hands, so to speak, than Schultz, the man who most exploited his capacity for violence. By the end of the film, Django isn't so much unchained as he is ignorant or unaware of his role as the now-activated violent agent of several institutions both within the film (slavery and bounty hunting) and outside of it (Hollywood).

The final film of my analysis is Steve McQueen's *12 Years a Slave*, which was adapted by screenwriter John Ridley from Solomon Northup's 1853 memoir *Twelve Years a Slave*. Various editions of Northup's book and references to it include a subtitle that reads *Narrative of Solomon Northup, a Citizen of New-York, Kidnapped in Washington City in 1841, and Rescued in 1853*, which is a useful summary for the events of the memoir, also categorized as a slave narrative. McQueen's film shares with *The Blind Side* and *Django Unchained* a hero whose potential for individual action is limited as a result of the individuals and institutions around him. But within that scenario, *12 Years a Slave* succeeds above the other films in expressing a multidimensional character for whom acts of resistance and compliance reveal a real and relatable self from whom the film never strays in its organization of action. This is a wise narrative design, as one of the key shifts in values present within Northup's memoir is the loss and restoration of self, with the assertion of individual identity and free status as the chief goals.

A large part of what makes the shift in values so powerful is the positivity of Northup's initial situation. In the book and the film adaptation, he is a free man. He is a family man. He is a musician. Dialogue from a supporting character in the film describes him as a "distinguished individual . . . an expert player on the violin." His own historical testimony states that before being "kidnapped and sold into slavery," he "for more than thirty years enjoyed the blessings of liberty in a free State."[17] Unlike the narratives of *The Blind Side* and *Django Unchained*, which begin with men in comparatively hopeless situations, the story of Solomon Northup is in its initial dramatic situation one of societal advancement, individual achievement, and personal happiness.

When reading and viewing the tale, I'm reminded of the language and imagery used by Sherry B. Ortner in her research on Generation X—the very same slacker generation identified by Biskind in his assessment of the late 1980s/early 1990s cultural shift away from films influenced by the civil rights era, resulting in a perspective that preferred *sex, lies, and videotape* to *Do the Right Thing*. In discussing her findings on social stratification of that era, Ortner observed:

> Lower-middle-class rage and depression, and upper-middle-class terror . . . are thus two sides of looking into the same abyss, an abyss portrayed in the public culture and theorized in accounts of class transformation and class reproduction. From the lower side this abyss seems increasingly impossible to cross; from the upper side it seems all too easy.[18]

If the comparatively privileged grouping known as Generation X was subject to and/or conscious of an abyss that existed between current state and possible future, then how much more consequential and daunting would have been that abyss of which Northup experienced a sudden realization? Spike Lee's resentment against Wenders's perspective on heroes resonates ever stronger when considered in this more historically complicated framework of class transformation from freedom to slavery to freedom. In the film, McQueen uses his signature long-take style to frame Northup's face staring almost directly at the audience. This wordless registering of the horrors of slavery is one of the most complex images in the film because the audience is forced to stare in the face of a character that stares back and sees only the abyss.

Chiwetel Ejiofor plays the role of Northup and locates the strength of the character in his refusal to admit to being anyone but himself. Despite being deceived, chained to the floor, and ferociously beaten, Northup holds on to the (idealistic) belief that a free man cannot cross the abyss into captivity. Fellow slaves who have more experience with the system provide him with advice and insight that will enable him to stay alive, but at a cost to his ideals.

Clemens (Chris Chalk) tells him, "If you want to survive, do and say as little as possible. Tell no one who you really are and tell no one you can read and write." When being transported on a boat, Northup discusses the possibility of a revolt with Clemens and Robert (Michael K. Williams). Clemens says the other slaves "got no stomach for a fight." While the line does fit within the narrative that writers like Jelani Cobb are trying to overturn, the impression of Northup's conversations with Clemens and their extinguished plan to revolt is that Northup has begun losing the power to shape his own destiny before he even gets off the boat. But he doesn't accept that reality. He equates "to live" with being who he is and "to survive" with hiding his identity. He feels it is more important to live than to survive.

From this point in the film, his twelve years as a slave are rendered as a series of challenges to that will to live. He takes the name Platt. His first master is Ford (Benedict Cumberbatch), who is regarded as benevolent, albeit within the evil institution of slavery. Ford is impressed by the engineering knowledge Northup displays as he designs and maneuvers a raft. He exclaims, "Platt, you are a marvel!" He also rewards Northup with a violin. But Eliza (Adepero Oduye), an enslaved woman who ended up at Ford's, warns Northup that his new reality is deceptive. A detailed description of their dialogue exchange reveals how quickly Northup has fallen victim to a system that disregards his individual will.

Eliza is overcome with sorrow because her children have been taken from her and sold within the slave market. Northup says to her, "If you let yourself be overcome by sorrow, you will drown in it." She retorts, "Have you stopped crying for your children?" He replies, "Master Ford is a decent man." Eliza says, "He's a slaver. But you truckle at his boot. You luxuriate in his favor–." At this point, Northup defends himself, declaring, "I survive! I will not fall into despair. I will offer up my talents to Master Ford. I will keep myself hearty until freedom is opportune." Having surrendered his name, and by using the word *survive*, he shows signs of retreating from his ideal to live, rather than merely survive. Eliza's reaction to his justification is to tell him he is "no better than prized livestock."

Sorrowful Eliza doesn't reproach Northup with self-righteousness. Her confrontation with him is an extension of her own turmoil. Racked by guilt, she once compromised herself in exchange for the "comfort" of her master. But that personal transgression did not earn her freedom from the institution. To the contrary, it put her in worse bondage. And now her children are gone. Northup, too, quickly learns that his ability to curry favor with Ford will not protect him from others on the plantation. When he does fight back against a villainous overseer, Northup finds himself being transferred to another plantation and under the ownership of Edwin Epps (Michael Fassbender).

In Epps's controlling presence, Northup experiences the full satanic force of slavery without any of the mediating aspects of his initial experiences as a slave. He experiences what screenwriting guru Robert McKee calls "negation of the negation."[19] McKee alleges that "a story that progresses to the limit of human experience in depth and breadth of conflict must move through a pattern that includes the Contrary, the Contradictory, and the Negation."[20] To use McKee's formula, we must first identify the positive value in Northup's life, which is clearly the value of human freedom. Following from this positive value, the contrary element would be limited human freedom (such as the sort he experienced at Ford's). The contradictory element is human captivity, which defines his experience from the moment he's kidnapped, but especially upon his transfer to Epps. Finally, the negation of the negation is utter dehumanization.

Though many aspects of life at Epps's plantation are dehumanizing, the worst is Epps's insistence that his dehumanized "property" participate in the violence that dehumanizes others. He orders Northup to whip Patsey (Lupita Nyong'o, in an Academy Award–winning performance), who is the object of Epps's sadistic lust and routine sexual attacks. It matters little to Epps that Patsey's crime consisted of going to an adjacent plantation to get some soap. Epps's own sadism and his wife's jealousy combine to mark Patsey as deserving of punishment. The scene in which Northup and Epps whip Patsey is stomach-churning in its violence. Yet the scene cannot be called excessive because within the source memoir, Northup himself isolates the event as the fullness of evil, beyond which worse cannot be conceived:

> Ropes were then brought, and the naked girl was laid upon her face, her wrists and feet each tied firmly to a stake. Stepping to the piazza, he took down a heavy whip, and placing it in my hands, commanded me to lash her. Unpleasant as it was, I was compelled to obey him. Nowhere that day, on the face of the whole earth, I venture to say, was there such a demoniac exhibition witnessed as then ensued.[21]

Northup's meeting of Epps's abuse against Patsey is the final step in his fall down into the abyss. Once free, he was captured and attempted to assert some rights, for which he was eventually punished by the removal of all freedom, and then used as an instrument of torture against another innocent slave. The strongest point of contrast between *Django Unchained* and *12 Years a Slave* is in the intended conclusion of each character's relationship to violence. Tarantino suggests that Django only becomes a free man by inflicting pain on others. McQueen, however, shows that letting oneself be used to inflict pain is the nadir of the arc of identity lost.

Solomon Northup's eventual return to freedom and family (in the memoir and film) is instructive for the reorientation of a narrative of powerlessness around positive values. To paraphrase Northup, freedom *is* an opportune conclusion for aspirational stories, and especially those involving or intended for a disenfranchised audience. *The Blind Side* errs by trusting too little in its hero to overcome his obstacles and express his goals. *Django Unchained* conceives of freedom as something to be enjoyed under institutional supervision or as the fuel for reckless vengeance. Only *12 Years a Slave* attests to the full humanity of its protagonist—as a man capable of freedom, capable of losing his way in the vise of captivity and historical evil, and ultimately triumphant in rising from the point of dehumanization to achieve his dreams anew.

In his farewell speech to the House of Representatives on January 29, 1901, Hon. George Henry White of North Carolina provided an aspirational framework that, though more than a century old, is worth revisiting:

> This, Mr. Chairman, is perhaps the Negroes' temporary farewell to the American Congress; but let me say, Phoenix-like he will rise up some day and come again. These parting words are in behalf of an outraged, heart-broken, bruised, and bleeding, but God-fearing people, faithful, industrious, loyal people—rising people, full of potential force.[22]

Contemporary politicians and filmmakers rarely use their positions of power to uphold such bold claims. Whenever we see a passive protagonist in a film that chooses as its dramatic action man's inhumanity to man, the response should be to demand multidimensional characters and stories "full of potential force." These could have the power to shift the national discussion from what we can and can't do, into that more difficult but necessary pursuit of how to do the right thing.

NOTES

1. John McWhorter, "Racism in America is Over," *Forbes*, December 30, 2008, http://www.forbes.com/2008/12/30/end-of-racism-oped-cx_jm_1230mcwhorter.html.
2. Topos Partnership, Marc Kerschhagel, and Opportunity Agenda, *Opportunity for Black Men and Boys: Public Opinion, Media Depictions, and Media Consumption* (New York: Opportunity Agenda, 2011), 1.
3. Kanye West, "New Slaves," from *Yeezus*, Roc-A-Fella, Def Jam, 2013, compact disc.
4. Pusha T, "Hold On," from *My Name is My Name*, GOOD Music, Def Jam, 2013, compact disc.
5. Ashraf H. A. Rushdy, *Neo-slave Narratives: Studies in the Social Logic of a Literary Form* (New York: Oxford University Press, 1999), 14.
6. Peter Biskind, *Down and Dirty Pictures: Miramax, Sundance, and the Rise of the Independent Film* (New York: Simon & Schuster, 2004), 79.
7. Lajos Egri, *The Art of Dramatic Writing: Its Basis in The Creative Interpretation of Human Motives* (New York: Touchstone, 2004), 34–35.
8. Cynthia A. Hamilton, "Models of Agency: Frederick Douglass and 'the Heroic Slave,'" *Proceedings of the American Antiquarian Society* 114, no. 1 (2005): 102.
9. John Lee Hancock, dir., *The Blind Side*, Blu-ray (2009; Burbank, Calif.: Warner Home Video, 2010).
10. Deirdre Donahue, "Ravens' Michael Oher Tells His Side in Memoir," *USA Today*, February 8, 2011.
11. Donahue, "Ravens' Michael Oher."
12. A. Timothy Spaulding, *Re-Forming the Past: History, The Fantastic, and the Postmodern Slave Narrative* (Columbus: Ohio State University Press, 2005), 5.

13. Jonathan Romney, "It's Good, Then It's Bad. Well, It Is Tarantino," *Independent*, January 20, 2013.

14. Romney, "It's Good, Then It's Bad. Well, It Is Tarantino."

15. Topos Partnership, Kerschhagel, and Opportunity Agenda, *Opportunity for Black Men and Boys*, 24.

16. Jelani Cobb, "Tarantino Unchained," *New Yorker*, January 2, 2013.

17. Solomon Northup, *Twelve Years a Slave*, ed. Sue Eakin and Joseph Logsdon (Baton Rouge: Louisiana State University Press, 1968), 3.

18. Sherry B. Ortner, *Anthropology and Social Theory: Culture, Power, and the Acting Subject* (Durham: Duke University Press, 2006), 101–2.

19. Robert McKee, *Story: Substance, Structure, Style, and the Principles of Screenwriting* (New York: HarperCollins, 1997), 319.

20. McKee, *Story*, 320.

21. Northup, *Twelve Years a Slave*, 196.

22. George H. White, "Defense of the Negro Race—Charges Answered. Speech of Hon. George H. White, of North Carolina, in the House of Representatives, January 29, 1901," *Documenting the American South* (Chapel Hill: University of North Carolina at Chapel Hill, 2002).

Index

9/11, 91, 163; post-911disaster films, 91, 94

12 Years a Slave, x, xi, 70, 73, 80, 227–289; "Burbanking", 255; double-consciousness, 241–250; Douglas, Orville Lloyd, 245; DuBois, W. E. B., 241; "The Fetishization of Lupita Nyong'o", 246; Holbein, Hans, *The Ambassadors*, 233; imaginative documentary, 257; Limbaugh, Rush, 245; long takes, 237; McQueen, Steve, x, 70, 73, 80, 251, 252; Northrup, Solomon, x, 70, 73, 80, 227–289, 251, 253, 285; political correctness, 242; *Privilege of Forgetting*, 254; repetitious nature of the trauma, 233; *Solomon Northup, a Citizen of New-York, Kidnapped in Washington City in 1841, and Rescued in1853*, 227–289, 253, 285

99%: The Occupy Wall Street Collaborative Film, 166

Alexander, Michelle, 16, 254. *See also* Cornel West
"All-American Skin Game", 19; Couch, Stanley, 18
American Dream, 171
American Winter, 161, 166
Amistad, 227
Angelou, Maya, 13; *I Know Why the Caged Bird Sings*, 14n24

The Autobiography of Miss Jane Pittman, 256

Baldwin, James, 33–40, 45–55; *Another Country*, 35; "The Artist Struggling for Integrity", 42n3; *Blues for Mister Charlie*, 35; "The Dangerous Road before Martin Luther King", 36, 42n14; "Everybody's Protest Novel", 36, 42n15, 45; *The Fire Next Time*, 35; *Go Tell It on the Mountain*, 35, 42n13; "Going to Meet the Man", 35; *If Beale Street Could Talk*, 35; *Just above My Head*, 35; Letter to Desmond Tutu, 42n6; "A Letter to My Nephew", 34, 42n9; *Notes of a Native Son*, 33, 42n4; *One Day When I Was Lost: A Scenario Based on Alex Haley's*The Autobiography of Malcolm X, 36; "Sonny's Blues", 35; "The Uses of the Blues", 42n10; "What It Means to Be an American", 35, 42n11
Barbershop, 107
Barnett, Ross Robert, Governor, 9
The Battle in Seattle, 151
The Battle of Algiers, 71
BBC.com, viii
Beasts of the Southern Wild, 111, 131–143, 277; climate change, 131–143; Zeitlin, Benh, 131–143
The Best Man, 107, 271n10

Birth of a Nation, 60, 227, 232, 252, 259
Biskind, Peter, 277
Black Caesar, 76
Black Dynamite, 59–64, 77–83, 259
Black Entertainment Television (BET), 149
The Black Gestapo, 79
Black Samson, 82
Blaxploitation, 58–83
The Blindside, 279–281; Hamilton, Cynthia, 280; *I Beat the Odds: From Homelessness to "The Blind Side" and Beyond*, 281; "The Negro Problem", 280; Oher, Michael, 279–281
Blue Jasmine, 165
Blomkamp, Neil, 149; *District 9*, 149; *Elysium*, 149
Blue Collar, 151
Bordwell, David, 46, 47; *Film Art*, 46
Boss Nigger, 84n15
Bound for Glory, 151
Bowman, James, 254, 260
Boys n the Hood, 107
BP Deepwater Horizon spill, 140
Brecht, Bertolt, 132
Brooks, Gwendolyn, 15–29; "A Bronzeville Mother Loiters in Mississippi. Meanwhile, A Mississippi Mother Burns Bacon", 16–29; "We Real Cool," 42n7
Brown v. Board of Education, 17
Bucktown, 75
Burton, Nsenga, x
The Butler, ix, xi, 70–80; Daniels, Lee, ix, xi, 70–80; Winfrey, Oprah, 72

Caffrey, Jane, xiin6
Campbell, Joseph, 37, 43n20; *Creative Mythology*, 43n20; *Hero of a Thousand Faces*, 43n20; *The Power of Myth*, 43n20
Cannes Film Festival, 277
Carmichael, Stokely, 9
Catch-22, 71
Cha-Ju, Sundiata Keita, 254
Clinton, Bill, 150, 158, 259, 263
Clinton, Hillary, 265
Coalition against Blaxploitation, 76
Cobb, Jelani, 285

Coffy, 77
Collins, Suzanne, 185; *The Hunger Games*, viii, 185, 201n34
Coogler, Ryan, 108
Cry Freedom, 111

Darabont, Frank, 85; *The Green Mile*(1999), 87; *The Mist*, 87; *Mob City*, 87; *The Shawshank Redemption*, 87; *The Walking Dead*, 87
Dargis, Manhola, xin1, 173, 241; "Movies in the Age of Obama", xin1
The Day after Tomorrow, 91
DeGeneres, Ellen, 242
Diawara, Manthia, 266; *Black American Cinema*, 266
District 9, 111
Dixon, Ivan, 80; *The Spook Who Sat by the Door*, 80
Django Unchained, viii, 31–43n29, 45–56n36, 60, 70, 227–290n22
domestic service, 3–22
double-consciousness, 69, 241
Douglas, Stephen, 41
Douglass, Frederick, 41, 124, 231, 280, 281; *The Heroic Slave*, 280; *Narrative of the Life of Frederick Douglass, an American Slave*, 231
Downey, Robert, Sr., 74; *Putney Swope*, 74
Dred Scott decision, 41
A Dry White Season, 111
DuBois, W. E. B., 41; double-consciousness, 241; *The Soul of Black Folk*, 244
Dylan, Bob, 17; "The Death of Emmett Till", 17

Easy Rider, viii
Ebert, Roger, 134, 151
Edge, Thomas, 265; "Southern Strategy 2.0", 265
Eliade, Mircea, 37; *Myth and Reality*, 43n19
Ellison, Ralph, 69; *Invisible Man*, 69
Emancipation Proclamation, 32, 228
Enron: The Smartest Guys in the Room, 151
Evers, Medgar, 23, 36

Farmer, James, 9
Fast, Omer, 22; *5,000 Feet Is the Best*, 22
Fessenden, Larry, 91; *The Last Winter*, 91
Five Easy Pieces, 71
Forché, Carolyn, 251, 254
Forrest, Nathan Bedford, 267
Forrest Gump, 72
Foucault, Michel, 14n23; *Power/ Knowledge: Selected Interviews and Writings*, 14n23
Foxy Brown, 76
Freedom Riders, 9
Friday Foster, 77
Fruitvale Station, 107–110; Coogler, Ryan, 107–110

Gates, Henry Louis, Jr., 55n15, 227, 239n20; "Interview with Quentin Tarantino", 55n15
Getino, Octavio, 258
Glass-Steagall Act, 157
Gleiberman, Owen, 13n3; "Inside Movies", 13n3
Glory, 75, 227
Gone with the Wind, 6, 10, 227, 232
Goodwin, Doris Kearns, 37; *Team of Rivals*, 37
The Grapes of Wrath, viii
The Great Gatsby, viii, 171–180; American Dream, 171–180; hip-hop, 179; Luhrmann, Baz, 171–180; *Washington Post*-Miller Center Poll, 180
Great Recession, 158, 159
Grier, Pam, 76

Hamilton, Cynthia, 280; "The Negro Problem", 280
Hancock, John Lee, 277–290n14; *The Blind Side*, 277–290n14
Harris, Trudier, 23; *From Mammies to Militants*, 31–40
Harris-Perry, Melissa, 8; "*The Help* Doesn't Help", 13n1
Helms, Jesse, 83n1
The Help, 3–29, 19, 22, 70, 277; Taylor, Tate, 3–29
Herodotus, 37
Hit Man, 76

hip-hop, 179
Hollinger, David, 264, 272n30
Hollywood Right and Left, 167
Holocaust, 257
Homeric myths, 37
hooks, bell, 135; "No Love in the Wild", 135
"house nigger", 70
Hughes, Langston, 17
The Hunger Games, viii, 185, 201n34; American reality television, 187; casting, 187–195; Collins, Suzanne, 185–200; *Essays on the Suzanne Collins Trilogy*, 188; merchandizing, 198
Hurricane Katrina, 139, 153, 172
The Hurt Locker, 71

If . . ., 71
I'm Gonna Get You Sucka, 77
I'm No Angel, 6
Imitation of Life, 6
In the Heat of the Night, 72
Indie Wire, ix
Inside Job, 156
Invictus, 111–128; Afrikaner, 111–112; Mandela, Nelson, 111–128; rugby, 111–128; Truth and Reconciliation Commission (TRC), 111–128
Iraq, 19
It's a Wonderful Life, 96, 168

Jackson, Jesse, 124
Jacobs, Harriet, 231; *Incidents in the Life of a Slave Girl*, 231
Jarhead, 71
Jay-Z, 26, 106
Jefferson, Thomas, 7, 14n16; Query XVIII: "Manners", 7
Joe, 71
Jung, Carl, 38
Justified, 162

Kansas–Nebraska Act of 1854, 41
Kennedy, John F., 23
Keynesian, 159
Killing Them Softly, 165
King, Martin Luther, Jr., 20, 21, 31, 34, 71, 72, 123, 278; "I Have a Dream", 73,

123
King, Stephen, 85–98; *The Mist*, 85–98
Klein, Naomi, 152
Koppelman, Alex, 172
Kopple, Barbara, 82; *Harlan County USA* (1976) and *American Dream*, 82
Ku Klux Klan, 23, 267. *See also* Forrest, Nathan Bedford
Kushner, Tony, 31–40; *Lincoln*, 31–40

Lacan, Jaques, 228, 231, 233, 239n13, 239n16, 239n18
Lawrence, Francis, 89; *I Am Legend*, 89
Lee, Spike, 248, 277; "American Slavery Was Not a Sergio Leone Spaghetti Western. It Was a Holocaust. My Ancestors Are Slaves. Stolen from Africa. I Will Honor Them", 248; *Do the Right Thing*, 277
Lehman Brothers, 158, 165
Leong, Nancy, 64; "Racial Capitalism", 64
Lincoln, viii, 31–40; Spielberg, Stephen, 31–40
Lincoln, Abraham, 31–40; Emancipation Proclamation, 32; Gettysburg Address, 39; Lincoln Bible, 32
Lincoln, Mary Todd, 39, 40
Little Big Man, 71
LL Cool J, 259; "Accidental Racist", 259
A Long Walk to Freedom, 111
Lorde, Audre, 17
Luhrmann, Baz, 171–181; *The Great Gatsby*, 171–181

Malcolm X, 75
Malcolm X, 278; *The Autobiography of Malcolm X*, 36
Mandela, Nelson, 111–130; *Invictus*, 111–130; Truth and Reconciliation Commission, 116
Mandingo, 60, 283
Margin Call, 164
Martin, Trayvon, xi, 107, 187
Marx, Karl, 83; *The Communist Manifesto*, 83
MASH, 71
McKee, Robert, 288
McQueen, Steve, x, 70, 73, 80, 227–289, 251, 252; *12 Years a Slave*, 70, 73, 80, 227–289, 251, 285–x; *Hunger*, 234; *Shame*, 234
McWhorter, John, 275
Menace II Society, 107
Meredith, James, 9
The Mist, 85–98; Darabont, Frank, 85–98; King, Stephen, 85–98; "magical negro", 88
Monster's Ball, 246
Moore, Michael, 152, 154, 160; *Capitalism: A Love Story*, 152, 154; *Fahrenheit 9/11*, 154; *Roger and Me*, 155
Morrison, Toni, 17, 47, 48; *Beloved*, 256; *Playing in the Dark: Whiteness and the Literary Imagination*, 55n8; "Romancing the Shadow", 47

NAACP, 75
Nama, Adilifu, 75; *SuperBlack: American Pop Culture and Black Superheroes*, 75
New Jack City, 107
New York Times, vii, xin1, 173, 241
Nietzsche, 70; *Beyond Good and Evil*, 70
Night of the Living Dead, 88
No End in Sight, 156
Norma Rae, 151
Northrup, Solomon, x, 70, 73, 80, 227–289, 251, 253, 285; *Solomon Northup, a Citizen of New-York, Kidnapped in Washington City in 1841, and Rescued in 1853*, 227–289, 253, 285; Wilson, David, 230

O Brother, Where Art Thou?, 255, 269
Obama, Barack Hussein: 2008 acceptance of the Democratic presidential nomination and address at the convention, 174; 2009 inauguration address, 140; 2013 inauguration address, 139; American Dream, 171–180; *The Audacity of Hope*, 138, 174; "Barack the Magic Negro", 142, 265, 272n31; "Birthers", 186; "closet Muslim", 265; Democratic National Convention 2004, 173, 176; *Dreams from My Father*, 264; Lincoln Bible, 32; "A More Perfect Union," 64n1, 106, 124; "Nobel Lecture: A Just and

Lasting Peace, 27n10; Nobel Peace Prize, 19; "The Nobel Peace Prize 2009 Presentation Speech", 27n5; Obama-specific horror imagery, 86; *Portrait of President Barack Obama*, 20; "Race Speech," 124; Remarks by the President on Trayvon Martin, 106; "Second Democratic Presidential Nomination Acceptance Speech, 180, 182n35; Thoughts on Reclaiming the American Dream, 171
Occupy Wall Street, 158
One Percenter, 159

Palin, Sarah, 265
Parks, Gordon, 271n13; *Solomon Northup's Odyssey*, 271n13
Peterson, Merrill, 40, 42n18; *The Image of Jefferson in the American Mind*, 40, 42n18; *Lincoln in American Memory*, 40
Pitt, Brad, xi, xiin10
plutonomy, 155
Poitier, Sidney, 72; *In the Heat of the Night*, 72
Precious, 277
Pusha T, 276; "Hold On," 276

The Queen of Versailles, 161

Raines, Howell, 28; "Grady's Gift" *New York Times*, 28
Rawls, John A., 28; *Theory of Justice*, 28
Reich, Robert, 158; *Aftershock: The Next Economy and America's Future*, 158; "Great Prosperity", 159; *Inequality for All: A Passionate Argument on Behalf of the Middle Class*, 158, 160, 167; Keynesian interventionist, 158; *The Work of Nations*, 158
Rise of the Planet of the Apes, 203–224; alienation, 220; capitalism, failure of, 203–224; films as public pedagogy, 206; Wyatt, Rupert, 204
Robinson, Jackie, ix
Rock, Chris, 76; *I Think I Love My Wife*, 76
Romero, George, 88; *Night of the Living Dead*, 88

Romney, Mitt, xi, 167
Roosevelt Franklin Delano, 159
Rosenberg, Alyssa, 28; "'The Help': Softening Segregation for a Feel-Good Flick", 28
Russell, Bertrand, 38

Sandburg, Carl, 39; *Abraham Lincoln, the Prairie Years, the War Years*, 39
Sankofa, 251, 254, 268; Gerima, Hallie, 251, 254
satyagraha, 72
Scott, A. O., xin1, 50; "The Black, the White, and the Angry", 55n20; "Movies in the Age of Obama", xin1
Shaft, 76
Shaft's Big Score, 76
Sharpton, Al, 124
Sherwood, Robert, 39; *Abe Lincoln in Illinois*, 39
The Shock Doctrine, 152
Shut Up and Sing, 154; the Dixie Chicks, 154
Sims, Yvonne, 76; *Women of Blaxploitation*, 76
Singleton, John, 74; *Boyz n the Hood*, 74
Singley, Bernestine, 28; "Sniffing Dirty Laundry: A True Story from 'The Help's' Daughter", 28
Slaughter, 76
Slotkin, Richard, 41, 51; *The Crater*, 41; *Regeneration through Violence*, 51; *The Return of Henry Starr*, 41; *The Young Lincoln*, 41
Smith, Bessie, 35
Smith, Lillian, 5
Soderbergh, Steven, 82; *Che*, 82; *Sex, Lies, and Videotape*, 277
South Africa, 31–33
Spielberg, Stephen, viii, 31–43n29, 75, 269; *Lincoln*, 31, 43n29, 269
Stockett, Kathryn, 22–29; *See also The Help*
Stockholm Syndrome, 53
Stone, Oliver, 162; *The Untold History of the United States*, 168; *Wall Street*, 163; *Wall Street: Money Never Sleeps*, 163
Stowe, Harriet Beecher, 36, 45; *Uncle Tom's Cabin*, 36, 45

Superfly, 75
Supreme Court, 83; 2010 Citizens United and 2014 McCutcheon, 83

Tarantino, Quentin, viii, 31–43n29, 49, 248, 282; *Django Unchained*, 31–43n29, 248; "Interview with Quentin Tarantino", 55n15
Taylor, Tate, 3–29; *The Help*, 3–29
Tea Party, 107
Thirteenth Amendment, 39
Till, Emmett, 15–29
Too Big to Fail, 165
Tutu, Desmond, 33

van Peebles, Melvin, 74
Vidal, Gore, 40; *Lincoln*, 40

Waiting for Superman, 152
A Walk in the Sun, viii
Warren, Elizabeth, 167
Washington, Booker T., 124
Watermelon Man, 74
Wayans, Damon, 77; *I'm Gonna Get You Sucka*, 77
Weinstein, Harvey, ix
Wells, Ida B., 41
West, Cornell, 20, 124; foreword to Michelle Alexander's *The New Jim Crow: Mass Incarceration in the Age of Color Blindness*, 16, 27n1
West, Kanye, 276; "New Slaves", 276
The West Wing, 169
Whitaker, Forest, ix; *Waiting to Exhale*, 76; *See also The Butler*
White, Armond, 267
White, Hayden, 36, 42n16; *Metahistory*, 36, 42n16
White, Michael Jai, 76; *Black Dynamite*, 76
will.i.am, 179
Wilson, Joe, 83n2
Winfrey, Oprah, 106
Winnie Mandela, 111
The Wire, 162
Witherspoon, Chris, 29; "Director: People Are Too Critical of 'The Help'", 29
Wolf, Naomi, 196; *The Beauty Myth*, 196
The Wolf of Wall Street, 166
Woodstock, 71
Wooley, Agnes, 132; "The Politics of Myth Making: *Beasts of the Southern Wild*, 132
A World Apart, 111
Wright, Jeremiah, 57, 58, 83n3

Zeitlin, Benh, 131–143. *See also Beasts of the Southern Wild*
Zimmerman, George, 107, 187

About the Editor and Contributors

David Garrett Izzo (http://www.davidgarrettizzo.com) is an English professor who has published seventeen books and sixty essays of literary scholarship, as well as three novels, three plays, a short story, and poems. He previously published (with Maria Orban) a book about African American author Charles Chesnutt. David has published extensively on the Perennial Spiritual Philosophy of Mysticism (Vedanta) as applied to literature. He is inspired by Aldous Huxley; Bruce Springsteen; his wife, Carol; and their five cats: Huxley, Max, Princess, Phoebe, and Luca. Two of his novels are fantasies with cats as characters: *Maximus in Catland* and *Purring Heights*.

* * *

Linda Belau is professor in the Department of English and director of the film studies program at the University of Texas–Pan American. She is the editor of *Topologies of Trauma: Essays on the Limits of Knowledge and Memory* and is the author of several articles on literary, cultural, and cinema studies.

Thomas Britt has taught at George Mason University since the beginning of its film and video studies BA program in 2007. His documentaries and music videos have screened internationally. His essays are available in edited volumes and print and online journals. He is a staff writer and columnist for PopMatters.

Sonya C. Brown is associate professor of English at Fayetteville State University. Her research interests include rhetorical theory and popular culture. Her publications have appeared in *Southern Communication Journal, Jour-*

nal for the Study of Popular Romance, Journal of Popular Culture, and Feminist Media Studies.

Brian E. Butler is the Thomas Howerton Distinguished Professor of Humanities at the University of North Carolina, Asheville. Previously he was the chair of the Department of Philosophy at the school. He has advanced degrees in fine art, philosophy, and law and regularly publishes on the intersection of these three disciplines. He recently edited an anthology on democratic experimentalism aptly titled *Democratic Experimentalism* (2012). In addition to his academic appointment, he is currently chair of the Black Mountain College Museum + Arts Center, an institution honoring the small experimental college founded upon a combination of the ideas of John Dewey and the Bauhaus tradition.

Ed Cameron is associate professor in the Department of English at the University of Texas–Pan American, where he teaches literature, theory, and film studies. He is the author of *Psychopathology in the Gothic Romance* and of several articles on literary, cultural, and cinema studies.

Kwakiutl L. Dreher is associate professor of English and ethnic studies at the University of Nebraska–Lincoln. She earned a bachelor's degree in English from the University of South Carolina–Columbia and her master's degree from Clark Atlanta University in Atlanta, Georgia. Dr. Dreher received her PhD from the University of California–Riverside. She conducts research in African American literature, including auto/biography; film, visual, and popular culture; and mass-marketed popular literature. She published her book *Dancing on the White Page: Black Women Entertainers Writing Autobiography* in 2008. She also published, among other journal articles, "Scandal and Black Women in Television" in *African Americans in Television: Race-ing for Ratings* (2013).

Rodney M. D. Fierce graduated in 2007 from Princeton University with a degree in English and a minor in theater and dance, and in 2012 from Simmons College with a master's degree in children's literature. He is currently a second-year PhD candidate in the University of Southern Mississippi English Department.

Andrew Grossman is the editor of the anthology *Queer Asian Cinema: Shadows in the Shade* and an editor of *Bright Lights Film Journal*. He has written chapters for many anthologies, including *Film and Literary Modernism* and *Chinese Transnational Cinema: Corporeality, Desire, and Ethics*. Currently he is co-editing (with Brian Bergen-Aurand) *The Encyclopedia of Queer Film*.

Peter Grosvenor, originally from Wales, holds a PhD in government from the London School of Economics. He is currently an associate professor of sociology and global studies at Pacific Lutheran University in Tacoma, Washington, where he teaches courses in social and political theory and in international relations.

Blake G. Hobby, associate professor of literature and language at the University of North Carolina–Asheville, has authored more than seventeen books, including the forthcoming *Anthology of Black Mountain College Poetry*, which will be published in 2015. An expert in modernism and in contemporary American literature, Dr. Hobby serves as the executive editor for *The Black Mountain College Studies Journal*. His recent work includes a MS on social justice in American fiction since 1990 and articles on a wide range of subjects and authors, from William Blake, James Joyce, and Franz Kafka to Eudora Welty, Flannery O'Connor, and Sylvia Plath. Dr. Hobby regularly teaches a course on social justice and power as part of the general education program at UNC–Asheville. In this course, Cultivating Global Citizenship, students transport classroom learning beyond the halls of academe into community settings, where they perform active roles in making a difference in others' lives.

David M. Jones is a professor of English and honors education at the University of Wisconsin at Eau Claire. He is also a faculty affiliate of the women's studies program and has served as campus fellow for equity, diversity, and inclusion. His research interests include the Black Arts Movement, critical race studies, literary regionalism, and American popular music. His recent publications include a volume of essays co-edited with Dr. JoAnne Juett: *Coming Out to the Mainstream: New Queer Cinema in the 21st Century*, which features an essay by Dr. Jones on the film *Boys Don't Cry* in its broader historical context. Previously, Dr. Jones has published essays on gender identity in the civil rights movement, musician Etta James, blues music in postmodern culture, and hip-hop intellectuals Nelson George and Joan Morgan. Dr. Jones is also a professional musician (a vocalist, guitarist, and songwriter with Davey J and the Jones Tones), and he is the former producer for two radio series broadcast on Wisconsin Public Radio: *Jazz, Blues, and Beyond* and *Wisconsin Wealth*.

Victoria McCollum is a final-year PhD candidate in the School of Media, Film and Journalism at the University of Ulster in Northern Ireland. Her research is concerned with why the American rural horror film resurged in an iconic post-9/11 era of city fear and urban terrorism.

Robert McParland is the author of *Charles Dickens's American Audience* and *How to Write about Joseph Conrad* and the editor of *Music and Literary Modernism* and *Film and Literary Modernism*. His previous essays on James Baldwin include "To the Deep Water: James Baldwin's Sonny's Blues" in *Interdisciplinary Humanities*. He is associate professor of English at Felician College in New Jersey and is a professional musician.

doug morris, PhD, teaches critical literacy and critical pedagogy at Eastern New Mexico University, in Portales, New Mexico. Interests include: the U.S. culture of militarism, film as public pedagogy, education for substantive democracy, Marxism, anarchism, and protest music (as performance and as inspiration).

Salvador Murguia is associate professor of sociology at Akita International University and a Paul Orfalea Center Fellow at UC–Santa Barbara. His research interests include popular culture and race. Selections of his work may be found in *American Behavioral Scientist*, *Journal for the Scientific Study of Religion*, and *Preternature*.

Irina Negrea is originally from Romania, where she received her BA in English and her MA in British cultural studies. She also received an MA in English from Kutztown University of Pennsylvania and a PhD in English from Lehigh University. Currently she is an assistant professor at Shaw University in Raleigh, North Carolina.

Mohanalakshmi Rajakumar has a PhD in literature from the University of Florida. Her research interests include gender and postcolonial literature. Mohana has published articles and chapters in a variety of academic journals including *The South Asian Review* and *The Annals of Urdu Studies*. Her first book, *Haram in the Harem* (2009), is a study of subversive use of Indian and Algerian women's domestic fiction by female writers. She has also been recognized for her fictional work: *Love Comes Later* (2012) is the first novel in English set in Qatar and won the 2013 Best Indie Book Award in the romance category. Her coming-of-age novel, *An Unlikely Goddess*, won the SheWrites New Novelist competition in 2011. Her nonfiction work has also been published in *Variety Arabia*, *Brownbook Middle East*, *AudioFile*, *Explore Qatar*, *Woman Today*, *The Woman*, *Writers and Artists Yearbook*, *QatarClick*, and *Qatar Explorer*. Mohana teaches writing and literature courses in Doha, Qatar. You can read more about her work on her website: http://www.mohanalakshmi.com.

Sohinee Roy is an assistant professor at North Central College. Her research interests center on the intersections of postcolonial theory and race theory in reading South African literature, particularly post-apartheid South African literature. Her essays have been published in *Modern Fiction Studies* and *Journal of Commonwealth and Postcolonial Studies*. Currently she is working on a monograph on the representations of reconciliation in post-apartheid literature from South Africa.

Alisha Saiyed is a graphic design student at VCUQatar with a passion for words and photography. She is a member of the social science research group run by Dr. Rajakumar and has served as a proofreader, database creator, and writer on a variety of research projects.

Cammie Sublette is associate professor and department head of English at the University of Arkansas–Fort Smith. She specializes in African American literature and cultural studies. Her publications include a co-authored article on American food elitism and another on pedagogy in the undergraduate theory classroom. She is currently co-editing a food studies book.

www.ingramcontent.com/pod-product-compliance
Lightning Source LLC
Chambersburg PA
CBHW030107010526
44116CB00005B/135